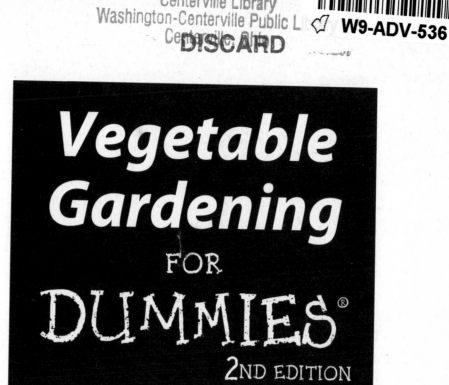

Vegetable Gardening

FOR

DUMMIES®

2ND EDITION

**by Charlie Nardozzi and the Editors of
The National Gardening Association**

WILEY

Wiley Publishing, Inc.

Vegetable Gardening For Dummies®, 2nd Edition

Published by
Wiley Publishing, Inc.
111 River St.
Hoboken, NJ 07030-5774
www.wiley.com

WILEY

About the Authors

Charlie Nardozzi has worked for more than 20 years bringing expert gardening information to home gardeners through radio, television, and the printed page. He delights in making gardening information simple, easy, fun, and accessible to everyone. His energy, exuberance, and love of the natural world also make Charlie an exciting public speaker and presenter. He currently is the senior horticulturist and spokesperson for the National Gardening Association (NGA). He also writes the *National News* as part of NGA's online publications, conducts media interviews about gardening and NGA, and provides horticultural consultation to NGA programs.

For 12 years Charlie was an editor with *National Gardening* magazine, writing stories on a variety of gardening topics from roses to tomatoes. He also has written for national magazines such as *Organic Gardening,* authored the first edition of *Vegetable Gardening For Dummies* in 1999 and *The Ultimate Gardener* in 2009, and contributed to other books such as *Gardening All-in-One For Dummies* (2003) and the Better Homes and Gardens' *Yard and Garden Owner's Manual* (Meredith Books, 2004).

Charlie's skills as a garden communicator extend beyond the printed page, however. In 2005, he was the host of PBS's television program *Garden Smart,* which reaches more than 60 million households. He also has been a gardening expert on many nationally syndicated television shows, such as HGTV's *Today at Home* and *Way to Grow,* Discovery Channel's *Home Matters,* and DIY's *Ask DIY.* He has appeared on QVC and the Home Shopping Network as well. At his home in Vermont, Charlie co-hosts the program "In The Garden," which offers weekly gardening tips on the local CBS affiliate television station, a weekly call-in gardening radio show on a local AM station, and gardening commentaries on public radio. He also hosts national and international gardening tours.

The National Gardening Association, founded in 1972, is a national not-for-profit leader in plant-based education, esteemed for its award-winning Web sites and newsletters, grants and curriculum for youth gardens, and research for the lawn-and-garden industry. NGA's mission is to advance the personal, community, and educational benefits of gardening by supporting gardeners, communities, and teachers with information and resources. For more information, please visit www.garden.org.

Dedication

I'd like to dedicate this book to everyone who has ever thought about vegetable gardening or tried to grow some of their own food. I particularly want to dedicate this book to my wife, Wendy, who is the best partner in the garden and in my life.

Author's Acknowledgments

I'd like to thank Mike Baker and Stacy Kennedy for sticking with this book idea and pursuing it so it finally became a reality. A big thanks goes to Georgette Beatty for her keen insights when reading this book and her organizational ability to keep the ball rolling. I appreciated Jessica Smith's thoughtful questions as the copy editor, especially because she's a budding vegetable gardener herself! Jim Schmidt kept me honest in the horticultural realm with his suggestions as the technical reviewer. Kathryn Born provided excellent updated illustrations. Suzanne DeJohn, my colleague at NGA, provided many beautiful color photos of vegetables and gardening techniques that make the words come to life.

Publisher's Acknowledgments

We're proud of this book; please send us your comments through our Dummies online registration form located at `http://dummies.custhelp.com`. For other comments, please contact our Customer Care Department within the U.S. at 877-762-2974, outside the U.S. at 317-572-3993, or fax 317-572-4002.

Some of the people who helped bring this book to market include the following:

Acquisitions, Editorial, and Media Development

Senior Project Editor: Georgette Beatty

   (Previous Edition: Kathleen M. Cox)

Acquisitions Editor: Stacy Kennedy

Copy Editor: Jessica Smith

   (Previous Edition: Kim Darosett, Gwenette Gaddis, Wendy Hatch)

Assistant Editor: Erin Calligan Mooney

Editorial Program Coordinator: Joe Niesen

Technical Editor: James C. Schmidt

Editorial Manager: Michelle Hacker

Editorial Assistant: Jennette ElNaggar

Art Coordinator: Alicia B. South

Cover Photo: Brand X Pictures

Cartoons: Rich Tennant (`www.the5thwave.com`)

Composition Services

Project Coordinator: Katherine Crocker

Layout and Graphics: Christin Swinford, Christine Williams

Special Art: Illustrations by Kathryn Born, M.A.

Proofreader: Toni Settle

Indexer: Joan Griffitts

Publishing and Editorial for Consumer Dummies

   Diane Graves Steele, Vice President and Publisher, Consumer Dummies

   Kristin Ferguson-Wagstaffe, Product Development Director, Consumer Dummies

   Ensley Eikenburg, Associate Publisher, Travel

   Kelly Regan, Editorial Director, Travel

Publishing for Technology Dummies

   Andy Cummings, Vice President and Publisher, Dummies Technology/General User

Composition Services

   Debbie Stailey, Director of Composition Services

Contents at a Glance

Table of Contents

Chapter 12: Growing Berries and Herbs for an Edible Landscape . . .181

Introduction

* *

*E*veryone loves good food. Fresh, tasty, nutritious food is our birthright. And what better way to have great food than to grow it yourself? You don't have to be a farmer to do so either. Whether it be a plot of land in the yard that's tilled up to grow vegetables, a few vegetables planted amongst your flowers and shrubs, or containers loaded with attractive, edible choices, growing your own food is a satisfying and rewarding activity.

Vegetable gardening isn't rocket science either. Heck, people have been growing their own vegetables for thousands of years. Like any pursuit, you just need some direction, good advice, and inspiration to get started. *Vegetable Gardening For Dummies,* 2nd Edition, is for anyone who already grows vegetables or who has ever dreamed of growing some of their own food. All it takes is some resolve to get started. You're already halfway there just by picking up this book!

About This Book

In this book, you can find all the basic information you need to grow a vegetable garden. It's great to read the book from front cover to back cover, but each section and chapter is complete in itself. So feel free to browse the vegetables or topics that you want to focus on first. I've been vegetable gardening my whole life, so throughout the book I try to impart some practical wisdom that's easily accessible. I also include some special tips and tricks that I've learned over the years and information on hundreds of vegetable varieties, many of which are beautiful to look at as well as tasty to eat. Of course, none of this matters if you can't grow the vegetables successfully. That's why a large part of this book is devoted to building soil, starting seeds, maintaining the garden, controlling pests, growing through the seasons, and harvesting. I like to encourage happy, healthy, successful gardeners who are willing to experiment, make mistakes, and enjoy sharing their bounty with their friends, family, and neighbors.

Conventions Used in This Book

To help you navigate this book, I include the following conventions:

  ✔ All references to temperature are in degrees Fahrenheit. As a reminder, I include the label with the first reference in each chapter. After that, I save space (and paper!) by leaving it out.

- ✔ Variety names for each vegetable are indicated by single quotation marks. These are the common names you'll see when buying vegetable seeds and plants.

- ✔ *Italics* highlight new terms (which I define right away) and the Latin names of vegetables, which I use only when necessary.

- ✔ **Boldfaced** text highlights the keywords of bulleted lists and the action part of numbered steps.

- ✔ Web addresses appear in `monofont`.

When this book was printed, some Web addresses may have needed to break across two lines of text. If that happened, rest assured that I haven't put in any extra characters to indicate the break. So, when using one of these Web addresses, just type in exactly what you see in this book, pretending as though the line break doesn't exist.

What You're Not to Read

I may think every word I've written on vegetable gardening in this book is intriguing, but I realize you have a life and may want to just get on with it. If you want only the basics, keep in mind that sidebars (in shaded gray boxes) and information tagged with the Technical Stuff icon aren't necessary to your basic understanding of vegetable growing and can be skipped, if you really have to.

Foolish Assumptions

Before I even put one word to the page, I was thinking about who may read this book. Here's what I assume about you, the reader:

- ✔ You want to create a vegetable garden that's filled with healthy, nutritious, beautiful plants to eat.

- ✔ You want to understand the basics of vegetable gardening and, for experienced gardeners, find new tricks to help you garden better.

- ✔ You want to grow vegetables in an environmentally friendly manner.

- ✔ You want to try vegetable gardening even if you only have a deck or patio to grow a few plants.

- ✔ You want to share your love of gardening with friends, family members, and neighbors because you feel that if more people grew some of their own food, the world would be a better place.

How This Book Is Organized

Like all *For Dummies* books, this book is broken into parts. Each part has a number of chapters related to a theme. Here's an overview to get you oriented with the organization.

Part 1: Digging Into the Basics of Vegetable Gardening

Vegetable gardening is about more than just growing tasty food. You can find many other reasons and benefits of vegetable gardening, and I explain them in this part. I also cover information you need to know to plan your garden, such as determining the importance of sun and soil, deciding what to grow, and exploring some sample garden designs.

Part 11: Vegging Out

Each chapter in this part explores vegetables grouped by botanical family (such as the squash family) or commonality (such as root crops). Each chapter is loaded with the best varieties to grow and specifics on how to grow them. I also provide information to help combat specific pests that may attack each crop. Chapter 12 is all about other edibles, such as berries and herbs. Food comes in many forms, and berries and herbs are some of the easiest and most reliable producers in your yard.

Part 111: Getting Down and Dirty in Your Vegetable Garden

Now for the good stuff: building your garden and getting it growing. In this part, I talk about starting seeds; improving your soil; maintaining your garden with proper watering, fertilizing, and mulching; using some extra-cool gardening techniques, such as succession planting; applying pest and disease controls; growing in containers; and harvesting and storage. Whew, that's a lot of great information!

Part 1V: The Part of Tens

This book wouldn't be a *For Dummies* book without the always-popular Part of Tens. The final chapters in this book look at the ten best tools to get the job done and nearly ten great season-extending techniques that enable you to garden earlier in spring and later into fall.

Icons Used in This Book

Like all *For Dummies* books, this book has icons that highlight great tips, warnings, and other specific topics. Here are the ones in this book:

Are you interested in growing plants in containers? If so, look for these icons throughout the book.

One of the best parts of vegetable gardening is involving kids. This icon marks plants that kids love or special gardening tips you can try with your little ones.

This icon highlights important information that helps you garden better. Don't forget this stuff!

If you want to go a little deeper in your knowledge of a plant or technique, read information marked with this icon.

This icon highlights information that saves time and money. Even experienced gardeners can learn something from these tidbits!

Sometimes you can make mistakes in the garden, and that's okay. To help minimize your mistakes, this icon alerts you to potential pitfalls.

Where to Go from Here

Start with the basics by taking in the information in Part I about seeds, plants, soil, your site, and garden planning. Then dive into your list of dream vegetables that you want to grow in your garden. Come back to the book periodically throughout the growing season to find out more about pest solutions in Chapter 17 and season extending in Chapter 21. And don't forget to keep harvesting the fruits of all your fine work.

This is just the beginning of your vegetable garden experience. Many resources are available for vegetable gardeners (the appendix can get you started). The key is to get started and keep learning. After tasting one of your first homegrown peas, you'll be hooked for life.

Part I

Digging Into the Basics of Vegetable Gardening

In this part . . .

In this part, I get your vegetable gardening juices
flowing. You first find out the environmental, social,
and health reasons for growing some of your own food.
Then you delve into planning your plot; I talk about the
right sun, soil, and growing conditions for your vegetable
garden and provide ideas for garden designs along with
some samples.

Chapter 1

Vegetable Gardening 101

In This Chapter

▶ Understanding why people grow veggies

▶ Beginning with the basics of planning

▶ Surveying some great vegetables to grow

▶ Keeping your garden growing well

I've been vegetable gardening my whole life. I've followed my grandfather picking stones out of the potato patch, weeded my mother's garden, taught my daughter to plant her first seeds, and built cold frames to maximize the amount of food my wife and I can grow in our yard with edible landscaping. I can attest that once you start, vegetable gardening becomes part of your life. It's not surprising that it grows on you.

In this chapter, I start you off with basics on site preparation, and I tell you what to grow and how to grow it. All the details that follow in subsequent chapters build on the information you need to know to be a successful vegetable gardener. Along the way I hope you are inspired to get some dirt under your fingernails and start your own garden. Dig in!

Why Have Your Own Vegetable Garden?

Over the years people had drifted away from vegetable gardening in the spirit of progress and affluence. However, more recently people are once again realizing that growing their own food, although not as critical to survival as it once was, is an important part of a healthy body, mind, spirit, lifestyle, and community. More people are again turning to vegetable gardening as a means of food and as a hobby. Even the president and first lady have installed a vegetable garden at the White House. Vegetable gardening is officially back!

Who can resist the flavor, smell, and texture of food literally picked minutes before you eat it? It you've ever sunk your teeth into a sun-warmed, ripe tomato and felt the juices and flavors explode in your mouth, you'll know what I mean.

But vegetable gardening isn't just about taste. It's about safe food that's produced close to home. It's about knowing what has been sprayed on that food. It's about feeding your friends and family nutritious food that's high in vitamins and *antioxidants* (cancer-fighting compounds). It's about connecting with your neighbors and community as you experiment with ethnic dishes using exotic ingredients grown in your not-so-exotic backyard. It's about reducing pollution and global warming by not buying produce that's shipped hundreds of miles to your local grocery store. Finally it's about reclaiming your ability to grow some of your own food, even if it's a container of basil, to have a little more control in your life.

If you're interested in finding out more about the popularity and benefits of vegetable gardening, be sure to check out Chapter 2.

The Basics of Planning a Veggie Garden

When's the best time to start vegetable gardening? Right now! Here are the basics on how to decide where to grow yours:

- ✔ Find a spot close to the house that you walk by daily so you don't forget about your project.
- ✔ Find a spot that gets at least 6 hours of direct sun a day.
- ✔ Find a spot that has great soil.

Keep your new garden small. You can be just as productive in a small raised bed garden, container, or small kitchen garden as you would be if you tilled your whole backyard. Start small, be successful, and then get bigger (if you want).

What should you put in your new garden? Well, you have many vegetable options when it comes to deciding what you can grow, so it's going to be tough deciding which ones to plant. The most important rule I can tell you is to grow what you like to eat. Yes, folks, this is all about taste. So no matter what people say about how easy beans are to grow, don't grow them if you hate to eat them. (Of course, after tasting fresh green beans from the garden, you may change your tune.) Grow a mix of varieties of favorite vegetables that you and your family will love. Also, try a few different ones to stretch your imagination.

Chapter 3 has plenty of pointers to help you plan your garden wisely.

A Cornucopia of Vegetables to Grow

You can grow many different types of vegetables in your yard — and not just in the backyard. These days veggies are pretty enough to be front and center.

The following sections describe some of the most popular to get you started. Hopefully you have plenty of room!

Tomatoes

Tomatoes are the most popular vegetable grown — and for good reason. The difference between a vine-ripened fruit and one picked green, gassed, and shipped hundreds of miles to your grocery store is incomparable. You can choose from container varieties that produce fruit the size of a pea and giant plants that grow to the height of a garage and produce fruits the size of a softball! You can even grow varieties of tomatoes with fruits every color of the rainbow except blue (however, I wouldn't be surprised to see that color someday either).

Tomatoes love the heat and sun and require fertile soil and support. Unless you're growing the dwarf varieties, stakes, cages, trellises, teepees, and arbors are essential for keeping plants growing upright and strong. You only need a few plants to keep your family in tomatoes most of the summer. Chapter 4 has the full scoop on growing tomatoes.

Peppers and eggplants

Peppers and eggplants are related to tomatoes, but they're a little more homogeneous in their plant size. However, what they lack in plant variety, they make up in fruit uniqueness. Pepper fruits come shaped as bells or as long and thin tubular shapes. Some are as sweet as candy and others are hot enough to burn your mouth.

Pepper fruits mostly start out green and end up red, but where they go, colorwise, in between is amazing. You can experiment with chocolate-, yellow-, ivory-, purple-, lavender-, and orange-colored fruits that can be eaten raw or used in a multitude of cooked dishes. Eggplants also have burst onto the scene with varieties that produce unique-colored fruits, including white, purple, striped, and even orange.

If you can grow a tomato, you can grow peppers and eggplants. They need similar growing conditions. Plus, I love them as ornamental edibles. Not only do they look good in flower beds and containers, but you can eat them too! Chapter 5 has more on peppers and eggplants.

Carrots, onions, and potatoes

Get to the root of the matter by growing carrots, onions, and potatoes. (I know, I couldn't resist the play on words!) Carrots, onions, and potatoes love cool soil and cool weather conditions. Start them in spring for an early summer crop or in summer to mature in fall. Here are a few fun facts on each group (Chapter 6 has more information):

- ✔ **Carrots:** Carrot varieties are either short and squat or long and thin. You can even get colors other than orange, including red, purple, yellow, and white. Because their seeds are so small and take a while to germinate, carrots can be difficult to get started. But once they're growing you'll soon be munching on roots.

- ✔ **Onions:** Onions are adapted to the north and south depending on the variety. Some are sweet and can be eaten out of hand, but others are pungent and best for cooking and storing in winter. You can grow onions from seed, sets (bulbs), or plants.

- ✔ **Potatoes:** Potatoes are an easy cool-season crop to grow because you plant part of the potato to get new plants. If you cover the tubers with soil, hill them up, and keep them watered, you'll be rolling in spuds come summer.

Peas and beans

Peas and beans are like brothers. They're in the same family and share similar traits, but in some ways they're very different!

- ✔ **Peas** are cool-season-loving crops that produce either plump or flat pods depending on the variety. With some pea varieties you eat pods and all. With others you eat just the peas inside.

- ✔ **Beans** love the heat. They're one of the easiest vegetables to grow. They come in bush and twining or pole bean forms.

Both are great vegetables in the garden because they require little fertilizer and care once they're up and running. Chapter 7 has details.

Cucumbers, melons, pumpkins, and squash

I affectionately call cucumbers, melons, pumpkins, and squash the "viners." They love to ramble about the garden, taking up space and producing loads of fruit. But even if you're a small-space gardener, you can still grow these space hogs. Newer varieties of cucumbers, squash, and melons can fit in a small raised bed or even a container.

One common trait of these vegetables is that they need heat, water, fertility, and bees. Bees? Yes, bees. Most of these squash family crops need to be cross-pollinated to produce fruit, so bees are critical to success. If you're growing other vegetables, flowers, and herbs, you're sure to have some bees flying about to do the dirty work.

Some members of this veggie family can be prolific, so don't plant lots of zucchinis, cucumbers, and pumpkins. Then again, if you really want to share the harvest you can plant a bunch to give away!

Head to Chapter 8 for plenty of pointers on growing vining veggies.

Broccoli, Brussels sprouts, cabbage, and cauliflower

Broccoli, Brussels sprouts, cabbage, and cauliflower are similar in how they grow and what they need to grow. However, their differences come in the parts you eat. Here's the lowdown:

- ✔ After you pick the heads of cabbage and cauliflower, the plant is finished and stops producing.
- ✔ After you pick broccoli heads, you'll keep getting more broccoli side shoots to eat all season long.
- ✔ Brussels sprouts are like your crazy Uncle Louis. He looks a little strange, and you don't know where he came from. Brussels sprouts produce cabbagelike balls all along a straight stem. Keep picking the sprouts starting from the bottom to the top of the stalk and working up until it stops producing because of the cold.

This group of veggies is productive and serves as a great addition to a cool-weather spring or fall garden. See Chapter 9 for more information.

Lettuce, spinach, Swiss chard, and specialty greens

If you're looking for quick rewards, go straight to Chapter 10 and grow greens: lettuce, spinach, chard, and wild greens, such as dandelions. Because you don't have to wait for greens to form fruits (you're just eating the leaves), you can pick them as soon as your stomach rumbles and the leaves are big enough to munch. They mostly love cool weather, so start early in spring and then keep planting and harvesting.

Greens are one of the best container vegetables to grow because they're easy and adaptable. You can mix and match lettuce varieties to produce different colors and textures that look beautiful and taste divine.

An assortment of other great veggies

In the previous sections, I just touch the tip of the iceberg when it comes to what to grow for vegetable varieties. There are so many more vegetables to grow; all you have to do is wander down the produce aisles at the local grocery store and think, do I like to eat that? Chapter 11 describes more than 30 other vegetables to grow — from asparagus to turnips. Watch out or you may get hooked and start growing so many vegetables you'll have to open a restaurant. Vegetable gardening really can become that much fun.

Non-vegetable edibles

Don't limit yourself to growing just vegetables in the vegetable garden. That would be silly! Berries, such as blueberries, strawberries, and raspberries, and herbs, such as basil, parsley, and chives, are great additions to your yard. They produce fruit, spice up a meal, and look beautiful. Need some inspiration? Here are some suggestions:

- ✔ Consider having a strawberry patch in your garden.
- ✔ Landscape your yard with blueberry bushes or a hedge of raspberries.
- ✔ Mix herb plants around vegetable plants or give them their own space in the garden. Herbs also grow well in containers mixed with flowers. I love growing rosemary in a deck planter each year for the attractive foliage and the enticing aroma.

Chapter 12 has plenty of details on growing berries and herbs in an edible landscape.

Getting Down to Growing

Are you excited to grow some of your own food? Not so fast! You need a roadmap to get a successful start. Just like driving, if you get off in the wrong direction, it takes lots of time and effort to get back on course. So you have to start out with a plan and stick to it. The following sections are a quick run-through from seed to table of growing vegetables. After you read this section, head to the chapters in Part II for all the nitty-gritty details that will ensure success.

Choosing between seeds and transplants

The easiest way to start a new garden is to grow those vegetables that can be planted from seed directly into the soil. For veggies that are best transplanted, buy the transplants locally. (Some vegetables can go both ways, too.) Here's a breakdown of the two groups:

- ✔ Some vegetables that can be sown directly into the ground as seeds include beans, peas, carrots, beets, and sweet corn.

- ✔ Some vegetables and herbs you can find in local garden centers as transplants include tomatoes, peppers, eggplants, broccoli, cauliflower, cabbage, lettuce, cucumber, squash, basil, and parsley.

If you have a small garden, go with the transplants. If you're growing a larger garden, you'll find it less expensive to grow veggies from seed.

Chapter 13 has details on growing seeds versus growing transplants.

Working the soil

After you have your vegetable seeds or transplants ready to go, the temptation is to simply turn the soil and then plant. However, soil building is one of the most important parts of your gardening experience. Your soil needs to be fertile, loose, dried out, and relatively weed and rock free to grow the best crops. If you take care of the soil in your beds, it'll take care of you by producing healthy, productive vegetables with few insect and disease problems.

Spend some time working the soil by hand or with a tiller. Amend it every year with compost to keep the fertility high and make it more workable. Test your soil to see if it needs other nutrients. Flip to Chapter 14 for more ways to coddle your soil.

Keeping your garden growing and enjoying the rewards

When your garden is up and running, you can lower your maintenance time and effort and raise your satisfaction level by doing the following (see Chapter 15 for the full scoop on maintenance):

- ✔ Mulch your beds.
- ✔ Water your plants deeply and consistently.
- ✔ Fertilize when necessary.

No matter how well you care for your garden, pests still may attack your plants. It's best to grow insect- and disease-resistant varieties when possible. And be sure to create barriers to block pests from attacking, clean up the garden well to remove overwintering insects and diseases, and only spray as a last resort. I provide more pointers on keeping your plants healthy in Chapter 17.

Finally, after all this serious stuff, comes the fun part: harvesting. Check the garden daily when plants are producing, and pick even if you don't have room in the refrigerator. With many vegetable plants, the more fruits you pick, the more you'll get. You always can give away the fresh produce to friends, family, and neighbors, so don't stop picking. Chapter 19 has details on harvesting and storing your veggies.

Trying tips for an even bigger bounty

To go further with your vegetable garden, try a few of the following techniques that help improve production and yield:

✔ **Use containers.** Growing in containers allows you to grow plants longer into the season and position your plants in the sunniest, most protected spots around your house. See Chapter 18 for the dirt on container gardening.

✔ **Practice cool farmer tricks, such as succession planting and interplanting.** *Succession planting* allows you to grow three or more crops in one season from the same spot. *Interplanting* is where you plant quick-maturing small plants, such as lettuce and radishes, around slow-growing larger plants, such as tomatoes and broccoli. The small plants are harvested before the larger plants shade them out. See Chapter 16 for more details.

Chapter 2

The Popularity and Benefits of Vegetable Gardening

In This Chapter

▶ Understanding why food gardening is a booming hobby

▶ Checking out a few advantages to food gardening

*I*f you're interested in growing your own food (of course you are; you're reading this book!), welcome to the club. Vegetable, fruit, berry, and herb gardening (collectively called *food gardening*) is booming across the United States and around the world. Why, you ask? Simply put, people enjoy the many benefits from food gardening. In this chapter, I paint a picture of food gardening's popularity in the United States and describe a few major advantages of growing your own food.

Food Gardening: It's Popping Up Everywhere

While food gardening is a great activity to do in your yard, it's also part of a growing trend of people wanting to eat better, grow some of their own food, and have more control on the quality of their food supply. What better way to ensure that you eat healthy food than growing it yourself?

In early 2009, the National Gardening Association (NGA) completed a survey that characterized food gardening in the United States. Here's what it found:

✔ Approximately 23 percent, or 27 million households, had a vegetable garden in 2008. That's 2 million more than in 2007. The number of food gardeners increases to 31 percent, or 36 million households, if you include those people growing fruits, berries, and herbs.

✔ The average person spends about $70 on their food garden every year. (I wish I could keep my spending that low!) The total nationwide is $2.5

billion spent on food gardening. I explain what you gain from that $70 in comparison to what you'd spend at the grocery store later in this section.

✔ The average vegetable garden is 600 square feet, but 83 percent of the vegetable gardens are less than 500 square feet. Nearly half of all gardeners grow some vegetables in containers as well.

✔ The typical vegetable gardener is college educated, married, female, age 45 or older, and has no kids at home. And almost 60 percent of vegetable gardeners have been gardening for less than five years.

✔ The typical reasons for vegetable gardening in order of importance are: to produce fresh food, to save money, to produce better-quality food, and to grow food you know is safe. (I go into detail on several important reasons to grow food later in this chapter.)

There you have it. Lots of food gardeners are out in their crops, and the numbers are growing faster than corn in July. You may grow only a small food garden, but when all the gardens are added together, the impact is enormous. Need more proof? Let me show you!

The *gross national garden product* (GNGP) is the combined amount of money that can be produced from America's food gardens. Here's how the NGA figured it out (time for some math fun!):

✔ About 36 million households grow vegetables, berries, fruits, and herbs. The average garden size is 600 square feet. The NGA estimates that you can produce about $1/2$ pound of vegetables per square foot of garden per year. That's about 300 pounds of vegetables in the average garden. The average price, in season, of vegetables is about $2 per pound, so the average vegetable garden produces $600 worth of produce. So, Americans invest an average of $70 to yield $600 worth of produce every year. Wow! That's a good return in my book!

✔ When you figure the numbers nationally, 36 million households spend $2.5 billion to yield a GNGP of more than $21 billion worth of vegetables each year. That's a stimulus plan I can live with! (You don't believe it? Go to the section "Save some cash" later in this chapter to see how you can save that kind of money by growing your own vegetables.)

A Few Good Reasons to Grow Your Own Food

It's almost predictable: When economic times are hard, people head to the garden. It happened in the 1920s with Liberty Gardens, in the 1940s with Victory Gardens, and in the 1970s with increases in oil and food prices. Similarly, with current concerns about food safety, global warming, carbon footprints, and pollution, along with a desire to build a link to the Earth and our own neighborhoods, food gardening has become a simple and tasty solution.

Food gardens aren't just in backyards anymore. People grow food in containers on decks and patios, in community gardens, at schools, at senior centers, and even in front yards for everyone to see. Food gardens are beautiful and productive, so why not let everyone enjoy the benefits? I describe the advantages to growing your own food in the following sections.

Improve your health

We all know we're supposed to eat more fruits and vegetables every day. It isn't just good advice from mom. Many vegetables are loaded with vitamins A and C, fiber, water, and minerals such as potassium. A growing body of research shows that eating fresh fruits and vegetables not only gives your body the nutrients and vitamins it needs to function properly, but it also reveals that many fruits and vegetables are loaded with phytochemicals and antioxidants — specific compounds that help prevent and fight illness.

While specific vegetables and fruits are high in certain nutrients, the best way to make sure you get a good range of these compounds in your diet is to "eat a rainbow." By eating a variety of different-colored vegetables and fruits, you get all the nutrients you need to be healthy.

While eating fruits and vegetables is generally a great idea, the quality and safety of produce in grocery stores has been increasingly compromised. Whether it's *Salmonella* on jalapeño peppers or *E. coli* in spinach, warnings seem to be happening every year. Also, some people are concerned about pesticide residues on their produce. A list called the "Dirty Dozen" points out the vegetables and fruits most likely to contain pesticide residues. Here's the list: apples, bell peppers, celery, cherries, imported grapes, nectarines, peaches, pears, potatoes, red raspberries, spinach, and strawberries. What better way to ensure a safe food supply free of biological and pesticide contamination than to grow your own? You'll know exactly what's been used to grow those beautiful crops.

Save some cash

You can save big money by growing your own vegetables and fruits. In fact, depending on the type and amount you grow, you can save hundreds of dollars. By spending a few dollars on seeds, plants, and supplies in spring, you'll produce vegetables that yield pounds of produce in summer. Instead of having to go to the grocery store to buy all that produce, you've got it ready for the picking for free in your yard. It's your own personal produce department! You'll save hundreds of dollars on your grocery bill each year by growing a garden.

Here's just one example of how a vegetable garden can save you some cash. The 20-foot-by-30-foot production garden in Figure 2-1 highlights many favorite vegetables. I also include some plans for succession cropping and interplanting. (See Chapter 16 for more details on these techniques.) When I indicate succession crops, I'm assuming two crops in one growing season. I'm also assuming 8-foot-long raised beds with rows with space to walk between the beds down the center.

To show you how the garden in Figure 2-1 saves you money, the following list provides vegetable yields and the price per pound of each crop. However, keep in mind that these are general averages. I've erred on the conservative side with many yields. Yields, after all, can vary depending on the location, variety, and growth of your crops. The prices are based on national average prices from the USDA Agricultural Marketing Service for those vegetables grown organically in summer. Again, these numbers may vary depending on the year and location in the country. However, even with all these variables, you can see that you grow more than 300 pounds of produce worth more than $600 just by working your own garden!

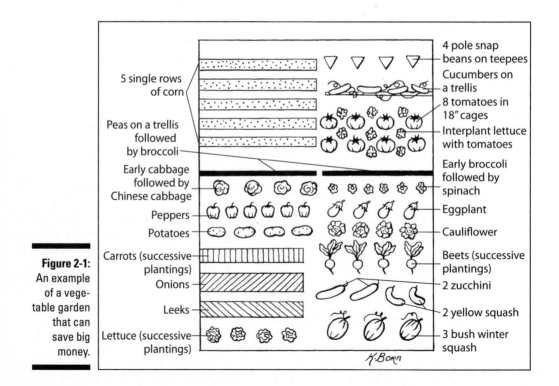

Figure 2-1:
An example of a vegetable garden that can save big money.

Vegetable	Yields	Dollars per Pound	Value
Beets	12 pounds	$1.50	$18
Broccoli	16 pounds	$2.50	$40
Cabbages	18 pounds	$1	$18
Carrots	16 pounds	$1.50	$24
Cauliflower	8 pounds	$3	$24
Cucumbers	10 pounds	$2	$20
Eggplant	12 pounds	$2	$24
Leeks	10 pounds	$1.50	$15
Lettuce	10 pounds	$2	$20
Onions	16 pounds	$1.50	$24
Peas (double row)	8 pounds	$3	$24
Peppers	30 pounds	$1.50	$45
Pole beans	12 pounds	$1.50	$18
Potatoes	25 pounds	$1	$25
Spinach	10 pounds	$3	$30
Summer squash/zucchini	25 pounds	$2	$50
Sweet corn (50 ears)	17 pounds	$0.50/ea	$25
Tomatoes	80 pounds	$2	$160
Winter squash (bush)	15 pounds	$2	$30
Totals	**350 pounds**		**$634**

If you grew the garden depicted in Figure 2-1, your initial investment of $70 to get started will yield 350 pounds of vegetables. If you purchased the same 350 pounds of vegetables in a grocery store, you'd have to pay more than $600. So, as you can see, you're saving money and getting great food to eat.

Help the environment

Your tomatoes, lettuces, and melons from the grocery store cost more than just the price to produce them. It's estimated that the average produce travels up to 1,500 miles to get from farm to grocery store, and that's just vegetables and fruits produced in the United States. Increasingly, produce is being imported from foreign countries, such as China and Chile. The fossil fuels used to transport these vegetables increases air pollution and global warming. So, one of the big-picture reasons for growing your own produce is to fight these effects on our planet.

Plus, by growing your own vegetables, fruits, and herbs, you also reduce the amount of pollution that's created on the farm. Regardless of it being a conventional or organic farm, many large operations tend to use lots of fertilizers, pesticides, and herbicides to grow their crops. Unfortunately, some of these additives end up as sources of pollution (and their creation requires fossil fuels). By growing your own produce using a minimal amount of these inputs (I show you how in Chapter 15), you can reduce the amount of chemical and fertilizer pollution that ends up in waterways around the country. For more information on gardening sustainably, check out *Sustainable Landscaping For Dummies* by Owen Dell (Wiley).

Increase your quality of life

A less tangible (but still important) reason to grow your own vegetables is related to quality of life. Vegetable gardening is a great way to unwind after a hard day. You can achieve a simple pleasure and satisfaction in roaming through your garden, snacking on a bean here and a cherry tomato there, pulling a few weeds, watering, and enjoying the fruits of your labors. It's an immediate, simple satisfaction in a world that so often is complicated and complex.

Also, if you garden with others in a community garden, you'll create new friendships and bonds with your neighbors. According to the NGA food gardening survey that I describe earlier in this chapter, more than a million community gardens exist across the country. Often community gardens become a focal point for neighborhood beautification, education, and development projects. When the gardens are sown, people start taking increased interest and pride in their neighborhood and how it looks. Often crime, graffiti, and vandalism are reduced just by creating a garden where people can gather together. And you thought all you were doing is growing a few vegetables!

For more information about starting a community garden or to find one in your area, contact the American Community Gardening Association at communitygarden.org.

Chapter 3

Planning Your Veggie Garden

*B*efore you go out and till up the whole yard to create a vegetable garden, you need to do a little planning. I know, I know. You're dreaming of luscious melons, mouth-watering tomatoes, and crisp salad greens picked fresh from your garden. But as my dad used to say, "You gotta have a plan, Charlie." So, in this chapter, I provide you with a basic plan for locating and mapping out the perfect vegetable garden to suit your yard and needs.

Deciding Where to Put Your Vegetable Garden

When considering where to plop down your plot, think of these three main elements, which are necessary for the perfect spot: site, sun, and soil. The following sections describe each of these and give you some things to think about when surveying your yard for the best possible spot for your plot. Figure 3-1 puts some of these ideas into visual perspective.

Don't be discouraged if you lack the ideal garden spot — few gardeners have one. Just try to make the most of what you have.

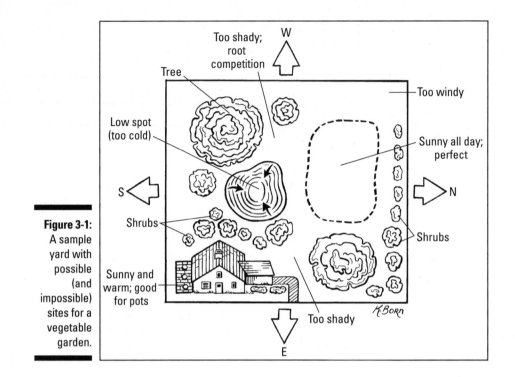

Figure 3-1:
A sample
yard with
possible
(and
impossible)
sites for a
vegetable
garden.

Considering different sites

Choosing a site is the important first step in planning a vegetable garden. This may sound like a tough choice to make, but don't worry; a lot of the decision is based on good old common sense. When you're considering a site for your garden, remember these considerations:

✔ **Keep it close to home.** Plant your garden where you'll walk by it daily so that you remember to care for it. Also, a vegetable garden is a place people like to gather, so keep it close to a pathway. (I talk about garden paths later in this chapter.)

Vegetable gardens used to be relegated to some forlorn location out back. Unfortunately, if it's out of sight, it's out of mind. I like to plant vegetables front and center — even in the front yard. That way you get to see the fruits of your labor and remember what chores need to be done. Plus, it's a great way to engage the neighbors as they stroll by and admire your plants. You may even be inspired to share a tomato with them.

✔ **Make it easy to access.** If you need to bring in soil, compost, mulch, or wood by truck or car, make sure your garden can be easily reached by a vehicle. Otherwise you'll end up working way too hard to cart these essentials from one end of the yard to the other.

✔ **Have a water source close by.** Try to locate your garden as close as you can to an outdoor faucet. Hauling hundreds of feet of hose around the yard to water the garden will only cause more work and frustration. And, hey, isn't gardening supposed to be fun?

✔ **Keep it flat.** You can garden on a slight slope, and, in fact, a south-facing one is ideal since it warms up faster in spring. However, too severe a slope could lead to erosion problems. To avoid having to build terraces like Machu Picchu, plant your garden on flat ground.

A bit of science also is involved in choosing the right site. *Microclimates* are small areas of your yard whose temperatures and related growing conditions are slightly different from the overall climate of your yard, neighborhood, or town. These differences usually are caused by large objects, such as your house, a wall, or a tree. For example, the south side of your house may be hotter than the rest of your yard, because the sun reflects off the walls and the house blocks prevailing cold winds. Or an area under a large tree may be cooler than the rest of the yard because of the shade provided by the tree's canopy.

How big is too big for a veggie garden? If you're a first-time gardener, a size of 100 square feet is plenty of space to take care of; I like to tell beginning gardeners to start small and build on their success. However, if you want to produce food for storing and sharing, a 20-foot-x-30-foot plot (600 square feet total) is a great size. You can produce an abundance of different vegetables and still keep the plot looking good.

Speaking of upkeep, keep the following in mind when deciding how large to make your garden: If the soil is in good condition, a novice gardener can keep up with a 600-square-foot garden by devoting about a half-hour each day the first month of the season; in late spring through summer, a good half-hour of work every 2 to 3 days should keep the garden productive and looking good. Keep in mind that the smaller the garden, the less time it'll take to keep it looking great. Plus, after it's established, the garden will take less time to get up and running in the spring. And if you use some of the time-saving tips throughout this book, you may be able to cut down the time commitment even more.

Letting the sun shine on your plot

Vegetables need enough sun to produce at their best. Fruiting vegetables, such as tomatoes, peppers, beans, squash, melons, cucumbers, and eggplant, need at least 6 hours of direct sun a day for good yields. The amount of sun doesn't have to be continuous though. You can have 3 hours in the morning with some shade midday and then 3 more hours in the late afternoon.

However, if your little piece of heaven gets less than 6 hours of sun, don't give up. You have some options:

- ✔ Crops where you eat the leaves, such as lettuce, arugula, pac choi, and spinach, produce reasonably well in a partially shaded location where the sun shines directly on the plants for 3 to 4 hours a day.

- ✔ Root crops, such as carrots, potatoes, and beets, need more light than leafy vegetables, but they may do well getting only 4 to 6 hours of sun a day.

If you don't have enough sun to grow fruiting crops, such as tomatoes and peppers, consider planting a movable garden. Plant these crops in containers and move them to the sunniest spots in your yard throughout the year. I discuss this technique more in Chapter 18.

Keep in mind that sun and shade patterns change with the seasons. A site that's sunny in midsummer may later be shaded by trees, buildings, and the longer shadows of late fall and early spring. If you live in a mild-winter climate, such as parts of the southeastern and southwestern United States where it's possible to grow vegetables nearly year-round, choosing a spot that's sunny in winter as well as in summer is important. In general, sites that have clear southern exposure are sunniest in winter (refer to Figure 3-1).

You can have multiple vegetable garden plots around your yard matching the conditions with the vegetables you're growing. If your only sunny spot is a strip of ground along the front of the house, plant a row of peppers and tomatoes. If you have a perfect location near a backdoor, but it only gets morning sun, plant lettuce and greens in that plot.

If shade in your garden comes from nearby trees and shrubs, your vegetable plants will compete for water and nutrients as well as for light. Tree roots extend slightly beyond the *drip line,* the outer foliage reach of the tree. If possible, keep your garden out of the *root zones* (the areas that extend from the drip lines to the trunks) of surrounding trees and shrubs. If avoiding root zones isn't possible, give the vegetables more water and be sure to fertilize to compensate.

Black walnut trees pose a particular problem to vegetable gardens because their roots give off a substance called *juglone* that inhibits the growth of some plants, including tomatoes. Plants growing in the root zones of black walnuts often wilt and die. Try to leave at least 50 feet between your garden and any walnut trees.

Checking your soil's drainage

After you've checked the site location and sun levels of your prospective garden, you need to focus on the third element of the big three: the soil. Ideally you have rich, loamy, well-drained soil with few rocks (as I describe in

Chapter 14). Unfortunately, that type of soil is a rarity. But a key that's even more essential to good soil is proper water drainage. Plant roots need air as well as water, and water-logged soils are low in air content. Puddles of water on the soil surface after a rain indicate poor drainage.

One way to check your soil's drainage is to dig a hole about 10 inches deep and fill it with water. Let the water drain and then fill the hole again the following day. Time how long it takes for the water to drain away. If water remains in the hole more than 8 to 10 hours after the second filling, your soil drainage needs improvement.

Soils made primarily of clay tend to be considered *heavy*. Heavy soils usually aren't as well drained as sandy soils. Adding lots of organic matter to your soil can improve soil drainage (I tell you a lot more about how to do that in Chapter 14). Or you also can build raised beds on a poorly drained site (see "Deciding on hills, rows, or raised beds," later in this chapter).

But slow water drainage isn't always a bad thing. Soil also can be *too* well drained. Very sandy soil dries out quickly and needs frequent watering during dry spells. Again, adding lots of organic matter to sandy soil increases the amount of water it can hold.

If you encounter a lot of big rocks in your soil, you may want to look for another spot. Or consider going the raised-bed route. You can improve soils that have a lot of clay or that are too sandy, but very rocky soil can be a real headache. In fact, it can be impossible to garden in.

Don't plant your garden near or on top of the leach lines of a septic system. I'm sure you know why. And keep away from underground utilities. If you have questions, call your local utility company to locate underground lines. If you're unsure what's below ground, visit www.call811.com to have lines or pipes identified for free.

Understanding Veggie Varieties

Before you go drooling over the luscious veggies in catalogs, in garden centers, and online, it's good to know a little about the varieties you can choose from. If you select your veggie varieties before you design your garden, you can ensure that you have the proper amount of space and the best growing conditions. (I explain how to design your garden later in this chapter.)

A *variety* is a selection of a particular type of vegetable that has certain predictable, desirable traits. These traits may include the following:

✔ **Adaptation:** Some varieties are particularly well adapted to certain areas and climates. For example, some tomato varieties produce good-tasting fruit in the cool, foggy coastal climates of the Pacific Northwest. And certain bean varieties are better adapted to the hot, dry deserts of the American southwest.

✔ **Appearance:** You can choose from a rainbow of fruit and leaf colors, such as purple peppers, yellow chard, and orange tomatoes. Leaf textures and shapes range from frilly to smooth to puckered. The flowers of some vegetables, such as okra and eggplant, are attractive in their own right. You get the idea. The more beautiful the vegetables, the more beautiful the vegetable garden — and the more stunning the food.

✔ **Cooking and storage characteristics:** Certain varieties of beans and peas, for example, freeze better than others. Some winter squash varieties may be stored for months, but others need to be eaten immediately.

✔ **Days to maturity (or days to harvest):** *Days to maturity* refers to the number of days it takes (under normal conditions) for a vegetable planted from seed (or from transplants) to mature and produce a crop. This number is especially important for vegetable gardeners who live in short-summer climates. Average days to maturity are listed for each type of vegetable in the appendix. You can find specific variety information on individual vegetables in Part II.

✔ **Extended harvest season:** A certain variety of corn, for example, may ripen early or late in the season. By planting varieties that ripen at different times, you can start harvesting as early as 60 days after seeding and continue for 5 or 6 weeks. Seed catalogs and packages often describe varieties as early season, midseason, or late season in relationship to other varieties of the same vegetable.

✔ **Pest resistance:** Many vegetable varieties are resistant to specific diseases or pests — a very important trait in many areas. Some tomato varieties, in particular, have outstanding disease resistance. See Chapter 17 for more on pest control. You also can read about specific pest-resistant varieties of individual vegetables in Part II.

✔ **Plant size:** The trend in vegetable breeding is to go small. Tomato, cucumber, and even winter squash varieties are available in dwarf sizes. These varieties are perfect for container growing or small-space gardens.

✔ **Taste:** Pick a flavor and you can find a vegetable that stars in it. You can grow fruity tomatoes, super-sweet varieties of corn, bitter melons, and spicy peppers. You'll discover flavors for every taste bud.

To realize the scope of your vegetable variety possibilities, see the individual vegetable descriptions in Part II. It's also important to note that you can categorize a variety as a hybrid, an open-pollinated, or an heirloom variety. Here's what these terms mean:

✔ **Hybrid:** *Hybrid seeds* (also known as *F-1 hybrids*) are the result of a cross of selected groups of plants of the same kind, called *inbred lines*. (A *cross* is when pollen from one flower fertilizes a flower from another similar plant, resulting in seed.) Hybrid seeds generally are more expensive than open-pollinated seeds, and they can't be saved and planted the next year because the offspring won't have the same characteristics as the parents. If you did plant them next year, you'd get a mix of characteristics — some desirable and some not. The plants are uniform, but they often lack a diversity of shapes, colors, sizes, and flavors. However, hybrid plants are more vigorous, productive, and widely adapted than other varieties.

✔ **Open-pollinated:** *Open-pollinated* varieties basically are inbred lines allowed to pollinate each other in open fields. They produce offspring that are similar to their parents. Before the arrival of hybrids, all vegetable varieties were open-pollinated. Some gardeners like these varieties for their flavor, their diversity, and the fact that they can save the seeds each year to replant. The resulting offspring are pretty predictable, but they don't provide the consistency of hybrids.

✔ **Heirloom:** Any open-pollinated variety that's at least 50 years old is generally considered an heirloom. Heirlooms are enjoying quite a revival because of the variety of colors, tastes, and forms that are available. They're worth trying, but keep in mind that some varieties may not have the disease resistance and wide adaptability that hybrids generally have.

One category generally available only to commercial farmers is that of the *genetically modified variety.* This kind of plant has a gene from a completely unrelated species inserted into it so that it exhibits a certain trait. For example, geneticists have inserted a gene of the biological pesticide Bt (see Chapter 17) into potatoes so that when the Colorado potato beetle (their biggest enemy) eats a potato's leaves, it also eats the pesticide and dies. Many questions exist about the long-term health risks and environmental safety of manipulating the gene pool so dramatically and quickly. For this reason, genetically modified organisms (GMOs) aren't allowed in organic gardening.

Timing Your Planting Wisely

As my dad used to say, "Timing is everything." This axiom is especially important for vegetable gardening, so file it where you can't forget it. Remembering it will save you lots of heartache and disappointment. For example, if you plant tomatoes too early, the plants will sit there like bumps on a log, not growing and possibly rotting in cold, wet soil or turning mushy and black after they've been zapped by frost. Plant lettuce too late, and it'll produce more flowers than leaves, and the leaves you harvest will be tough and bitter. I can give you examples like this for every vegetable, but I'll spare you the monotony. Just know that planting at the wrong time of year is a recipe for disaster.

If you follow the rhythms of nature and plant when conditions are perfect for proper growth, growing vegetables is a breeze. But how are you supposed to know about these rhythms? Start tapping your foot, because the following sections will have you moving like Fred Astaire.

Some like it cool, some like it hot

Vegetables can be divided into the following two categories based on the temperature conditions in which they grow best:

- ✔ **Cool-season vegetables:** These vegetables, such as lettuce, spinach, peas, potatoes, broccoli, and cabbage, grow best in the cool weather of spring and fall. As vegetables go, they're fairly hardy and survive despite freezing temperatures. In most areas, cool-season vegetables are usually planted in early spring so they mature before the onset of hot weather, or in late summer to early fall for maturation in the cool months of fall or early winter. However, in areas where summers are very cool and winters are mild, such as in coastal areas of the western United States and the far north, cool season vegetables can be grown year-round and may be the only vegetables that can thrive in this climate.

  What happens if you plant a cool-season vegetable when it's too warm? Not a lot of good. Lettuce will *bolt,* meaning it starts to flower before you get a chance to harvest it. In other words, instead of producing tender, crisp leaves, lettuce will send out a tall flower spike. Any leaves that are left on the plant will be bitter-tasting and tough. Broccoli will form loose clusters of yellow flowers instead of forming nice tight heads. And peas won't properly fill their pods with sweet, succulent peas. You get the idea!

- ✔ **Warm-season vegetables:** These vegetables, such as beans, tomatoes, peppers, cucumbers, melons, squash, okra, and corn, like it hot and grow best in the warm months of summer. They need warm soil and air temperatures to grow their best; if they're planted while the weather is still too cool, they'll suffer and not grow. Because freezing temperatures kill these vegetables, they're usually planted after the threat of frost in spring. In warm areas, they also can be planted in late summer for a fall harvest.

To push along warm-season veggies, wait until the soil and air are the proper temperature. Or consider using season extenders to trap heat around the plants. Season extenders also help in cool summer climates such as the Pacific Northwest, where the weather rarely gets warm enough even in summer to ripen heat-loving vegetables like melons. (Chapter 21 has more ideas on season-extending techniques.)

Frost dates and the length of the growing season

You should know two very important weather dates for your area if you want to grow vegetables successfully:

- ✔ The average date of the last frost in spring
- ✔ The average date of the first frost in fall

These frost dates tell you several important things:

- ✔ **When to plant:** Cool-season vegetables are generally planted 4 to 6 weeks before the last spring frost. Fall planting of cool-season vegetables is less dependent on frost dates, but it's usually done 8 to 12 weeks before the first fall frost. Warm-season vegetables are planted after the last spring frost or in late summer in warm areas for a fall harvest.

- ✔ **When to protect warm-season vegetables:** Frosts kill warm-season vegetables. So the closer you plant to the last frost of spring, the more important it is to protect plants. And as the fall frost gets closer, so does the end of your summer vegetable season — unless, of course, you protect your plants. I show you how to provide frost protection in Chapter 21.

- ✔ **The length of your growing season:** Your *growing season* is the number of days between the average date of the last frost in spring and the average date of the first frost in fall. The length of the growing season can range from less than 100 days in northern or cold winter climates to 365 days in frost-free southern climes. Many warm-season vegetables need long, warm growing seasons to properly mature, so they're difficult, if not impossible, to grow where growing seasons are short.

  How are you to know whether your growing season is long enough? If you check mail-order seed catalogs or even individual seed packets, each variety will have the number of days to harvest or days to maturity (usually posted in parentheses next to the variety name). This number tells you how many days it takes for that vegetable to grow from seed (or transplant) to harvest. If your growing season is only 100 days long and you want to grow a melon or other warm-season vegetable that takes 120 frost-free days to mature, you have a problem. The plant will probably be killed by frost before the fruit is mature. In areas with short growing seasons, it's usually best to go with early ripening varieties (which have the shortest number of days to harvest).

  However, you also can find many effective ways to extend your growing season, such as starting seeds indoors or planting under *floating row covers* (blanketlike materials that drape over plants, creating warm, greenhouselike conditions underneath). Various methods of extending growing seasons are covered in Chapter 21.

There you have it; now you know why frost dates are so important. But how do you find out dates for your area? Easy. Ask a local nursery worker or contact your local Cooperative Extension office (look in the phone book under *county government*). You also can look in the appendix of this book, which lists frost dates for major cities around the country.

Frost dates are important, but you also have to take them with a grain of salt. After all, these dates are averages, meaning that half the time the frost will actually come earlier than the average date and half the time it will occur later. You also should know that frost dates are usually given for large areas, such as your city or county. If you live in a cold spot in the bottom of a valley, frosts may come days earlier in fall and days later in spring. Similarly, if you live in a warm spot or you garden in a microclimate, your frost may come later in fall and stop earlier in spring. You're sure to find out all about your area as you become a more seasoned vegetable gardener and unearth the nuances of your own yard. One thing you'll discover for sure is that you can't predict the weather.

Listening to your evening weather forecast is one of the best ways to find out whether frosts are expected in your area. But you also can do a little predicting yourself by going outside late in the evening and checking conditions. If the fall or early spring sky is clear and full of stars, and the wind is still, conditions are right for a frost. If you need to protect plants, do so at that time. Frost-protection techniques are covered in Chapter 21.

Designing Your Garden

After you've found the best spot for your plot, selected a few veggie varieties, and figured out when you need to plant those varieties, it's time to map out your garden. Designing a vegetable garden is a little bit of art and a little bit of science. Practically speaking, plants must be spaced properly so they have room to grow and arranged so taller vegetables don't shade lower-growing types. Different planting techniques fit the growth habits of different kinds of vegetables. You also should think about the paths between rows and plants. Will you have enough room to harvest, weed, and water, for example?

On the other hand, having fun with your vegetable garden design is important too. Many vegetables are good looking on their own, but you also can get creative with combinations of vegetables with different flowers and herbs.

In the following sections, I give you the basics so you can start to sketch out a garden plan. I also provide some sample designs to get your juices flowing. If you stick with your plan, you'll be a vegetable gardening wizard in no time.

 These sections give you the nuts and bolts information you need to create a final vegetable garden design. Don't stop here though. The descriptions of individual vegetables in Part II suggest ways to grow various types of vegetables — information that will probably influence your design. And the information on planting times earlier in this chapter, the scoop on succession planting in Chapter 16, and the lowdown on watering techniques in Chapter 15 can influence the way you arrange and plant your garden.

Deciding on hills, rows, or raised beds

Before you sketch a plan, you need to decide how to arrange the plants in your garden. You can use three basic planting arrangements:

✔ **In rows:** Planting vegetables in rows is the typical farmer technique. Any vegetable can be planted in straight rows, but this arrangement works best with types that need quite a bit of room, such as tomatoes, beans, cabbages, corn, potatoes, peppers, and summer squash.

✔ **In hills:** Hills are typically used for vining crops such as cucumbers, melons, pumpkins, and winter squash. You can create a 1-foot-wide, flat-topped mound for heavy soil, or you can create a circle at ground level for sandy soil. You then surround the soil with a moatlike ring for watering. Two or three evenly spaced plants are grown on each hill. Space your hills the recommended distance used for rows of that vegetable.

✔ **In raised beds:** Raised beds, which are my favorite, are kind of like wide, flat-topped rows. They're usually at least 2 feet wide and raised at least 6 inches high, but any planting area that's raised above the surrounding ground level is a raised bed. Almost any vegetable can benefit from being grown on a raised bed, but smaller vegetables and root crops, such as lettuce, beets, carrots, onions, spinach, and radishes, really thrive with this type planting. On top of the raised bed you can grow plants in rows or with broadcast seeding (see Chapter 13 for more on seeding techniques).

A raised bed can be a normal bed with the soil piled 5 or 6 inches high. I call this a *temporary raised bed.* Or you can build a *permanent raised bed* with wood, stone, or masonry sides, as shown in Figure 3-2.

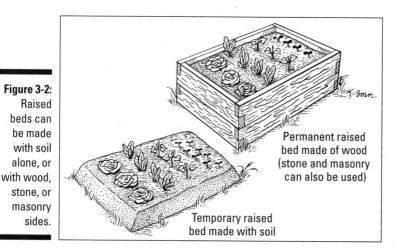

Figure 3-2: Raised beds can be made with soil alone, or with wood, stone, or masonry sides.

Permanent raised bed made of wood (stone and masonry can also be used)

Temporary raised bed made with soil

Raised beds have several advantages, including the following:

✔ **They rise above soil problems.** If you have bad soil or poor drainage, raised beds are for you. You can amend the garden soil in the raised bed with compost or the same sterile potting soil you use for containers (see Chapter 18). And because you don't step on the beds as you work, the soil is more likely to stay light and fluffy, providing the perfect conditions for root growth — especially for root crops such as carrots and beets.

✔ **They warm up quickly.** Because more of the soil in raised beds is exposed to the sun, the soil warms early and dries out faster, allowing for early planting and extended harvest seasons.

If you're in a hot climate and have sandy soil, raised beds may not be for you, because they'll dry out and heat up too much.

✔ **They reduce your work.** By growing your vegetables in raised beds, you can maximize your fertilizing and watering so that more nutrients and water are actually used by the plants rather than wasted in the pathways.

✔ **They're easy on your back and knees.** If you design the beds properly (about 18 to 24 inches high and no wider than 4 feet), raised beds can make vegetable gardening a lot more comfortable. You can sit on the edge and easily reach into the bed to weed or harvest. You can even cap the edge to make it more benchlike.

✔ **They're attractive.** You can make raised beds in almost any shape you like — rectangle, square, triangle, circle. Your garden can take on a whimsical design with a little creativity. Just keep the width less than 4 feet so you can easily reach the center of the bed without stepping on the soil.

Wooden raised beds should be made of rot-resistant woods, such as redwood or cedar, or recycled plastic timbers. I like to use two 2-x-10 boards for the sides, and then I anchor them with lag screws at the corners with short 4-x-4 posts buried a foot deep. (You don't necessarily need the posts, however.) If you plant several raised beds, leave at least 3-foot-wide paths between them for access. (I discuss garden paths in more detail later in this chapter.)

Some gardeners use pressure-treated wood or creosote-treated railroad ties to construct raised beds; check with your local lumberyard for these materials. I prefer not to use woods treated with chemicals. They'll last a long time, but research has shown that some of these chemicals leach into the soil and can adversely affect your plants.

The one downside of permanent raised beds is turning the soil. Lifting a tiller onto the bed can be difficult, so they're best turned by hand with an iron fork. (I like to "fluff" my beds each spring with an iron fork.) You also can use a minitiller, which I discuss in Chapter 20.

In dry areas such as the desert Southwest, the traditional bed isn't raised — it's sunken. These *waffle beds* are created by digging into the soil about 6 inches deep and making a small wall of soil around the outside edge of the bed. This design allows the bed to catch any summer rains, protects young plants from the drying winds, and concentrates water where the vegetables grow.

Spacing your plantings properly

After you know what you're planting and how to arrange the plants, it's time to talk spacing. Make a list of the different types of vegetables that you want to grow, and then pay attention to these columns in Table A-1 in the appendix:

- ✔ **Plants/Seeds per 100 ft. of Row:** This column tells you how many plants/how much seed you need to purchase.

- ✔ **Spacing between Rows/Beds (Inches):** This column includes the ideal distance you should leave between rows or beds of different vegetables. This is usually a little more than the distance you should leave between plants.

- ✔ **Spacing between Plants (Inches):** In this column, you find the ideal distance to allow between individual vegetable plants within a row or planting bed.

- ✔ **Average Yield per 10 ft. of Row:** This column shows you how much you can expect to harvest.

The vegetable spacing information that I provide in Table A-1 in the appendix is more like guidelines than hard-and-fast rules. If you're growing on raised beds or growing dwarf varieties (see Part II for examples of these types of varieties), you can plant a little closer together, because you'll be concentrating the fertilizer and water in a smaller space.

Even though closer planting is possible, don't plant so close that plants have to compete with each other for food, water, and light. If you do, you'll eventually get smaller harvests or lower-quality vegetables.

Following the paths

You can get so involved in the beds, rows, hills, and vegetable varieties that you forget about the paths between everything. Keep the paths at least 2 to 3 feet wide so you can easily walk on them. For larger gardens, consider a few main paths that are wide enough for a passing garden cart.

Be sure to use mulching materials on the paths to keep weeds at bay and make for easier walking. The last thing you want to do is weed your garden paths! Most gardeners tend to use whatever materials are cheap and widely available. Pine straw in the South, hay in the North, and gravel in the arid West are all possibilities for garden paths. I prefer organic materials (everything from ground bark and straw to sawdust, leaves, and grass clippings) because they add organic matter to the soil, helping my garden prosper. Check out Chapter 15 for more information on mulching your beds.

Sketching it out

After you determine the location and dimensions of your garden, you need to sketch out a simple garden plan. Your drawing doesn't have to be a work of art, just functional. All you need is a piece of graph paper and a pencil, a list of vegetables you want to grow, and maybe a seed catalog or two. Then just grab your pencil and graph paper and start drawing. First, draw the garden to scale. Leave space from the edge of the paper, draw in the first row, leave room for a path, and then create your next row. Continue filling in the rows with your favorite crops, taking into account the space requirements of the crops you want to grow (refer to Table A-1 in the appendix); whether you want to plant in rows, beds, or hills; and how much of each vegetable you want to harvest.

Here are a few things to keep in mind as you sketch out your garden plan:

✔ **You can't plant everything.** Choose your crops carefully, and only grow what you like to eat. And grow only how much you think you can eat. Eating broccoli for breakfast, lunch, and dinner can get old fast.

✔ **Not all plants have it made in the shade.** Tall crops like corn should be placed where they won't shade other vegetables. The north end of the garden is usually best.

✔ **These roots aren't made for walking.** Plan your garden with walkways so you can get to plants easily without damaging roots. (For more about walkways, see the previous section.)

Planning on paper helps you purchase the correct number of seeds or transplants and use space more efficiently. It's a good way to see the possibilities for *succession planting* (following one crop with another) and *interplanting* (planting a quick maturing crop next to a slower-maturing one and harvesting the former before it competes for space). For example, you may see that you can follow your late peas with a crop of late broccoli, and you'll be ready with transplants in July. Or you may see that there's space to tuck a few lettuce plants among your tomatoes while the vines are still small. You can find out more about these techniques in Chapter 16.

In the following sections, I provide some sample garden designs for inspiration. If you're looking for a basic veggie garden design, flip to Chapter 2. Keep in mind that you can alter the designs in these sections to fit the size of your garden; you also can substitute similar-sized vegetables for those that you don't like. The options are endless!

A raised-bed greens garden

The 6-foot-x-10-foot garden in Figure 3-3 is an easy one to tuck along a house or garage or in a small space near your kitchen. It's composed of four 2-feet-x-4-feet beds with mulched paths in between. The raised beds make this garden easy to access and care for.

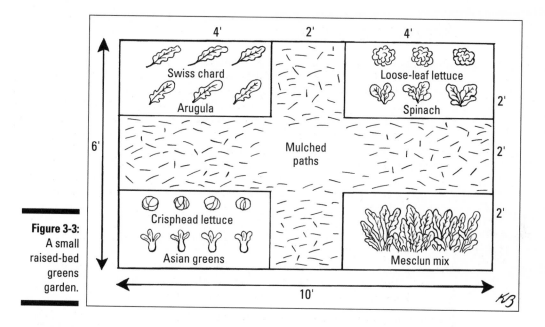

Figure 3-3:
A small
raised-bed
greens
garden.

The key to getting the most from the raised beds in this plan is to succession crop. For example, after the spinach crop is finished, plant summer lettuces or chard. Some greens, such as the loose-leaf lettuces and mesclun, can be cut and allowed to regrow for a second or third crop (see Chapter 10 for more information on cut-and-come-again lettuce). With a little forethought you can have fresh greens and salad fixings from spring through fall.

An edible-landscape garden

The garden in Figure 3-4 is beautiful and functional. I designed it to be around the front entrance of the house. It allows you to have blueberries, dwarf apple trees, and raspberries close to the house rather than way out in the backyard.

I created permanent raised beds on either side of the walkways leading to the front door. The paths between the beds are growing grass and are wide enough for a mower to pass through. In the beds are a combination of edible flowers, herbs, vegetables, and fruits, all selected with beauty and productivity in mind.

For example, you can grow colorful heirloom tomatoes, a combination of sweet and hot peppers, purple and yellow beans, basil and other herbs, cut-and-come-again greens, strawberries, and vivid root crops. You also can try growing edible flowers such as nasturtiums, marigolds, calendula, and pansies in their own bed and scattered throughout. See Chapter 12 for more on edible landscaping and growing fruits and herbs in your garden.

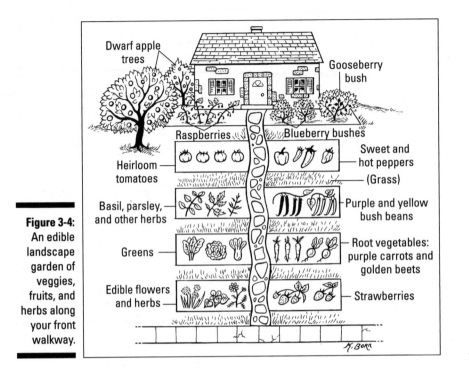

Figure 3-4:
An edible landscape garden of veggies, fruits, and herbs along your front walkway.

Dwarf apple trees

Gooseberry bush

Raspberries

Blueberry bushes

Heirloom tomatoes

Sweet and hot peppers

(Grass)

Basil, parsley, and other herbs

Purple and yellow bush beans

Greens

Root vegetables: purple carrots and golden beets

Edible flowers and herbs

Strawberries

K. Born

An ethnic pizza garden

The garden in Figure 3-5 uses the pizza garden theme from kids' gardens, where each "slice" is a potential topping on a pizza. In my case, each "slice" of this 20-foot-diameter pizza is composed of specialty varieties of different ethnic vegetables. Ethnic cooking is booming as people discover cuisines from around the world. Many of the special varieties and ingredients in ethnic cooking aren't readily available in grocery stores, but you can grow them at home.

The mulched pathways (each 3 feet wide) allow for 3 beds to be in each slice. The four cuisines are Asian, Italian, Mexican, and French/Continental. Not all the vegetables you need for cooking are represented in this garden, but it has some key ingredients that you can't do without, such as chili pepper for Mexican cooking, basil for Italian dishes, and pac choi for Asian cuisines.

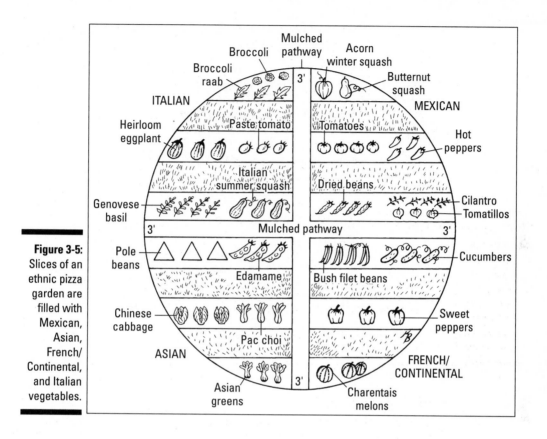

Figure 3-5: Slices of an ethnic pizza garden are filled with Mexican, Asian, French/Continental, and Italian vegetables.

Part II
Vegging Out

The 5th Wave   By Rich Tennant

In this part . . .

*E*ach chapter in this part looks at the most popular groups of or individual vegetables. I show you lots of varieties you can experiment with and the best ways to grow them successfully to harvest. I even talk about other edibles, such as berries and herbs, that are easy and beautiful to grow in your yard or garden.

Chapter 4

Tomatoes: The King of Veggies

As I mention in Chapter 2, tomatoes are hands down the most popular vegetable grown in the garden. After you've picked and tasted a juicy, vine-ripened fresh tomato, you'll understand why. You can't compare the bland supermarket tennis balls that most people make do with to the taste and texture explosion of the homegrown tomato. The best news is that tomatoes are even easy to grow! Just give them a good start and a little attention during the growing season, and you'll be rewarded with more delicious ripe fruits than you can eat.

Tomatoes are no longer limited to the round red fruits we're accustomed to seeing. Through breeding and the rediscovery of heirloom varieties, tomatoes now come in almost every color of the rainbow, from black to white, and in a variety of sizes, from as tiny as a blueberry to as large as a grapefruit. Modern breeding practices have created tomato varieties that are well adapted to heat, cold, and even containers. Great taste, disease resistance, and ease of growing make tomatoes the most rewarding to grow of all the vegetables.

Even though we all call the tomato a vegetable, botanically it's considered a fruit. Any edible plant part that develops from the ovary of the plant (found behind the flower) after fertilization is considered a fruit, so tomatoes, cucumbers, squash, peppers, and eggplant are considered fruits; lettuce, carrots, onions, and spinach are technically considered vegetables. Of course, this discussion is a moot point, because most folks categorize fruits and vegetables by their uses, not by their botany. (Case in point: A Supreme Court ruling in 1893 declared the tomato a vegetable.) So be it.

Checking Out Tomato Varieties

Before deciding which tomato variety to grow, you first need to consider the growth habits of the different plants. Plants can grow into huge monsters or tiny pot plants. So first decide how much room you have to plant tomatoes, and then decide on the right variety for that space. Whether a cherry tomato, paste tomato, or red slicing variety, tomatoes all fall into one of these categories:

- **Indeterminate:** *Indeterminate* tomato plants keep growing and growing and growing. The side branches and shoots continue to grow even after fruit is *set* (in other words, after the flower has been pollinated and the young tomato fruits begin to grow), and they can be stopped only by frost, insects, disease, or an ax. Most main crop tomatoes are of this type.

    These tomato varieties do produce a ton of fruit, but the tomatoes tend to mature later in the season than those born by the shorter plant varieties. Varieties such as 'Better Boy' and 'Brandywine' are good examples of indeterminate tomato types.

- **Determinate:** Unlike indeterminate varieties, *determinate* varieties tend to stop growing once the shoots set fruit. Varieties vary in the degree that they're determinate, but these plants generally tend to be shorter and produce less fruit. However, they do mature fruit earlier than indeterminates. Varieties such as 'Solar Fire' and 'Oregon Spring' are good examples of determinate types.

- **Dwarf:** These stronger determinate plants tend to reach only a few feet tall, produce all of their fruit at once, and then stop producing for the season. These plants are excellent as patio or container plants, producing cherry tomato–sized fruits. The 'Patio' and 'Tiny Tim' varieties are examples of dwarf tomatoes.

- **Dwarf-indeterminate:** The best of both worlds, these plants stay dwarf, only reaching about 3 to 4 feet tall, but continue to produce full-sized tomatoes all season long. They grow well when planted in containers or in the garden. Some dwarf-indeterminate varieties include 'Bush Big Boy' and 'Husky Gold'.

In Figure 4-1, you can see the differences between determinate, indeterminate, and dwarf plants.

When in doubt about a variety's quality, look for the All-America Selections (AAS) winner label in the variety's description. This group evaluates new varieties yearly by conducting trials all across the country for outstanding growth and flavor. A variety with this label will likely perform well in your garden.

Tomato varieties also can be classified as hybrids or open-pollinated plants (see Chapter 3 for more information):

- *Open-pollinated* refers to varieties that have the ability to cross-pollinate among themselves naturally and produce plants that resemble the parents. All heirlooms are open-pollinated and are generally considered varieties that were grown prior to the 1940s.

✔ *Hybrid* varieties are the products of crosses between two varieties that wouldn't necessarily naturally cross. Hybrids are an invention of post–World War II plant breeders to make varieties more productive, uniform, and disease resistant.

One more way to classify tomatoes is by their color, shape, and use:

✔ **Color:** What was once exclusively a red fruit now comes in orange, yellow, green, black (really dark brown), white, and striped colors. The only color not represented is blue; however, give breeders a little time, and it may show up someday!

✔ **Shape:** Tomatoes have been traditionally available as a round fruit, but new shapes pop up all the time. Some shapes that are available today include oblong, egg, cherry, grape, pear, and flattened.

✔ **Use:** While I mostly like to eat tomatoes fresh off the vine, some varieties are better suited to sauces, canning, and drying. (Check out the later section "Studying some saucy tomatoes" for more on varieties that are great for processing.)

With so many distinctions, how do you decide which varieties to plant? In this section, I help you decide by listing some of my favorites.

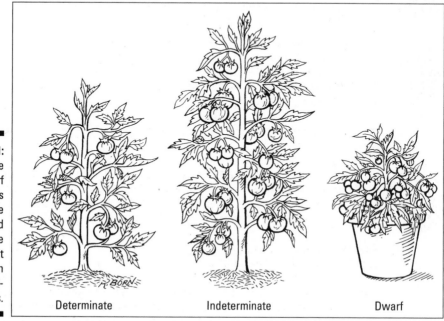

Figure 4-1: Determinate and dwarf plants tend to be shorter and produce less fruit earlier than indeterminate plants.

Determinate   Indeterminate   Dwarf

Enjoying classic red, round tomatoes

When you say the word "tomato," most people think of red, round tomatoes. They're the classic, bright red, juicy, meaty tomatoes that we all want to grow. You have hundreds of varieties to choose from, so deciding can be difficult. But, don't worry! The following list includes some of my favorites that you may want to try:

- ✔ **'Better Boy':** This hybrid indeterminate produces smooth 8- to 12-ounce fruits 72 days after transplanting that are great for slicing. This variety has good disease resistance.

- ✔ **'Big Beef':** This All-America-Selections-winning, indeterminate hybrid is loaded with disease resistance, producing blemish-free 8- to 10-ounce fruits. This variety matures 70 days from transplant.

- ✔ **'Bush Big Boy':** This hybrid dwarf-indeterminate variety produces 10-ounce fruits on a 4-foot-tall plant 71 days after transplanting.

- ✔ **'Cold Set':** If you're trying to grow tomatoes in a cold climate, try this open-pollinated variety. The 4- to 6-ounce fruits set 65 days after transplanting on determinate plants that can tolerate a light frost.

- ✔ **'Costoluto Genovese':** This Italian indeterminate heirloom is close to my heart and taste buds. The 8-ounce fruits are deeply ribbed, juicy, and have a strong tomato flavor. The plants love the heat and produce fruits 80 days after transplanting.

- ✔ **'Delicious':** If you want to grow "the big one," this indeterminate heirloom is for you. The plant produces fruit 77 days after transplanting, and those fruits often weigh more than 2 pounds each. This variety holds the world record for the largest tomato: 7 pounds, 12 ounces.

- ✔ **'Early Girl':** Despite being an indeterminate hybrid (which generally matures later in the season), this plant produces 4- to 6-ounce fruits only 52 days after transplanting. You can experiment with the 'Bush Early Girl' version as well, which has the same characteristics except that it only grows 2 feet tall.

- ✔ **'Oregon Spring':** This determinate, open-pollinated variety is bred for cold tolerance and relatively few seeds in each fruit. The 7- to 8-ounce fruits are produced only 58 days after transplanting.

- ✔ **'Solar Fire':** This determinate hybrid was bred at the University of Florida, so it's heat tolerant. The large, 7- to 10-ounce round fruits are disease resistant and mature 72 days after transplanting.

- ✔ **'Stupice':** This Czechoslovakian indeterminate heirloom is an early and cold-tolerant variety that bears 1- to 2-ounce fruits 52 days after transplanting.

- ✔ **'Super Bush':** This determinate, 3- to 4-foot tall hybrid plant is great in containers. Unlike many other container-adapted varieties, the 'Super

Bush' variety produces large, 8- to 10-ounce fruits on disease-resistant plants. Fruits are produced 85 days after transplanting.

When in doubt about choosing a variety to grow in your garden, ask your local garden center, farmer's market, or neighbor who's growing tomatoes for suggestions about what grows best in your region.

Surveying all the other colors of tomatoes

Tomatoes of a different color (other than red that is) are very popular. The flavor of many of these varieties is comparable to the red varieties, but the colors can be outstanding in salads and casseroles, or just by themselves. Here are some beautifully colored varieties you might try:

- ✔ **'Black Krim':** This indeterminate Russian heirloom has unique, 12-ounce, dark reddish-brown fruit. Both the skins and the flesh are colored this way, and the fruit color darkens in hot weather. Fruits are produced 80 days after transplanting. This tomato is something really different!

- ✔ **'Brandywine':** This Amish indeterminate heirloom has unique potato-leaf foliage and produces 1- to 2-pound pink fruits with red flesh — reportedly the most flavorful of all varieties — 80 days after transplanting. You also can buy a similar 'Yellow Brandywine' and 'Red Brandywine' if you'd like all the colors of 'Brandywine' tomatoes in your garden.

- ✔ **'Cherokee Purple':** This heirloom indeterminate bears 10-ounce dusky rose- or purple-colored fruits with thin skins about 80 days after transplanting.

- ✔ **'Great White':** This indeterminate heirloom plant produces 10- to 12-ounce white-colored fruits 85 days after transplanting. The meaty fruits, whose skins and flesh are white, have a mild flavor, few seeds, and a creamy texture. When combined with 'Black Krim' it makes an interesting black-and-white tomato salad.

- ✔ **'Green Zebra':** These 3-ounce fruits are produced 75 days after transplanting. The skin and flesh are green even when ripe. The flavor of this indeterminate heirloom is tangy and sweet and makes a mean fried green tomato dish.

- ✔ **'Husky Gold':** This AAS-winning dwarf-indeterminate hybrid plant only reaches 4 feet tall, but it produces deep golden-colored, 8-ounce fruits 70 days after transplanting.

- ✔ **'Lemon Boy':** The first lemon-yellow-colored tomato, this hybrid indeterminate produces 7-ounce fruits with lots of disease resistance 72 days after transplanting.

- ✔ **'Long Keeper':** These determinate, open-pollinated plants produce 6- to 7-ounce orange-red fruits 78 days after transplanting. When unblemished fruits are gathered before the first frost, they can last in winter storage for up to 3 months. (Flip to Chapter 19 for more on storing fruits and vegetables during the winter months.)

- ✔ **'Striped German':** This German heirloom indeterminate variety produces 16- to 32-ounce fruits with beautiful yellow-orange skin and red marbled flesh 78 days after transplanting.

Sweetening the pot with cherry, grape, and pear tomatoes

Cherry, grape, and pear tomatoes sound like fruits, and they may as well be for their sweet, melt-in-your-mouth flavor. Nothing is more satisfying to me than going into the garden and munching on handfuls of cherry tomatoes. Rarely do these babies even make it to the kitchen.

The latest newcomer on the small tomato scene is the grape tomato. Originally from Thailand, these tomatoes have a grape shape and are smaller than most cherry tomatoes. However, grape tomatoes have a thicker skin and are less juicy, which means they squirt less when you munch down on them. Because they're easier to eat, they're often found in place of cherry tomatoes in salad bars and restaurants.

Pear tomato varieties have been around for years. These red- or yellow-colored fruits look like small pears and are flavorful, but they generally aren't as sweet as cherry tomatoes.

Cherry, grape, and pear tomatoes can be very productive, so often, only one or two plants are enough to keep your family happy all season. If you're growing dwarf, patio-type tomatoes, they do best in containers. (See Chapter 18 for more on growing vegetables in containers.) Cherry, grape, and pear tomato fruits do tend to crack more easily than larger-sized tomatoes, so make sure that they have plenty of water and mulch (see Chapter 15 for watering and mulching tips).

Here are some of my favorite small tomato varieties:

- ✔ **'Black Cherry':** These 2- to 3-ounce black-red skinned and fleshed fruits have a complex flavor. The heirloom indeterminate plants produce cherry-shaped fruits 65 days after transplanting.

- ✔ **'Golden Sweet':** This indeterminate hybrid grape tomato features 1-ounce golden yellow fruits with a mild, sweet flavor and no cracking. Fruits mature 60 days after transplanting.

✓ **'Juliet':** This 1-ounce red, indeterminate hybrid, AAS-winning grape tomato is crack and disease resistant. It matures 60 days after transplanting.

✓ **'Patio':** This hybrid, dwarf plant produces grape-sized red fruits all at once about 70 days after transplanting.

✓ **'Sun Gold':** This hybrid indeterminate plant produces fruity tasting 1- to 2-inch-diameter orange-colored cherry tomato fruits 57 days after transplanting.

✓ **'Sweet Million':** This prolific hybrid indeterminate, 1- to 2-inch-diameter, red-fruited cherry tomato variety has good disease and crack resistance and matures early at 60 days after transplanting.

✓ **'Tiny Tim':** These open-pollinated, dwarf, 18-inch-tall plants are great for containers. They produce 1-inch-diameter red cherry tomato fruits 60 days after transplanting.

✓ **'Window Box Roma':** This hybrid determinate plant produces 2-ounce, roma-type, cylindrical-shaped fruits 70 days after transplanting on 18-inch-tall plants. This variety is perfect for producing a container of sauce-making tomatoes.

✓ **'Yellow Pear':** This is an heirloom indeterminate that produces yellow, 2-inch-diameter pear-shaped fruits on huge plants about 78 days after transplanting. Kids love the shape of these tomatoes.

Studying some saucy tomatoes

Eating tomatoes fresh from the garden is pure joy. However, you may want to preserve some of that fresh taste for cooking in the off-season like my mama used to do. If making tomato sauce, paste, salsa, and juice is for you, the following paste tomato varieties are bred to order. Even though any tomato variety can be processed, these pear- or plum-shaped types are meatier and thicker-walled and usually have less juice, so they're perfect for cooking. Many of these varieties are now bred to be good for fresh eating in salads and on sandwiches as well:

✓ **'Amish Paste':** These large, teardrop shaped red fruits are produced on indeterminate heirloom plants 85 days after transplanting. The fruits are meaty and flavorful, so they're super for making pastes.

✓ **'Golden Mama':** This 4- to 5-ounce, golden-yellow sauce tomato is produced 68 days after transplanting. These productive plants are indeterminate hybrids. The yellow sauce you can make from this beauty is appealing to the eye and has a sweet flavor.

✓ **'Roma':** This is one of the most popular processing tomatoes around. This open-pollinated determinate produces 3-ounce, plum-shaped fruits on compact vines 78 days after transplanting.

✔ **'Super Marzano':** A hybrid version of another popular paste tomato, this hybrid indeterminate has 4- to 5-ounce pear-shaped fruits that are more disease resistant and productive than their heirloom cousins. The fruits mature 70 days after transplanting.

✔ **'Viva Italia':** This sauce tomato is as good fresh as it is processed. It's a determinate hybrid that produces pear-shaped, 3- to 4-ounce fruits with great disease resistance 80 days after transplanting.

Elongated plum- or pear-shaped tomatoes tend to be more susceptible to blossom-end rot (see "Weather-related problems," later in this chapter, for more on this condition). To prevent blossom-end rot, keep the plants well watered, and mulch with a 4- to 6-inch-deep layer of hay or straw to keep the moisture levels constant. Pick off and throw away any affected fruits, and the new ones that develop should be fine.

Introducing the tomato's relatives

Just like in any family, tomatoes have some odd relatives. Following are descriptions of three of the most commonly known tomato relatives. They're all grown similar to tomatoes, but the flavors are much different. Try one of these varieties:

✔ **'Husk Cherry'** (*Physalis peruviana;* also known as 'Strawberry Tomato' or 'Cape Gooseberry'): These sprawling plants produce tons of small, papery husks similar to Chinese lanterns. Inside each husk is a cherry tomato–sized fruit that matures to yellow or gold. The flavor is like a sweet wild berry. Kids love these fruits. And because they self-sow readily, once you plant them in the garden, you'll have them forever. They mature 75 days after transplant.

✔ **'Tomatillo'** (*Physalis ixocarpa*): The standard ingredient in salsa, these tomato relatives produce papery husks like the 'Husk Cherry,' but the fruits inside are ping-pong-ball size and tart rather than sweet. Varieties come in yellow and purple fruit colors. Fruits mature 65 days after transplant.

✔ **'Tree Tomato'** (*Cyphomandra betacea-amarillo*): Although technically in the tomato family, this tropical plant is as unfamiliar as the uncle you rarely see. It's a small perennial tree native to the Peruvian Andes that produces tons of hen's-egg-sized fruits that range from yellow to red when mature. The flavor isn't like a tomato but more like a tropical fruit.

'Tree Tomato' plants need 18 months of warm weather to mature a crop, so unless you have a greenhouse, growing this variety is limited to gardeners who live in zone 10 areas. (Flip to the appendix to find out more about zones.)

Growing Tomatoes with Ease

After you decide on and purchase your tomato varieties, it's time to get them growing. In this section, I explain how to start your tomato plants; plant, fertilize, and maintain them; handle insects, diseases, and weather-related issues; and harvest them for your enjoyment.

Jump-starting tomatoes

Tomatoes require such a long season to mature that they're best bought as transplants through the mail or from local garden centers. You also can start them from seed indoors 4 to 6 weeks before your last frost date (I cover starting seeds indoors in Chapter 13; see the appendix for average frost dates in your area). Either way, you simply want to have a stocky, 6- to 10-inch tall, dark-green-leafed, flowerless transplant ready to go into the garden after all danger of frost has passed.

For gardeners in subtropical areas, such as southern Florida, you can plant two crops of tomatoes: one in the spring and another in the fall. Start seedlings indoors in January and February for planting outside in March and harvesting in May and June. For a fall harvest, start your seeds in July, or buy transplants for a late August or September planting. By late fall or winter, you'll be enjoying ripe tomato fruits while colder areas are eating snow.

Tomatoes love to be patted. If you're starting your tomatoes from seed at home, keep the plants short and stocky by brushing your hands over the tops of the seedlings ten strokes daily starting when they're 2 ½ inches tall. Research has shown that this brushing strengthens the stem and causes the seedling to stay short and squat, suffering less transplant shock when planted in your garden.

Tomatoes (and their roots in particular) love heat. To give tomatoes a jump-start, preheat the garden soil by covering it with dark plastic mulch. Lay the plastic sheet over the garden bed, pull it tight, cover the edges with soil, and let the plastic heat the soil for 2 weeks before transplanting. While you're waiting for the soil to heat up, *harden off* your transplants (in other words, gradually make them accustomed to the outdoor growing environment) with the guidelines in Chapter 13.

Planting, trellising, and pruning

Tomatoes are one of the most forgiving vegetables to grow. But to get the best crop, you need to plant properly, keep the fruits off the ground by trellising, and even prune the most vigorous bushes to keep them inbounds. I discuss some simple guidelines in the following sections.

Planting

Here are the basic steps for planting tomato plants:

1. **Dig a hole twice the diameter and depth of the tomato root ball.**

2. **Place a small handful of all-purpose organic fertilizer or compost into the hole.**

3. **Plant the tomato transplant up to its first set of leaves.**

   Tomatoes have a unique ability to form roots all along their stems. So even if you have a tall, leggy, lanky seedling, just bury the stem either vertically or horizontally in the ground, leaving at least two sets of leaves poking out (see Figure 4-2).

If you're using plastic mulch, cut (or burn with a propane torch) a 6-inch-diameter hole in the plastic, and plant your tomato transplant directly through the plastic mulch using the same technique that I walk you through earlier.

Research has shown that red plastic mulch increases tomato yields by 20 percent. How? The red mulch reflects specific light wavelengths back into the tomato plant stimulating it to produce more fruit.

Figure 4-2: A lanky tomato planted horizontally in the ground.

Place a small handful of organic fertilizer in the hole.

K. BORN

Trellising

As the weather warms, tomatoes grow quickly. So soon after you transplant, you have to decide which trellising method you'll use to keep your tomatoes off the ground. All but the dwarf and dwarf-indeterminate varieties need to be staked, caged, wired, or generally held off the ground to minimize the amount of rot and pest damage that the plants suffer. Figure 4-3 shows two basic trellising methods, which work well with tomatoes (see Chapter 15 for details):

✔ **Staking:** To stake your tomato plant, you simply drive a wooden or metal stake into the ground right next to the tomato transplant when you first plant it. Fasten the main trunk of the tomato to the stake with flexible rubber or plastic ties, and then continue adding ties as the plant grows. Staking is often combined with pruning to produce fewer, but larger fruits.

✔ **Caging:** To cage your tomato plant, buy a large, three-ringed metal cage and insert it into the soil around your tomato transplant when you plant. Keep any errant branches inside the cage by gently reorienting them. This method requires less work than staking, and unless pruned, caged plants produce more but smaller fruits.

Pruning

In addition to staking, another way to keep vigorous plants (especially inde-terminates, which continue to grow all season) in bounds is to prune them. Removing extra side branches called *suckers* (see Figure 4-4) helps direct more energy to fruit production and less to leaf and stem production. When the suckers are 3 to 4 inches long, remove them from the plant by pinching them back to the main stem with your fingers or a pair of scissors.

Pruning suckers reduces the overall yield of your tomato plant, but the fruits you do get will be larger and will ripen slightly earlier than if you didn't prune them.

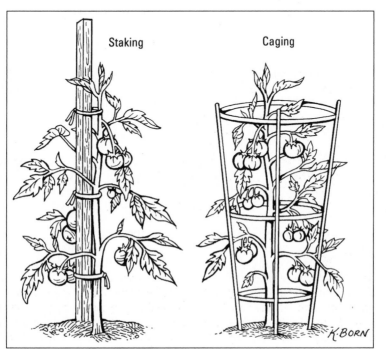

Figure 4-3:
The basic staking and caging methods.

Staking   Caging

K. BORN

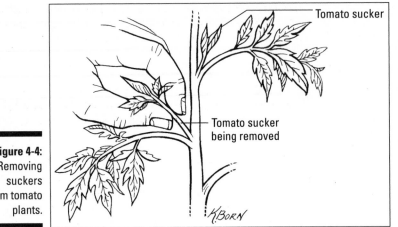

Tomato sucker

Tomato sucker
being removed

K.BORN

Figure 4-4:
Removing
suckers
from tomato
plants.

Fertilizing and maintaining your plants

Tomatoes are generally heavy-feeding plants. They like a soil rich in organic matter and compost, but they also respond well to side-dressing with fertilizers during the growing season. Maintaining proper moisture and mulching also are crucial for producing the best tomatoes possible. I explain everything you need to know in the following sections.

Side-dressing

Side-dressing is adding a small amount of fertilizer around or "on the side" of plants after they're growing. Side-dress with a complete organic fertilizer, such as 5-5-5, by sprinkling a small handful of the fertilizer around each plant. Apply the first side-dressing when the tomatoes are golf-ball sized, and then apply another side-dressing every 3 weeks after that. Scratch the granular fertilizer into the top few inches of soil. (Refer to Chapter 15 for more on fertilizers.)

Use fertilizers with lower rates of nitrogen; higher rates cause tomato plants to sport lots of dark green leaves and produce few tomatoes. Also, try not to get any fertilizer on the foliage; it can burn the leaves.

If you prefer to spray your plants, treat your tomatoes to a *foliar feeding* by mixing the fertilizer with water and then spraying it on the plant foliage; this is a quick way to get nutrients to your tomato plants. Using fish emulsion or seaweed mix, dissolve the fertilizers according to the recommendations on the bottle and spray the plants every 3 weeks. Plants can take up nutrients faster through their leaves than through their roots, but the effects don't last as long. Some research suggests that spraying plants with a seaweed mixture can also help reduce leaf diseases.

Tomatoes also like Epsom salts. Research has shown that 1 tablespoon of Epsom salts dissolved in 1 gallon of water and sprayed on the transplants after planting and a month later makes for greener and more productive tomatoes.

Watering and mulching

Watering is critical if you want your tomatoes to produce the best quality fruits. In general, tomatoes need 1 inch of water a week, but they may need more in areas with hot, dry, windy summers. Chapter 15 discusses watering strategies in detail.

One of the best things you can do to conserve moisture is to mulch around your tomato plants. Plastic mulch conserves some moisture but is best used in conjunction with soaker hoses or the ditch watering method (see Chapter 15 for details). The best water-conservation mulch is a 4- to 6-inch layer of hay or straw. The mulch is thick enough to prevent weeds from germinating and stop soils from drying out.

Hay and straw mulches keep soil cool, but tomatoes love heat. So, if you're in an area that has cool summers, wait until the soil has warmed and the plants are thriving before mulching with these materials.

Mulching and watering evenly also prevents many fruit problems, such as blossom-end rot and fruit cracking. See the section "Weather-related problems," later in this chapter, for details on these conditions.

Eliminating pests and other problems

Tomatoes grow so vigorously that they often outgrow any problems and still give you a harvest. But to get the most out of your plants, look out for the troubles in the following sections, which are caused by insects, diseases, or weather. (For a general description of and a plan of action against common insects and diseases, see Chapter 17.)

Spray with pesticides only as a last resort; many plants can withstand a small infestation of bugs or a few diseased leaves.

Insects to watch for

Here are a few insects that are a particular problem with tomatoes:

- ✔ **Tomato hornworm:** These huge, green caterpillars, which sometimes grow to 4 inches long, look like the monster that ate Tokyo (see Figure 4-5). They eat leaves and fruits of tomatoes, and I swear that if you're quiet enough, you can hear them chewing. A few hungry hornworms can devastate a tomato plant quickly.

TIP

The simplest control is to handpick the caterpillars off the plants and wrestle them into a can of soapy water to drown. Early morning is the best time to remove these pests from plants — like many people, they're still sluggish at this time of day.

✔ **Tomato fruitworm:** This green, 1-inch-long caterpillar with white or yellow stripes feeds on foliage and fruits. They can be handpicked from plants as with the hornworm; however, for a severe infestation, you also can spray plants with Bt.

✔ **Stink bug:** A problem mostly in warmer areas, these ½-inch-long gray or green shield-shaped insects primarily feed on fruits, causing hard, white or yellow spots on the tomato skin. To control stink bugs, keep your garden weed-free — the pests hide in weeds around the garden — and spray plants with pyrethrin.

Figure 4-5:
A tomato
hornworm
makes its
way to a
meal.

Chapter 17 discusses pests and ways to rid your garden of them, such as using Bt and pyrethrin, in more detail. Flip there to read more.

WARNING!

Got a disease?

Leaf diseases, such as the ones in the following list, can devastate tomatoes:

✔ **Blights and leaf spots:** The devastation starts with the lower leaves getting brown spots, turning yellow, and eventually dying. The symptoms of leaf spot look similar to the symptoms of late and early blight. The disease slowly spreads up the plant, eventually defoliating the whole plant. These fungal diseases are particularly active during warm, wet weather. To control blight and leaf spots:

• Clean up and destroy all diseased foliage in the fall.

• Rotate crops, as described in Chapter 16.

- Mulch the plants with plastic, hay, or straw after planting to prevent water from splashing the spores from the ground onto the leaves.

- Before the condition gets severe, spray with an organic fungicide, such as copper or *Bacillus subtilis.*

✔ **Verticillium and fusarium wilt:** These soil-borne fungal diseases cause yellowing, wilting, and early death of tomato plants. Once infected, the plants will likely die and should be removed. The best prevention is to rotate your plantings and plant wilt-resistant plants (indicated by the letters V and F after the variety name).

Luckily, many varieties of tomatoes now are resistant to some of these diseases. Use the guidelines in Chapter 17 to reduce the amount of disease in your garden.

Weather-related problems

Not all problems with tomatoes are related to insects or diseases. Too much or too little water, too much fertilizer, cold temperatures, and varietal differences can all contribute to deformed fruits. Here are a few of the more common problems and some solutions:

✔ **Blossom drop:** Your tomatoes are flowering beautifully, but the blossoms all seem to drop without forming any fruit. This condition, called *blossom drop,* is caused by air temperatures above 90 degrees Fahrenheit or below 55 degrees Fahrenheit. At these temperatures, most tomato flowers will not set fruits. The solution is to grow varieties adapted to the heat (such as 'Solar Fire') or cold (such as 'Cold Set'). Or you can protect the plants during flowering with floating row covers.

✔ **Blossom-end rot:** With this condition, the bottom, or *blossom end,* of tomatoes turns brown and rots. Blossom-end rot is caused by fluctuating moisture conditions in the soil, so the best cure is to mulch the plants well, plant them in well-drained soil, and keep them evenly watered.

✔ **Fruit cracking:** Many types of fruit cracking affect tomatoes, but all involve fluctuating moisture conditions and exposure to cold temperatures early in the season. To avoid this problem, plant varieties that are less likely to crack (such as 'Big Beef'), reduce nitrogen fertilization, mulch the plants to keep the soil moisture even, and protect flowering plants from cold nights with row covers (see Chapter 21).

✔ **Sunscald:** You'll know that your tomatoes have sunscald if the top surfaces of the fruit skins have lightly colored patches. These patches, which are caused by direct exposure to the sun, eventually rot. To avoid sunscald, grow indeterminate varieties that have lots of foliage to shade the fruits (such as 'Better Boy'), avoid pruning the leaves, and provide afternoon shade with shade cloths. Or you can grow the plants in cages instead of staking them.

Harvesting tomatoes

Harvest tomatoes when they're fully colored and still firm to the touch. Tomatoes don't need direct sun to ripen, just warm temperatures. Tomatoes will continue to ripen indoors if they're picked too early, so it's better to err on the early side when harvesting. As long as they show some color when picked, they'll ripen indoors with that vine-ripened flavor.

If you want to push the harvest along, you can prune off some new branches and tiny fruits to redirect the plant's energy to the larger, maturing fruits. You also can root-prune the plant, cutting 6 inches into the soil in a circle one foot away from the stem of the plant. Root-pruning severs some of the roots, shocking the plant and forcing it to ripen its fruits faster. It will, however, stop the production of new fruits, so this technique is best used at the end of the season.

If you live in an area with bright sunshine, don't prune off tomato foliage. Removing too much foliage results in sunscald, a condition in which the tomato skin literally gets sunburned. Sunscald itself doesn't ruin the tomato crop, but it opens the door for other rot organisms to attack the fruit. (See the previous section for more details.)

Chapter 5

Meeting the Tomato's Cousins: Peppers and Eggplants

*P*eppers and eggplants, which are two tomato relatives (they're all in the nightshade, or *Solanaceae,* family), may not have the popularity of their big, red tomato cousins, but their varieties do have a similar diversity of tastes, colors, and shapes.

Peppers, in particular, are experiencing a resurgence of interest, and breeders have responded to that interest by creating new and improved varieties. Whether they be sweet or hot peppers, you have many new varieties to choose from. No longer simply green, yellow, or red, sweet pepper varieties come in a rainbow of colors, including orange, purple, and chocolate. The new varieties adapt better to cold and hot temperatures and have more ornamental qualities. With the popularity of salsa (which is now the number-one condiment in the United States, according to the U.S. government), nachos, and spicy foods in general, hot peppers are gaining heaps of attention as well. From the mildest jalapeño to the hottest 5-alarm habañero, varieties are available for all taste buds and heat tolerances.

Eggplants (named because some varieties have fruits the shape and color of hens' eggs), aren't as popular as peppers, but they have gained a lot of attention because of the discovery of varieties other than the traditional dark purple, teardrop shape. Long, thin, Oriental types make excellent grilled snacks, skin and all. Small, round, green, Asian eggplants are great in soups and casseroles. You can even find unusual round, orange, Turkish types that are used in specialty ethnic cooking.

Both peppers and eggplants are beautiful plants to grow in your garden, and they make excellent container plants if you have limited space. Some pepper varieties have purple stems, leaves, and fruits; eggplants have beautiful purple flowers, and the fruits can be a variety of colors, including white, purple, striped, green, and orange. So, reserve a spot in the vegetable or flower garden for these beautiful, edible fruits.

Producing Plenty of Peppers

An abundance of pepper varieties are available to home gardeners, including many new varieties of hot peppers. In the following sections, I classify peppers into four groups: sweet bell peppers, sweet nonbell peppers, hot peppers, and ornamental peppers. Most of these pepper plants grow to 2 to 3 feet tall unless otherwise noted.

Those sweet bells

Bell pepper fruits come in blocky, round, or elongated shapes. Most fruits start out green but mature through a variety of colors before ripening to their final color.

The days to maturity given in the following variety descriptions represent the time from transplant in the garden to full size. Add 2 weeks to this number to know when they'll mature to their final color. Sweet bells have the sweetest flavor when harvested at the mature color stage, but they still can be harvested green and taste good.

Variety descriptions for sweet peppers frequently use words such as lobes and blocky. No, I'm not talking about ear shapes. When you cut a pepper crosswise near the stem, you'll notice that the walls divide the pepper fruit into sections. Pepper experts call these sections *cells* or *lobes*. Well-defined lobes or cells make peppers blocky. Most bell peppers have three to four lobes. Blocky fruits are best used for stuffing or slicing into pepper rings. The thick-walled varieties are best for stuffed-pepper recipes.

Here are a few of my favorite varieties of sweet bells, all of which offer good disease resistance:

- ✔ **'Ace':** This early, 3- to 4-inch-long hybrid bell matures within 50 days and grows well in cooler climates.

- ✔ **'Bell Boy':** These four-lobed, thick-walled All-America Selections, or AAS, winners yield fruits that turn red on *compact* (smaller than usual) hybrid plants. They mature in 70 days.

✔ **'Blushing Beauty':** This AAS winning hybrid features 4-inch-long-by-4-inch-wide blocky fruits that mature in 72 days. The fruit color is amazing. It starts out ivory white, turns to gold, turns to orange, and then finally turns to red. It tastes great at any stage.

✔ **'California Wonder':** These classic, thick-walled, 4-inch-by-4-inch blocky hybrid bells mature to red in 75 days and are great for stuffing. They also come as a yellow-fruited variety called 'Golden CalWonder'.

✔ **'Chinese Giant':** These old-fashioned, thick-walled, huge (6 inches by 6 inches) heirloom bell peppers mature to red and are very sweet. They're good stuffing peppers and mature in 75 days.

✔ **'Chocolate Bell':** These 3- to 4-inch-long hybrid bells mature in 70 days to a rich chocolate skin color with red flesh. The fruits have a smokey-sweet flavor, but sorry, they don't taste like chocolate.

✔ **'Golden Summer':** These blocky, thick-walled, four-lobe hybrid fruits are lime green in color and mature to gold in 67 days.

✔ **'King of the North':** This variety is reportedly one of the best open-pollinated bell peppers for cool areas with short growing seasons. It takes only 57 days to mature the 3- to 4-inch-long, thick-walled fruits that start out green and mature to red.

✔ **'Islander':** This unique, light lavender–skinned and pale yellow–fleshed hybrid bell pepper also has yellow and orange streaks before turning bright red at maturity. These three-lobed fruits are produced within 80 days.

✔ **'Jingle Bells':** These hybrid bells mature in 60 days. Compact plants are loaded with miniature (1 to 2 inches in length and width) bell peppers that mature to red.

✔ **'Purple Beauty':** This 4-inch-long heirloom features a short, bushy plant with fruits that start out purple and mature to red. The thick-walled, sweet fruits are ready to harvest within 75 days.

✔ **'Valencia':** These hybrid plants have good foliage cover and produce large, 5-inch-by-5-inch peppers with thick walls and sweet, orange flesh. They mature in 70 days.

✔ **'Vidi':** These French hybrid bells mature in 70 days. The plants mature into red, 5- to 7-inch-long peppers that withstand less-than-ideal growing conditions.

✔ **'Whopper Improved':** It ain't called a "whopper" for nothin'. This classic green hybrid bell pepper that turns to red is widely adapted and matures in 72 days. The bushy plant has good foliage cover to reduce *sunscald* (lightly colored patches on the fruit caused by direct sun exposure that eventually rot), and it produces reliably large yields of 4-inch-long-by-4-inch-wide fruits.

Long and round sweet peppers

Sweet peppers are more than big, blocky bells. Some of the sweetest peppers I've ever tasted have been long, tapered (or blunt-ended), thin-walled, Italian frying types. These types of peppers have gone through a renaissance of late, with more varieties available for outdoor grilling, frying, and sautéing than ever before. Other great sweet peppers come in round, cherry shapes and short, fat heart shapes. Both long and round varieties of pepper plants grow 2 to 3 feet tall and most mature to the color red, which is when they're the sweetest. So heat up the frying pan, fire up the grill, and dive in! Here are some of my favorites:

- ✔ **'Biscayne':** These 6-inch-long, 2-inch-wide, Cubanelle-type (which feature a blunt end) hybrid bells mature in 65 days. They're good for frying.

- ✔ **'Carmen':** An AAS-winning hybrid variety, these bull's horn–shaped fruits are 6 inches long and 2 inches wide. Fruits turn red in 75 days and are very productive, making this a great variety for cool-summer gardeners.

- ✔ **'Corno di Toro':** These bells are original Italian "bull's horn" peppers. They received their name because the fruits are 8 to 10 inches long and are curved like the horn of a bull. Three-foot-tall plants ripen yellow or red fruits in 68 days. These peppers are great for frying. 'Sweet Toro' is a newer hybrid version; and now you can purchase a golden version called 'Corno di Toro Yellow'.

- ✔ **'Cubanelle':** These 6-inch-long, light green, open-pollinated fruits have thin walls and blunt ends, making them perfect for frying. They mature in 65 days.

- ✔ **'Giant Marconi':** This AAS-winning variety, which stretches to 8 inches long, is known as one of the largest Italian frying peppers available. It matures early at 63 days and is high yielding and flavorful. It's the perfect grilling sweet pepper. These hybrid plants are also disease resistant.

- ✔ **'Gypsy':** These AAS-winners produce 4-inch-long, wedge-shaped fruits early in the season; the fruits mature from yellow to orange-red in 60 days. This hybrid variety is very productive and adapts to many growing conditions.

- ✔ **'Jimmy Nardello':** Okay, so I couldn't resist a pepper close to being my namesake. This tasty variety features very sweet, 8-inch-long, open-pollinated peppers that mature to red in 90 days. Long, thin, and sweet — just like me!

- ✔ **'Paprika Supreme':** Care to make your own paprika powder? Well, here's the pepper for you. These 7-inch-long, flattened, thin-walled hybrid fruits are perfect for drying after they mature; maturation takes 100 days.

- ✔ **'Peperoncini':** These 4-inch-long, wrinkled, open-pollinated peppers are best known as the pickled, light green peppers served in Italian antipasto. They take 62 days to mature.

✔ **'Sweet Banana':** Probably the most well-known of the long, tapered, open-pollinated sweet peppers, these 6-inch-long fruits, which mature from yellow to red, are born on compact 1 1/2-foot-tall plants. They take 72 days to mature. 'Banana Supreme' is a hybrid version.

✔ **'Sweet Red Cherry':** These thick-walled, 1 1/2-inch-round sweet open-pollinated peppers are often available at salad bars and pickled. The plants are compact — 1 1/2 feet tall — and are very productive. They mature in 78 days.

Peppers that turn on the heat

At one time, the only hot peppers you'd see people eating were the dried flakes sprinkled on pasta in Italian restaurants. How times have changed! With the growing interest in cuisine from around the world — such as Mexican, Korean, Thai, and Indian — hot peppers are enjoying widespread popularity.

Speaking generally about hot peppers is difficult, because the flavor and level of hotness varies with each type of pepper. But, here's one general fact to keep in mind: Hot pepper plants usually are easier to grow and produce more peppers than sweet pepper plants. And because some varieties are so hot that they could strip paint, you won't need to add very many to your cuisine. In the following sections, I discuss the factors behind the fire, provide a chart for measuring a pepper's heat, and list some popular varieties.

Understanding the fire of the hot pepper

Before getting into hot peppers, you need to understand the heat in hot peppers. The active ingredient that causes all the fire is called *capsaicin* (the tiny, blisterlike sacs on the inner wall of the fruit, as shown in Figure 5-1), which is located on the pepper's *placental wall*. You find fewer sacs at the tips of hot peppers, so you could bite off the tip of a hot pepper and be fooled into thinking it's not that hot. If you cut into the pepper or handle it roughly, however, you break the inner-wall lining, releasing capsaicin throughout the fruit — even to the tip.

To counteract the hotness of hot peppers, try eating dairy products such as yogurt, ice cream, or milk with your hot dishes.

Some pepper varieties, such a habañero, are so hot that you can get serious burns in your mouth. If you get the capsaicin in your eyes or in a wound, you can get burns there also. Check out the new, less hot habañero in the later section "Picking some hot peppers to grow."

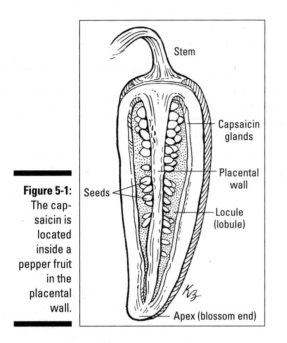

Figure 5-1:
The cap-
saicin is
located
inside a
pepper fruit
in the
placental
wall.

Stem

Capsaicin
glands

Placental
wall

Seeds

Locule
(lobule)

Apex (blossom end)

Measuring heat with the Scoville scale

To help you decide how hot you want to go with hot peppers, the Scoville Heat Scale was developed in 1912. The scale ranges from 0 to 350,000 and measures pepper hotness in multiples of 100. Table 5-1 shows some of the most popular hot pepper types and their hotness ratings. The chart gives a range for each rating because weather, growing conditions, and pepper variety can all affect how hot a pepper is. This chart can help you decide how hot you want your peppers.

Table 5-1	Scoville Heat Scale
Pepper Types	*Scoville Rating Range*
Bell	0–100
Hot cherry	100–500
Jalapeño	400–2500
Anaheim	500–2,500
Ancho/poblano	1,000–1,500
Serrano	10,000–25,000
Hot wax	10,000–40,000
Cayenne	30,000–50,000
Habañero	100,000–350,000

Picking some hot peppers to grow

Here are some hot pepper varieties that you can grow:

- ✔ **'Anaheim TMR 23':** These moderately pungent, open-pollinated, smooth-skinned, 7-inch-long-by-2-inch-wide peppers are produced on 3-foot-tall, leafy, tobacco mosaic virus resistant (TMR) plants. They mature in 75 days. You can use the dried pods to make the *ristras* (wreaths of dried peppers) popular in the Southwest.

- ✔ **'Ancho 211' (Poblano):** These open-pollinated, red, mildly hot, 4-inch-long, wrinkled, heart-shaped peppers often are stuffed and served as chile rellenos. You also can dry them and make them into wreaths or powder. They take 80 days to mature.

- ✔ **'Big Chili II':** This hybrid Anaheim-type roasting pepper is 8 to 10 inches long and mildy pungent. Yields are high and early at 68 days.

- ✔ **'Cherry Bomb':** These mildly hot, 2-inch-round, thick-walled hybrid fruits mature in 65 days to a bright red.

- ✔ **'Habañero' (*Capsicum chinense*):** These are some of the hottest peppers known to mankind! These 1-inch-by-1-inch, lantern-shaped fruits mature to orange on 3-foot-tall open-pollinated plants. They thrive in the hot weather and take a long season to mature — 100 days. The hottest variety of this type is a red variety called 'Caribbean Red,' which tops 445,000 on the Scoville scale.

  These hot peppers can be dangerous, so take care when handling and eating them.

- ✔ **'Hungarian Hot Wax':** These medium-hot, 7- to 8-inch-long, tapered open-pollinated peppers mature from yellow to red and are great for pickling. They take 70 days to mature.

- ✔ **'Jalapeño M':** The classic salsa, nacho, and pizza hot peppers. These moderately hot, 3-inch-long, round-tipped open-pollinated fruits taste great when eaten green or red. 'Jalapa' is a more productive hybrid version, and 'Tam Jalapeño' is a milder variety. These peppers take 75 days to mature.

- ✔ **'Mariachi':** This AAS-winning hybrid hot pepper features high yields of 4-inch-long and 2-inch-wide mild fruits that are very attractive. The peppers start yellow and mature to red in 66 days.

- ✔ **'NuMex Joe E. Parker':** A very productive open-pollinated variety of a popular breeding line from New Mexico State University. The 6- to 7-inch-long fruits have a mild to medium spice. They mature in 65 days.

- ✔ **'Serrano del Sol':** These candle-flame-shaped, 3½-inch-long, hot peppers are born abundantly on 3-foot-tall plants. This new hybrid version matures 2 weeks earlier and is more productive than the original 'Serrano'. With the same heat as jalapeños, they're great in salsa and often are used in sauces. They mature in 64 days.

- ✔ **'Super Cayenne III':** These 3- to 4-inch-long, fiery hot hybrid fruits taste great when eaten green or at mature red. The attractive plants are 2 feet tall and look good in containers. These peppers take 75 days to mature. A similar yellow-fruited variety called 'Yellow Cayenne' is also available.

- ✓ **'Super Chili':** These AAS winners produce an abundance of 2-inch-long, cone-shaped, hybrid hot fruits that you can dry or eat fresh. These peppers take 75 days to mature.

- ✓ **'Thai Hot':** These 1-inch-long, fiery hot peppers from Thailand mature in 80 days. Compact 1 ½-foot-tall open-pollinated plants bear tons of fruit, making them attractive ornamentals as well. You also can try other varieties of this pepper, including 'Giant Thai Hot', which produces larger-sized fruit.

- ✓ **'Zavory Habañero':** This open-pollinated, first-ever mild habañero pepper registers only 100 on the Scoville scale. Red fruits are produced abundantly within 90 days. You can really eat them out of your hand!

Pretty peppers: The ornamentals

Most peppers are produced on plants that are small enough to grow in containers (see Chapter 18 for more on container gardening) or in the flower garden. Not only does their size make them a good fit for container growing, but they make an attractive addition as well. Some varieties have been specifically bred for their attractive fruits, stems, and leaf colors as well as their fruit shapes. The ornamentals in the following list are also edible. Here are some of my favorites:

- ✓ **'Black Pearl':** This All-American Selections hybrid pepper with purple leaves and stems bears ³/₄-inch-round fruits that start out purple and mature to red in 60 days. The purple color holds up well in the heat, making this a good variety for the South and West.

- ✓ **'Bolivian Rainbow':** These 2- to 3-foot-tall plants have purple leaves and stems and beautiful 1-inch-long fruits. The fruit color starts out purple, but changes to yellow and orange, finally maturing to red. You'll see all color stages of fruit on the plants at the same time, making this variety a rainbow-colored showstopper. Fruits mature within 80 days.

- ✓ **'Pretty in Purple':** The leaves, stems, and fruits of these 2½-foot-tall open-pollinated plants are dark purple. Upon maturity (which takes 75 days), the 1-inch-long, fiery hot peppers turn red, creating a gorgeous ornamental effect.

- ✓ **'Riot':** These 2- to 3-inch-long open-pollinated hot peppers sit atop short, compact plants and blaze from yellow to bright red when mature (70 days). The effect looks like a riot of color.

- ✓ **'Sweet Pickle':** Surprise — these aren't hot ornamental peppers, but sweet ones! Two-inch-long, oval, thick-walled fruits on open-pollinated plants mature from yellow to orange, purple, and red, often having all three colors present on one plant. They take 65 days to mature.

Distinguishing Eggplants by Shape

Lest you think peppers are the only international travelers with variety and a zest for life, eggplants also come in a range of shapes, colors, and sizes. I arrange the varieties in this section by shape so you can choose the variety that's right for your taste and use. The days to maturity in the variety descriptions represent the time from transplant to harvest.

Large and oval

Large, oval eggplants are the varieties that most people are familiar with. They're the dark purple, teardrop-shaped fruits that you see in grocery stores. The plants grow 3- to 4-feet tall, each producing an average of eight to ten fruits. These eggplants are great in casseroles. Here are some of my favorite varieties to grow:

- **'Black Beauty':** These large heirloom purple-skinned eggplants grow best in areas with long, hot growing seasons. They mature in 75 days.

- **'Black Opal':** This hybrid, dark purple, teardrop-shaped variety is a bit smaller than the 'Black Beauty,' but it has a similar creamy texture and flavor. Very productive plants have fruits produced in 65 days.

- **'Cloud Nine':** This hybrid has pure-white skin and a delicate flavor with no bitterness. The fruits are best harvested when they're 7 inches long. They mature in 75 days.

- **'Florida High Bush':** This is an heirloom variety from Florida that loves the heat. Large, upright plants produce 10-inch-long, black-purple-skinned fruits in 85 days.

- **'Purple Rain':** These beautiful, white-striped, lavender-skinned hybrid eggplants mature early at 66 days and are productive.

- **'Rosa Bianca':** This Italian heirloom features white fruits with lavender streaks. These fruits, which are best adapted to warm regions, mature in 75 days.

Cylindrical

Traditionally called Oriental eggplants, these cylindrical fruits are long and thin (2 inches wide and up to 10 inches long). The plants are smaller than the oval-shaped varieties, reaching only 2 to 3 feet tall, and produce about 15 fruits. They're great grilled or used in hors d'oeuvres. These are a few of my favorite varieties:

✔ **'Fairy Tale':** This early-maturing (50 days), AAS-winning hybrid variety features purple-and-white-striped fruits that form in clusters. They're best when harvested at 3 to 4 inches long. The fruits are free of bitterness, have few seeds, and are highly productive.

✔ **'Hansel':** This AAS-winning hybrid variety features deep-purple, finger-shaped fruits that can be harvested when they're 3 to 4 inches long, which usually takes 55 days. This variety is very productive. A sister to 'Hansel' is 'Gretel', which has the same characteristics except that the fruit has white skin.

✔ **'Ping Tung Long':** These long, lavender-skinned fruits grow in areas with good heat and humidity. The open-pollinated plants are disease resistant, and the fruits take 65 days to mature.

✔ **'Raveena':** This hybrid variety features vigorous plants that yield light green, cylindrical fruit in clusters in 70 days. They're best when harvested before they reach 9 inches long.

✔ **'Vittoria':** This hybrid has purple-black skin and is best when harvested at 10 inches long. The fruit matures in 61 days.

Small and round

The plants in this category grow only 1 to 2 feet tall, making them great for container culture. Each plant produces 20 to 25, 1- to 3-inch-round fruits. Even though the following eggplants are novelties, they're also great for skewering and pickling:

✔ **'Calliope':** This hybrid features a heavy crop of round, 2-inch-diameter, purple-and-white-striped fruits in 64 days on a spineless plant.

✔ **'Easter Egg':** These open-pollinated plants produce white-skinned, egg-shaped fruits that kids marvel at. They received their name because they resemble chicken eggs. They turn yellow at maturity, which takes 65 days, but they're best when eaten white; they taste bitter if you allow them to mature to yellow.

✔ **'Kermit':** These Thai specialty hybrid fruits have green skin with white stripes — very unusual. They take 60 days to mature.

✔ **'Turkish Orange' (*Solanum gilo*):** These bushy, 2- to 3-foot-tall open-pollinated plants have good insect resistance and produce fruits that mature from green to orange. The fruits are best when eaten green, before their skin turns orange and bitter. They take 80 days to mature.

Growing Peppers and Eggplants

Many of the *cultural instructions* (instructions on how to grow a plant) for producing tomatoes (see Chapter 4) hold true for peppers and eggplants as well. But, of course, peppers and eggplants have some of their own special requirements as well, as you find out in this section.

A few guidelines for starting and planting

Peppers and eggplants are warm-season crops, so you don't need to rush to plant them until the ground has warmed up sufficiently. Here are some guidelines you can follow:

✔ In most areas, you need to start peppers and eggplants from seed indoors, usually 6 to 8 weeks before the last frost date for your area (see the appendix for first and last frost dates). You also can purchase them from a local nursery or through the mail as transplants. (See Chapter 13 for seed-starting basics.)

✔ If you live in zone 9 or 10, you can sow the seeds directly into your garden. If you keep the plants healthy and have no frost in your area, peppers and eggplants can actually be *perennials* (plants that grow year-round) and will bear fruit all season.

However, even in cold climates, I've dug up pepper plants and eggplants in fall, placed them in pots in my greenhouse all winter, and then transplanted them back out in spring. Even after three years these plants remain attractive and healthy.

Peppers and eggplants are more finicky than tomatoes are about temperatures, fertilization, and general growing conditions, so they're less forgiving of mistakes. So, you need to be extra cautious about starting pepper and eggplant seedlings early indoors. Give them ample light, fertilizer, and water; harden them off well; and wait to plant until the soil temperature is at least 60 degrees Fahrenheit. You should purchase or have grown a 4- to 6-inch-tall, dark-green-leafed, stocky transplant that isn't *root-bound* (roots growing around the container).

One handy product you may want to purchase is a *soil thermometer.* Usually costing less than $20, a soil thermometer can help you gauge when to plant warm-season crops such as peppers and eggplants. Place it in a shady spot and take readings in the morning for accuracy.

If your peppers have flowered or set fruits before you've transplanted them or when the seedlings still have only four to six leaves each, remove any blossoms or fruits. The plants will then send more energy to grow more leaves and roots to support a larger harvest later rather than maturing only a few peppers early.

Peppers and eggplants grow best in raised beds (see Chapter 3) because the soil warms faster and drains quicker. The following guidelines can help you get the soil temperature right depending on your climate:

- ✔ **Cold areas:** Cover the top of the beds with black or dark green plastic mulch to preheat the soil a few weeks before planting. (See Chapter 15 for details on how to use mulch in your garden.)

- ✔ **Warm areas:** Mulch with straw, white plastic, or aluminum foil in summer to help keep the soil cool. Aluminum foil also reflects light back into the sky, confusing insects trying to find plants.

To plant eggplant and pepper transplants, use scissors to cut holes in the plastic mulch every 1 to 1½ feet (wider for taller varieties) for peppers and every 2 to 3 feet for eggplants. If you're using mulch that isn't plastic, plant at the same distances as you would in plastic mulch. Plant eggplant and pepper transplants at the same soil level as they are in their containers. Cover the plantings with a floating *row cover* (a lightweight, cheesecloth-like material that lets air, water, and sunlight through to keep the air warm and bugs out; see Chapter 21).

Even though pepper and eggplant plants are usually strong enough to stand on their own without supports, I like to either stake or cage tall, heavy-yielding varieties such as 'Carmen' and 'Black Beauty'. Staking or caging the plants keeps fruits off the ground, making them less likely to rot during wet weather. I find that I get heavier yields this way as well. Use small stakes or tomato cages to keep your plants vertical (see Chapter 15 for more supporting your vegetables).

Fertilizing and watering tips

Peppers and eggplants are sensitive to excessive fertilizer, in particular nitrogen. Plants fertilized with too much nitrogen will grow large but have few fruits. However, don't neglect fertilizing your plants; simply avoid using high rates of nitrogen fertilizers. Instead, apply a 2- to 3-inch layer of compost over the bed and a small handful of 5-5-5 organic fertilizer around each transplant. (Chapter 15 has more on fertilizing.)

Water your plants well, following the suggestions in Chapter 15. Watering is particularly important during 90-degree weather when water stress and high temperatures can cause flowers to drop. *Side-dress* (add fertilizer around the plants during the growing season) around the *drip line* (where water naturally drips off the ends of leaves) of the plant with a tablespoon of organic fertilizer, such as 5-5-5.

To give your peppers a boost, mix 1 tablespoon of Epsom salts in 1 gallon of water and spray the pepper plants when they're flowering.

Pest patrol

If you see holes in a pepper fruit and find a small, white worm inside the fruit, consider it your introduction to the *pepper maggot*. The adult fly lays eggs on the fruit in midsummer. After the eggs hatch, the larvae tunnel into the fruit. To control these pests, do the following:

- ✔ Rotate crops
- ✔ Cover young plants with row covers
- ✔ Grow varieties such as 'Serrano' and 'Jalapeño' that are less attractive to the maggots
- ✔ Hang yellow sticky traps before the adult flies lay eggs. Remove rotten fruits that may harbor the flies before you hang the traps.

Peppers and eggplants generally have fewer pest problems than their tomato cousins, but they share such pests and diseases as blossom drop, sunscald, blossom-end rot, fruitworms (also called corn earworms), and Verticillium wilt (see Chapter 4). Flea beetles (see Chapter 17) and Colorado potato beetles (see Chapter 6) love eggplants. Chapter 17 describes other insect and disease problems that affect all vegetables.

Harvesting tips

Peppers and eggplants are great to grow because you don't have to wait until the fruits are fully mature before you pick them. Consider your options for both fruits:

- ✔ **Peppers:** You can pick and enjoy sweet peppers green or wait until they ripen to orange, yellow, or red for a sweeter taste. Hot peppers vary in their hotness depending on stress. Stressed peppers tend to be hotter, so if you withhold water and fertilizer when the hot peppers are ripening, you can increase the heat in the peppers' flavor. Cool, cloudy weather tends to make hot peppers less hot.

- ✔ **Eggplants:** You can pick eggplants at almost any stage. The key is to not let them become overmature; otherwise the texture will become soft and mushy. To check eggplant maturity, watch the fruit's skin. A dull-colored skin means it's overmature. Double-check by cutting into the fruit and looking at the seeds. Brown-colored seeds are another sign of overmaturity.

A simple test for maturity is to push the eggplant's skin with your fingernail. If the skin bounces back, the fruits are ready to harvest. If your nail indents the skin, the fruits are overmature. If your fruits are really mature and rotting on the vine, just pick them and throw them out; they won't taste very good.

The key to harvesting is to do it often. The more often you harvest, the more peppers and eggplants you get. To harvest, cut peppers and eggplants with a sharp knife just above the top of the green cap on the fruit. The fruits will continue to ripen after you harvest them, so store them in a cool place. If you want to dry your peppers, pick them when they mature and hang them to dry in a warm room with good air circulation. See Chapter 19 for more tips on preserving your harvest.

Harvesting hot peppers and eggplants can be tricky, so use gloves when harvesting them. Hot peppers need careful handling because they contain capsaicin, which can easily cause burning, especially in your eyes or in open cuts. (Believe it or not, I've known of gardeners having to go to the hospital to be treated for burns from hot peppers.) Some eggplant varieties have sharp spines on their stems, so be sure to work around them when harvesting the fruits. Or consider growing spineless varieties such as 'Fairytale' and 'Hansel'.

Chapter 6

Growing Underground Crops: Carrots, Onions, and Potatoes

Root-crop vegetables are an example of those good things in life that you can't actually see. Their tops are green, unassuming, and may even be mistaken for weeds — but oh, when you give them a yank! I can still remember the look on my daughter's face when she first helped me dig potatoes and discovered that they grow underground. Digging for potatoes was like a treasure hunt. I think that most gardeners feel that same sense of wonder and excitement when they dig or pull up their root crops. The result is always something marvelous.

You can grow many different root crops, but the big three are carrots, onions, and potatoes. They aren't botanically related like peppers, eggplants, and tomatoes are (see Chapters 4 and 5); what these crops do have in common, however, is that they're grown for their underground parts: roots, bulbs, or *modified stems* (underground stems that expand to produce large, edible areas; potatoes' stems are called *tubers*). I provide plenty of growing tips for carrots, onions, and potatoes in this chapter; I discuss other root crops in Chapter 11.

A Rabbit's (and Gardener's) Favorite Root: Carrots

Carrot (*Daucus carota*) varieties are categorized by their shape. You can grow long, thin carrots; short, stocky carrots; and even little, round, baby carrots. A few varieties are supercharged with vitamins, and many hybrids have added vigor and disease resistance. The latest trend in carrots is colorful roots. Roots no longer come in just orange — now you can grow varieties that are white, yellow, red, and purple, too!

If you're trying to decide which carrot variety to grow, consider your type of soil as well as the use you plan for the carrots. Loose, sandy soil is good for growing any root crop. If you have heavy, clay soil, consider a variety that's shorter in length, such as 'Short 'n Sweet'. It's easier for this short carrot variety to push into the heavy soil than a long, thin, tapered root variety. (Chapter 14 has more information about soil types.)

Classifying carrots by type

Carrots often are described as a certain type, such as baby carrots. If the carrot type is part of a variety name, you can determine what the carrot will look like when it matures. Table 6-1 shows the common types of carrots and their characteristics. All the types listed, except baby carrots and Imperators, range in size from 6 to 8 inches. Aside from eating the carrots fresh, you can best use certain varieties for juicing and storing; some even grow well in containers.

Table 6-1	Carrot Types	
Type	*Size and Uses*	*Best Soil Type*
Baby	Short (3 to 4 inches); early maturing; grows well in containers; great for salads and roasting.	Grows best in heavy, clay soil.
Chantenay	Wide *shoulders* (the top of the carrot root) and tapered to a point; good grated in salads or cooked.	Grows well in heavy soil.
Danvers	Tapered to a point; thinner and longer than Chantenay; good for storing.	Grows best in sandy, loose soil.
Imperator	Similar to Danvers, just longer (10 to 12 inches); good cooked and in soups and stews.	Grows best in sandy soil.
Nantes	Cylindrical shape with blunt end; good for juicing.	Grows well in sandy soil.

Most short varieties that you find in grocery stores are baby carrots, and the longer carrots may be any of the other types mentioned in Table 6-1. The bagged "baby-size" carrots in grocery stores are often just normal-sized carrots peeled down to a small, rounded size. Look for carrots with the tops still showing for true baby carrots. Baby carrots may be varieties that are naturally short or larger varieties harvested at an immature stage.

Examining some carrot varieties

Knowing what type of carrot a certain variety is can help you when deciding which variety to grow. With some of the most widely known carrot varieties, you can easily identify the carrot type because it's part of the variety's name; some examples include 'Scarlet Nantes' and 'Danvers 126'. Otherwise, you simply read the description to find out.

The carrot varieties in the following list fall into one of the five types of carrots identified in Table 6-1, but they also have special characteristics that may make them perfect for your garden; they're flavorful, disease resistant, and easy to grow. All are good for baking. The days to maturity are from seeding in the ground until first harvest; however, early season carrot varieties are flavorful even when you harvest them before they fully mature:

- ✔ **'Atomic Red':** This Imperator-type, open-pollinated carrot features 9-inch-long roots that are red from skin to core. The color deepens and flavor becomes milder when cooked. This variety matures in 70 days.

- ✔ **'Bolero':** This hybrid, Nantes-type carrot produces 6-inch-long roots and 8135*has extra disease resistance and stores well. It matures in 72 days. 'Yaya' is a newer hybrid Dutch variety that's sweeter and matures earlier (60 days) than 'Bolero'.

- ✔ **'Danvers 126':** These heat-resistant, open-pollinated roots produce heavy yields of 7- to 8-inch-long carrots 70 days after planting.

- ✔ **'Healthmaster':** This hybrid, Danvers-type variety grows up to 10 inches long and contains 30 percent more vitamin A than other carrot varieties. It matures in 110 days.

- ✔ **'Kuroda':** This hybrid, 6-inch-long, Chantenay-type produces heavy yields of tender carrots that are good for juicing and storing. It matures in 79 days.

- ✔ **'Little Finger':** This open-pollinated variety is an early (65 days), 3-inch-long, smooth-skinned, small-cored baby carrot that's sweet. 'Little Finger' carrots are great for planting in containers.

- ✔ **'Merida':** This hybrid, Nantes-type, 7- to 8-inch-long carrot can be planted in spring for fall harvest. However, it's most often grown as a fall crop and in mild-winter areas, such as the Pacific Northwest, where it can *overwinter* (live through the winter) and be harvested in spring. It matures in 75 days.

- ✔ **'Parmex':** This hybrid, baby-type carrot features 1½-inch-diameter round roots that are harvested in 50 days. Great for planting in shallow soils.

- ✔ **'Purple Haze':** This hybrid, 10- to 12-inch-long Imperator has purple skin and an orange core. This sweet variety's purple color fades when cooked. It matures in 70 days.

- ✔ **'Scarlet Nantes':** This heirloom, Nantes-type variety has bright red-orange flesh with a small core. The 6- to 7-inch-long roots mature in 65 days.

- ✔ **'Short 'n Sweet':** This 4-inch, open-pollinated, Chantenay-type carrot grows well in heavy clay soil and containers. It matures in 68 days.

- ✔ **'Sugarsnax':** This hybrid, Imperator-type variety is as tender and sweet as a Nantes variety, yet it grows up to 9 inches long, is disease resistant, and is high in beta carotene. It matures in 68 days.

- ✔ **'Thumbelina':** This unusual hybrid, baby-type, All-America Selections winner (see Chapter 4) has a round root that's the length of a silver dollar; it's especially good for baking. It grows well in containers and in heavy clay or rocky soil. It matures in 65 days. Kids love this variety for its small size and easy-growing nature.

- ✔ **'White Satin':** This hybrid, Nantes and Imperator cross features 8-inch-long crisp, textured white roots that grow under a wide range of soil and weather conditions. It matures in 68 days.

Onions: The Bulbs with Layers of Sweet and Pungent Goodness

The two most important factors to consider when choosing onion (*Allium cepa*) varieties are flavor of the onion and location of your garden. Although most people use taste as their first criterion, the old advice about "location, location, location" has greater relevance when growing onions. Onions are particular about how much sunlight they get, forming bulbs in response to the number of daylight hours. As a result, onion varieties are classified by day length — *long day, short day,* or *intermediate day* (also known as *day neutral*) — as well as by taste — sweet (which are good for eating raw or freshly cooked) or pungent (which are good for storing).

In general, short-day onions grow well in the southern United States, long-day onions grow well in the northern United States, and intermediate-day onions grow well in the in-between regions.

See the later sidebar "What a difference a day makes!" if you really want to get into a discussion on day length and onions. If you want to avoid the whole issue, try growing some fun onion relatives, such as leeks, garlic, and shallots, which I discuss in Chapter 11.

Choosing your onion varieties

In the following lists of my favorite onion varieties, I distinguish between onions that are long day, short day, and intermediate day (or day neutral). Within each group are sweet and pungent varieties. These varieties are the most *widely adapted* (able to grow in a wide variety of geographic regions under various weather conditions) and easiest to grow. Keep in mind that pungent onions are much better for storage than sweet varieties. (You can read more about storage in Chapter 19.)

I also indicate whether you can purchase the variety as a *set* (small onions that have been pregrown so that they mature faster) or as a plant (or both). (Check out the appendix for a listing of companies that specialize in onion sets and plants.) The days to maturity are from either directly seeding in the garden or *setting out* (placing outdoors) sets or plants. Short-day onions are generally planted in fall to grow through the winter, so they take longer to mature than other types. Long- and intermediate-day onions are usually planted in spring. All the onions have yellow skin and white flesh unless otherwise noted.

Short-day onions include the following varieties:

- ✔ **'Giant Red Hamburger':** This open-pollinated, sweet, short-day variety features dark red skin and red-and-white flesh. It matures in 95 days from seeding and can be purchased as a plant.

- ✔ **'Granex 33' (Vidalia):** This classic hybrid sweet onion is a well-known short-day variety. It is available as a plant and is popular in the Southeast. It matures in spring, 180 days after fall seeding.

- ✔ **'Texas Grano 1015' (Texas Supersweet):** This sweet, short-day, hybrid variety can grow as large as a baseball and still remain sweet. It's also available as a plant and is popular in Texas and in the Southwest. It matures 175 days from fall seeding.

Intermediate-day (or day-neutral) onion varieties include the following:

- ✔ **'Candy':** This sweet, hybrid, intermediate-day onion is widely adapted. It's also available as a plant. It matures 85 days after seeding.

- ✔ **'Italian Red Torpedo':** This sweet, Italian heirloom, intermediate-day, red onion forms a bottle-shaped bulb with a mild taste and pink flesh. It matures 110 days after seeding.

- ✔ **'Superstar':** This All-America Selections winning, hybrid, white-skinned, sweet onion produces a 1-pound, disease-resistant, uniform, mild-tasting bulb 109 days from planting. It's isn't good for long-term storage because of its extra sweetness.

Long-day onion varieties include the following:

- ✓ **'Ailsa Craig Exhibition':** This yellow-skinned, open-pollinated variety is known for its sweet, 2-pound bulbs that mature 105 days after seeding. It tolerates cool weather well.

- ✓ **'Borrettana cipollini':** Cipollini are unique heirloom, Italian, flat-shaped varieties. The 'Borrettana' variety produces 2-inch-diameter yellow sweet onions that are great braided and good caramelized and sautéed. It matures 110 days after seeding. 'Red Marble' is a good red cipollini-type variety.

- ✓ **'Copra':** You can store this hybrid, pungent variety until spring. It matures 104 days after seeding.

- ✓ **'Purplette':** This open-pollinated, purple-skinned mini-onion is best harvested when 3 to 4 inches in diameter 60 days after seeding. It has mild, sweet pink flesh and is a good one for pickling. It also can be used as a scallion (see the next section).

- ✓ **'Yellow Sweet Sandwich':** This hybrid variety actually gets sweeter in storage and comes in a white-skinned version called 'White Sweet Sandwich'. Both versions are available as plants. The variety matures 100 days after seeding.

- ✓ **'Walla Walla Sweet':** This sweet, hybrid variety has light yellow flesh and good cold tolerance. It's available as a plant and is popular in the Northwest. It matures 115 days after seeding.

- ✓ **'Yellow Stuttgarter':** This pungent, standard, open-pollinated storage variety often is sold as a set. It matures in about 90 days from a set and 120 days after seeding.

Looking at scallions and perennial onions

You may have run across some other onion types in restaurants or produce markets. For example, *scallions* (also called bunching onions, spring onions, or green onions) are picked for their delicate, juicy, green tops before they form bulbs. Scallions take up less space in your garden than regular onions because you can plant them closer together, and they can give you a quick crop when planted in spring or fall. Growing scallions is a good way for novice onion growers to start.

Any onion variety grown from a seed can be harvested as a scallion, but here a few varieties that are especially widely adapted as scallions:

- ✓ **'Evergreen Hardy White' (*Allium fistulosum*):** This hardy, white-stalked variety is a great one for cold climates (USDA zone 5), and it can overwinter if protected and used as a perennial. It matures 65 days after seeding.

✔ **'Red Beard' (*Allium fistulosum*):** This tender variety has unique coloring: a red stem with a white tip and green leaves. It matures 45 days after seeding.

✔ **'White Spear':** This heat-resistant scallion features blue-green leaves and thick white stems. Good for warm climates. It matures 65 days after seeding.

Multiplier, or perennial, onions come back year after year and reproduce easily. Here are the two main types:

✔ **Egyptian top-set onions (also known as walking or tree onions):** These onions reproduce by forming clusters of onion sets on the tips of their growing stalks, as shown in Figure 6-1. As the weight pulls the stalks down, the clusters root wherever they land, making the onions look like they're walking slowly across your garden. During the winter months, Egyptian top-set onions primarily are eaten as scallions, but the top-sets make good, small, sweet onions when you pick them in summer. They're also very cold hardy.

✔ **Potato onions:** These onions form a main onion in summer from a fall planting. They're hardy to USDA zone 4 and produce many smaller sets that you can replant after summer harvest to produce more onions the following year.

What a difference a day makes!

The long-day, short-day, intermediate-day onion issue can get confusing. Short-day onions form bulbs when they receive 11 to 12 hours of daylight, while long-day onions form with 14 to 16 hours of daylight. Generally, gardeners north of 35 degree latitude (a line running from northern North Carolina through Oklahoma and Arizona to central California) grow long-day onions because their summer days are long enough to initiate bulb formation. Gardeners south of that line grow short-day onions because they're closer to the equator and their day lengths are pretty steady at 12 hours. Gardeners in the South also have the luxury of planting short-day onions in fall, overwintering them (because of their mild winters), and harvesting in late spring.

Northern gardeners need to plant long-day onions in spring for a summer harvest. If you were to plant long-day onions, such as the 'Copra' variety, in the South, they'd never receive enough daylight hours to bulb up. Likewise, short-day onions, such as the famous 'Vidalia' onions, grown in spring in the North, would bulb up quickly while the plants were small because they'd receive the necessary 12 hours of daylight early in the season. The end result would be small bulbs.

Modern plant breeders have made this whole task a bit easier by introducing intermediate-day varieties that aren't as dependent on certain amounts of daylight hours to form bulbs. These varieties like intermediate lengths of daylight (12 to 14 hours) and grow best in hardiness zones 5 through 8 (see the appendix for more about zones).

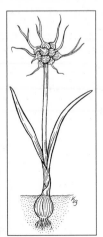

Figure 6-1:
An Egyptian
top-set
onion plant.

Potatoes: No Longer a Boring Spud

If I had to vote on the most underrated vegetable in the world, I would choose the potato (*Solanum tuberosum*). Potatoes have a reputation for being common, widely available, inexpensive, and just plain brown and boring. Why bother growing them? Well, first of all, the flavor and texture of fresh potatoes dug from the soil is much better than the bagged spuds that sit on grocery-store shelves for weeks. It's also fun to grow the many different varieties, including novelty potatoes such as purple-, red-, or yellow-fleshed varieties. You'll surely astound your family and dinner guests with these not-so-plain potatoes.

Potatoes are one of the most foolproof crops to grow. Start planting early, while the weather is still cool, by placing a piece of the tuber (called a *seed potato*) in a furrow, or trench. After the potatoes start growing, if you *hill* them (push soil around the plants), water them, and keep the bugs away, you're almost guaranteed some great tubers. I explain more about planting potatoes and provide tips on growing sweet potatoes, a special kind of root crop, later in this chapter.

Potatoes classified

Potato varieties usually are classified as early-, mid-, and late-season from the time you plant the seed potato to harvest. If you have a short growing season, grow early-season plants. If you have a longer growing season, you'll be safe with the late-season plants. If you want to have a constant supply of potatoes all summer, grow a few of each. Table 6-2 shows the approximate number of days to maturity for each category.

Table 6-2	Potato Maturity
Type	*Days to Maturity*
Early	65 days
Midseason	75 to 80 days
Late	90+ days

Selecting a few potato varieties

So many potato varieties are available that narrowing the field is often difficult. However, you may want to try some of my favorites, which I describe in the following list. I've included some fingerling varieties that are the latest rage; they produce an abundance of small, fingerlike tubers that are great roasted, fried, or steamed. Here are my favorite potato varieties in terms of flavor, color, and ease of growing:

✓ **'All Blue':** This mid- to late-season spud has blue skin and flesh. It has a mealy texture, so it's best as a mashed potato. Yes, blue mashed potatoes! You also can grow a similar 'All Red' (also known as 'Cranberry Red') variety that has red skin on the outside and pink flesh on the inside. Combined with 'All Blue' potatoes and a white variety, you can create a red, white, and blue mashed potato extravaganza!

✓ **'Butte':** This late-season variety is the classic Idaho baking potato. It's a great *russetted* (has rough, brown-colored skin) baking variety that features 20 percent more protein and 58 percent more vitamin C than other varieties. It's also tolerant of scab disease and late blight. (See the later section "Keeping Your Root Crops Healthy and Pest-Free" for more on these problems.)

✓ **'Caribe':** This early, lavender-skinned, white-fleshed variety produces large tubers. A great masher.

✓ **'Kennebec':** This all-purpose midseason variety with white skin and flesh is dependable, resists disease, and is good for almost any use.

✓ **'King Harry':** This early-season, gold-skinned and white-fleshed variety is unique for its hairy leaves that reportedly ward off insects, such as Colorado potato beetles, leafhoppers, and flea beetles (see Chapter 17). Oh, and the spuds taste great, too!

✓ **'Red Norland':** This early variety has red skin and white flesh. Harvested early when plants are just flowering, this variety is commonly sold in markets as a new red potato. It tastes best boiled or mashed.

✓ **'Rose Finn Apple':** This late-maturing fingerling variety features rose-colored skin and yellow flesh. It has a firm, moist texture and is great baked or boiled.

- ✔ **'Russian Banana':** This late-season, fingerling-type variety has a banana shape with a waxy yellow skin and flesh. You'll find it great for roasting and boiling.

- ✔ **'Superior':** This early-season tuber has buff-colored skin and white flesh. It's scab disease–resistant, grows under a wide range of conditions, and stores for a long time. A keeper!

- ✔ **'Viking Purple':** This midseason, purple-skinned, white-fleshed variety can endure dry weather and stores well. It tastes great boiled or mashed.

- ✔ **'Yukon Gold':** This very early variety with yellow skin and flesh produces high yields and is drought tolerant. It's a great keeper; in fact, I've been known to still be eating this variety from storage 8 months after harvest. This moist-fleshed potato is best in salads or boiled. Plus it makes a great chip!

Even though most potatoes are grown from seed potatoes, you can grow potatoes from seeds just as you do with tomatoes and peppers. One hybrid, late-maturity, true-seed variety that's currently available is called 'Catalina' (which is very similar to 'Kennebec'). For best results, start seeds indoors a month before planting. You grow your crop the same way that you grow other potatoes. Growing potatoes from seeds is a bit trickier but less expensive than planting seed potatoes, and you reduce the chance of passing on any tuber-borne diseases to your new crop. (See the later section "Keeping Your Root Crops Healthy and Pest-Free" for more on potato diseases.)

Growing and Gathering Root Crops

Root crops are easy to grow if you have good soil, water, and proper spacing. The mystery of root crops is that you can't see the reward until you dig them up. But that's half the fun of growing them.

General guidelines for all your root crops

The keys to growing great root crops are preparing the soil bed well and giving the plants room to grow. You also need to keep the crops clear of weeds and make sure they have enough water. Here are further details on each of these important points:

- ✔ **All root crops like well-drained, loose, fertile soil.** And with the exception of potatoes, which grow best in hills (as you find out later in this chapter), root crops grow best in raised beds (see Chapter 3 for more on these special beds). They also can grow if you have a gardening spot that gets only 4 to 6 hours of direct sun a day. Try some carrots and onions in that patch.

To prepare the soil, add a 3- to 4-inch layer of compost or manure at least 2 to 3 months before you're ready to plant. If you wait until just before planting to add fresh compost or manure, you're likely to get poor growth. Why? Too much nitrogen fertilizer on carrots and potatoes in spring promotes foliage growth but not good tuber and root formation. Instead, root crops enjoy phosphorous, which promotes root growth, so perform a soil test (see Chapter 14), and based on the results, add bone meal or rock phosphate fertilizer before planting to keep your roots happy.

Onions in particular like lots of fertilizer, and they can stand some extra nitrogen, which promotes leaf growth. Add extra fertilizer when the transplants are 6 inches tall and the bulbs begin to swell. Then add a complete organic fertilizer, such as 5-5-5, at 1 pound per 10 feet. (See Chapter 15 for more on fertilizers.)

✔ **Root crops, especially carrots and onions, require proper spacing to grow at their best.** Thin out the young seedlings when they're 3 to 4 weeks old by pulling them out or snipping them until they're properly spaced (see Chapter 13 for details on thinning seedlings). Onions should be 4 inches apart, scallions 2 inches apart, and carrots 3 inches apart. Potatoes don't need thinning and should be planted 8 to 10 inches apart when planted.

I know that thinning your hearty crops sounds cruel, but if you don't do it, the roots won't have enough room to expand, causing you to get lots of plants but few roots — and fewer roots means fewer carrots and onions.

✔ **You'll be rewarded with lots of crisp roots in no time if you regularly weed your root crop patch.** After a good thinning, hand-weed beds of carrots and onions; potatoes can be weeded with a hoe. Mulch the bed with hay or straw. You don't have to mulch in between individual onion and carrot plants. Simply mulch around the beds, and keep them well watered.

Carrots, onions, and potatoes are root crops that like cool temperatures. They grow best and have the best flavor when temperatures stay below 80 degrees Fahrenheit.

Cultivating carrots

Carrot seeds are small and take up to 2 weeks to germinate, so you run a greater risk of poor germination with them than with other vegetables. To get your carrots off on the right foot, try these tips:

✔ **Prevent forked roots in carrots by making sure the soil is free of rocks, sticks, and hard pieces of soil.** If carrot roots come in contact with a hard object as they're growing, they fork, creating a multipronged carrot. Even though they're interesting to look at and a conversation piece at dinner, forked roots are harder to clean and yield fewer carrots. No soil can be completely free of rocks and sticks, but when building a raised bed try to remove as many as possible. And be sure to amend the soil with compost to make the soil looser so the roots stay straight. If your soil is heavy clay or a rock jungle, try growing round varieties such as 'Thumbelina'.

✔ **For easier germination of small carrot seeds, try purchasing pelleted seeds.** These seeds are covered with a biodegradable coating, making the seed larger and easier to handle. However, the seed germination isn't affected. Sprinkle carrot seeds on the top of the soil and then cover them with a thin layer of potting soil or sand. Potting soil and sand are lighter than garden soil, enabling tender seedlings to more easily grow through.

✔ **Keep your soil moist.** If it dries, the seedlings can quickly die. (See Chapter 15 for more on watering.)

✔ **Grow carrots as a fall crop, starting 1 to 2 months before your first frost date.** They germinate faster in the warmer soil of summer, and their flavor is sweeter when they mature in cooler fall weather. In hot-summer areas, you may need to shade your newly sown soil with a shade cloth; hot soil temperatures hinder proper seed germination. (The appendix has more on frost dates.)

If your carrot tops break off during harvest (some always do), use a garden fork to dig up their roots. Pull the largest carrot roots first to leave room for the smaller roots to fill out. And if you can't eat all your carrots before the first freeze, lay a 6- to 8- inch-thick layer of hay or straw over the carrot bed. This layer of protection will keep the soil thawed, allowing you to go out on a winter's day and harvest fresh carrots right until spring.

If you're really hungry for carrots and can't wait until they fully mature, you can harvest young carrots anytime after the roots have formed. They just won't taste as sweet unless you grow the baby types.

Growing onions

The simplest way to grow onions is from a set or plant. But you can also directly sow onion seeds in spring, 2 weeks before your last frost date, or start them indoors 8 weeks earlier. For a fall planting of onions, start seedlings indoors or buy transplants. Plant the onion plants 4 to 6 weeks before the first frost. If you're starting your own seeds for a fall planting, start them indoors 8 weeks earlier.

If you start onions indoors, keep the plants stocky and short; whenever they get long and straggly, cut the tops with scissors so the plants are 3 inches tall. Trimming encourages better root growth and keeps the plants at a manageable size. Keep the seedlings moist and grow them under lights (Chapter 13 has more on growing seedlings indoors). Then *harden off* the transplants — gradually introduce them to the outdoor growing environment by bringing them outside for longer amounts of time each day for up to 1 week; then plant them 4 to 6 inches apart.

What makes onions pungent or sweet? The sulfur, not the sugar. Sweet onions have less sulfur than pungent varieties, so they taste sweeter. Even though the sulfur can make the onion more pungent, it also makes those varieties great storage onions. To keep your sweet onions as sweet as they can be, don't apply any sulfur fertilizers. Also keep the onion plants stress free by controlling weeds and making sure that the plants receive enough water and fertilizer (such as 5-5-5). If you do so, they will thrive and be sweet.

You can harvest onions anytime if you want scallions or small, baby onions, but for the largest bulbs, wait until about 80 percent of the tops have naturally started to fall over. Pull the bulbs out on a dry day if possible and then let them dry out in a warm, shady spot. For more on harvesting, see Chapter 19.

Producing potatoes

Potatoes are mostly grown from seed potatoes, which are either small potatoes or larger ones cut so that each piece has two *eyes* (those small indentations on a potato's skin). Eyes are dormant buds from which roots and shoots grow. Plant pieces about 8 to 10 inches apart in rows.

Don't try to plant potatoes that you purchase from a grocery store. These spuds have been treated with a chemical sprouting inhibitor, so they either won't grow any plants or the plants will be weak and not productive. It's best to purchase seed potatoes from a mail-order catalog, nursery, or garden center.

In this section, I describe essential techniques for growing potatoes.

Protecting your taters with the hilling technique

If you weed your root crop patch, mulch it with hay or straw, and water it well, crisp roots will be yours for the taking in no time. However, potatoes do require one more special technique, called hilling. *Hilling* is the technique of mounding up the soil with a hoe around the plants as they grow (see Figure 6-2). Hill at least twice during the growing season — about 1 week after the leaves emerge from the soil and again 2 to 3 weeks later. Hilling promotes the production of bigger potatoes and more of them, kills weeds, and keeps the sun off the tubers.

After your final hilling, lay a 3- to 4-inch-thick layer of hay or straw around your potatoes. Not only will this layer reduce the amount of weeding you do the rest of the summer, but it also will keep the soil cool and moist — perfect tuber-forming conditions! This layer also helps create larger tubers with fewer problems, such as *hollow heart* (when the center of the potato is hollow due to moisture stress).

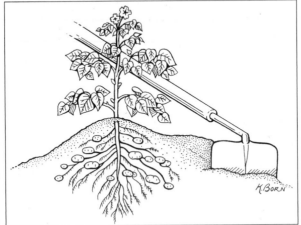

Figure 6-2:
Hilling
potatoes
encourages
more of
them to
form.

Any direct sun on potatoes causes chlorophyll to form, turning the potato skins green and giving them an off taste. Tubers actually are mildly poisonous after they've formed chlorophyll, but you'd have to eat a truckload to really get sick. Keep the potatoes hilled and mulched when in the ground, and store them in the dark after harvest to avoid this problem. If you have a small green patch on your potato, just cut if off; the rest of the tuber is fine to eat.

Applying a space-saving planting technique

Don't have room in your garden but want to grow potatoes? Instead of planting in rows, try growing potatoes vertically in potato towers (see Figure 6-3). Here's how:

1. **Place a 3-foot-diameter heavy wire cage over cultivated soil.**

2. **Add a 2- to 3-inch layer of soil to the bottom of the cage, and line the sides of the cage with hay. Plant four seed potatoes in the bottom of the cage and cover them with soil.**

3. **As the potato plants grow, continue adding soil over them and adding hay around the inside of the cage until you reach the top of the tower. Keep the soil well watered.**

4. **In the fall, open the cage and watch your tubers roll out!**

Digging up the fruits (er, vegetables) of your labor

Harvesting potatoes is like going on an archeological dig. After a potato plant dies, use a metal garden fork and dig up the area 1 foot away from the row so you don't spear the tubers. You'll be amazed at the number of tubers you find — on average, 10 to 20 per plant. Dry the potatoes for an hour or so in the shade, and then store them in a dark, airy, 60-degree area for *curing* (the process of letting the skin toughen so the vegetables store better). After 2 weeks, move the potatoes to a shed or room that's 40 to 50 degrees to store for up to 9 months (depending on the variety). Always eat any damaged tubers first, because they'll be the first to rot in storage.

Figure 6-3: You can grow potatoes in towers if you don't have much room in your garden.

New potatoes are just young potatoes, and with their soft skin and texture, they make a great summer treat. If you can't wait until the main harvest is ready, steal a few new potatoes the second time you hill. Just reach into the soil and feel for small, round tubers. Taking a few won't kill the plant, and you'll still get some larger spuds later on.

The sweetest of tubers: Planting sweet potatoes

Sweet potatoes (*Ipomoea batatas*) are a root crop with a reputation for being grown only in the South. However, if you choose the right varieties, you can grow sweet potatoes just about anywhere — even in cold climates like Minnesota. Sweet potatoes are easy to grow and store well indoors in winter. The orange- or yellow-fleshed tubers can be baked, mashed, or sliced and deep fried for a nutritious and delicious snack. Some short-season varieties (90 days) to grow are 'Beauregard', 'Centennial', and 'Georgia Jet'. Other varieties that mature 1 to 2 weeks later are 'Bush Porto Rico', Jewel', and 'Vardaman'.

To grow sweet potatoes, you don't plant seeds. Instead, you buy small plants called *slips*. Slips are available at local nurseries or garden centers in spring or through the mail. You can start your own at home, but it's better to purchase certified disease-free slips from commercial growers to avoid disease. Sweet potatoes love the heat, so wait until the soil temperature is at least 60 degrees before planting. The vines of your sweet potatoes will create a dense, mat-like groundcover, making this an attractive and edible plant to grow.

To plant and grow your sweet tubers follow these steps:

1. **Create raised beds at least 6 inches tall and amend the soil with compost.**

2. **Plant the slips up to their bottom leaves, 1 foot apart in the raised beds.**

   In cold-winter areas, consider laying black plastic over the beds, punching holes, and planting the slips through the plastic so the soil will heat up faster and the tubers will grow and mature sooner.

3. **Side-dress the plants once, a month after planting.**

   When side-dressing, use an organic fertilizer, such as 5-5-5, or a mix of blood and bone meal fertilizer. And be sure to keep your plants well weeded and watered. Keep the soil on the slightly acidic pH side to avoid some diseases. (Check out Chapter 15 for details on side-dressing and fertilizing.)

4. **Before the first frost, or about 100 days after planting, dig under the plants and check for roots.**

   Pull plants that have formed good-sized roots and cure (dry) these in a warm (80-degree) room for 2 weeks. The curing process not only helps the skin toughen, but also converts starches to sugars, giving sweet potatoes their characteristic taste.

   After curing, eat the tubers or store them in a humid, 55-degree basement (or in any other cool area of your house) all winter.

Keeping Your Root Crops Healthy and Pest-Free

Many of the same pests and diseases that you find on other vegetable crops — such as aphids, flea beetles, thrips, mosaic virus, and nematodes — also occur on root crops. Other potentially damaging root crop pests are animals — such as rabbits, mice, and chipmunks — that enjoy the underground snacks out of sight of predators. I lost most of my potato crop one year due to an overpopulation of hungry chipmunks looking for food. (I discuss insect and animal pests as well as common diseases in more detail in Chapter 17.)

Check with your local Cooperative Extension Service office or the folks at your local nursery or garden store to find out what specific diseases and insects may be problems in your area. Then, as with any vegetable, you can plant varieties that are resistant to those diseases and insects.

Besides the usual suspects that attack vegetable gardens, a few pests and diseases specifically harm root crops. Here are descriptions of them as well as the appropriate controls:

✔ **Blight:** This fungal disease can wreak havoc on potatoes. Late blight, in particular, is the infamous disease that destroyed potatoes in Ireland in the 1840s, causing the Irish potato famine. This disease thrives in cool, humid weather, and infection starts in the form of water-soaked black spots on the leaves.

Unfortunately, once blight starts, you can't treat it; the plants can die, and any tuber that they produce also may be infected and inedible. To avoid this disease, mulch, rotate crops, pull up any *volunteer* potatoes that sprout from old tubers in the ground, and plant certified disease-free seed potatoes.

✔ **Carrot rust fly:** If your carrots' roots have holes bored into them, they may be infected with carrot rust flies. The adult flies lay their eggs on the soil near carrot plants, and then when the young larvae hatch, they tunnel into the soil to feed on the carrot roots. If your carrots have these holes in them, you can eat the carrots as long as the disease hasn't started rotting the root.

To avoid this problem, rotate crops, grow resistant varieties, and cover the plants with a *floating row cover* (a cheesecloth-like material that lets air, water, and sun in, but keeps bugs out; see Chapter 21).

✔ **Colorado potato beetle:** The most destructive potato pests, these ½-inch-long, tan- and brown-striped adult beetles lay yellow eggs in clusters on the undersides of potato leaves, starting in early summer. After the eggs hatch, the dark-red larvae feed on the leaves and can quickly destroy your crop (see Figure 6-4).

Figure 6-4: Colorado potato beetle eggs, larvae, and adults love potato leaves.

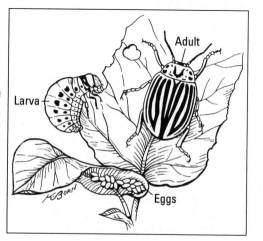

Control these insects by growing resistant varieties, crushing their eggs on sight, handpicking the young beetles, mulching with a thick layer of hay to slow their spread, and spraying the biological spray Bt 'San Diego', which is specifically designed to kill young potato beetles but doesn't harm other insects, animals, or people, on the larvae. Potatoes can withstand significant potato beetle leaf damage and still produce. You just won't receive as large of a crop.

- **Onion maggot:** This pest's larvae attack the bulbs of developing onions, causing holes, opening the bulb to infection from disease, and making them inedible. Onion maggots like cool, wet weather. To control onion maggots, place a floating row cover over young seedlings after the weather warms to around 70 degrees. Doing so prevents the adult flies from laying eggs on the young plants.

- **Potato scab:** This fungal disease causes a potato's skin to turn brown with a corky texture. Tubers with potato scab are unattractive but still edible. Control this cosmetic disease by planting resistant varieties and rotating your crops.

- **Wireworm:** These jointed, hard-shelled, tan-colored, 1-inch worms feed on underground tuber roots as well as the bulbs of a number of crops. They're generally a problem with recently sodded soil. Control this pest by setting potato traps before your root crops begin maturing. Spear a potato piece on a stick and bury it 2- to 4-inches in the ground; the wireworms should infest the potato piece. Dig up the piece after 1 week and then destroy it.

Chapter 7

Sweet and Simple: Beans and Peas

. . . .

In This Chapter

▶ Growing bean and pea varieties of different heights, colors, and flavors

▶ Planting beans and peas in your garden

▶ Caring for your beans and peas

▶ Harvesting your crop

. . . .

*O*ne vegetable that you can always rely on is the bean. So for ensured success in your first garden, plant some bean seeds. When I teach gardening to beginner groups, the first plants that I talk about are bean plants — and for good reason. Bean seeds are large and easy to plant, they grow easily, and they don't require lots of extra fertilizer or care. Within 60 days, you're bound to have some beans to eat. With beans, satisfaction is as guaranteed as it gets in the vegetable gardening world. In fact, they're even more forgiving than tomatoes!

Peas are in the same legume family as beans; other crops in this family include clover and alfalfa, but you don't eat them (unless you grow sprouts!). Like beans, peas also have large seeds and require little care. The only difference between the two is that peas like cool weather to grow and mature, whereas beans like it warm. If you get the timing right for beans and peas, you'll have lots of legumes rolling through your kitchen door; just use the guidelines in this chapter to get started. (See the appendix for a general planting guide for selected beans and peas.)

A Bevy of Beans: Filling Your Rows with Bean Family Plants

All bush, pole, and dried beans are members of the *Fabaceae* family. In this section, I classify beans according to their growth habits and usage (that is, whether you eat them fresh or dried). Here are the categories:

- ✔ **Bush beans:** These beans get their name because they grow on a bush. They tend to produce the earliest crops, maturing all at once (within a week or so of each other); you have either feast or famine with these types.

- ✔ **Pole beans:** These beans need staking and usually grow on poles. They tend to mature their crops later than bush beans, but pole beans continue to produce all season until frost or disease stops them. (Luckily, home gardeners generally don't have to worry about disease resistance with their bean plants.)

- ✔ **Dried beans:** These are actually varieties of bush or pole beans. You can eat them fresh, like bush or pole beans, but they're better if you allow them to dry and then just eat the bean seeds. Growing dried beans is easy: Just plant them, care for them, and harvest them when the pods are dried and the plants are almost dead.

Bush and pole beans actually are the same type of bean, just with different growth habits. Bush and pole beans often are called *snap beans* because they snap when you break their pods in half. Another name for these beans is *string beans,* because early varieties had a stringy texture. (Modern varieties don't have this texture, so this name isn't commonly used today.) Yellow snap varieties mature to a yellow color and are called *wax beans.* Don't get lost in the snap versus string discussion. Those are just names people have given to a bean eaten before the seeds inside begin to form.

Beans harvested at different stages can be called different names. Consider the following:

- ✔ A bean harvested when it's young, before seeds have formed, is called a *snap bean.* They come in green, yellow, or purple depending on the variety.

- ✔ If a bean matures further and you harvest it when it's still young but the bean seeds are fully formed, it's called a *shell bean.*

- ✔ If the pod dries on the plant and then you harvest it, it's called a *dried bean.*

Some bean varieties can be harvested at all stages. However, most bean varieties are best harvested at one particular stage — snap, shell, or dried — depending on their breeding (see the later section "Keep on pickin': Harvesting your crop" for details).

Just for fun in this section — in addition to the bush, pole, and dried beans, I also list some other bean relatives that are tasty and have novel colors and shapes (they're unique). The days to maturity for all these beans represents the time from when you plant the seeds in the ground to when you harvest them. Bean appétit!

Bushels of bush beans

Bush bean plants generally are less than 2 feet tall and produce handfuls of beans at their one main harvest of the season. Depending on the variety, the beans are green, yellow, or purple. Most *pods* (the part of the bean that you eat) are 6 to 8 inches at maturity, but you can harvest beans that are flavorful sooner. If you need lots of beans all at once for canning or preserving, grow bush beans. Selecting among the various types is really just a matter of color and experimentation; try one and see if you like it. Here are a few of the most reliable varieties to grow:

- ✔ **'Blue Lake 274':** This big, meaty, green bean variety matures high yields (about 12 pounds for every 10 feet of row) in 55 days — even under adverse weather conditions. It also comes in a pole bean version.

- ✔ **'Derby':** This disease-resistant green bean is an All-America Selections winner (see Chapter 4) and features extra-tender pods and high yields 57 days from seeding.

- ✔ **'Improved Golden Wax':** This disease-resistant, yellow-bean variety produces broad, flat golden pods 52 days from seeding.

- ✔ **'Jade':** This heat-tolerant green bean produces huge yields of pencil-straight beans 60 days after seeding. It produces high-quality beans later into the season than other green bush beans, allowing you to extend your harvest time.

- ✔ **'Kentucky Wonder':** This classic green bean's round, green pods are produced prolifically on sturdy plants 57 days from seeding. It also comes in a pole bean variety.

- ✔ **'Nash':** This heavy yielding, disease-resistant variety grows well in the heat, so it's a good choice in hot-summer areas. Its green pods mature 54 days from seeding.

- ✔ **'Provider':** This variety has great disease resistance and can grow in adverse weather. Its green pods mature 50 days from seeding.

- ✔ **'Roc d'Or Wax':** This variety produces long, slender, round, bright yellow pods on sturdy plants in 53 days.

- ✔ **'Roma II':** This Romano-type bush bean has tender, flat pods and high yields earlier than Romano (53 days after seeding). The pods are slow to develop seeds and strings, so they stay tender longer.

> ✔ **'Romano':** This long, flat green bean is an Italian classic and also comes in a pole variety. The pods are known for their strong flavor and ability to stay tender even when they're large. This variety matures in 60 days. 'Romano Gold' and 'Romano Purpiat' are yellow and purple varieties, respectively, that grow similar to the original just with different-colored pods.
>
> ✔ **'Royal Burgundy':** This attractive purple-podded bean also has a purple tinge on its leaves, stems, and flowers. It matures in 55 days and turns dark green when cooked.

Pole beans: The long and tall crop

Many pole bean varieties share the names and characteristics of their bush bean counterparts. Pole beans mature more beans overall but start a week or so later than bush beans and produce only a handful of beans per day, which makes them great for small families. Pole beans keep producing beans until frost, in all but the hottest summer areas. You also can plant them in summer for a fall crop in warm areas.

In the following list, I mention the pole beans that also have bush forms, plus some other well-producing and attractive pole varieties:

> ✔ **'Blue Lake':** See the bush variety in the preceding section.
>
> ✔ **'Emerite':** Think of this variety as a green filet bean (see the later section "Other beans") on poles. The tender, pencil-thin, 4- to 5-inch-long pods are produced 64 days from seeding.
>
> ✔ **'Fortex':** This variety produces extra-long (11-inch) pods that are stringless, tender, nutty, and savory. A French favorite, this productive green bean matures 60 days from seeding.
>
> ✔ **'Goldmarie':** This early yielding, wax pole bean variety produces 8-inch pods 54 days from seeding.
>
> ✔ **'Kentucky Wonder':** See the bush bean variety in the preceding section for a description. 'Kentucky Wonder' also is available in a wax pole bean variety.
>
> ✔ **'Purple Pod':** This unique purple-colored variety grows on a 6-foot-tall plant. When you cook the bean, its color changes from purple to dark green. It matures 65 days from seeding.
>
> ✔ **'Romano':** See the bush bean variety in the preceding section.
>
> ✔ **'Scarlet Runner':** This beautiful, vigorous pole bean is actually in a different species than other pole beans (*Phaseolus coccineus*). It produces attractive scarlet red flowers, large hairy pods, and bean seeds that are edible 70 days from seeding. The pods can be eaten when young and the

bean seeds are edible when dried. This variety tastes okay, but it usually is grown as an ornamental for its attractive flowers and colorful red and black bean seeds.

The versatile shell and dried beans

Shell and dried beans are some of the most versatile beans to grow because you can eat them at the snap, shell, or dried stages. Eaten at the shell stage (fully matured seeds in the pod, but the pod is still green) or dried stage, you're eating the seed inside the pod. These seeds come in colors from white to red and can even be striped and spotted. Dried beans are great baked and in soups and chowders.

Most of the varieties in the following list are grown for their dried beans but also taste good at their shelling stage, too. They're the dried beans that most people are familiar with eating, and they're the tastiest to grow. The days to maturity represent the time from seeding to dried bean harvest. Most of these varieties are bushy plants:

- ✔ **'Black Turtle':** This small black bean matures 85 days from seeding and grows best in warmer climates. Each pod produces seven to eight beans, which are often baked as well as used in soups and casseroles.

- ✔ **'Blue Speckled Tepary':** This Southwest variety grows great in hot, dry conditions. The brown seeds with red speckles mature 90 days from seeding.

- ✔ **'Cannellini':** This famous white, kidney-shaped bean is often used in minestrone soups. Large plants produce beans that are best when eaten at the shelling stage, which is 80 days from seeding.

- ✔ **'French Horticultural':** An old-time favorite, this tan-colored bean matures in 90 days. You also can eat this variety earlier as a shelling bean.

- ✔ **'Jacob's Cattle':** This bean gets its name from the cattle that Jacob, the biblical character, tended. It's white with splashes of maroon. This bean is best adapted to cooler weather. You'll find 'Jacob's Cattle' great in baked bean dishes.

- ✔ **'Navy':** This small, semi-vining plant produces white, oval beans 85 days from seeding. These beans are excellent baked.

- ✔ **'Pinto':** A vining plant produces buff-colored, brown-speckled, dried beans 90 days from seeding; these beans are widely used in Mexican dishes. You also can grow this variety as a pole bean.

- ✔ **'Red Kidney':** This bushy plant produces large, red, kidney-shaped beans 100 days from seeding. These beans are used in many baked dishes. 'Red Kidney' also comes as a white-seeded variety.

✔ **'Soldier':** This white, kidney-shaped bean with red markings produces 6 beans per pod 85 days from seeding. This bean is great baked and in stews.

✔ **'Tongue of Fire':** These 6- to 7-inch, red-streaked pods can be eaten shelled or dried. They mature to the shell stage 70 days from seeding.

✔ **'Vermont Cranberry':** This red, brown-speckled, New England classic dried bean is one of the most popular beans to grow. It matures 90 days from seeding and is *widely adapted* (can grow in a variety of geographic regions under a variety of weather conditions).

Miscellaneous beans not to be forgotten

Some variations on the common bean are exotic and fun to grow. The beans in this section are grown similarly to bush or pole beans but come in different shapes and flavors. Some of these beans aren't even in the same species as bush and pole beans, but they're grown the same way. The following sections show you a few of the best ones to try.

Asparagus bean

The asparagus bean (*Vigna unguiculata sesquipedalis,* or Yard-Long bean) is a pole bean that grows more than 10 feet tall and produces extremely long beans (up to 3 feet tall!). This variety is popular in Europe and Asia and is catching on in the United States. The asparagus bean takes a longer growing season to mature than traditional pole bean varieties, however. Most mature within 80 days from seeding. Some good varieties to look for include 'Chinese Green Noodle' and 'Red Noodle'. 'Chinese Green Noodle' features long, thin green beans. The 'Red Noodle' variety features burgundy-colored pods that hold and deepen their color to purple when cooked.

Edamame

Edamame (*Glycine max*), or Green Vegetable soybean, started as a novelty bean from Japan and has turned into a favorite in many home gardens and kitchens. Unlike the commercial soybean that's grown for animal feed, oil, and so on, this soybean is meant to be eaten at the green shell stage; it has a buttery, lima-bean flavor. Some varieties have green seeds and others black.

'Envy' is the earliest maturing of the edamame varieties (75 days from seeding). 'Black Pearl' is smaller than other soybean seeds and has a rich and distinctive flavor. Maturing in 85 days, it grows up to 3 feet tall and wide, so it needs more room than other varieties. 'Butterbean', which matures in 90 days, is a high-yielding soybean with a sweet and buttery flavor and well-branched plants. 'Sayamusume', which is a Pacific Northwest favorite, produces high yields of large soybeans with 3 to 4 soybeans per pod. This variety matures in 85 days.

Edamame beans are a kid-sized treat. Children of all ages love to pop these buttery-flavored beans in their mouths after they're steamed.

Fava bean

The fava bean (*Vigna acontifolia,* or English Broad bean or Horse bean) is a popular English bean that grows on plants that are 2 to 3 feet tall; unlike other beans, the fava bean likes cold weather. You can harvest the 7-inch pods as snap or shell beans; they mature 85 days from seeding. Fava beans are a good alternative to lima beans in cold climates. 'Windsor' is a good variety that produces 3 to 5 green seeds per pod 75 days after seeding.

French filet

The French filet bean (*Haricot Vert*) is a classic bean from France that has really caught on in the United States. This bean has been bred to be tender and stringless. Compact bush plants produce an abundance of these thin, textured, "melt-in-your-mouth" beans when harvested young. Pick them when they're less than $1/4$-inch-thick, or they'll have started to mature, leaving the pods tough and stringy.

You can choose from a number of varieties of French filet beans. Some of the best include the following: 'Maxibel' (high yields of 7-inch-long, round beans); 'Nickel' (heat and cold tolerant plants produce 4-inch-long beans); 'Tavera' (very slender, 4- to 5-inch-long beans); and 'Soleil' (a unique 4-inch-long, yellow-podded variety). All filet beans mature between 50 and 60 days from seeding.

Lima bean

Once you've eaten a fresh lima bean (*Phaseolus lunatus,* or Butter bean), you'll never settle for the canned version again. Lima beans come in bush and pole varieties and love a long, warm growing season. Fat pods, which are 4 to 8 inches long, produce 4 to 6 beans each that you harvest at the shell stage.

One of the best bush varieties is 'Fordhook 242', which matures in 75 days. It produces 3 to 5 white seeds per pod and is tolerant of both heat and cold. Another is 'Jackson Wonder'. This "baby" lima produces 3 to 4 beans per pod and matures in 75 days, which makes it good for cooler climates. A good pole variety is 'King of the Garden', which matures 88 days from seeding. It yields 4 to 6 large, cream-colored seeds per pod. 'Florida Speckled Butter', another pole bean, matures in 85 days. Each pod produces 3 to 5 light-brown seeds speckled with maroon. The plant is heat- and drought-tolerant, making it a good Southern variety.

Southern pea

Although it's called a pea, the southern pea (*Vigna unguiculata,* or Cowpea) actually is more like a bean in growth and usage. Like limas, southern peas grow best in warm climates. The plants are either bush or semi-vining, and you harvest the pods about 60 days from seeding at the shell or dried stage.

Some of the more famous types are Black-Eyed peas such as 'Pink-Eyed Purple Hull', which is named for the black speck on the seed; Crowders such as 'Mississippi Silver', named for the way the seeds grow jammed in the pod; and Cream peas such as 'Lady', named for their smooth pod.

More Peas, Please!

One vegetable that's truly a treat to grow yourself is the pea, which is *Pisum sativum* botanically. In grocery stores, peas are available for only a short time, and their flavor isn't as sweet and tender as freshly picked pea pods. Some varieties grow to be huge and bushy, needing extra support to stand tall. Others are short and bushy and don't require fencing or support. Viny pea plants produce a grabbing shoot called a *tendril* that holds onto whatever it comes in contact with. Some novel types don't even bother growing leaves. In the following sections, I divide peas into three groups: English, snap, and snow. Mind your peas and take a look at some excellent varieties.

A pea is described by the type of pods it has. Here are the categories:

- An *English,* or garden, pea has a tough pod with tender peas inside.

- A *snap* pea has tender peas inside but also an edible, sweet pod.

- A *snow* pea is harvested flat (that is, harvested before the pea seeds inside the pod form) mainly for its tender pea pod.

English peas: The reliable standby

Sometimes called the garden pea, the English pea is the pea that gardeners are most familiar with and that's most widely grown. In the following list, the days to maturity represent the time from seeding to harvest. Here are some of the most reliable varieties of English peas:

- **'Alderman' (Tall Telephone):** This old heirloom matures in about 74 days. Six-foot-tall vines produce a large number of 4- to 5-inch pods with 6 to 8 peas per pod.

- **'Blondie':** This new variety features 3-inch-long pods with 8 peas per pod. The yellow leaves and pale green pods and peas make this an eye-catching variety in the garden. It matures in 65 days and needs trellising (which I discuss in the later section "Spacing properly and providing support").

- **'Feisty':** This 30-inch-tall vine has few leaves and many tendrils, which makes the medium-sized pea pods with 6 to 8 peas per pod easier to harvest. The plant matures in 61 days.

- ✔ **'Little Marvel':** Even though it's a dwarf plant that grows only 18 to 20 inches tall, this pea plant produces heavy yields of 3-inch pods with 6 to 8 peas per pod. The plant matures in 62 days.

- ✔ **'Maestro':** A prolific early variety matures in 60 days and reaches only 2 feet tall but produces 4- to 5-inch pods with 9 to 11 peas per pod on powdery mildew–resistant plants.

- ✔ **'Mr. Big':** This All-America-Selections-winning (see Chapter 4), disease-resistant variety is a big producer that matures in 67 days. The 5- to 6-foot-tall vines produce 4- to 5-inch-long pods with up to 10 peas per pod.

- ✔ **'Petit Pois':** This novel *baby* pea (the pea seed inside the pod is smaller than the normal pea seed) is extra sweet and tender. It produces 6 to 7 peas per pod. The plants are 20 inches tall and produce peas in 58 days.

- ✔ **'Wando':** This very productive, warm weather variety grows 3 feet tall and produces 7 to 8 peas per pod in 68 days.

Sweet and tender snap peas

Snap peas were once the new peas on the block. Now they have become a mainstay in many gardens. Snap pea pods *fill out* (the pea seed inside the pod forms) like an English pea, but they have a sweet, tender pod like a snow pea. Some newer varieties are considered stringless. The plants range from the original 'Super Snap' that grows to 8 feet tall to the diminutive 'Sugar Bon' that grows to less than 2 feet tall. Kids love snap peas, and they're as easy to grow as English peas.

Try these varieties of sweet and flavorful snap peas:

- ✔ **'Cascadia':** These 2-foot-tall vines resist the pea enation virus disease (a problem in the Pacific Northwest; see the later section "Pesky pea problems") and produce 3-inch, dark green peas 58 days after planting.

- ✔ **'Sugar Ann':** The earliest maturing snap pea, this variety is ready for harvest in 52 days. The plants grow only 2 feet tall, producing sweet, 2- to 3-inch pods. Because this snap pea is a dwarf variety, it doesn't need support and can be grown in containers. 'Sugar Sprint' is similar to 'Sugar Ann' but doesn't produce stringy pods.

- ✔ **'Sugar Bon':** A 1- to 2-foot-tall snap pea, this plant matures in 56 days and resists powdery mildew disease. Because of its size, this variety is super for containers.

- ✔ **'Sugar Lace II':** These 30-inch-tall vines have few leaves and many tendrils, making the 3-inch-long pods easy to see. The plant is self-supporting and disease resistant. It matures in 68 days.

✔ **'Super Sugar Snap':** These vines grow to 6 feet tall, producing tons of sweet, long pods and peas 65 days after planting. This variety is shorter and more disease resistant than the original 'Sugar Snap', which is still available.

An earlier harvest: Snow peas

If you've eaten a vegetable dish in a Chinese restaurant, you've probably tried these sweet-tasting, flat-podded peas. Snow peas are the easiest peas to grow because you don't have to wait for the pea pods to fill out to harvest them. They're tender, stringless, and best when harvested before the peas inside begin to swell. Here are some of the best producing varieties to try:

✔ **'Dwarf Gray Sugar':** This viny, 2- to 3-foot-tall plant needs support but produces 3-inch, dark green pods 57 days after planting. The pink flowers this plant produces are ornamental, so you'll enjoy how they dress up your garden.

✔ **'Golden Sweet':** This Indian heirloom features unique golden-colored pods on 6-foot-tall green vines that mature in 65 days. The pods stay golden when cooked, making them beautiful additions to stir-fry and salads.

✔ **'Mammoth Melting Sugar':** This 4- to 5-foot-tall heirloom features 5-inch-long pods that stay sweet longer than other varieties. It matures in 68 days after planting.

✔ **'Oregon Giant':** These large 4- to 5-inch sweet pods grow on disease-resistant, 3-foot-tall vines 60 days after planting.

✔ **'Oregon Sugar Pod II':** Another large-podded, sweet-tasting snow pea, this variety grows to 4 feet tall and matures its pods 68 days after planting. Like 'Oregon Giant', it's also disease resistant.

Get 'Em in the Ground: Growing Beans and Peas

Peas and beans are like siblings: They have a lot in common but also have some different preferences. For instance, both peas and beans like moderate moisture throughout the growing season and well-drained soil that isn't heavily *amended* (nutrient-improved) with fertilizer. And neither is very demanding at all. The fundamental difference between pea and beans, however, is that peas like cool climates and beans prefer warm ones. If you get the timing right — by planting peas so they mature when it's cool and beans when it's hot — these two siblings will reward you with a bounty of legumes.

Planting legumes for an ample harvest

When planting legumes, choose a sunny spot with well-drained soil and create a raised bed (see Chapter 3). Raised beds help keep pea seeds from getting soggy while they germinate in cool spring soil; at the same time, raised beds also warm up the soil for bean seeds, which you plant in late spring and summer. In the following sections, I explain how to prepare the soil for your legumes, figure out when to plant, and discover how to give them the proper support.

Preparing the soil

Plants need nitrogen to grow, and most of the time they get it from the soil. Legumes are unique, however, in that they can use the nitrogen in the air through a special relationship with a type of bacteria called a *rhizobium*. This bacteria naturally occurs in soil and attaches itself to legume roots, living off the plants. In exchange, the bacteria takes the atmospheric nitrogen and changes it into a form that the plants can use. Beans and peas get the nitrogen they need, and the bacteria gets a home. So don't worry about adding more nitrogen fertilizer to legumes; they can take care of themselves. If you see bumps or nodules on the roots of your plants, you know that bacteria is at work.

Books and catalogs often suggest that you buy your own bacteria inoculant powder to add to bean and pea seeds when planting. This powder really isn't necessary. Soil already has bacteria in it, so usually you don't need to add any extra to your seeds. The exception, however, is with very sandy or poor soil. These types of soil need a one-time *inoculation* (the mixing of powder with seeds at planting), which peppers the soil with bacteria and gives plants the boost they need. After the rhizobium is in the soil, you don't need to add it yearly.

Even though legumes don't need extra nitrogen, they benefit from a 2- to 3-inch layer of composted manure worked into the soil before planting. For poor soils with low fertility, add an organic fertilizer high in phosphorous and potassium, such as 5-5-5 (see Chapter 15).

Determining when to plant

With beans, wait until the soil is at least 60 degrees Fahrenheit before planting. Beans planted in cool soil rot before germinating. Stagger your bush bean planting dates by planting small batches of seeds every week or so (see Chapter 16 for more on succession planting). By staggering the plantings, you'll have a continual harvest all summer.

Peas like cool soil; in fact, they can germinate in 40-degree soil. As soon as the soil dries out, build your raised beds and plant your seeds. You can determine whether your soil is dried out by squeezing a handful of it; if no water trickles out and the soil clump feels moist and breaks up easily when poked with your finger, the soil is dried out.

You can plant peas 3 to 4 weeks before the last frost date in your area if the soil is ready. Pea seeds germinate better in 60- to 70-degree soil, but if you wait until the soil is warmer, the plants will get off to a late start. By the time the peas would begin flowering, the air temperature would be too warm (above 80 degrees), and your plants and production would suffer.

You also can grow peas as a fall crop, which you start in summer so the plants mature in the cool days of autumn. I've had success planting snow peas as a fall crop. You can harvest these legumes sooner than English and snap peas because you can eat the flat pea pods as soon as they form and before the freezing weather hits.

To help pea seeds germinate in cold or hot soils, try *pregerminating* the seeds (see Figure 7-1). Place the pea seeds in a moist paper towel in a dark, warm spot for a few days. Check the seeds daily; when you see a small root begin to grow, plant the peas in the ground. Pregerminating helps the peas get off to a faster start and reduces the chance that they'll rot in cool soil.

Figure 7-1:
Pregerm-
inate pea
seeds
indoors by
soaking
them in a
dark, warm
spot.

Spacing properly and providing support

How close you plant your legumes depends on the varieties you've chosen. The following guidelines can help:

- ✔ **Bush beans grow best in rows on top of a raised bed.** In rows 1 to 2 feet apart, plant the individual seeds within 1 to 2 inches of each other. Then thin the beans to 4 to 6 inches apart after they germinate and emerge from the soil. (Chapter 13 provides pointers on how to thin your vegetable seedlings.)

- ✔ **Because you plant peas when the soil is cooler, the germination percentage may be less than with beans.** So, on your raised bed, plant your peas less than 1 inch apart in rows 6 inches apart.

Tall vining varieties of beans, such as pole beans, and tall varieties of peas need support to grow their best. The type of support needed depends on the plant (see Figure 7-2). Pole bean shoots spiral and wrap themselves around objects that they can climb, and peas attach themselves to objects with *tendrils* (grabbing shoots that hold onto whatever they come in contact with). Generally, beans like to climb poles, and peas like to climb fences. The height of your fence or pole depends on the varieties that you're growing: A 4- to 5-foot fence is good for most peas, and a 6- to 8-foot pole is good for pole beans.

Keep your fences and poles within reach because if the plants grow too tall, you'll need to use a ladder to harvest. For more information on trellises, fences, and teepees, see Chapter 15.

Plant both pea and bean seeds 1 to 2 inches deep. Plant pole beans around individual poles; you should have 4 to 6 pole beans around each pole, about 6 inches away from the pole (see Figure 7-3). In between the pea rows, place your trellis or chicken wire so the peas can climb both sides of a fence (or whatever you have for them to climb on).

Figure 7-2:
Climbers versus twiners.

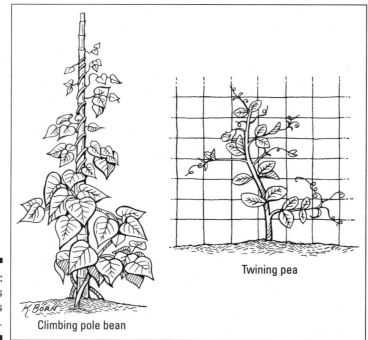

Twining pea

K. BORN

Climbing pole bean

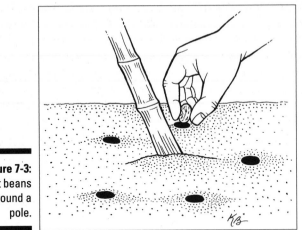

Figure 7-3:
Plant beans
around a
pole.

After they start to grow, beans and peas need little attention other than regular watering and weeding. Both benefit from a layer of hay or straw mulch placed around the rows. The hay or straw mulch reduces the need for weeding and keeps the soil moist. (See Chapter 15 for more on mulch and other maintenance.)

Be careful when weeding around peas because they have shallow root systems. Instead of digging in the soil around the roots, pull any weeds by hand or bury young weeds with soil as they germinate.

Thwarting pests and diseases

One nice thing about beans and peas is that they're susceptible to only a few serious pests or diseases. However, some of the common problems that plague other vegetables, such as damping off, fusarium wilt, powdery mildew, and leaf blight, also can be problematic for peas and beans (see Chapter 17). You can avoid many of these problems in vegetables by rotating crops, tilling in the fall, and growing resistant varieties; see Chapter 16 for details. The following sections describe some problems specific to beans and peas.

Battles for beans

Here are the most troublesome of the bean problems along with some advice on how to solve (and prevent!) them:

✔ **Bald heading:** If your bean seedlings emerge from the soil without leaves, they may have a condition called *bald heading*. Insects can cause this condition and so can seed that has been damaged. It can occur when you plant the seeds too deep in the ground or in gravel soil, which causes the leaves to rip off as they try to break through the soil. To prevent this condition, prepare the seed bed by removing rocks, sticks, and clods of soil before planting; and don't plant too deep. Leafless beans don't produce any crops, so if you see any leafless beans, pull them out and replant.

✔ **Mexican bean beetle:** This ladybug relative has an orange-yellow shell with 16 black spots on it. The adult beetles lay masses of orange eggs on the undersides of maturing bean plants. When the eggs hatch, the $1/3$-inch, spiny yellow young that emerge feed on the bean leaves, defoliating the plant. To control these pests, do the following:

  • Plant early maturing varieties that are finished producing before the bean beetles become plentiful.

  • Crush any egg masses that you see.

  • Clean up old bean plant debris where the plants *overwinter* (live throughout the winter).

  • Spray the adult beetles with *pyrethrin* (a botanical insecticide made from pyrethrum flowers).

✔ **Rust:** If your plants have red or orange spots on their leaves and then they yellow and die, you may have rust disease. This fungal disease overwinters on bean plant debris left in the garden and infects new plants in summer when the weather is right (warm temperatures and high humidity). To prevent rust disease, clean up plant debris and till your garden in fall. The next growing season, rotate bean plantings to another section of the garden. Also, don't work in your garden when the leaves are wet; wet leaves provide the moisture that rust disease spores need to be able to spread.

Pesky pea problems

Peas don't have many disease or pest problems, but here are a few to watch out for:

✔ **Pea aphid:** These pear-shaped, $1/8$-inch, green insects suck the juices from pea leaves and stems and can stunt a plant's growth and cause it to wilt. If your plants are severely affected by these insects, spray the plants with Safer's insecticidal soap.

✔ **Pea enation virus:** Pea enation virus is a particular problem for peas grown in the Pacific Northwest. The virus, which is spread by aphids (another reason to control the pest), causes plants' leaves and pods to be stunted and deformed. The best solution is to grow disease-resistant varieties such as 'Cascadia'.

Keep on pickin': Harvesting your crop

As you probably know, when it comes to harvesting vegetables, timing is everything. Keep a close eye on your beans and peas as they start to mature and pick often. Beans and peas can get overmature, tough, and stringy quickly, especially in warm weather. Here's how to tell when the beans you've planted are ready for harvest:

- **You can harvest snap beans when the pods are firm and crisp and the seeds inside are undeveloped.** (If the pod is smooth and not bumpy, you know that the seeds haven't developed yet.) Carefully hold the bean stem with one hand and pull the individual beans off with your other hand to avoid breaking the plants.

  The more beans you pick, the more you'll get. That's because the plant wants to produce mature seeds and you keep frustrating it by picking the pods. So be sure to harvest even if you're not going to eat all the beans immediately. Remember, you can always share your crop with hungry friends and family.

- **Harvest shell beans when the pods are full, green, and firm but haven't dried out yet.** You can store the beans in a refrigerator for a few days before cooking them.

- **Let dried bean pods dry on the plant until they naturally begin to split and then harvest them.** Break the bean seeds out of the pods by rubbing the pods in your hands, which shatters them. Store the beans in glass jars in a cool place; you can either eat them or save them to plant next year.

Peas lose quality quickly, so picking them when they're undermature rather than overmature is better. Also, try to cook them the same day; they turn starchy quickly if you keep them for more than 1 or 2 days. Here are some guidelines for harvesting peas:

- **You harvest English and snap peas when the pods are full and before they fade in color.** Upon harvesting snap peas, cut off the cap (stem end) of the pod and take the string (along the seam) out of the pod; these are the only two parts of the pod that are chewy.

- **You can pick snow peas anytime before the pea seeds inside the pods begin to form.** After the peas begin to fill out, the pods get tough and stringy.

- **You can harvest the tender shoots and tendrils of peas.** Harvest from the end of the shoots back 2- to 3-inches including the leaves and tendrils. The shoots and tendrils are great sautéed or mixed raw in salads. It's a way to get the pea flavor without the peas and to use more parts of the pea plant.

Chapter 8

Vigorous Vines: Cucumbers, Melons, Pumpkins, and Squash

- -

In This Chapter

▶ Choosing the best vining varieties for your garden

▶ Understanding how to grow and maintain your viners

- -

*I*f the heat is on, it's time to grow your vining veggies. This group of vegetables is part of the cucumber family (*Cucurbitaceae*), and it includes cucumbers, melons, squash, and pumpkins. Gourds also are in this family, but I discuss them in Chapter 11.

What all these vegetables have in common is their love of heat, their ability to grow long stems (and vine to great lengths), and the fact that they have separate male and female flowers on the same plant. Unlike the other vegetables that I mention in this book (which have both male and female parts in the same flower), the viners need someone to play Cupid and bring pollen from the male flower to the female flower in order to produce fruit. This process is called *pollination,* and usually bees play the role of the chubby cherub. Of course, there are exceptions to the Cupid rule, and I discuss them in the sections about the individual vegetables in this chapter.

This large family of vegetables is known for producing lots of fruits and taking up lots of room in the process. However, modern plant breeders have responded to the need for smaller, space-saving vegetable plants by breeding *bush* (nonvining) varieties of some favorite cucumber-family crops. So now you have one more reason to grow some cucumbers and squash. Actually, if you've ever tasted a vine-ripened melon or cucumber or baked a homegrown winter squash, you're probably hooked. Their flavor and texture are much better than anything you can buy in stores, and if you grow too many vegetables, you can always give them away to hungry neighbors.

Checking Out Cool Cukes

Cucumber varieties usually are categorized two ways: as slicers and picklers. Slicing-cucumber varieties are long, smooth-skinned cucumbers that tend to be larger, a darker shade of green, and have thicker skin with fewer bumps (spines) than pickling varieties, which are short and prickly. Slicing cucumbers are the ones you're probably most familiar with from grocery stores; they're great in salads and other recipes, but they're also super for munching. Of course, you can use pickling varieties the same ways you use slicing varieties, and they're great when eaten fresh, but if you want to make pickles, the pickling varieties have better textures for it.

The easiest cucumber varieties to grow are the hybrid bush types. These varieties, such as 'Salad Bush', are good producers, are disease resistant, and produce a small vining plant that can grow in a container. Bush types don't produce as many cucumbers as larger vining varieties, nor do they produce them all summer long. But if you have a small family, a few bush varieties should be plenty.

To round out the cucumber field in this section, I describe some unusual *heirloom* (old-fashioned) varieties and some modern, seedless cucumber varieties that produce fruit without pollination. If you plant one of the seedless varieties (these varieties actually have seeds, but the seeds aren't developed), avoid planting any other cucumber varieties in your garden. If a seedless variety gets pollinated by bees, edible but seedy fruits will result. For that reason, gardeners often grow these varieties in greenhouses, which protect the plants from bees. (See the section "Ensuring proper pollination," later in this chapter, for more information.)

Before you choose: Brushing up on some cucumber vocabulary

When you're reading about cucumber varieties, you may notice some words — such as *gherkin* and *gynoecious* (guy-NEE-shous) — that would challenge even the best Scrabble player. Fortunately, you don't need to memorize these terms to grow good cucumbers. However, they do enable you to figure out the type of cucumber that you're buying — and impress your friends! Here are some terms to be familiar with:

✔ **Burpless:** This thin-skinned cucumber type has a long, slender shape and a mild flavor that isn't bitter. It's said to produce less intestinal gas than other varieties, which clearly explains where it got its name.

- ✔ **Gherkin:** Actually, this type is a whole different species of cucumber (*Cucumis anguria*). It's used commercially as a pickling cucumber. Gherkins have small, oval shapes and prickly skin. As far as the home gardener is concerned, this species difference has no effect.

- ✔ **Gynoecious:** This type of cucumber has only female flowers and requires the presence of a male pollinating cucumber variety to produce fruit. Usually, seed companies include seeds of a pollinating variety in packets of gynoecious cucumbers; the seeds are marked with a bright-colored coating.

- ✔ **Monoecious:** This cucumber type has both male and female flowers on the same plant. Most cucumber varieties are of this type.

- ✔ **Oriental cucumbers:** This type of cucumber tends to be a thin, long-fruited variety with ribbing on its skin.

- ✔ **Parthenocarpic:** This cucumber type is seedless, producing fruit without pollination. Varieties of this type produce only female flowers and need to be separated from other cucumber varieties. Otherwise, if they're pollinated, they may produce misshapen fruits and form fruits with seeds. (You can still eat them; they'll just look funny.) This cucumber type is often grown in greenhouses.

Surveying common cucumber varieties

After you know a bit of the language, take a look at some of my favorite cucumber varieties. Most of these varieties vine 4 to 5 feet unless I note otherwise. Regular production of cucumbers is about 12 pounds per 10-foot row (about 10 cukes per plant). Choose varieties based on disease resistance, size, productivity, and adaptability. The days to maturity are from seeding in the ground until first harvest. Consider these varieties:

- ✔ **'Armenian':** This unique heirloom, which also is known as the snake cucumber or yard-long cucumber, actually is part of the melon family (*C. melo*). 'Armenian' produces 5-foot-long vines and burpless, nonbitter, 12- to 15- inch-long ribbed slicing fruits in 60 days. It sets fruits even in high temperatures when cucumbers normally won't set fruit, making it a good choice for hot summer climates.

- ✔ **'Bush Pickle':** This hybrid bush pickling variety produces 4-inch pickles all at once on 2- to 3-foot-diameter plants that mature in 45 days.

- ✔ **'County Fair':** This hybrid pickling variety produces 3-inch-long cukes on 2- to 3-foot-long vines. It's best known for its disease resistance, especially to bacterial wilt (see "Controlling pests and diseases" later in this chapter). Choose this variety if cucumber beetles (which spread the disease) are a problem in your area. It matures in 50 days.

- ✔ **'Diva':** This All-America Selections (AAS; see Chapter 4) winner is a hybrid bush slicing cucumber that has it all. It's parthenocarpic, nonbitter, mildew and scab resistant, and has a thin, no-peel skin. It produces 5-inch-long cukes in 58 days.

- ✔ **'Fanfare':** This AAS winner is a hybrid slicing cucumber that grows on a *semi-bush plant* (bigger than a bush variety, but not as rambling as other slicers). It vines to 4 feet, has lots of disease resistance, and produces 8-inch fruits in 63 days.

- ✔ **'Homemade Pickles':** This disease-resistant monoecious, open-pollinated pickler produces 5-foot-long vines and heavy yields of 6-inch-long fruits throughout the season. This variety matures in 55 days.

- ✔ **'Lemon':** This unique monoecious, heirloom variety produces yellow, lemon-shaped fruits that are crisp and mild flavored. This slicer matures in 64 days.

- ✔ **'Little Leaf':** This unique parthenocarpic, open-pollinated pickling variety has compact, multibranched vines that yield well even when stressed. The leaves are half the normal cucumber leaf size, making it easier to find and harvest the 3- to 4-inch-long fruits. This pickler matures 55 days from seeding.

- ✔ **'Salad Bush':** This AAS winner is a hybrid, bush slicing variety that needs only 2 square feet to produce its 8-inch fruits. It matures in 57 days.

- ✔ **'Suyo Long':** This unusual Oriental-type slicing cucumber is burpless, mostly seedless, and produces 15-inch fruits. It matures in 61 days.

- ✔ **'Sweet Success':** This AAS winner is a seedless, parthenocarpic slicing variety with slender, 14-inch-long fruits that have tender skin and good disease resistance. It matures in 54 days.

- ✔ **'Tasty Jade':** This is a vigorous-growing hybrid bush Oriental cucumber that produces thin-skinned, 11-inch-long ribbed, parthenocarpic fruits. This good greenhouse variety matures in 54 days.

Melons: The Sweet, Juicy Vining Plant

Compared to cucumbers with their various sexual combinations and vine lengths, melons are, well, easy. They all have separate male and female flowers on each plant (which categorizes them as *monoecious*), and they all need about 6 to 8 feet of space to vine. Many different types of melons with many unique flavors are available. A number of melons can be harvested on the unripe side and left to mature off the vine while still producing their sweet flavor. (See the later section "Harvesting your vining crop" for more on harvesting melons.) In the following sections, I describe several kinds of melons and share some of my favorite melon varieties.

Distinguishing different types of melons

Most gardeners are familiar with the two most popular types of melons: muskmelons (also known as cantaloupes) and watermelons. But more and more exotic melon types continue to show up in produce markets and seed catalogs. These exotic types include crenshaw, honeydew, and charentais. They're similar to muskmelons, but they offer a tropical, juicy flavor. Watermelons come in the traditional "let's have a picnic" oblong shape as well as the more compact, round shape (also called an icebox shape). Yellow-fleshed and seedless watermelon varieties also are available. Most muskmelons tend to weigh between 2 and 5 pounds, but watermelons can run from 8 pounds to between 20 and 30 pounds. And you thought all melons are alike!

When is a cantaloupe not a cantaloupe? When it's a muskmelon. The round, netted, tan-colored, orange-fleshed fruits that you see in grocery stores usually are sold as "cantaloupes." However, true cantaloupes are tropical fruits that have green flesh and hard skin and are rarely seen in this country. What people from the United States refer to as cantaloupes technically are muskmelons.

Here's a description of some specialty melons you might like to try:

- **Charentais:** This traditional French melon has modern varieties that look like muskmelons. It has deep orange flesh and a honeylike flavor.

- **Crenshaw:** This salmon-fleshed, oval-shaped melon with dark green skin turns mottled yellow when ripe. It needs a long season (about 4 months) to mature.

- **Honeydew:** This sweet, juicy melon has smooth tan skin and pale green flesh; unlike other melons, it doesn't continue to ripen off the vine. These melons store longer than muskmelons.

- **Mediterranean:** This group of melons includes many types, such as Israeli, Galia, Piel de Sapo (Christmas), Canary, and Middle Eastern. This is a large group of tropical melons that generally have yellow skin and sweet, aromatic, pale green or white flesh when mature.

Perusing popular melon varieties

Like all cucumber-family crops, melons need warmth, water, space, and sun. For these reasons, they grow well in the Southeast and the Southwest United States. But with the right variety selection and some growing tricks (see the "Growing Those Vines" section later in this chapter), cool-climate gardeners also can enjoy these sweet, juicy fruits. The days to maturity noted in the following sections are from seeding in the garden until first harvest.

Muskmelons and specialty melons

Here are some popular muskmelon and specialty melon varieties:

- ✔ **'Alaska':** This early hybrid muskmelon variety grows well in areas with short growing seasons. It produces 4-pound fruits in 70 days.

- ✔ **'Ambrosia':** This 5-pound hybrid muskmelon has sweet, salmon-colored flesh and good resistance to powdery mildew disease. It matures in 86 days.

- ✔ **'Amy':** This AAS-winning hybrid muskmelon is firm and deliciously scented. The vines tolerate poor soils and only grow 6 feet long, maturing 3- to 4-pound fruits with white flesh and canary-colored skin in 70 days.

- ✔ **'Early Crenshaw':** This hybrid early-maturing crenshaw-type melon produces 14-pound fruits with mild-flavored, peach-colored flesh. It matures in 90 days.

- ✔ **'Earli-Dew':** This early-maturing hybrid honeydew-type melon has lime green flesh and produces 2- to 4-pound fruits. It matures in 85 days.

- ✔ **'Hale's Best':** This popular heirloom muskmelon features 3- to 4-pound fruits with succulent, deep salmon-colored flesh in 80 days.

- ✔ **'Lambkin':** This hybrid AAS-winning Piel de Sapo or Christmas melon hails from Spain. This variety features 2- to 4-pound fruits with beautiful mottled green- and gold-colored skin and honey-sweet white flesh. It matures quickly in 70 days.

- ✔ **'Passport':** This hybrid Galia-type, 5- to 6-pound melon has light green flesh. It has good disease resistance, is widely adapted, and matures in 73 days.

- ✔ **'Savor':** This hybrid Charentais-type melon features 2-pound fruits with sweet, orange flesh. This great, small melon matures in 78 days.

- ✔ **'Sugar Nut':** This hybrid Canary-type melon produces 2-pound fruits with sweet, white flesh. Because of their diminutive size, they're perfect for snacking. This variety matures in 77 days.

Watermelons

The following are popular watermelon varieties:

- ✔ **'Crimson Sweet':** This oval-shaped, open-pollinated watermelon variety produces sweet, red-fleshed, 25-pound fruits and has good disease resistance. It matures in 90 days.

- ✔ **'Moon and Stars':** This heirloom oblong-shaped watermelon features 25-pound fruits with dark green skin with yellow "moon and stars" markings (squint and you can see them — or what passes for them) and has very sweet, pink flesh. The variety matures in 95 days.

- ✔ **'Orange Sunshine':** This very sweet, oval, seedless, orange-fleshed variety produces 10- to 15-pound fruits in 85 days.

✔ **'Sugar Baby':** This round, compact, open-pollinated watermelon variety produces icebox-size (8- to 10-pound), red-fleshed fruits with a mottled green skin in 85 days. Youngins love this sweet, kid-sized fruit.

✔ **'Sweet Beauty':** This AAS-winning, oval-shaped, red, seedless variety features 5- to 6-pound fruits that mature in 80 days.

✔ **'Yellow Doll':** This hybrid, oval-shaped, yellow-fleshed watermelon produces 4- to 8-pound fruits in 70 days.

Seedless watermelon varieties may germinate more slowly than other varieties, especially in cool soils (below 65 degrees Fahrenheit). So wait until the soil is warm before seeding and give them a few more days than the other watermelon varieties to germinate.

Unearthing the Humble Squash

Squash may not be as glamorous as their melon cousins, but boy can they produce. Whether you're growing summer squash or winter squash, they'll produce an abundance of fruit and flowers with seemingly little attention. Just ask any gardener friend who has grown zucchini before, and he or she will attest to how prolific these vegetables are. In the following sections, I define different kinds of squash and describe many popular squash varieties.

One way to slow squash production is to eat the flowers. They taste great stuffed with cheese and herbs or sautéed with olive oil and garlic, along with some Italian bread.

Different squash types

Before setting out to incorporate squash into your garden, the first order of business is to define the different types. They're generally broken into two categories — summer squash and winter squash. From there you'll find all sorts of different types. The following list should help:

✔ **Summer squash** are bush-type plants whose fruits are harvested when they're tender and immature. Summer squash usually are separated into yellow, straight, or crookneck varieties; green zucchini varieties; or green-, white-, or yellow-skinned, scallop-shaped, "patty-pan" fruit varieties, as shown in Figure 8-1. (This last group got its name because the fruits resemble the pie shells used in England for baking vegetable, meat, or fish "patties.") Summer squash usually mature within 2 months of planting and continue to produce all season long. Summer squash don't store well, however.

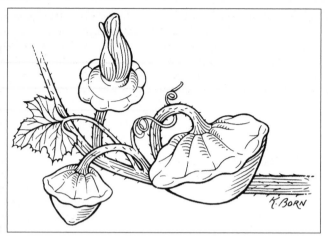

Figure 8-1:
A scalloped or "patty-pan" summer squash, so named because the fruits look like crimped pie pans.

✔ **Winter squash** have vining or bush-type plants whose fruits are harvested when they're fully mature. They mature after 3 months or more of growing and are best harvested after the cool, fall weather sets in. You can store them for months in a cool basement — hence the name winter squash. They're also good for baking.

You can easily get lost in the maze of winter squash types, so here's a quick list of the most popular types. I include the botanical names, too, for you Latin buffs.

- **Acorn (*Cucurbita pepo*):** This squash type has black, dark green, or white skin and an acorn-shaped, ribbed fruit. It has pale yellow flesh.

- **Buttercup (*Cucurbita maxima*):** This green or orange, turban-shaped type has a "button" on the end of its fruits. It has dry, orange flesh.

- **Butternut (*Cucurbita moschata*):** This bottle-shaped squash has smooth, tan-colored skin and moist, orange flesh at maturity.

- **Delicata (*Cucurbita pepo*):** This small, green- and yellow-striped, zucchini-shaped squash has sweet, pale yellow flesh.

- **Hubbard (*Cucurbita maxima*):** This large, blue or green, oval-shaped squash has a long neck and dry yellow or orange flesh.

- **Kabocha (*Cucurbita maxima*):** This buttercup-like squash has drier and sweeter flesh than other types. It's the latest winter squash craze.

- **Spaghetti (*Cucurbita pepo*):** This oblong, tan-colored squash has yellow flesh with a stringy, spaghetti-like texture. Kids think it's cool that a squash could look like spaghetti, so consider impressing your own children (or your neighbor's) by growing this type.

Keep your squash areas weeded and watered, and you'll be rewarded with super squash. Just remember to give the plants room to grow. Summer squash varieties tend to stay in a bush form, but they still need a few feet to spread out. And even though winter squash do come in bush forms, most of the best-flavored varieties have at least 6-foot vines. Check out the later section "Planting and feeding" for the full scoop on growing squash and other viners with ease.

Popular squash varieties

The lists of summer and winter squash varieties in the following sections include some of my favorites; they're easy to grow, produce well consistently, and have a sweet flavor. The days to maturity are from seeding in the garden until first harvest.

Summer squash varieties

The following are my favorite summer squash varieties:

- ✔ **'Black Beauty':** This standard open-pollinated, zucchini-type variety produces tons of dark green, slender fruits on open, easy-to-harvest bush plants in 60 days. Zucchinis can be gold-colored as well, such as with the AAS-winning 'Gold Rush' variety. This golden variety matures in 50 days.

- ✔ **'Magda':** This hybrid, light-green-skinned summer squash is a variation on the traditional straight-neck squash. It's shorter and more blocky. It's often called the cousa or Lebanese squash and has a sweet, nutty flavor. The fruits mature in 48 days.

- ✔ **'Portofino':** This classic, deeply ribbed, green- and white-striped hybrid Italian zucchini has a crisp, nutty flesh on open plants. This variety takes 55 days to mature.

- ✔ **'Sunburst':** This hybrid, yellow-skinned patty pan summer squash has tender, scallop-shaped fruits that mature in 50 days. For a green patty pan variety, try the AAS-winning 'Peter Pan', which matures in 50 days.

- ✔ **'Yellow Crookneck':** This heirloom, smooth, yellow-skinned crookneck squash has a delicate texture and flavor. (*Crookneck* squash have a bent top, or neck.) The variety takes 50 days to mature.

Winter squash varieties

Good winter squash varieties include the following:

- ✔ **'Baby Blue Hubbard':** This scaled-down version of the typical heirloom 12- to 20-pound 'Blue Hubbard' winter squash produces 4- to 5-pound fruits with dry, sweet, yellow flesh and a very hard shell. This variety, which matures in 100 days, is especially great for storage and baking.

- ✔ **'Burgess Buttercup':** This 3- to 5-pound open-pollinated winter squash has sweet, fiberless (not stringy), orange flesh. This variety, which matures in 95 days, is one of my personal favorites. (Its sweet flavor and dry flesh taste great with a little maple syrup mixed in!) 'Bon Bon' is a good hybrid variety.

- ✔ **'Cornell's Bush Delicata':** This AAS-winning variety features bushy plants that are resistant to powdery mildew disease. The green- and white-striped oblong fruits mature in 100 days and have a sweet orange flesh. I love to eat this variety baked.

- ✔ **'Red Kuri':** This attractive, teardrop-shaped, 4- to 7-pound open-pollinated 'Baby Red Hubbard' squash has orange skin and flesh. It's great for pies and purees and matures in 92 days.

- ✔ **'Spaghetti':** This ivory-skinned, yellow-fleshed, 4- to 5-pound open-pollinated winter squash has stringy, spaghetti-like flesh. Try this one baked and covered with pasta sauce! It takes 88 days to mature.

- ✔ **'Sweet Sunshine':** This hybrid kabocha-type winter squash has bright orange skin and produces 3- to 5-pound fruits with sweet, dry, flaky, deep orange flesh. This variety takes 95 days to mature.

- ✔ **'Table King':** This 6-inch-diameter, green-skinned, open-pollinated acorn winter squash grows on a bush plant. It takes 80 days to mature. A similar gold-colored variety is called 'Table Gold'.

   A newer, smaller-sized hybrid acorn squash called 'Honey Bear' is great for single servings. It matures in 85 days.

- ✔ **'Waltham Butternut':** This heirloom variety produces light-tan-colored, 5-pound fruits that have smooth-textured orange flesh. It takes 105 days to mature.

Great Pumpkins: Counting the Uses for This Versatile Squash

Pumpkins are the quintessential fall crop in many areas, and most peoples' favorite winter squash. (Yes, pumpkins are squashes, too. Most pumpkin varieties are in the *Cucurbita pepo* species, directly related to the acorn- and spaghetti-type winter squash that I describe earlier in this chapter.) Pumpkins are used in pies, soups, and casseroles or carved into ghoulish shapes on Halloween. Even their seeds are edible!

Because people are so interested in pumpkins, modern breeders have created many different varieties. Some varieties are great for carving into jack-o'-lanterns, some are bred for cooking, and still others are known for their tasty seeds. When my daughter Elena was young she loved to roast batches of 'Triple Treat', naked-hulled (thin-hulled) pumpkin seeds because they pop like popcorn. You can bake any pumpkin seeds, but in my opinion, the hulless types are best for flavor and crunchiness. (In case you're wondering, the *hull* is the coat of the seed.) Other types of pumpkins, like 'Atlantic Giant', are bred to win awards; they can grow to such huge sizes that they could practically break a truck's suspension.

Pumpkins are grown similar to winter squash and require plenty of space to vine. Here are a few of the most popular pumpkin varieties:

- ✔ **'Atlantic Giant':** This is the pumpkin that sets world records. Technically, it's called a *Cucurbita maxima* (similar to Hubbard squash). It requires lots of water, heat, and fertilizer to reach the mammoth 1,600-pound, world-record size. This variety looks like a flat tire when it matures. Even though your pumpkin may not weigh 1,600 pounds, a few hundred pounds is still a lot of pumpkin. 'Atlantic Giant' is open-pollinated and takes 115 days to mature. This is one large vine.

- ✔ **'Baby Bear':** This is the smallest pumpkin variety, so naturally kids are attracted to it. 'Baby Bear' is an AAS-winning, 2-pound, open-pollinated, minipumpkin that's great for cooking. Its semi-naked (thin-hulled) seeds taste great roasted. This variety matures in 105 days.

- ✔ **'Connecticut Field':** This classic 20-pound, open-pollinated, flat-bottomed, jack-o'-lantern pumpkin is great for carving and baking. It matures on large vines in 115 days.

- ✔ **'Lumina':** This unusual, white-skinned, orange-fleshed, open-pollinated, 20-pound pumpkin can be made into a ghostly looking jack-o'-lantern. It takes 95 days to mature.

- ✔ **'Rouge Vif d'Etampes':** This attractive, red-skinned, French heirloom pumpkin variety, which is also known as 'Cinderella', is in the *Cucurbita maxima* species. The 10-pound fruits are short and squat (like a wheel of cheese) and are good in pies. The variety takes 115 days to mature. Another similarly shaped variety is 'Long Island Cheese', which has tan-colored skin.

- ✔ **'Small Sugar':** Known as the pumpkin for pies, this 4- to 6-pound, open-pollinated variety features smooth-textured flesh and a small seed cavity. It takes 95 days to mature.

- ✔ **'Triple Treat':** This open-pollinated pumpkin is grown especially for its thin-hulled, naked seeds, which are great roasted. You also can carve this 8-pound pumpkin and use its flesh in a pie or bake it. This variety takes 110 days to mature.

The seeds of this all-purpose pumpkin are slower and more finicky about germinating than other pumpkin varieties. So wait until the soil is 65 degrees to plant; you may even want to start it indoors for 3 to 4 weeks before planting outside.

To find out how to grow giant pumpkins and for details about yearly competitions, visit The Pumpkin Patch at www.backyardgardener.com/pumkin.html or Big Pumpkins.com at www.bigpumpkins.com.

Growing Those Vines

Warmth, water, and proper pollination are the keys to growing cucumber-family crops. In the following sections, I explain how to plant, feed, water, pollinate, and harvest your viners; I also provide tips on how to keep pests and diseases under control.

Planting and feeding

Because vining vegetables love the heat, you don't need to rush the season and plant early. Wait until your soil temperature is at least 60 degrees at seeding depth before planting these vegetables. Here are some guidelines for starting viners, based on your climate zone (see the appendix for more about these zones):

✔ **Zones 3 and 4:** If you live in zones 3 or 4 and have a very short growing season, you may want to start cucumbers, melons, pumpkins, and squash indoors 3 to 4 weeks before your last frost date. Or consider buying transplants at a garden center. To get a jump on the season in cool areas such as zones 3 and 4 (though zones 5 and 6 can also benefit), lay black or dark green plastic mulch on your soil 1 or 2 weeks before planting to heat up the soil (see Chapter 15 for details).

✔ **Any other zone:** If you live in other climate zones, sowing seeds directly in your garden should work fine. In warm areas such as southern Florida and Texas, you can even start a fall crop of cucumbers or summer squash. Pull out the first group of plants when the summer heat, insects, and diseases become too intense; then plant a fall crop in August to mature 3 or 4 months later.

Plant seeds about 1 inch deep in the soil, and space them far enough apart so they have room to ramble. For vining varieties of cucumbers, melons, squash, and pumpkins, plant hills at least 6 to 10 feet apart. For bush varieties, plant seeds about 2 to 4 feet apart. Follow the spacing guidelines for individual vegetables in the appendix.

Planting in *hills* is really a misnomer. It means planting four or six seeds in a 1-foot-diameter circle. After germination, you thin these seedlings to two plants per hill.

You also can plant cucumber-family crops in rows, but the hill method is better with the vining types because it enables you to thin the weakest plants and not throw off the spacing between the remaining plants. However, if you're using black plastic mulch (which is necessary in cool areas), your best option is to plant in rows (see Chapter 13 for details).

If you don't have a lot of room in your garden (viners require 4 to 6 feet), but you really want to grow pumpkins, melons, and vining varieties of cucumbers and squash, try these space-saving techniques:

- ✔ Pinch off the tips of the vines after the fruits have set to keep them from extending too far (see Figure 8-2).
- ✔ Physically pick up the vines and direct them back toward the plant.
- ✔ Plant along the edge of your garden so that the vines run into your lawn. That way you don't have to mow as much lawn either.
- ✔ Grow cucumbers and melons on an A-frame trellis (see Chapter 15 for trellising options), which helps plants grow straighter and stay cleaner. You may need to support melons with a nylon or fabric sling, shown in Figure 8-3, after they form.

Figure 8-2:
Pinch off the ends of vines to keep them in bounds and mature your fruits faster.

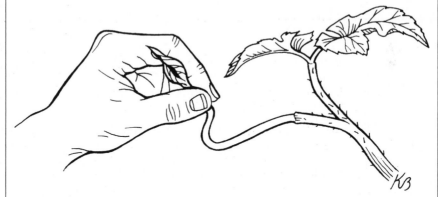

The cucumber-family responds better than any other vegetable family to extra doses of manure and compost. Cucumber-family crops love organic matter, so add a generous 3- to 4-inch-thick layer of compost to each planting bed. Sometimes pumpkin plants vine out of old compost or manure piles, which is evidence of how much this vegetable family loves manure. If you don't have a source for manure or compost, work in a handful of balanced organic fertilizer, such as 5-5-5, around each plant. To help increase the fruit count and size, add a side-dressing of the same fertilizer after the plants begin vining. Chapter 15 discusses side-dressing and fertilizer in more detail.

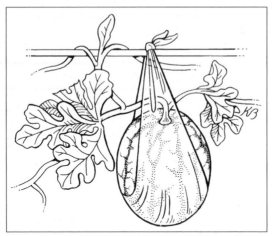

Figure 8-3:
Supporting
melon fruits
with a sling
helps make
trellising the
vines easier
and makes
for simpler
harvesting.

Water, water, water!

Cucumber-family crops are like camels; they're almost 95 percent water at maturity. Without a consistent supply of water, your melons won't taste sweet, your winter squash and pumpkins won't grow large, and your cucumbers will taste bitter. To get the best-sized and best-tasting vining crops, give your plants a consistent supply of water. The general rule is to water so that the soil is wet 6 inches deep. If you're growing your crops with black plastic mulch, consider placing a soaker hose or drip irrigation hose underneath the plastic to ensure that the water gets to the plants. (See Chapter 15 for more watering ideas.) After the soil has warmed, mulch around the plants with a 3- to 4-inch-thick layer of hay or straw to help conserve moisture and keep weeds away. (You don't need to mulch with hay if you're using black plastic, however.)

If you want the sweetest melons, water consistently until a week or so before maturity and then reduce your frequency of watering; the melon fruits will have less water and taste sweeter.

The great thing about this group of vining crops is that after they start growing and running to their hearts delight, they shade the ground, preventing weeds from germinating and keeping the soil moist. They're their own best friends!

Ensuring proper pollination

Proper pollination is a key to growing successful cucumber-family crops, which can pose particular problems. Because most cucumber-family vegetables have separate male and female flowers on the same plant, they need Mother Nature's help to pollinate the female flowers and produce fruit.

Most of the problems that I hear from gardeners — like zucchini rotting before it starts growing, too few fruits on squash plants, and misshapen cucumber fruits — are due to poor insect pollination. Bees are the solution as well as the problem: Honeybees, bumblebees, and many other wild bees carry out pollination, but they're finicky. For example, bees don't fly when the weather is cloudy or too cool. Also, native bee populations are declining because of a variety of environmental and pest problems. Fewer bees mean fewer chances that your flowers will be pollinated. And each cucumber-family crop flower opens for only 1 day.

So what's a gardener to do? Either try to attract bees to your garden by growing a variety of bee-attractive flowers and herbs or else pollinate the flowers yourself! And no, you don't have to buzz around and dress up in a bee costume to fool the plants. Here's a simple way to pollinate crops if you're having trouble getting fruit:

1. **Identify the male and female flowers on your plant (see Figure 8-4).**

   Don't be discouraged if you don't see female flowers at first. Male flowers form about a week ahead of the females. The female flowers will come along; just be patient.

2. **Before noon on the morning that the male flower first opens, pick the male flower and then remove the petals to reveal the sexual parts of the flower (the stamen), which contain the yellow pollen.**

   You use this male flower to pollinate a female flower from the same variety of plant. For example, don't try to use a cucumber flower to pollinate a pumpkin plant.

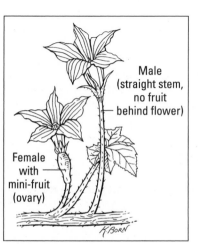

Figure 8-4:
Male flowers are long and thin, whereas female flowers are short and have a minifruit behind their flowers.

Male (straight stem, no fruit behind flower)

Female with mini-fruit (ovary)

K.BORN

3. **Choose a female flower that has also just opened and swish the stamen around inside that flower. Repeat this process with other female flowers, using the same male flower for two to three pollinations.**

Voilà; you've done it. Congratulations, have a cigar!

If your squash and pumpkins are growing close together, and bees cross-pollinate them, will you get a squakin? Not this year at least. Cross-pollination happens when the pollen from one variety or type of plant goes to a different variety or type of plant. Only the same species of *Cucurbits* can cross-pollinate each other. For example, a cucumber can't cross-pollinate a pumpkin. However, squash (such as an acorn and zucchini type) and pumpkins in the same species can cross-pollinate each other. (You can tell the species by looking at the second word in the plant's botanical name.) However, this cross-pollination won't affect your crop for this year. Your acorn squash will still look and taste like an acorn squash, even if it was pollinated by a pumpkin flower. However, if you save the squash seed and plant it the following year, you may get an interesting creation. But that's why gardening is fun!

Controlling pests and diseases

Dampening the success of a good vine crop is tough. Once established, vining crops don't have any more pest problems than other vegetables. Modern, disease-resistant varieties help ward off fungi, bacteria, and viruses. However, you still need to watch out for powdery and downy mildew, wilt, and viruses that affect all vegetables (see Chapter 17). Also, stay out of the vine crop patch when the leaves are wet because you can easily spread disease as you move. Finally, remember that common insect pests, such as aphids and cutworms, attack young plants.

Here are a few diseases and pests that particularly love vining crops:

- ✔ **Anthracnose:** This fungus attacks many vegetables, but it especially loves cucumbers, muskmelons, and watermelons. During warm, humid conditions, the leaves develop yellow or black circular spots, and fruits develop sunken spots with dark borders. To slow this disease, space plants a few feet further apart than normal so the leaves can dry quickly in the morning. Also, destroy infected leaves and fruits. You also can avoid this disease by rotating crops yearly.

- ✔ **Bacterial wilt:** This devastating bacterial disease is found mainly on cucumbers and muskmelons. Sure signs of the disease are well-watered plants that wilt during the day but recover at night. Eventually, the plants will wilt and die. If you cut open a wilting vine, the sap will be sticky and white. To control this disease, plant resistant varieties and control the cucumber beetle, which is the pest that spreads bacterial wilt in your garden.

✔ **Cucumber beetle:** This ¹/₄-inch-long, yellow- and black-striped (or spotted) adult beetle feeds on all cucumber-family crops. The adults feed on the leaves, and the young larvae feed on the roots. Cucumber beetles are the chief culprits for spreading bacterial wilt and virus diseases; they're especially devastating to young plants.

To control cucumber beetles, cover young plants with a *floating row cover* (a cheesecloth-like material that keeps insects out but lets in air, light, and water; see Chapter 21 for details) as soon as they emerge. After the plants flower, remove the row cover so bees can pollinate the flowers. You also can apply a botanical spray such as pyrethrin on the adult beetles.

✔ **Squash bug:** These ¹/₂-inch-long, brown or gray bugs love to attack squash and pumpkins, especially late in the growing season. The adults and smaller-sized young feed on leaves and stems, sucking out the plant juices. These insects move in packs, and their feeding can quickly stunt your plants. Squash bugs usually start laying eggs when the plants begin to vine. To control these pests, crush the masses of reddish-brown eggs on the underside of leaves. Also, rotate crops and clean up plant debris in fall where the squash bugs *overwinter* (live through the winter).

✔ **Squash vine borer:** This pest mostly affects squash and pumpkin plants. In early summer, the adult moths lay their eggs on stems near the plants' bases. After the eggs hatch, white caterpillars with brown heads tunnel into the plants' stems to feed. They can cause well-watered vines to wilt during the day and eventually die. Look for entry holes and the sawdust-like droppings at the base of your plants to see if vine borers are present. Consider growing butternut squash, which is less susceptible to vine borers.

To control these pests, try one of the following methods:

- Slit your plant's stem lengthwise from the entry hole toward the tip of the vine with a sharp razor, and physically remove the caterpillar. Then cover the stem with soil; it will reroot itself.

- Cover the plants with a floating row cover until they begin to flower, which keeps the moths from laying their eggs.

- Inject Bt (*Bacillus thurengiensis;* a naturally occurring bacterium that attacks only caterpillar-family insects) into the stem with a syringe to kill any young caterpillars.

Harvesting your vining crop

One of the keys to a good cucumber-family crop is harvesting the fruits at the right time. Here are some guidelines for you to follow:

- ✔ **Cucumbers:** The fruits are best when harvested small — slicers when they're 6 inches long and picklers when they're 4 inches long. If they grow too large and begin to turn yellow, the seeds inside the cucumber are maturing, and the plant will stop producing flowers and fruits. Pick off and compost any large fruits that you missed so you can keep the young ones coming.

- ✔ **Summer squash:** Harvest summer squash as small as possible, even if the flower is still attached. Doing so helps you avoid the glut of zucchinis that always happens by midsummer.

- ✔ **Winter squash and pumpkins:** Harvest winter squash and pumpkins after they change to the expected color of their variety and their skin is thick enough that your thumbnail can't puncture them. If you want to store winter squash and pumpkins through the fall and winter, don't let them get nipped by frost, or they'll rot. Leave 2 inches of the stem attached for best storing.

Deciding when to harvest muskmelons can be tricky. After their skin color turns from green to tan and the *netting* (the ribbing on the skin that's slightly raised) becomes more pronounced, gently lift the melons up. If they're ripe, the fruits will slip, or easily detach, from the vine. If you aren't sure, harvesting early rather than late is better because most melons continue to ripen off the vine.

Watermelon harvesting is even more complicated because it's often not obvious when the fruits are ready to harvest. Follow these tips:

- ✔ **Watch for changing colors:** Two signs that it may be time to harvest watermelons are when the skin color turns from shiny to dull and when the color of the spot where the watermelon rests on the ground turns from white to yellow.

- ✔ **Thump the watermelons:** I love watching the old-time gardeners thump watermelons with their fingers to figure out when they're ripe. Whether this test is consistently accurate is another story. Here's what to look for: Unripe watermelons have a sharp sound, and ripe ones have a muffled sound. The rest is experience!

- ✔ **Look for brown tendrils:** The surest way to tell whether your watermelons are ripe is to look at their tendrils. *Tendrils* are the little curlicues coming off the stems that attach to whatever weeds and plants are around. When the tendril closest to the ripening watermelon turns brown, it's harvest time!

Chapter 9

Cool Weather Staples: Broccoli, Brussels Sprouts, Cabbage, and Cauliflower

. . . .

In This Chapter

▶ Selecting cole crop varieties

▶ Caring for your cole crops, from planting to harvesting

. . . .

*B*roccoli, Brussels sprouts, cabbage, and cauliflower: All these hardy vegetable are in the same family, so they get lumped together in this chapter. Even though they may look different, they all require similar growing conditions. So if you can grow one, you probably will have success with the others. These crops love it cool, so they thrive in northern areas or when grown in spring, fall, and even winter in southern areas. This group is often referred to as the "cole" crops, because *cole* is the German word for cabbage — and since all these vegetables are related to cabbage, they often are referred to as the cabbage family of crops.

In this chapter, I discuss the major cole crops. Other related but less popular cole crops, such as collards, kale, kohlrabi, and Chinese cabbage, are covered in Chapter 11. All fall in the *Brassica oleracea* botanical family.

Paying Attention to the Often-Overlooked Cole Crops

In the beginning there wasn't anything glamorous about cole crops. They weren't as colorful, succulent, or sensuous as tomatoes or melons. Cole crops were simply known for being rugged, tough, good-for-you plants. Just look at variety names such as 'Snow Crown' cauliflower and 'Stonehead' cabbage, and you get the picture.

However, that reputation has begun to change. With the advent of interesting-shaped heirloom and hybrid varieties and the coloring of cauliflower into orange, green, and purple heads, cole crops are becoming trendy. They may never be as sexy as the melons, but they're getting a facelift.

Even with a new look, cole crops are still reliable staples in any vegetable garden. Given cool conditions, fertile soil, and proper watering, these plants produce lots of nutritious and delicious vegetables (as you find out in the later section "Growing Your Own Cole Crops").

However, many people still haven't warmed up to cole crops. I don't understand this aversion. Cole crops are tasty, easy to grow, and capable of producing over long periods of time. Plus, with the exploding interest in eating nutritious foods and the discovery of the great potential health benefits of broccoli and other vegetables in its family (see Chapter 2), more and more people are dipping, steaming, and stir-frying their way to health with cole crops. In the following sections, I provide details on different varieties of broccoli, Brussels sprouts, cabbage, and cauliflower.

Easing into cole crops with broccoli

Broccoli is one of the easiest cole crops to grow, and it's one that's close to my heart. Like my ancestors, broccoli hails from Italy. My mother and I still enjoy a good meal of garlic sautéed in olive oil and tossed with broccoli, accompanied by a loaf of fresh Italian bread. She likes the smaller-headed, old-fashioned, sprouting broccoli varieties such as 'DeCicco', whose stems and leaves are so tender that they're eaten along with the head.

Modern broccoli varieties have been bred to form one large main head. This head is simply a tight cluster of flower buds. Once the main head is cut off, multiple side branches and mini heads form along the plant. In most areas, the side branches and mini heads continue to form until the plant is killed by frost, insects, or disease. So from one plant, you can harvest right through summer, fall, and winter (if your climate is warm enough). I explain how to harvest broccoli in more detail later in this chapter.

Choosing the right broccoli variety for your garden depends on a number of factors, including where you live and what you plan to do with the crop. Here are a few guidelines to follow when choosing a broccoli variety:

✔ If you plan to stock up for the winter by freezing broccoli heads, choose a variety with large heads that mature mostly at the same time. Try 'Green Magic' or 'Premium Crop'.

✔ Broccoli, like all cole crops, likes cool weather. Warm weather makes the heads flower too quickly, resulting in a bitter flavor. Gardeners in warm climates should choose varieties that withstand heat or mature early, before the heat of summer. 'Packman' is a good choice.

✔ If you want a long, steady production of small but tender side shoots, choose an old-fashioned variety with good side-shoot production, such as my mom's favorite, 'DeCicco'.

✔ If you live in a humid climate (such as Dallas) or a coastal area that has lots of fog and mist (such as San Francisco), broccoli heads can rot before maturing. Choose varieties with added disease resistance and tightly clustered flower heads that shed water easily, such as 'Arcadia'.

Here's a list of some of the best broccoli varieties to grow. The days to maturity listed for each variety refers to the number of days from transplanting a seedling into the garden until the harvest of the main head. If you sow the seeds directly into the garden, add another 20 days to estimate the maturity date. Of course, the actual number of days varies depending on weather and soil conditions. All plants listed grow to about 1 to 2 feet:

✔ **'Arcadia':** A large, 8-inch-diameter, blue-green-colored head is formed high on stems above the foliage, making this variety easier to harvest than other broccoli varieties. 'Arcadia' is a hybrid variety (see Chapter 3 for more on hybrids), so it's a vigorous grower, producing uniform-sized heads in 63 days, and has excellent disease resistance. It's also tender and tasty.

✔ **'Belstar':** This hybrid is a favorite of commercial organic growers. It's widely adapted, produces 6-inch-diameter heads equally well in spring or fall, and it also has good side-shoot production. This variety matures in 66 days.

✔ **'DeCicco':** This heirloom, old-fashioned Italian variety produces a 3-inch-diameter main head and multiple side shoots in 48 days and has tender leaves and stems.

✔ **'Green Magic':** This early-maturing hybrid broccoli is very heat tolerant, making it a good summer and fall crop. The plant produces a 6-inch-diameter head in 57 days.

✔ **'Packman':** A hybrid, this variety produces a 9-inch-diameter main head earlier (52 days) than other large-headed varieties such as 'Premium Crop'. It also has excellent side-shoot production and heat tolerance.

✔ **'Premium Crop':** An All-America Selections (AAS) winner (see Chapter 4 for more about this designation), this hybrid broccoli produces a large, 9-inch-diameter head late in the season (after 62 days). However, it's slow to flower, so you don't have to rush to pick it.

✔ **'Purple Sprouting':** This Italian heirloom produces a 2-foot-tall plant with multiple 3-inch-diameter purple heads late in the season (after 125 days). It's best grown in cool northern areas to mature in late fall. Or, in mild-winter climates, you can plant it in fall and grow it through the winter to mature in early spring. (Refer to the section "Giving cole crops what they want," later in this chapter, for planting tips.) The head turns green upon cooking.

✔ **'Small Miracle':** This early hybrid variety grows less than 1-foot- tall, so the plants only need to be spaced 8 inches apart, which makes this variety great for small gardens. It produces 6- to 8-inch heads in 55 days.

Brussels sprouts: The little cabbages

Rows of Brussels sprout stems standing tall in the garden loaded with sprouts are a sure sign of fall. Although the sprouts take a whole season to mature, they're relatively maintenance-free, and the sprouts turn a sweet, nutty flavor after they're touched by cold weather.

To the untrained eye, a Brussels sprout plant can look like a strange life-form from another planet. Small, cabbagelike sprouts grow in clusters along the 3-foot-tall stem, and often gardeners remove most of the leaves so that the sprouts grow larger. The plants look like miniature palm trees (see Figure 9-1), with mini-cabbages on the stalk. In fact, if you like cabbage, you'll love the similar flavor of the smaller and more manageable Brussels sprouts.

The key to growing Brussels sprouts is having a long growing season and a cool fall to induce the best flavor. The flavor actually benefits from a light frost.

Figure 9-1:
Sprouts form along the stem of a Brussels sprout plant.

The following varieties are widely adaptable and worth a try in any garden. The days to maturity are from setting out seedlings to first harvest. Add 20 days to the maturity if direct seeding into the garden.

 ✔ **'Diablo':** This hybrid is a standout in American and European gardens. The 3-foot-tall plants produce heavy crops of medium-sized sprouts later in the season (after 110 days). The sprouts stay firm when mature and hold well in the garden (can be left on the plant in the garden until you need them in the kitchen).

✔ **'Jade Cross E':** A hybrid AAS winner, this variety's 2½-foot-tall plants produce good-sized sprouts all the way up their stalks in 90 days.

✔ **'Oliver':** One of the earliest-maturing varieties, this hybrid matures in 85 days on 2-foot-tall plants. It is well adapted to many climates.

✔ **'Red Rubine':** Yes, even Brussels sprouts have color variations. This heirloom variety produces very tasty and attractive red sprouts on a hardy, purplish-red-colored 2-foot-tall plant. The red color remains even after cooking. This variety matures in 95 days.

Choosing cabbage: The age-old and dependable cole crop

When many people think of cole crops, they first think of cabbages. Broccoli and cauliflower may be gaining in popularity, and Brussels sprouts may be novel, but cabbage is a long-time, solid vegetable citizen. It has been an easy-to-grow staple in Europe for hundreds of years and for centuries before that in the Middle East.

Cabbage-growing isn't as popular as it once was, and you rarely find cabbage on the menus of finer restaurants, but the sweet, tender flavor of freshly harvested cabbage makes it worthy of a spot in your garden. With so many varieties to choose from, you can have fresh and delicious cole slaw, sauerkraut, and boiled cabbage almost all season long — from summer into winter.

Cabbage requires the same conditions as other cole crops — cool weather, fertile soil, and proper watering — but the variety that you select is a bit more important to ensure a continuous harvest. By selecting early-, mid-, and late-season varieties, you can extend your cabbage harvest season by weeks. You can easily get lost in the dizzying array of cabbage varieties:

✔ Early-, mid-, and late-season varieties

✔ Round, pointy, and flat-headed varieties

✔ Smooth-leafed and *savoyed* (crinkle-leafed) varieties

✔ Green and red-colored varieties

Growing two or three different varieties that mature at different times allows you to spread out the harvest over the growing season. And by spreading out the harvest, you avoid getting yourself into the "six heads of cabbage ready all the same week" situation. (Even the most ardent cabbage lover would have a hard time eating all that cabbage!)

To get you started on the right foot, in the following list I describe ten varieties that represent the universe of cabbages. (Note, however, that I cover Chinese cabbage in Chapter 11.) Cabbage plants can spread to 3 feet in diameter, and they all have green leaves and white centers unless otherwise noted. The late-maturing and fall-planted varieties are best for storage. (I talk more about storing cabbages in Chapter 19.) The days to maturity for each variety are from setting out seedlings in the garden to first harvest. Add 20 days to the maturity date if you directly seed in the garden. Without further ado, here are some varieties to try:

- ✔ **'Danish Ballhead':** This old-time favorite produces 8-inch-diameter, round, smooth-leafed heads late in the season (after 100 days) and is great for winter storage. This variety is good for sauerkraut and slaw recipes.

- ✔ **'Early Jersey Wakefield':** This early heirloom smooth-leafed cabbage with a pointed head measures 5 inches in diameter and has compact plants that are slow to split. (For more on splitting, see the later section on harvesting cabbage.) This variety matures in 65 days.

- ✔ **'Famosa':** This hybrid midseason, round-headed crop produces 2- to 4-pound, dark blue-green, savoyed heads with a yellow tinted interior and tender leaves in 75 days.

- ✔ **'Golden Acre':** This early-maturing, open-pollinated, round-headed variety produces 3- to 4-pound disease-resistant heads that are great in salads. The leaves are smooth. It matures in 58 days.

- ✔ **'Gonzales':** This popular European variety grows to be only 4 to 6 inches in diameter, making it a great selection for small spaces. This early-season hybrid produces round, softball-sized, smooth-leaved, aqua-green-colored heads in 66 days.

- ✔ **'Late Flat Dutch':** This heirloom, late-maturing, 10-inch-diameter variety features a flattened head and smooth leaves. It's excellent for sauerkraut and storage and matures in 100 days.

- ✔ **'Red Acre':** This red, early-maturing, 6-inch-diameter, round, open-pollinated cabbage with a dense interior, smooth leaves, and deep color has good disease resistance and is great for storage. The cabbages mature in 76 days.

- ✔ **'Ruby Perfection':** This red, midseason hybrid variety produces attractive 5- to 6-inch-diameter, smooth-leaved, reddish-purple round heads in 80 days.

- ✔ **'Savoy Express':** This early hybrid, AAS-winning, sweet-tasting, savoy-leafed variety produces 1- to 2-pound round heads that are perfect in slaw and salad. The variety matures in 55 days.

- ✔ **'Stonehead':** This widely grown, early-maturing hybrid variety produces 5- to 6-inch-diameter solid, smooth-leaved, round heads on compact plants in 60 days.

Considering cauliflower in a rainbow of colors

Think of cauliflower as broccoli's hard-to-get-along-with brother. Both are from southern Europe, require similar growing conditions, and are closely related botanically. However, cauliflower plants produce only one head and no side shoots, and they have a reputation for being a bit tougher to grow. (See the later section "Giving cole crops what they want" for more information.) But don't worry! With the right varieties, proper soil conditions, appropriate watering, and well-timed planting, cauliflower can be a joy to grow in your vegetable garden. It's especially exciting for young gardeners who are amazed to find a beautiful snow-white-colored head hidden under the green leaves. And if you're tired of pure-white heads, purple-, green-, and even orange-headed varieties are now available.

Broccoli and cabbage plants produce *heads,* and Brussels sprout plants produce, well, *sprouts,* so what does a cauliflower plant produce? A *curd.* (But I'll refer to them as heads throughout this chapter, because that's what folks are used to.) No, it's not a Middle Eastern ethnic group or something that Little Miss Muffet ate with her whey. Like a broccoli head, a cauliflower curd is comprised of miniature flower heads tightly clustered together.

On white cauliflower varieties, the heads stay white and tender only if you stop the sun from hitting them by covering the head. (This technique is called *blanching;* see the later section "Nurturing cole crops" for details.) If exposed to the sun, the heads turn yellow and develop a mealy texture.

Like cabbage, cauliflower comes in early-, mid-, and late-season varieties. All the varieties in the following list produce 6- to 7-inch-diameter heads. The days to maturity for each variety are from setting out seedlings in the garden until first harvest. Add 20 days to the maturity date for direct seeding in the garden. Consider these popular varieties:

- ✔ **'Cassius':** A favorite among commercial organic growers, this hybrid variety features vigorous, sturdy plants and picture-perfect, snowy white heads. The variety matures in 65 days.

- ✔ **'Cheddar':** Here's where the cauliflower color revolution started. The 'Cheddar' hybrid has orange heads that become even brighter as they mature; the color even holds when cooked. The orange coloring is from the presence of *carotene* (the same substance that causes carrots to be orange), so this variety is also high in vitamin A and has a sweet flavor. The heads mature in 58 days.

- ✔ **'Fremont':** A self-blanching hybrid variety, 'Fremont' is known for dependable midseason production (after 62 days), even under adverse weather conditions.

✔ **'Graffiti':** For eye-popping color, grow some purple cauliflower! The brilliant purple-colored head of this hybrid is great raw in salads. However, the color fades when cooked. This variety matures in 80 days.

✔ **'Panther':** Not to be outdone by its colorful cousins, 'Panther' features lime-green-colored heads on hybrid plants. Large, uniform heads produce early (in 75 days) and hold well in the garden.

✔ **'Snow Crown':** This is the standard white hybrid variety that's easy to grow, early (60 days), widely adaptable, and dependable.

If you're looking for a cauliflower with class, try growing the Romaneseco types. Originally only grown around Rome, Italy, in fall, this cauliflower is getting broader play today. The heads are sweeter than white cauliflower, but take longer to mature (85 to 90 days). The reward for your patience is a pale to dark-green head consisting of mini-spirals that look like minarets. This variety is almost too beautiful to eat! 'Veronica' is a new hybrid variety, and 'Minaret' is an attractive heirloom.

Growing Your Own Cole Crops

As long as the weather is cool, cole crops are a snap to grow. They thrive in most parts of the country as a spring or fall crop just for that reason. Start with a rich, fertile soil; keep them well weeded and watered; and keep pests such as the cabbageworm at bay. You'll be rewarded with an abundant harvest. I explain what you need to know in the following sections.

Giving cole crops what they want

The keys to growing all cole crops are cool weather and fertile soil. Cole crops are cool crops: They grow and taste best when temperatures are below 80 degrees Fahrenheit, especially when the crops are maturing. Cole crops grow best in raised beds (see Chapter 3) and are also fairly demanding of nutrients, so be generous with manure and fertilizers (after you've done a soil test as indicated in Chapter 14 and know what nutrient adjustments need to be made), and they'll reward you with plenty of growth and production.

Because cole crops thrive in cool weather, many gardeners can grow all of them to mature as a summer crop and then some as a fall crop. That's two crops in per year! I explain how to plant summer and fall crops in the following sections.

Two caveats apply:

✔ Brussels sprouts may be hard to mature as a fall crop in far northern areas, but they're commonly grown in fall in most other areas of the country.

✔ If the weather gets too cold or too warm when cauliflower plants are forming heads, all you end up with are scraggly, small heads. Temperatures in the 70-degree range are ideal, so it's best to avoid growing cauliflower when it will mature in the heat of summer. For that reason, many gardeners like to grow cauliflower only as a fall crop started in summer to mature in the cooler, autumn weather.

Planting summer cole crops

Even though you can *direct seed* most summer-maturing cole crops in spring — that is, plant the seed directly in the garden — it's easier to get a jump on the season by starting the plants indoors 6 to 8 weeks before your last frost date (see the appendix for first and last frost dates in your area). Then you can plant the seedlings in your garden 2 to 4 weeks before that date. Spring-planted summer-maturing cole crops can withstand a light frost, and planting them early gives them a jump-start on growing. After the plants have at least four leaves, cultivate around the plants to kill any weeds and mulch with hay or straw. (Check out Chapter 14 for information on battling weeds and Chapter 15 for mulching techniques.)

Here's a rule-of-green-thumb when it comes to spacing cole crops, especially cabbage: The closer the plants are to one another, the smaller their heads will be (the appendix provides plant spacing guidelines). A dwarfed crop isn't necessarily bad — you may want to produce smaller, more manageable heads of cabbage. So, instead of planting cabbages 12 to 24 inches apart, try 8 to 12 inches. You'll get smaller, more manageable heads.

Planting fall cole crops

For gardeners in all but the coldest areas, a fall-maturing crop of broccoli, Brussels sprouts, cabbage, and cauliflower may be easier to manage than a similar summer-maturing crop. Fall weather provides the perfect temperatures to mature cole crops to their sweetest flavor.

For fall cole crops, start seedlings indoors about 3 months before your first frost and then transplant the seedlings to the garden 1 month later. For example, if your first frost is November 1, you should start seeds indoors on August 1 and then transplant them in your garden on September 1. (Starting the seedlings indoors and letting them grow until they're 3 to 4 weeks old helps them withstand the shock of being planted in the garden in summer.) To protect the young seedlings from the harsh summer sun, mulch them with hay or straw immediately after planting, and shade them — especially in the afternoon — with a shade cloth or *floating row cover* (a plastic or fabric material that lets light through but insulates the plants). (Refer to Chapter 21 for information on row covers.)

In very mild-winter areas such as the U.S. West coast and the Gulf coast, try growing *overwintering* varieties of broccoli (varieties that can withstand cold temperatures better than other varieties and need a longer season to mature) such as 'Purple Sprouting', which I discuss earlier in the chapter. Planted in fall, such varieties slowly grow all winter and mature in spring.

Nurturing cole crops

Cole crops like full sun and well-drained soil that's built into raised beds. Most importantly, though, cole crops really like fertile soil. A week or so before planting your seedlings, work a 3- to 4-inch layer of composted manure into the bed. About 1 month after you transplant your cole crop seedlings, apply about 3 to 4 pounds of an organic fertilizer, such as 5-5-5, to every 100 square feet of garden. (Chapter 15 has more on fertilizing.) Keep the soil moist, and a week or so after transplanting, apply an organic mulch such as hay or straw. These types of mulches keep weeds at bay and keep the soil cool and moist — just how cole crops like it.

I stress the importance of cool weather for cole crops throughout this chapter, but mild temperatures can be too cool for some cole crops. Even though mature cole crop plants can withstand temperatures into the 20s, young plants may not be so hardy. If broccoli plants are exposed to several days of 40-degree temperatures when they're still young, they can form flower heads prematurely when the weather warms (which is called *buttoning*). Cauliflower does the same thing when exposed to cold temperatures or other stresses, such as crowding, when young. In either case, you're left with a small plant and head. To avoid this premature flowering, plant in summer for a fall crop or cover young spring-planted crops with a row cover to keep them warm.

With older cauliflower varieties, such as 'Snow Crown', you have to wrap the leaves over the head and tie them with twine, as shown in Figure 9-2. However, many newer varieties, such as 'Fremont', are *self-blanching* (the leaves naturally grow to cover the head and avoid light) as well as disease resistant. However, even newer varieties benefit from careful inspection to ensure that the leaves are tightly covering the heads once they form.

Keep the plants well watered, weeded, and mulched so they grow steadily through the season. Side-dress cole crops with an organic fertilizer such as 5-5-5 about 1 month after transplanting in the garden. (For more on side-dressing, flip to Chapter 15.) Nurture your plants, and they'll reward you with a bountiful harvest.

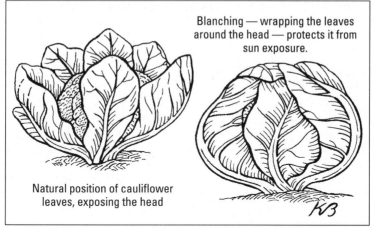

Figure 9-2: You can keep older cauliflower varieties white by wrapping the leaves over the developing heads to keep them away from the sun.

Blanching — wrapping the leaves around the head — protects it from sun exposure.

Natural position of cauliflower leaves, exposing the head

Putting a stop to pesky pest problems

In general, cole crops have only a few problems that home gardeners need to watch out for. Many modern hybrid varieties have added disease resistance, so choose these varieties if diseases are a problem in your garden. I discuss general vegetable diseases and pests, such as cutworms, aphids, nematodes, flea beetles, and mildews, in Chapter 17, but the following list warns you about some specific cole crop pests:

✔ **Black rot:** This bacterial disease is a problem particularly with cabbage and cauliflower. It causes the plant or head to rot before maturing. The telltale signs are a foul smell, a yellowing of the lower leaves, blackening of the leaf veins, and triangular yellow areas on the leaf edges. You can control this problem by *rotating crops* (planting other unrelated crops such as tomatoes, beans, or lettuce in that area for 3 years) and removing all old cole crop plant debris.

✔ **Cabbage maggot:** If plants are stunted, pull one up and look at the roots. If you see small, white larvae (maggots) feeding there, you probably have *cabbage maggots.* The adult fly lays eggs on the stems at the soil line and then when the eggs hatch, the larvae tunnel into the soil and start feeding on the roots. The maggots are especially dangerous to young seedlings. To control the cabbage maggot, place a floating row cover over the young seedlings. After the weather warms, remove the row cover.

✔ **Club root:** If your plants are stunted, pull one up and check the roots. If the roots are gnarled and disfigured, a fungus called *club root* may be to blame. To prevent this disease, rotate crops and raise the soil pH to 7.2 by adding lime (see Chapter 14 for more on acceptable pH ranges for vegetables).

✔ **Imported cabbageworm and cabbage looper:** These two insects are the number-one problem with cole crops. The adult of the cabbageworm is a seemingly harmless white butterfly that lays single white eggs on the undersides of leaves. The eggs hatch, and then green caterpillars crawl out and begin to feed on the leaves. The adult of the cabbage looper is a gray-brown moth. These pests can quickly destroy your crop. As soon as you see signs of feeding — including the caterpillars or their dark green droppings — spray the crop with a biological control called *Bacillus thuringiensis* (Bt). Bt is an effective bacteria that attacks only the larvae of caterpillar family insects and is safe to other insects, animals, and humans.

Harvesting cole crops

If all goes well, cole crops should be ready to eat after a few months. However, be sure to check the days to maturity for the varieties you choose. In this section, I share some tips to help you get the best harvests.

Broccoli

Harvest broccoli by cutting the main head when the flower buds are still tightly clustered together without any signs of blossoming. Even if the head is smaller than you would like it to be, cut it now. After the yellow flowers open, the flavor turns bitter. If you leave a few inches of the main stem on the plant, many broccoli varieties respond by growing side branches that produce little heads (see Figure 9-3). Keep harvesting, and the broccoli keeps producing! When you harvest the side shoots, cut the shoot back to the main stem. Doing so creates fewer, but larger side shoots that are easier to use.

Brussels sprouts

Brussels sprouts taste best after cool weather helps turn some of their carbohydrates into sugars. Following a frost, pick off the marble-sized sprouts from the bottom of the plant first, moving up the stalk. The more sprouts you pick from below, the larger the sprouts above will get. Pull off the lower leaves for easier picking.

To make the sprouts mature faster, snip off the top few inches of the plant once sprouts have formed on the bottom 12 inches of the stalk.

Because Brussels sprouts tolerate temperatures into the 20s, you can harvest right into New Year's in some areas. I've picked frozen sprouts off plants for Christmas, and they tasted great. The flavor actually gets sweeter with cool temperatures! Just cook and eat them immediately; if you try to store them, they'll rot.

Cabbage

Harvest cabbage heads when they're firm when squeezed. By periodically squeezing your cabbages through the growing season, you'll be able to tell when they're firm. (Don't worry — they won't mind!) To harvest, cut the head from the base of the plant with a sharp knife. When harvesting early-maturing varieties in summer, don't dig up the plants. Cabbages have the ability to grow smaller side heads on the plant after the main head is harvested; you harvest these side heads the same way that you do the main head.

Sometimes, cabbage heads split before you can harvest them. *Splitting* occurs when the plant takes up too much fertilizer or water, especially around harvest time. This "overdose" causes the inner leaves to grow faster than the outer leaves, splitting the heads. Harvest splitting heads as soon as possible. To stop splitting once it starts, grab the head and give it a one-half turn to break some of the roots. You also can *root prune* the plant by digging in a circle about 1 foot from the base of the cabbage. Both of these methods slow the uptake of water and fertilizer to preserve the head.

Cauliflower

When heads are between 6 and 12 inches in diameter and blanched white (for white varieties) or fully colored (for colored varieties), pull up the whole plant and cut off the head. Cauliflower, unlike cabbage and broccoli, won't form side heads after the main head is cut.

Chapter 10

A Salad for All Seasons: Lettuce, Spinach, Swiss Chard, and Specialty Greens

*I*f you're a beginning gardener and have never grown a vegetable in your life before, try greens. You'll find no easier group of vegetables to grow than greens. Unlike other vegetables that require weeks or even months of nurturing, greens are good things that come even to those who can't wait. Because you don't have to wait for flowering and fruiting to enjoy their green goodness, you can just pick the leaves at any stage, and — voilà! — you have dinner.

In many growing areas, you can have fresh greens year-round from your garden with just a little planning. Sure, it's easy to buy a head of lettuce at the grocery store or farmer's market, but the pure joy of running out to the garden in the evening and plucking a fresh head for dinner gives you a great sense of satisfaction while introducing you to unusual varieties and flavors not readily available from most supermarkets. Plus you don't have to push a shopping cart with a bad wheel or break up any arguments in the cereal aisle just to gather basic salad ingredients.

And speaking of salad, for most people, lettuce and salad are synonymous. Lettuce is definitely the number-one green, but in this chapter, I also discuss two other major greens crops: spinach and Swiss chard. In addition, I talk about my favorite unusual wild greens, including dandelions and sorrel. (Flip to Chapter 11 for details on other unusual yet more mainstream types of greens, such as arugula, collards, and endive.)

Greens, by nature, are cool, moisture-loving crops. When the weather heats up to above 80 degrees Fahrenheit for several days in a row and the plant is mature enough, annual greens such as lettuce and spinach think the end is near and send up a seed stalk. This process is called *bolting*. Bolting doesn't just mean getting out of the house quickly. It's also a term used to describe a greens crop gone bad. During this process, the flavor of the greens quickly becomes bitter, so plan to plant and harvest your greens while the weather's cool or else grow varieties that are tolerant of the heat. I provide guidelines for growing all types of greens at the end of this chapter.

Lettuce Get Together

Originally from the Mediterranean area, lettuce (*Latuca sativa*) was eaten at the tables of Persian kings in 550 B.C. and was once thought to be an aphrodisiac. I can't attest to its aphrodisiacal qualities, but I do know that lettuce is considered the quintessential salad crop around the world.

The four basic types of lettuce — crisphead, loose-head, loose-leaf, and romaine lettuce (all shown in Figure 10-1) — offer a number of tasty varieties to delight the palate. The most common are green-colored leaf varieties, but you can grow many red- and burgundy-colored leaf varieties and those with a mixture of colors, too. Some varieties form solid heads, but others don't. Varieties have smooth, frilly, or deeply cut leaves.

The following sections describe the four basic types of lettuce along with their days to maturity and some of my favorite varieties. They all are best in cool weather conditions, but some varieties can tolerate the heat. Just remember that lettuce can be eaten much younger, depending on your needs and appetite.

Crisphead lettuce

The crisphead group is most widely known as the "iceberg" lettuces, so named because when the lettuce was shipped from California (the main lettuce-growing region in the United States) to the East Coast in the early 1900s, mounds of ice were used to keep it cool and fresh.

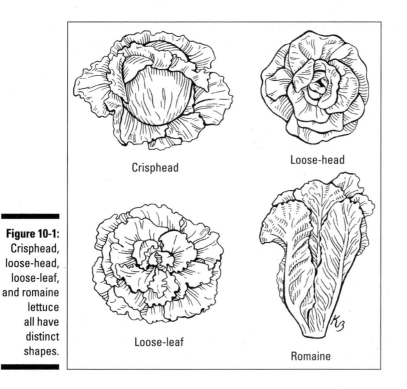

Crisphead

Loose-head

Loose-leaf

Romaine

Figure 10-1:
Crisphead,
loose-head,
loose-leaf,
and romaine
lettuce
all have
distinct
shapes.

'Iceberg' is the most widely known variety, but many other crispheads are just as tasty and easy to grow. This type of lettuce forms a solid head when mature, with white, crunchy, densely packed inner leaves. Crispheads tend to take at least 70 days to mature from seeding in the garden. Following are some popular varieties of crisphead lettuce:

- ✔ **'Iceberg':** Famous in grocery stores across the country, these compact heads have tightly-packed smooth leaves and white hearts. They're best when grown in cool conditions (below 70 degrees), because then they form solid heads. (Find tips for growing head lettuce in the section "Growing Great Greens," later in this chapter.)

- ✔ **'Nevada':** This French crisphead features upright, bright green ruffled leaves with a nutty flavor. These cool-weather plants resist tip burn, rot, and bolting.

- ✔ **'Summertime':** So named for its ability to form solid heads in the heat of summer, 'Summertime' has green, frilly leaves and a crisp texture.

Romaine lettuce

Romaine was named by the Romans, who believed in the healthful properties of this type of lettuce. Emperor Caesar Augustus even built a statue in praise of romaine lettuce, so it's no surprise that this is the type of lettuce featured in Caesar salad. The alternative name, "Cos," comes from the Greek island of Kos, where it's popular.

Romaine lettuce grows tall, upright, solid heads and long, thick green or red leaves with solid *midribs* (the middle vein of the leaf). This type of lettuce tends to take at least 70 days to mature from seeding and can withstand summer heat. It can be grown as a "cut and come again" type of lettuce. Here are a few common varieties:

- ✔ **'Outredgeous':** Bright red, thick, glossy, ruffle-edged leaves form the red color best on this open-pollinated variety when grown in partly shaded areas.

- ✔ **'Parris Island Cos':** This smooth, green-leafed, open-pollinated romaine lettuce has 10-inch-tall, thick, green leaves.

- ✔ **'Rouge D'Hiver':** An old French heirloom with bronze-red smooth leaves and a buttery texture. It tolerates cold better than heat.

- ✔ **'Winter Density':** This variety is a green smooth-leaf lettuce that's actually a cross between a loose-head and a romaine-type lettuce. This 8-inch-tall plant is both heat and cold tolerant.

Loose-head lettuce

Loose-head or Butterhead lettuce features dark or medium green leaves or red leaves and smooth, thick outer leaves folded around a loosely-formed, yellow-to-white head. The heads of loose-head lettuce aren't solid like a crisphead type, but they're easier to grow, especially during the summer heat. This type matures starting at 60 days from seeding. Here are a few popular varieties:

- ✔ **'Bibb':** 'Bibb' is an heirloom, dark green, smooth-leafed, loose-head lettuce that dates back to the 1800s.

- ✔ **'Buttercrunch':** A bolt-resistant, open-pollinated, loose-head type, 'Buttercrunch' has thick, juicy, ruffled leaves; it's best grown as a summer crop.

- ✔ **'Deer Tongue':** This heirloom, loose-head type lettuce with tongue-shaped, smooth-edged, green leaves is slow to bolt, making it a good choice in warm weather. Kids are fascinated by this variety because of its unique shape and name.

> ✔ **'Four Seasons' (Merveille des Quatre Saisons):** This heirloom has beautiful deep burgundy, smooth-edged, puckered outer leaves covering a creamy green-leaved heart. The plants are compact and sweet.
>
> ✔ **'Speckles':** An unusual Amish heirloom Bibb-type lettuce with red speckles on olive green, smooth-edged, slightly puckered leaves and a blanched green heart.

Loose-leaf lettuce

Loose-leaf lettuce doesn't form a solid head and is best harvested by picking off the mature outer leaves, allowing new leaves to continue growing. This type is often cut and allowed to "come again" (I discuss this technique later in this chapter) to provide multiple crops of greens from one head. You can start harvesting this type about 45 days from seeding. Some popular varieties include the following:

> ✔ **'Black Seeded Simpson':** This widely adapted variety is an heirloom lettuce with crinkled, light green leaves. 'Simpson Elite' is a more heat-resistant strain of this classic variety.
>
> ✔ **'New Red Fire':** This unusual, open-pollinated variety has extremely frilly, burgundy-red puckered leaves. It's slow growing and disease resistant.
>
> ✔ **'Red Salad Bowl':** This is a red version of the classic 'Salad Bowl'. It's a loose-leaf, open-pollinated lettuce that features frilly green leaves and a mild, tender taste. This attractive burgundy-red-leafed version grows and looks best in cooler weather.
>
> ✔ **'Royal Oak Leaf':** An improved version of the old-fashioned oak leaf, the 'Royal Oak Leaf' is open-pollinated, has bigger, more defined, darker green, deeply cut leaves and is slower to bolt, making it better for warm-weather growing.

Popeye's Pal: Spinach

Spinach is a Middle Eastern vegetable that has been cultivated for centuries. The dark green leaves of spinach (*Spinacia oleracea*) are nutritious (just ask Popeye, Olive Oyl, and Brutus of comic book fame) and stronger tasting than lettuce. It's one of the first crops many gardeners plant in spring. In fact, when the heat comes, spinach quickly bolts. However, if you love spinach and want to eat it throughout the summer, you can grow warm-weather spinach look-a-like crops that produce all summer, such as New Zealand spinach (*Tetragonia tetragonioides*) and Malabar spinach (*Basella rubra*). Though not in the spinach family, they have a similar look and taste.

You can grow two different leaf types of spinach: savoy (crinkled) and smooth. Which is better is a matter of personal preference. The savoy-leaf types give you more leaf surface to hold that salad dressing, but the smooth-leaf types are easier to clean.

Unless otherwise noted, the varieties in the following sections mature in about 30 to 45 days from a spring planting. As with lettuce (which I describe earlier in this chapter), you can always harvest the young, tender greens earlier if you just can't wait.

Savoy spinach

The following are popular savoy-type (crinkled-leaf) spinach varieties:

- ✔ **'Bloomsdale Long Standing':** This heirloom variety has thick-textured, glossy, crinkled, dark green leaves.

- ✔ **'Melody':** This hybrid, All-America Selections winner (AAS; see Chapter 4 for more) features large semi-savoy leaves and good disease resistance.

- ✔ **'Tyee':** This hybrid, slightly savoy-type is a vigorous grower. It's a personal favorite because it's easy to grow and slow to bolt.

Smooth spinach and some spinachlike friends

Following are a few smooth spinach varieties and a couple of good look-and-taste-alikes that are easy to grow:

- ✔ **'Malabar Red Stem':** Although this plant isn't botanically related to spinach, its vining red stems produce spinachlike leaves all summer. This heat lover grows to 6 feet tall, so it must be trellised and grown like a pole bean (see Chapter 7 for details on growing beans). It can be used as a spinach substitute raw or cooked.

- ✔ **'New Zealand':** This 1- to 2-foot-tall plant resembles spinach in looks and flavor, but it's able to withstand summer heat. It can be cut repeatedly and still regrow, a method called *cut and come again*. I talk more about this method later in this chapter.

- ✔ **'Oriental Giant':** This hybrid variety produces large, smooth, 12- to 15-inch-long leaves and yields up to three times more foliage than other spinach varieties.

✔ **'Reddy':** This smooth-leafed hybrid spinach variety has red stalks and veins that contrast nicely with its deep green, arrow-shaped leaves.

✔ **'Renegade':** This smooth-leafed hybrid spinach variety is faster growing and more disease resistant than the similar 'Space' variety.

The Attractive and Hardy Swiss Chard

Swiss chard (*Beta vulgaris*) has finally come of age. With the recent introduction of more colorful varieties, this green is now a top specialty treat in many gardens. (Even Aristotle wrote about the virtues of this lovely plant!) Swiss chard hails from southern Europe, where it grew up next to its close cousin, the beet. In fact, the only differences between the two vegetables are that chard (sometimes known as "spinach beet") doesn't have the bulbous root of the beet, and its greens are more tender and prolific.

I've grown Swiss chard for years because it has so many wonderful characteristics: It's easy to grow; doesn't bolt like spinach; has a consistent flavor, even in the hot summer; and has leaves that keep producing until frost. I also grow chard for the gorgeous color of its *midribs* (the middle part of the leaf). Varieties such as 'Rhubarb' and 'Bright Lights' make this garden green a real showstopper.

The color of the midrib is evident even at a young stage, so picking them as baby greens still yields the attractive look. These colorful varieties look so beautiful I sometimes grow them as ornamentals in my flower garden.

The following varieties all mature between 50 and 60 days from direct seeding in the garden, but the baby greens can be harvested as early as 1 month after seeding:

✔ **'Bright Lights':** This AAS-winning hybrid variety features a mix of plants with red, pink, yellow, gold, or orange midribs on leaves that taste as good as they look. These leaves have a milder texture than other chard varieties.

✔ **'Bright Yellow':** This open-pollinated variety's yellow midrib contrasts beautifully with the dark green leaves.

✔ **'Fordhook Giant':** This open-pollinated variety features a thick, celery-like midrib with large, dark green savoy (crinkled) leaves. It's a heavy producer.

✔ **'Rhubarb':** An heirloom, burgundy-red midrib variety with dark green leaves, this variety is a bit smaller than other chards, but it's still tasty and good looking.

Mixing it up with mesclun

Mesclun is a French term that means "mixture." It caught on in the 1990s as a way to enliven salads by mixing in various colored and flavored greens and has gone mainstream ever since. Mesclun isn't actually an individual green but a mix of different greens. The flavors can be mild to piquant, depending on the ingredients in the mix. You can purchase mild, savory, and spicy individual mesclun mixes to name a few. Traditional mesclun may include a blend of lettuces, endive, arugula, cress, dandelion, and mache. Today the list of possibilities has expanded to include herbs, kales, radishes, and Chinese greens such as mizuna and pac choi. You also can get mixtures of different colored

and shaped lettuce varieties that offer a mild taste. And there are even *microgreen mixtures* (greens harvested when only 1 to 2 inches tall) that can be quickly grown and added to salads.

The key to any of these flavorful blends is to harvest the greens when they're small and tender — while they're still "baby" size. This usually is within 3 weeks of seeding. Because most of these greens are cold-weather tolerant, mesclun is usually the first green harvested from my garden in spring. The greens quickly regrow after cutting for a number of harvests. The greens taste great doused with a balsamic vinegar and olive oil dressing.

Going Wild with Specialty Greens

Salad has gone through a revolution in the past 20 years. At one time, salad meant simply lettuce, spinach, and maybe Swiss chard. No longer. With the growing interest in exotic Chinese and European greens, salad palettes have expanded to include many ethnic greens, including arugula and mizuna (see Chapter 11 for more on these particular greens). Folks are even becoming interested in greens previously thought to be weeds, such as sorrel and — the scourge of lawn lovers — dandelions.

Eating these wild greens isn't a new idea; in fact, when I was a boy, my Italian grandmother picked wild dandelion greens in spring to be sautéed with garlic and olive oil. I don't bother cultivating these greens in the garden; I just eat my lawn! It's loaded with dandelions, sorrel, and plantain. Even my cultivated gardens have great annual weeds that I harvest young and mix in salads, including lamb's quarters, chickweed, and pigweed. I'm not alone; such culinary practices are being rediscovered and embraced as the interest in ethnic dishes grows.

For many wild greens, you can just go into your garden or lawn and munch away, but *never* eat greens from lawns treated with pesticides.

You have good reason to cultivate and enjoy unusual greens. In fact, many types aren't considered weeds, and you actually can cultivate them in your garden. Many of these are very easy to grow (some can even withstand freezing temperatures), they're more nutritious than traditional lettuce, and their flavors are unique and sometimes quite surprising.

Many of the most popular and more mainstream specialty greens like endive are discussed in Chapter 11. But if you're curious about growing some of the wild ones, try a few of the eyebrow-raising varieties listed here. Most can be harvested starting about 1 month after direct seeding in the garden. (Seeding gives you better varieties and more control than just waiting for the weed to pop up.) You also can find many of these varieties commercially. Check out some of my favorites:

- **Asian greens:** This catch-all phrase refers to a number of different greens. I cover mizuna in Chapter 11, but here are some lesser-known types that are great eaten on their own or tossed into mesclun mixtures (see the nearby sidebar):

  - **'Tatsoi'** produces a tight rosette of mild-flavored leaves. It's a cool-season green.

  - **'Komatsuna'** has mild, fleshy, rounded dark green leaves with rounded stems. It tolerates heat well.

  - **'Shungiku'** is an edible chrysanthemum. The leaves are harvested when less than 8 inches tall and used in salads, sushi, and pickles. This variety likes cool weather.

- **Miner's lettuce (*Claytonia perfoliata*):** Heart-shaped leaves encircle a white-flowered stem. This variety grows best in cool weather and regrows after harvesting. It's good planted in fall as a winter salad green.

- **Dandelion:** Yes, you can plant the same dandelions that dad has spent years pulling out or mowing over. Harvest them young during cool weather in spring or fall — when the leaves are about 4 to 6 inches long — so the greens are only slightly bitter. Varieties from France and Italy, such as 'Ameliore', grow taller and are easier to harvest.

- **Mache (corn salad or lamb's lettuce):** This cool-weather-loving and cold-tolerant green features small, dark green, tender leaves in a rosette shape with a mild, nutty flavor. It's often the first green to start growing. Some varieties to try include 'Vit' (especially good for cold and wet conditions) and 'd'Etamps', which has large, rounded leaves.

- **Mustard:** These beautiful, 1- to 2-foot-tall, upright-growing, spicy greens grow best in cool weather and make a bold statement in the garden. They're great used in salad mixes. The spicy-hot, raw flavor mellows when cooked. Some of the best varieties include 'Green Wave' (heavily curled, spicy green leaves), 'Red Giant' (large, purple-tinted, mildly flavored leaves), and 'Osaka Purple' (red, mildly flavored leaves that are more compact than 'Red Giant').

   ✔ **Sorrel (*Rumex sanguineus*):** The 8-inch-long, arrow-shaped greens start growing in early spring and continue until fall. They have a distinct, lemony flavor that's great in salads and soups. This green *perennializes* (comes back each year on its own) and can grow in light shade. A beautiful, red-tinged variety is 'Red Veined' sorrel.

   ✔ **Vegetable amaranth:** This is a variety of the ancient grain amaranth that's harvested young for its oval-shaped, coleuslike leaves. The leaves may be all green, green-and-red colored, or all red, depending on the variety. These greens germinate best in warm weather.

Growing Great Greens

Fertile soil and consistent watering are essential to growing great greens. Given those two factors, greens have to be one of the easiest vegetables to grow. The biggest problem gardeners have with greens is too much success — in other words, an overabundant harvest that you can't eat! The following sections offer tips for getting the most out of your greens.

Timing is everything: Determining when to plant your greens

In areas with mild summers and winters, such as the West Coast, greens are easy to grow year-round. For most other areas, spring and fall are the best times to grow greens.

Greens can be direct sown in the garden starting in spring and, in cool areas, planted throughout the summer until September. If you want to get a jump on the season, start seeds 4 to 6 weeks before the last frost date in your area (see the appendix for a listing of first and last frost dates) so they can be planted 2 to 3 weeks later.

Gardeners in mild winter areas such as Arizona, Texas, and Florida may prefer a winter crop of greens because the weather is more favorable. Summer is too hot to germinate the seeds and grow the traditional types of lettuce and greens. For a winter crop, sow seeds indoors in fall to be transplanted into the garden a month later.

If you don't have the right climate for year-round growing but love fresh greens, here are some guidelines for growing your own salad 12 months of the year in spite of cold winters and hot summers:

   ✔ **Choose the right varieties.** To grow a winter greens crop in cold-winter areas (hardiness zone 5 or 6) without season extenders (see Chapter 21), plant spinach, arugula, claytonia, mizuna, and winter lettuce varieties such as 'Winter Density'. To grow greens through summer in warm areas (hardiness zone 7 and warmer) choose greens that like the heat, such as Malabar or New Zealand spinach.

✔ **Time your planting.** Start heat-loving greens in late spring so they mature during summer's heat. For winter greens in the cold areas, start cold-tolerant plants in fall so they mature to full size before the bitter cold weather of December. The greens don't have to grow during the short winter days and cold temperatures — they just need to stay alive.

✔ **Keep the soil fertile.** Successive crops of greens will take nutrients out of the soil, so after every crop you remove, add a 2- to 3-inch layer of compost to the soil and work it in well.

✔ **Protect the plants.** During the summer heat, use shade cloth to block the afternoon sun. In the North, protect greens through the cold winter by growing them in cold frames (see Chapter 21 for cold frame designs).

Here are a couple of other tips for planting greens at the right time:

✔ **Stagger your plantings to avoid producing too large a supply.** I remember planting a 10-foot row of lettuce all at once, watching it germinate and grow, and feeling very smug about my success. My satisfaction evaporated when I was inundated a month later with lettuce, lettuce, and more lettuce. I got sick of eating salads for breakfast, lunch, and dinner, and most of my crop eventually bolted and tasted bitter. I learned my lesson that year.

Planting small, 2-to-4-foot patches of greens every 2 weeks throughout the growing season, which is referred to as *succession planting* (see Chapter 16), is the best way to ensure a manageable supply of lettuce all summer long. In warm areas, you may want to skip planting in midsummer because lettuce will bolt from the heat.

✔ **Give crisphead lettuce the environment it needs to thrive.** Growing great crisphead or iceberg lettuce can be a challenge for many gardeners. The problem is that crisphead lettuce likes cool temperatures (50 to 60 degrees) throughout the growing season, especially when it's trying to form a head. For northern and southern gardeners, fall planting is the key. In warm areas, start seeds indoors in September; then place the seedlings in the garden in October or November. In cooler climates, start seeds indoors in July to plant in the garden in August or September. Keep plants well watered and feed them every 3 weeks with fish emulsion (which I discuss later in this chapter). By the cool days of fall, your iceberg lettuce heads should form.

Putting your greens to bed

Greens are easiest grown in raised beds (see Chapter 3 for more on raised beds). The beds are flat and smooth on top with most of the rocks and debris removed. Raised beds drain water well, which greens love, and they're easy to work. Instead of planting in a straight row (which is okay, by the way), you can broadcast the seeds over the top of the entire bed. This *wide row planting technique* is described in Chapter 13. By using the wide row planting technique, you get more greens per square foot sooner with less weeding and watering.

If you don't have room for greens with all those other gorgeous vegetables growing, get creative about where you plant. Because greens plants are generally small and fast growing, you can tuck them in all kinds of empty patches in your garden. For example, you can plant greens in between newly planted tomato, broccoli, or cabbage seedlings; under a pole bean teepee; between rows of corn; or around carrots in the carrot patch. The greens mature and are harvested before the other plants get too large to shade them. In the carrot patch, harvesting the greens gives room for these root crops to enlarge and mature. In summer, after your crop of beans or peas is finished, yank out the exhausted plants and plant a quick crop of lettuce to harvest later in late summer or fall.

Adding nitrogen-rich fishy fertilizer

Greens have simple fertilizing needs. You eat the leaves. Leaves need nitrogen to grow. So the soil needs to be rich in nitrogen. Any questions? That being said, it's important to remember balance in all things, including fertilizer in your lettuce patch. So applying an organic fertilizer, such as blood meal, that's high in nitrogen is a good practice. (Chapter 15 provides more information on organic fertilizers.) I suggest working in a 3- to 4-inch layer of compost and applying soluble nitrogen fertilizer, such as fish emulsion, every few weeks. By doing so, your greens stay lush and mature quickly.

Thin and bare it: Thinning your greens

Whether you plant in straight rows or wide rows, greens need thinning. Generally, spinach and loose-leaf lettuces need 3 to 4 inches between plants; crisphead and romaine lettuce like 6 to 10 inches. Thinning isn't critical if you're harvesting your greens when small or "baby" size.

Thin the seedlings as soon as each plant has four leaves. (Don't throw out those thinnings, though. They make great "baby" greens for salad.) After the plants are properly spaced, mulching with a 2- to 3-inch layer of hay or straw is a good way to conserve vital moisture, prevent weeds, and keep the leaves clean of splashing soil after rain. (Check out Chapter 13 for more information on thinning seedlings.)

Watering to win the war against wilt

Keeping the soil consistently moist after planting is a good way to avoid a common complaint with lettuces: The seeds never came up.

Greens need moist soil to germinate. Once growing, the plants generally have small root systems, so they're the first vegetable to wilt when the soil is too dry. Water deeply — 5 to 6 inches deep — and mulch to keep greens crisp. A simple way to water is to use soaker hoses or drip irrigation (Chapter 15 describes watering techniques). To preserve moisture, especially if it's hot, lay a *floating row cover* (a lightweight, cheesecloth-like material that lets air, water, and sunlight through and keep the bugs out) over the bed until the seedlings emerge.

Working out the bugs (and other common ailments)

Greens have some of the problems that plague other vegetables. Insects such as aphids and white flies and diseases such as white mold and viruses can quickly destroy a crop. Because greens tend to have shallow and relatively small root systems, they can succumb easily to damage. Slugs are a threat to young seedlings in moist areas such as the Pacific Northwest, and rabbits and woodchucks are critters that love greens anywhere. All these problems are covered in depth in Chapter 17, but remember that fertile, well-drained soil that's kept moist and fertilized is usually your best bet against any problems with your greens crop. And don't hesitate to yank out an insect-infested or animal-chewed crop: Greens grow and mature so quickly, it may be better to start over than to nurse a sick crop.

Here are a few specific problems that plague greens:

- ✔ **Bottom rot:** This condition, caused by a fungus, makes lettuce (especially head lettuce) wilt and rot before maturing. It's mostly seen in poorly drained soil during wet conditions. To avoid this problem, rotate crops, keep your soil well drained, and grow lettuce in raised beds.

- ✔ **Spinach leaf miner:** This small fly lays eggs on spinach and Swiss chard leaves. The eggs hatch, and the tiny larvae tunnel in between the leaf layers. Pick off and destroy tunneled leaves, and cover the crop with a floating row cover after germination to prevent damage.

✔ **Tip burn:** Tip burn causes the leaves of head lettuce to turn brown at the edges. This condition is seen during hot weather when soil moisture tends to fluctuate, creating a calcium deficiency in plants. Don't bother adding calcium to the soil, but do pick off burned leaves, choose varieties that resist tip burn, and keep the soil evenly moist to control this problem.

Your bowl runneth over: Harvesting greens

Harvesting greens couldn't be easier. After all, you eat the leaves. Except for crisphead lettuces, harvest greens while they're young and tender to avoid a common complaint of lettuce growers: bitter-tasting lettuce. Bitter taste usually develops in older plants, so start picking when the leaves are 4 inches long. Harvest the outer leaves first to allow the inner leaves to continue to develop. Also, wait until you're almost ready to prepare your meal to harvest. That way, the greens will be fresh and crisp in your salad bowl.

Some lettuces, such as loose-leaf varieties and Swiss chard, are examples of "cut and come again" greens (see Figure 10-2). You can cut these greens at the ground level — they'll sprout new leaves from their bases — or you can just harvest the mature leaves, leaving the immature leaves to continue growing. Cutting the leaves at ground level is a great alternative to replanting, and you can cut the plants up to four times.

Crisphead or iceberg lettuce can be harvested young, before heads form. However, to get the solid, blanched heads seen in grocery stores, wait until full maturity when heads are firm when squeezed.

Figure 10-2:
Cut and come again for more lettuce greens.

Chapter 11

Sweet Corn and an A to T of Other Worthy Veggies

The preceding seven chapters cover the most popular and widely grown vegetables. But part of the fun of vegetable gardening is trying new and unusual crops. These "experiments" can be as commonplace as corn or as exotic as mizuna.

This chapter starts with one of the most popular vegetables of summer: corn. Corn isn't related to any of the vegetables mentioned in Chapters 4 through 10, so I give it a special place in this chapter. Although corn is as traditional as apple pie, any vegetable that's closely related to lawn grass has some unique qualities!

In this chapter, I also include an alphabetical listing of other fun and unusual vegetables to help you decide which ones to try and how to grow them. Each listing provides a description of the vegetable, a list of sample varieties to look for, and some basic growing tips. (*Note:* The planting times for each of these vegetables depend on the weather in your area. Refer to seed packages for planting times. See the appendix for information about hardiness zones and first and last frost dates.)

As a bonus, I include cooking tips with many of the vegetables. Like my mom used to say, "You'll never know if you like it unless you try it." Happy gardening, and bon appétit!

Sweet Corn and Its Relatives

Corn (*Zea mays*) has a reputation of being grown only in large fields, but you also can grow a great crop of corn in a small garden in your backyard. The satisfaction of harvesting your own fresh-picked corn and steaming it for dinner is one of the joys of summer. In the following sections, I discuss sweet corn along with popcorn.

Sweet corn

If all you've ever eaten is sweet corn from the supermarket, you're missing one of summer's true delights. Fresh-picked, steamed sweet corn has a sweet flavor that brings a smile to old and young faces alike. You also can roast corn on an open fire or grill to give it a woodsy flavor.

By selecting the right varieties to grow, you can have sweet corn maturing all summer long. And you don't need a 10-acre field to grow it. Five to six short rows are all you need to get plenty of ears for your family.

Varieties

The kernels of the sweet corn plant are actually seeds. Most sweet corn varieties come with white, yellow, or bicolor (yellow and white mixed) kernels. Some heirloom varieties that are mostly used for corn flour and roasting feature red and blue kernels, which is where the red- and blue-colored corn tortilla chips come from. The color of corn that you choose depends on what flavor you like and what varieties grow well where you live. Varieties mature in 65 to 100 days, so choose a sampling that will mature over time in your garden. Gardeners in cold climates should stick with quick-maturing varieties, such as 'Quickie' and 'Early Sunglow'.

As with many vegetables, corn has open-pollinated heirloom varieties as well as many modern hybrids (see Chapter 3 for more about open pollination and hybrids). The following two newer hybrid groups, which hold their sweetness and tenderness, are now commonly found in grocery stores, and their seeds are available in garden centers and seed catalogs:

- ✔ **Sugar-enhanced (se) varieties** have a special gene in their makeup that increases the tenderness and sweetness of the ears.

- ✔ **Supersweet (sh2) varieties** have a gene bred into the variety that makes the ears even sweeter than sugar-enhanced, and they can be stored for a week in the refrigerator without losing their sweetness. However, many feel that what supersweets gain in sweetness, they lose in "real corn" flavor.

Even though these newer, sweeter varieties are a bit more finicky about growing, especially the sh2 varieties, they do allow you to eat your corn over time without worrying about it getting starchy. Still, for best flavor, eat your sweet corn as soon as possible after harvest.

Following are some sweet corn varieties you may want to try:

- ✔ Some standard heirloom yellow varieties to grow are 'Golden Bantam' and 'Ashworth'. White-kerneled standard heirloom varieties include 'Country Gentleman' and 'Stowell's Evergreen'. One uniquely colored heirloom variety is 'Black Aztec' (black).

- ✔ A few standard sugary hybrids include 'Early Sunglow' (yellow), 'Honey and Cream' (bicolor), and 'Silver Queen' (white).

- ✔ If you're interested in sugar-enhanced varieties, try 'Quickie' (bicolor), 'Sugar Buns' (yellow), 'Sugar Pearl' (white), and 'Ruby Queen' (red).

- ✔ For some good supersweet varieties, grow 'Early Xtra Sweet' (yellow), 'Honey N' Pearl' (bicolor), and 'Xtra Tender' (white).

Whew, that's a lot of choices! This list is actually only the tip of the iceberg, so don't be afraid to try other varieties to see which grow best in your area.

Growing guidelines

Sweet corn is a warm-weather crop, so don't rush to plant it. The soil temperature should be at least 65 degrees Fahrenheit for the best germination.

You may notice that some companies coat their seeds with a brightly colored fungicide to prevent rotting while the seed germinates — rotting during germination is a big problem in wet, cool weather with heavy clay soil. If you're a strict organic gardener, select corn from companies that sell untreated or organic seed. You also can plant in slightly raised beds to hasten the soil in drying out and the seeds in germinating. (See Chapter 14 for more on raised beds.)

Corn is in the grass family, so, like your lawn, it needs plenty of nitrogen fertilizer to grow best. Before planting, amend the soil with composted manure, and then side-dress the patch with a 5-5-5 fertilizer when the plants are knee-high and again when *silks* (fine hairs on the ears) appear.

Corn was traditionally planted in hills following the Native American technique, but for the best production, plant corn in groups of short rows called *blocks*. Blocks consist of at least four straight rows of corn about 10 to 20 feet long. Rows should be 2 feet apart, with walkways 2 to 4 feet wide between blocks so you can easily harvest. Plant the seeds 6 inches apart in a full-sun location in 2-inch-deep furrows. After germination, thin the plants to 12 inches apart.

Each corn kernel needs to be pollinated by pollen from the *tassel* (the antennae-like flower at the top of the corn plant). If corn plants are grouped together, the wind blows the pollen down to the silks on the ears, and the pollen moves along the silks to pollinate the kernels. If you plant only one or two long rows, chances are some kernels won't get pollinated, and your ears will look like mouths that are missing a few teeth. Plant only one variety in each block to ensure that the tassels drop pollen when the silks are ready. If you mix varieties within a block, you may not get proper pollination, because the pollen may drop when the ears aren't ready. You can stagger the planting dates of your varieties by 2 weeks or plant other blocks of early-, mid, or late-season varieties to extend the harvest season.

Don't plant supersweet varieties within 250 feet of any other corn variety. If non-supersweet pollen pollinates the corn, the supersweet corn will lose its extra sweetness.

When the corn plants are about 8 inches tall, *hill* them (mounding soil up to the lower leaves) to help kill weeds and reduce the likelihood of the tall stalks blowing over when older. (You can see this technique illustrated in Chapter 6.) Keep the corn well-watered, and watch for leaf-yellowing. Yellowing leaves are a sign of nitrogen deficiency, so you should add more nitrogen fertilizer, such as fish emulsion or blood meal, to correct it.

When the husks are bright green and the silks turn brown, your ears are ready to check. Feel the ears to ensure they're filled to the tips; you can even pull back the husk at the tip to check the kernels. If you can pinch the kernels and the juice is a milky color, the ear is ready to pick. For the best flavor, right after picking, remove the leaves and the silks and steam or boil the corn in water for about 5 minutes (for the whole pot); then chomp away for a true taste of summer.

Corn is notorious for attracting certain pests. Caterpillars such as the corn earworm and corn borer can devastate a patch, and animals such as raccoons and birds love sweet corn. Check Chapter 17 for tips on thwarting insects and animals that thrive in the corn patch.

Popcorn

Popcorn is an educational and tasty vegetable to grow. Sure it's easier to go to the local store and buy popcorn seed (kernels), but with unusual varieties and the opportunity to show your kids where popcorn really comes from, I think it's worth growing. If you can grow sweet corn, you can grow popcorn. Newer varieties have unusual-colored kernels that are good in crafts as well as in your tummy. However, they all still pop into white kernels. Some varieties to try are 'Robust 128YH', 'Tom Thumb', and 'Japanese Hulless'. All are 4- to 8-feet tall and need 85 to 120 days to mature.

The only difference between growing sweet corn and popcorn occurs at harvest time. Leave popcorn ears on the stalk until the stalks and husks are brown and dry. Before the first frost, harvest and strip away the husks. Hang the ears in mesh bags in a warm, airy, indoor location to continue drying for 4 to 6 weeks. Twist the kernels off the cob and store them in glass jars. You can do a sample pop to see if they're dry enough. You pop them as you would store-bought corn — but home-grown popcorn has a fresher taste. Your kids will never look at movie popcorn the same way.

A Variety of Other Great Vegetables

Whether you're interested in the tame or the exotic, the following sections give you information for growing a cornucopia of other great vegetables in your garden.

Arugula

Arugula (*Eruca vesicaria*) is also known as roquette or rocket salad. It's one of the main greens found in mesclun mixes (refer to Chapter 10 for more about mesclun). Arugula is one of the easiest, most cold-tolerant, and quickest-to-mature greens you can grow. The plant is small, with an *open habit* (it doesn't form a head-like lettuce), and its dark green leaves have a slight peppery and nutty flavor. Arugula adds an interesting zip to everyday salads and is a nice addition to soups and stir-fries.

Most gardeners buy arugula without a named variety. However, with its increased popularity, a number of named varieties are now available. 'Astro' is an early, heat-tolerant selection. 'Sylvetta', or wild arugula, is slower growing with smaller, more pungent leaves.

Arugula, like most greens, grows best in cool weather. When growing it, follow the guidelines for growing greens in Chapter 10. In mild-winter climates, you can plant arugula seeds in fall, winter, and spring. In cold-winter climates, start arugula in spring as soon as you can work the soil; take the summer off and then begin sowing again in fall. Arugula will overwinter in a cold frame very well — even in cold climates. (See Chapter 21 for more on cold frames.)

Seed small patches every 2 weeks, and in 30 to 40 days, you can harvest the 4- to 6-inch-long leaves. In the heat, arugula quickly *bolts* (forms a flower head with bitter leaves), but you can eat the flowers if you like a strong, peppery flavor. The only major pest to bother arugula is the flea beetle. Flip to Chapter 17 for tips on controlling this insect.

Asparagus

One of the joys of spring is picking fresh asparagus (*Asparagus officinalis*) spears from the garden. I give you the scoop on varieties and growing guidelines in the following sections.

Unlike most of the vegetables mentioned in this book, asparagus is a perennial plant: It comes back year after year from the *crown* (the short stem near the roots) and the roots. In fact, the crown actually expands with age, producing more spears each year. After the spring harvest, let the spears grow into towering ferns that feed the roots for next year's crop.

Varieties

Asparagus has male and female plants. Female plants produce spears that eventually grow to produce flowers and seeds that not only take extra energy to produce, reducing spear production, but also sow seeds that create a jungle of little asparagus plants. Unfortunately, these young seedlings aren't productive and are mostly just weeds. Male plants don't have flowers and seeds and are therefore more productive than the female plants.

Older varieties of asparagus such as 'Martha Washington', which has both male and female spears, were the standards for years. In the past 20 years, breeders have developed new varieties that are more productive and better adapted to tough soil conditions. Many of these varieties are in the "Jersey" series from a breeding program in New Jersey. These are touted as all-male varieties even though they may have a few female plants mixed in. These male varieties are superior for production and growth:

- ✔ 'Jersey Giant' is one of the first Jersey introductions. It's well adapted to most gardens, but it thrives in cool-temperature locations. It's disease resistant and frost tolerant.

- ✔ 'Jersey Knight' has high-quality spears produced on disease-resistant plants. It's particularly well adapted to growing in heavy soils.

- ✔ 'Jersey Supreme' is a new variety that matures earlier than the other Jersey series varieties. It's also higher yielding and has fewer female plants.

For a little extra color, try 'Purple Passion'. This variety produces sweet-tasting purple spears that turn green when cooked. For California and warm-weather gardeners, the University of California has a variety called 'UC 157' that was born and raised in warm soils and performs very well.

Growing guidelines

Asparagus crowns are generally available for purchase in late winter and spring at garden centers or through the mail. Because asparagus is a perennial, you need to pay particular attention to it when planting and take special care when preparing the planting site. You'll find it easier to amend the soil before planting rather than trying to alter it after you plant the crowns. To ensure planting success, follow these steps:

1. **Choose a location with full sun, and then pay special attention to removing all the weeds.**

2. **Dig a trench that's 1 foot deep and as long as you like.**

3. **Backfill the trench with 6 to 8 inches of finished compost and soil mixed together.**

4. **Using the added compost form volcano-like mounds (4 to 6 inches high) every 18 inches and lay the spiderlike crowns and roots of the asparagus on top of the mounds so the roots drape over the sides of the mounds and the crowns sit on top (see Figure 11-1).**

5. **Cover the crowns with soil and periodically backfill the trench as the asparagus spears grow, until the crowns are about 3 inches below the soil surface.**

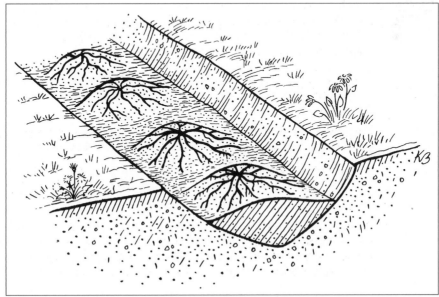

Figure 11-1:
Plant your asparagus crowns in trenches.

Keep the bed well watered, and fertilize each year with manure or a complete organic fertilizer such as 5-5-5 after harvest each year. Because asparagus is a perennial, you start harvesting in spring when the spears emerge and stop 6 to 8 weeks later. Here's how to handle the harvest in the first couple of years:

- ✔ **The first year:** Let all the spears grow into ferns.

- ✔ **The second year:** Harvest only those spears whose diameters are larger than a pencil; your harvest window is about 2 weeks in the spring. Snap off the spears by hand at the soil line when they're 6 to 8 inches tall.

- ✔ **The third year:** Begin harvesting only the pencil-diameter-sized spears for 4 to 6 weeks each spring. Stop after that and let the spears grow into ferns to replenish the crown and roots.

The ferns may be cut down after a hard frost in fall or winter. Weeds are the number-one downfall of most asparagus beds. If you keep the beds well weeded each year and use a light mulch, you'll lessen the chances of disease and insects reducing your yields.

If you've ever been served white asparagus tips in a restaurant and loved the flavor, you can easily grow your own. All you need to do is *blanch* the spears (block light from the plant, stopping chlorophyll from forming and leaving that part of the plant white) by covering the bed with black plastic after the spears begin to break ground. Check them every day or so and harvest as usual. The blanched spears are more tender and have a milder flavor.

Beets

Beets (*Beta vulgaris*) are best known for their deep-red-colored roots and sweet flavor. However, their leaves (called *greens*) also are very tasty and can be used as a substitute for Swiss chard or spinach (see Chapter 10 for more about these greens). Try slicing beet roots or greens in salads or cooking the roots in classic beet dishes such as *borscht* (beet soup). In the following sections, I describe different beet varieties to try and provide pointers on growing beets.

Varieties

Beets tend to mature about 50 to 65 days from seeding. Some good varieties to try are 'Red Ace', 'Detroit Dark Red', and 'Lutz Green Leaf'. For a long, thin, red root, try 'Cylindra' or 'Forono'. These varieties are consistent producers and widely adapted to various growing conditions.

If you're interested in beets of different colors, try growing white-fleshed 'Blankoma', which is very sweet. Or try yellow-fleshed 'Touchstone Gold' or red-and-white-striped 'Chioggia', which are sweet, too, but are mostly grown for their looks.

If you're mostly interested in beet greens, try 'Bull's Blood'. The blood-red leaves produce a baby beet. This variety is great in salads and beautiful in the garden.

Growing guidelines

Beets grow best in cool, moist conditions. Two weeks before the average date of your last frost, prepare a raised bed by working in a 2- to 3-inch layer of composted manure. Then sow seeds ½ inch deep and 2 inches apart. (Even though you eventually thin them to 4 inches apart, it's better to plant close in case the seeds don't geminate uniformly.) Cover the seeds with soil, and keep them well watered. Plant seeds again every 2 weeks into summer to ensure a continual supply of beets. (See Chapter 16 for more on this succession planting technique.)

Beet seeds are actually tiny dried up fruits with many seeds inside. For this reason, one seed produces many plants. These plants really need to be thinned early. After the seedlings stand 2 to 3 inches tall, thin them to 2 inches apart; thin the seedlings to 4 inches apart a month later. Because many beet plants grow in the same area, try snipping off the seedlings that you don't want with scissors instead of pulling them out and disturbing the roots. Use the thinned greens in salad mixes to add color and flavor. (Chapter 13 provides more information on thinning seedlings.)

Thinning root crops is essential if you want the roots to grow into beets, carrots, onions . . . whatever. If they don't have adequate space, you'll get a small vegetable or no vegetable forming in the roots.

Harvest the roots when they're golf-ball sized and the most tender. To see whether the beet is large enough to harvest, brush the soil off around the beet root; beets grow right at the surface of the soil, so it's easy to see the tops of the roots. But make sure you leave some beets, especially the 'Lutz Green Leaf' variety, to experience the cool weather that produces the sweetest fruits.

Broccoli raab

Broccoli raab is one vegetable that I had to include in this book. My mother loves it, and of course she's going to read this book, so I better write about it. Actually I love broccoli raab, too, not only for its quick and easy growing habit but also for the mustardy, broccoli taste of the greens. Unlike regular broccoli, you can eat the whole shoot of broccoli raab (*Brassica rapa*): stems, leaves, head, and all. It matures in about 40 days, so you can grow many crops throughout the year. If you still aren't convinced about growing and eating broccoli raab, come visit my momma, and we'll sit down to a plate of cavatelli and broccoli raab.

Varieties of broccoli raab come in two forms: spring raab and fall raab. 'Spring Raab' is a good spring and summer variety producing large plants that are slow to bolt. 'Sessantina Grossa' is a good fall variety with thick, tender shoots and fat buds. Choose the variety that corresponds to your planting season.

Like broccoli, broccoli raab grows best in cool weather. In mild-winter areas, you can plant it in fall, winter, and spring. In cold-winter areas, plant in spring and fall. Plant every few weeks to ensure a continuous supply of these tasty greens. Direct seed broccoli raab in the garden and grow it as you would broccoli (see Chapter 9). Just before the small head containing flower buds opens, clip the whole plant and sauté away.

Celeriac

If you like the flavor of celery but have a difficult time growing it, try celery's cousin, celeriac (*Apium graveolens*). Instead of growing an edible stem, celeriac grows a large, round, white-fleshed root. Once harvested, cleaned, and peeled, it reveals a creamy-white flesh with pure celery flavor. Celeriac tastes great in soups, stir-fries, and salads. Some of the newer varieties that produce consistently good-sized roots include 'Brilliant' and 'Diamant'.

Celeriac likes cool weather and needs a long growing season (100+ days) to mature. In cold-winter climates, start seeds indoors 8 to 12 weeks before your last frost date. In mild-winter climates, start seeds in early summer indoors, and then transplant the seedlings in late summer. Plant the seedlings 8 inches apart in raised beds, and amend the soil with plenty of compost. Keep the plants mulched with hay or straw and water them well, especially during hot spells. When the roots are about 2 to 3 inches in diameter, you can start harvesting. Pull the whole plant, discard the tops, and peel and chop the root.

The roots develop the best flavor when they're left in the garden until after a few frosts.

Celery

Celery (*Apium graveolens*), although found in so many dishes, is rarely grown by home gardeners. It can be a challenge to grow because the young plants can die easily and the stems often get stringy. However, growing celery can be very rewarding. You can use the leaves and stalks in soups or in raw vegetable dips. If you're growing celery for leaves and stalks, you usually won't get the seeds. Check out some celery varieties and growing guidelines in the following sections.

Varieties

Like celeriac, celery needs a long-growing season (120+ days). For some widely adapted varieties of celery, try 'Ventura', 'Utah 52-70 Improved', and 'Tango'.

For a uniquely colored type, try 'Golden Self-Blanching' or 'Giant Red Reselection'. These varieties produce either golden-yellow or red-colored stalks. Their flavor is more distinct than other varieties, but they aren't as mild as fully blanched varieties. These varieties make a great color addition to salads.

There's also a type of celery called "cutting celery" (*Apium graveolens*) that's grown for its leaves rather than its stems. This celery isn't common, but it's easier to grow than regular celery.

Growing guidelines

Celery grows best in areas with moderate summers or winters — it doesn't like extremes of heat or cold. Start celery seed indoors in winter in cold-winter areas and indoors in midsummer in mild-winter areas. Transplant the seedlings outdoors when they're 3 inches tall (about 10 weeks after seeding indoors), spacing them 6 inches apart.

Celery requires fertile soil and a constant water supply. Apply plenty of compost or a complete organic fertilizer, such as 5-5-5, at planting, and mulch the plants well. Side-dress bimonthly with the same fertilizers to ensure good-sized stalks (see Chapter 15 for more on side-dressing).

If temperatures get too cold (below 55 degrees) or too warm (above 80 degrees) for weeks, celery will suffer, causing the stalks to become tough and stringy. After 3 months or so, begin harvesting your celery stalks, either by pulling up the entire plant or just selecting outer stalks.

Gardeners may not know that the white stalks of celery are blanched. Home-grown, unblanched celery has a stronger flavor and better nutritional value than store-bought types, but if you like the white stalks, it's easy to blanch your celery, too. To blanch, place an empty metal can or milk carton with the ends removed over the stalks 10 days before harvesting. You don't need to cover the leaves.

Chinese cabbage

Chinese cabbage (*Brassica rapa*) combines the best of two worlds. It blends the mild, mustardy flavor of cabbage (see Chapter 9) with the texture of lettuce (see Chapter 10). Chinese cabbage tastes great in stir-fries, Asian soups, sukiyakis, and salads. It likes cool temperatures and is best grown as a fall or winter crop. Because it takes only 40 to 55 days to mature, it's easy to get a good crop of Chinese cabbage from your fall garden.

Chinese cabbage falls into two categories: heading and non-heading. The heading types can be tall and torpedo-shaped and called "Michihli," or they can be short and barrel-shaped and called "Napa." Some good Chinese cabbage varieties that mature in about 45 days include 'Jade Pagoda' and 'Monument' (which are both Michihli type) and 'Minuet' and 'China Express' (which are Napa type). (I discuss the non-heading types, known as pac choi, later in this chapter.)

In cold-winter areas, Chinese cabbage seed of the heading type is best sown indoors in spring for an early summer harvest or indoors in late summer for an early fall harvest. In warm-winter areas, sow the seed in late summer for a fall harvest. Transplant 6-week-old seedlings so they're spaced 1 foot apart, and fertilize them every 3 weeks with a complete fertilizer, such as 5-5-5. Mulch with hay or straw to keep the soil cool and moist. Start harvesting when the plants are 10 inches tall.

The biggest pest of heading-type Chinese cabbage is the flea beetle. You can read up on controlling these insects in Chapter 17.

Collards

Collards (*Brassica oleracea*) are an ancient cabbage-family crop that's a stalwart in many Southern gardens. Unlike cabbages, they don't form heads and can withstand heat and still grow well. The whole plant can be eaten at any stage, and the large, smooth oval leaves, in particular, taste great steamed or mixed in soups. Healthwise, they're one of the best greens you can eat; they're high in vitamin A, iron, and calcium. Some good varieties for production and vigor include 'Champion', 'Georgia', and 'Flash'.

Collards like cool weather and mature quickly within 60 to 80 days after seeding. Sow seeds directly in the garden 4 to 6 weeks before the last frost date for a spring harvest, and again in mid to late summer for a fall harvest. Thin the seedlings to 10 inches apart. Use the thinnings in soups and casseroles. Fertilize, water, and mulch collards as you would cabbage, which I discuss in detail in Chapter 9.

Endive

Endive (*Cichorium endivia*), a French cool-season green from the chicory family, has a reputation for being bitter, but if you grow it yourself, the flavor is mild, and the texture is crunchy. Endive is distinguished from its sister escarole (discussed in the following section) by its deeply cut and curled leaves. Both mature in 45 to 55 days. You'll find endive in many mesclun seed mixes (see Chapter 10 for more on mesclun) and blended with lettuce at restaurant salad bars. Some varieties to try are 'Rhodos', 'Galia', and 'Neos'.

Growing endive is similar to growing lettuce, and endive matures in the same time frame (see Chapter 10). As an added benefit, if you let the heads become large, the centers naturally blanch, resulting in tender, mild-flavored, creamy-white leaves. If the weather is heating up, harvest the greens young (when they're about 6 inches in diameter) before the flavor becomes bitter and the texture becomes tough.

Escarole

Escarole (*Cichorium endivia*) is endive's sister, with the only true distinguishing feature being the larger heads with broad, thin, smooth leaves of the escarole. It's grown like endive and has the same uses, but it's sweeter and crunchier than endive. Some Italian cooks, like my mom, use escarole in soups, creating a flavorful, sweet, and slightly bitter broth. Escarole also can be blanched by covering the leaves 5 days before harvest to create an even milder flavor and texture. Escarole matures in 45 to 50 days. A good variety to look for is 'Full Heart Batavian'. For growing instructions, see the previous section on endive.

Florence fennel

Florence fennel (*Foeniculum vulgare*) produces a bulging area at the stem near the soil line called a bulb (technically it isn't a bulb but an enlarged stem). There's also a leaf-type herb called sweet fennel that's grown for its ferny leaves and doesn't produce a bulb. If you like anise flavor, you'll love fennel.

This cool-season crop produces bulbs 80 days after sowing and can be grown as a spring or fall crop. The crunchy bulbs are great sliced in salads, marinated in oil and balsamic vinegar, grilled, or just eaten raw. (My fennel crop never makes it into the house because my daughter Elena likes to pick and eat it while wandering around the yard.)

Even though Florence fennel is grown mostly for its bulbs, you also can use its ferny leaves to add a licorice flavor to salads and casseroles. If you let the plant bolt, the flowers that form produce anise-flavored fennel seeds; you can then eat or cook with these great-tasting seeds. The flower heads also are beautiful in the garden and attract beneficial insects that can protect your plants from pests (more on that in Chapter 17). The best varieties are the newer ones, which are slower to bolt in the heat and more productive. 'Orion', 'Perfection', and 'Zefa Fino' are good choices.

Fennel likes cool weather to mature the largest and sweetest-tasting bulbs. Prepare the soil, fertilize, and water as you would for lettuce (see Chapter 10). Start fennel indoors in early spring for transplanting outdoors a month later, just before your last frost date. For fall planting, start seeds indoors in late summer. Space transplants 6 to 8 inches apart; harvest a few months later — when the fennel bulbs are 3 to 4 inches in diameter — by pulling the plants out of the ground, cleaning off the soil, and removing the roots and tops.

Garlic

If any vegetable has experienced a renaissance lately, it has to be garlic (*Allium sativum*). In recent history, garlic was poo-pooed as a low-class herb that needed to be masked on your breath, or you'd risk social embarrassment. Now it's the chic ingredient in many gourmet restaurants and touted as a major medicinal herb to cure everything from earaches to high cholesterol. Garlic also is a key ingredient in some insect and animal repellents and is very effective at repelling vampires (just kidding, I think). These uses come as no surprise to anyone who knows the history of garlic. It has been used medically for centuries, but only recently did people rediscover its benefits.

For some unknown reason, many also believe that garlic is difficult to grow. That isn't true. I describe some popular garlic varieties and explain how to grow garlic in the following sections.

Varieties

Even though you could grow your own garlic from bulbs bought in grocery stores, most of those varieties are adapted to a California climate. Unless you live in central California where most garlic is commercially grown, it's best to select varieties from catalogs and local garden centers.

The beauty of growing your own garlic is being able to sample the selection of varieties now available. Choosing the variety adapted for your area is the first step, but then you also can try varieties from around the world. The flavors of these different varieties can vary from mild to spicy hot.

Garlic comes in two basic types:

- ✔ **Softneck:** This type of garlic produces 12 to 18 cloves per bulb in several layers around a main stem. Softneck varieties tend not to produce a flower stalk and are the best types for long-term storage and *braiding* (twisting the garlic tops in a braid so they're easy to hang in the kitchen). Some varieties include 'New York White', 'Inchelium Red', 'Silverskin', and 'Early Red Italian'. 'Susanville' is a good variety for hot-summer areas.

✔ **Hardneck:** This type produces fewer cloves per stem than softneck garlic (6 to 12), but the cloves are larger. They grow in a single circle around a woody stem. The hardneck varieties also produce an attractive flower stalk called a *scape* that forms small bulblets at the end. The bulblets and scape are edible (see Figure 11-2). Hardneck varieties don't store as long as softneck varieties, but I've never had any trouble getting the bulbs to last through winter.

The hardneck group has more diversity in clove flavor and color. Varieties to try include 'German Extra Hardy', 'Russian Red', 'Ajo Roja', and 'Persian Star'. 'German Extra Hardy' is particularly cold hardy and good for severe-winter areas. 'Ajo Roja' is particularly well adapted to growing in California and the South.

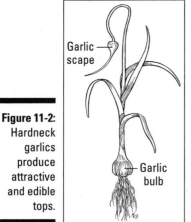

Garlic scape

Garlic bulb

Figure 11-2:
Hardneck garlics produce attractive and edible tops.

You may come across a third type of garlic that's more closely related to leeks than garlic. Called 'Elephant' garlic (*Allium ampeloprasum*), this type is grown like other garlics but isn't as winter hardy. 'Elephant' garlic plants produce huge white bulbs weighing up to a half pound, with large, easy-to-peel cloves. The flavor is milder than regular garlic, and you can store the bulbs for up to 1 year.

Growing guidelines

The key to a good crop of garlic is planting at the right time for your area. Garlic likes cool weather conditions and requires a long time to mature its bulbs. For gardeners in cold areas or areas with hot summers, fall is the best time to plant garlic. For gardeners with mild summers and winters, garlic also can be planted in spring.

Prepare the soil as you would for onions, forming raised beds and adding composted manures (see Chapter 6 for details on onions). Garlic needs well-drained soil — if the crop fails, it's usually due to the cloves rotting in wet, cool soil. Fertilize the beds as you would for onions.

Plant individual cloves a few inches deep and 3 to 4 inches apart about 4 to 6 weeks before the ground freezes for fall planting or as soon as the ground can be worked for spring planting. For fall planting in cold-winter areas, wait for a few hard freezes and then mulch the beds with a 2- to 4-inch-thick layer of hay or straw to protect the cloves over winter. As the cloves start growing in spring, remove the mulch. Once the soil warms, apply a side-dressing of a soluble high-nitrogen fertilizer, such as blood meal or fish emulsion (see Chapter 15 for more on side-dressing). In spring- or fall-sown beds, keep the patch well weeded and watered; you may want to mulch in between plants for weed control and moisture retention. Harvest starts when most of the leaves have yellowed, but before the cloves begin to separate from each other in the bulb.

After harvest, let the bulbs *cure* (toughen their skins) in a warm, dry, airy place for a few weeks. Then braid (just like you do hair) the softneck varieties or remove the tops of the hardneck bulbs, and store them in a cool, slightly damp basement for use as needed. The bulbs last longest in a slightly damp area, but you can store them in a cool, dry place — they just don't stay hard as long.

Garlic flavor is enhanced in storage; cloves often taste best after stored for a few months.

Globe artichokes

You don't have to live in California (the artichoke capital of the world) to grow globe artichokes, which are a thistle relative. Globe artichokes are beautiful, bushy perennial plants that produce baseball-sized, edible flower buds. I love eating them steamed and dipped in melted butter. They're a gourmet treat.

Globe artichokes are only hardy in warm climates, but you now can grow varieties that mature in one growing season (annuals), allowing northern gardeners a chance to grow and enjoy fresh "chokes" from the garden. Most varieties mature about 90 days from transplanting. 'Green Globe Improved' is a standard, widely adapted variety. 'Imperial Star' has been bred for annual production and is good for northern growers. 'Violetto' features violet-colored buds.

To plant globe artichokes, amend the soil with a 2-inch-thick layer of compost. Start transplants indoors from seed 6 to 8 weeks before setting outdoors. In mild-winter areas, set out transplants in fall to grow through winter and mature next spring. Everywhere else transplant seedlings in spring. In cold areas, the transplants need 10 days of temperatures between 32 degrees and 50 degrees to induce flower buds to form. Space plants in mild areas 6 to 8 feet apart. In cold areas, space them closer, at 2 to 3 feet apart. Keep the soil consistently moist, but not soggy.

Fertilize with an organic product such as 5-5-5 after harvest in mild areas. In cold areas, fertilize when planting in spring. Always keep plants well watered and mulched.

Harvest the buds with a sharp knife before they open. Plants grown as perennials will yield two crops (spring and fall) and up to 20 buds per plant. Annual plants yield 6 to 8 buds from midsummer to fall. Cut back perennial plant stalks to the ground in fall after harvest.

Gourds

Certain vegetables, such as gourds, are grown not for eating — because they taste like cardboard — but for crafts, decorations, and fun. Gourds are great to grow with kids because of all the fanciful creations they can make after the gourds are dried.

Gourds come in two general types:

- ✔ **Small-fruited gourds (_Cucurbita pepo_):** These come in a variety of shapes — egg, pear, apple, turban — mature in 96 days, and are used for decorating and crafts. Unlike large-fruited gourds, you don't have to follow special drying instructions; you can use small-fruited gourds right after harvest.

- ✔ **Large-fruited gourds:** These gourds are not only decorative but functional as well. Some examples of functional gourds are the birdhouse gourd (_Lagenaria siceraria_), dipper gourd (_Lagenaria siceraria_), and luffa gourd (_Luffa aegyptiaca_). In some countries these gourds are used for making musical instruments! Large-fruited gourds require longer growing seasons (140 to 150 days) than the small-fruited gourds, and you must follow special drying instructions before you can use them.

Most gourds are ornamental, but some can be eaten when young and have unique flavors. Asian gourds grow like cucumbers (see Chapter 8) and feature strong flavors that are often used in Indian, Chinese, and Southeast Asian soups and stews. Some types to try in your garden include the bitter gourd and calabash gourd.

Grow gourds as you would winter squash (see Chapter 8). The seeds have particularly thick skins, so nicking them with a file helps water penetrate them and hastens germination. Because gourds love to vine, consider growing them on a trellis or at the edge of your garden to roam the lawn. If you're growing large-fruited gourds in a cold-winter climate, start the plants indoors 4 weeks before the last frost date to get a jump on the season.

Wait until the fruit skins are hard and the stems are brown (but before a frost) to harvest. Large-fruited gourds can survive a light frost, but small-fruited ones can't. When harvesting, cut the vines, leaving 1 inch of stem on the fruit, and clean the skin.

Small-fruited gourds can be used as decorations immediately after harvest, but large-fruited gourds need to dry in a warm, dry, airy room for a few weeks. When you can shake the gourds and hear the seeds rattling around inside, they're ready to carve, paint, and decorate. If you want to accelerate the drying process, try drilling a hole in the bottom of the large-fruited gourd.

Horseradish

Of the few commonly grown perennial vegetables, horseradish is probably the easiest to grow. These roots are hardy in northern climates, last for years in your garden, and actually can become a nuisance as they spread over time. The spicy-sweet flavor of horseradish is a favorite condiment. It can be grated and combined with vinegar to make a condiment sauce, which can be stored for months in the refrigerator. A good variety to try is 'Bohemian'. It's hardy and produces high-quality roots a year after planting.

Choose a location for planting that has partial to full sun, and then amend the soil with compost, digging the soil deeply since these roots grow best in loose soil. Plant horseradish roots 3 inches deep and 12 inches apart in spring after danger of frost has passed.

In spring, fertilize the plants with compost and mulch with hay or straw to keep the soil weed free and moist. Then in the fall, dig up roots taking the largest (6- to 12-inches long) for eating and replanting smaller roots to grow new plants. Roots taste sweetest if harvested after a few frosts, but they may take two seasons to grow large enough to eat. The dark green leaves make an attractive ornamental. Mulch the plants after harvest for winter protection in cold areas.

Kale

If there's one vegetable to grow for purely the health benefits alone, kale (*Brassica oleracea*) is it. Kale offers the highest amount of protein, calcium, iron, vitamin A, and antioxidants (cancer-fighting compounds) of any cultivated vegetable. Luckily, it tastes good too! Lightly steamed or added to soups and casseroles, kale adds a crunch and a mild cabbage flavor to dishes.

Like its cousin, collards (which I describe earlier in this chapter), kale is technically a non-heading cabbage. It's grown like collards, matures in 50 to 60 days, but has smaller and more fringed leaves. Some new varieties with red and purple leaf coloration are now available. Just imagine: a vegetable that tastes good, is good for you, and looks good in the garden, too! Here are a few popular varieties:

- ✔ Some standard curly-leafed varieties are 'Siberian', 'Winterbor Hybrid', and 'Starbor Hybrid'.

- ✔ Some of the newer flat-leafed varieties are 'Red Russian', with oak-shaped, reddish-purple leaves, and 'White Russian', a white version of 'Red Russian'.

- ✔ For curly-leafed varieties with different colored leaves, try 'Lacinato' with curly, dark, blue-green leaves. It's often called dinosaur kale. 'Redbor Hybrid' has curly, reddish-purple leaves with deep purple veins. The color gets deeper as the weather cools.

Grow kale as you would collards, planting in late summer for a fall harvest. The flavor and sweetness of the leaves improve after exposure to near-freezing temperatures, so I often grow it as a fall crop by planting in late summer, picking and eating the plants into the winter.

Kohlrabi

Now here's something different: a vegetable that looks like a flying object from War of the Worlds. It's kohlrabi (*Brassica oleracea*), a cabbage relative that's also called a "stem turnip" because the stem near the soil line forms a round, turniplike globe, which you eat. Once you get over kohlrabi's odd appearance, you may be won over by its taste and crunchiness. Peeled and sliced, it's excellent in dips and stir-fries.

The plant is easy to grow and very hardy. Some standard varieties are 'Early White Vienna' and 'Kolibri', which has attractive purple skin and coloring in the leaves. If you fall in love with kohlrabi and can't get enough, try growing 'Superschmelz', a football-sized variety that stays tender and doesn't get woody (tough) even though it's large. The other varieties that I mention get woody if they grow too large or they're exposed to excessive heat.

Like all cabbage-family vegetables, kohlrabi likes cool weather. It's best grown as a spring or fall crop, avoiding the heat of summer that causes the globes to get woody. Start seeds indoors as you would broccoli and cabbage (see

Chapter 9), and kohlrabi will mature 50 to 60 days after transplanting in the garden. The fertilizing, watering, and pest control are similar for cabbages. Harvest the globes when they're about 2 to 3 inches in diameter (unless, of course, you're growing the football-sized variety).

Leeks

Leeks (*Allium ampeloprasum*) haven't received a lot of press in North America, but they're considered a staple in every vegetable garden in England and Europe. I love them because you transplant the seedlings in spring, as you would onions, keep them weed-free and watered, and then forget about the crop until fall. They grow slowly all summer, and by the time cool temperatures arrive, they've formed thick stalks that can be harvested and sautéed in butter or added to soups, such as potato-leek. The flavor is milder than that of onions and takes on a slightly sweeter flavor after a few cold nights.

Some leek varieties are very cold-tolerant, so you can harvest right through the winter in many areas. Varieties such as 'Bandit' are winter hardy and have attractive blue-green-colored foliage that makes leeks a beautiful ornamental as well. Some other good varieties to try are 'King Richard', 'Lancelot Hybrid', and 'Giant Musselburg'.

Leeks need a long season to mature — nearly 100 days for many varieties. For cold-winter areas, start seeds in early spring as you would for onions — about 8 to 12 weeks before your last frost date. For mild-winter areas, start seeds in late summer for a fall planting and winter harvest. Transplant the seedlings 6 inches apart into 6-inch-deep trenches filled halfway with compost. Fill in the rest of the trench with garden soil as the leeks grow.

Leeks are commonly purchased as plants, allowing you to skip the step of seeding them so early.

Like onions, leeks don't compete well with weeds, so be diligent about weeding. Water and fertilize as you would onions (see Chapter 6). When the stalks have thickened and after a few cool nights, begin harvesting. Certain hardy varieties such as 'Bandit' can withstand temperatures below 20 degrees and can be harvested and eaten all winter in mild-winter areas. Other varieties can be mulched with hay to allow you to keep harvesting into the winter, even in cold areas. Even if leeks freeze, they can still be eaten as long as they're cooked right away.

Hilling the stalks two to three times during the growing season will blanch the bottom of the stems white (see Chapter 6 for more on hilling). The flavor of the blanched stems is milder, and the texture is more tender than the green stems.

Mizuna

Mizuna (*Brassica rapa*) is a leafy-type, Oriental green that's often found in mesclun mixes. Mizuna has a small white stem and deeply cut leaves with a mild, mustardy flavor. 'Kyoto' is a deeply fringed, white-stemmed variety. A purple-fringed variety, 'Purple Mizuna', is now available as well.

Mizuna matures from direct seeding in about 40 days. As with lettuce, you can plant successive crops of mizuna to add zip to salads and stir-fries. It also can be cut and allowed to regrow many times. Treat it like any green (see Chapter 10) as far as seeding, watering, and fertilizing, and watch out for flea beetles eating the leaves.

Okra

Okra (*Ablemoschus esculentus*) is a classic southern vegetable that loves the heat. In fact, it's one of the few vegetables that keeps producing during the dog days of summer in the South. This tall (4 to 10 feet), stalky plant produces attractive, trumpetlike flowers along the main stem that mature into okra pods, making it a beautiful addition to a flower garden. Some varieties, such as 'Red Burgundy', have colorful leaves to boot! Each flower potentially produces one pod. The pods can be fried, pickled, baked, boiled, and eaten on their own or used in soups and stews such as gumbo. Some people don't like the sticky nature of the insides of the pod, but I love them broiled with a little oil.

The standard okra variety is 'Clemson Spineless', which matures in 60 days. But for gardeners with a short growing season, better choices are 'Annie Oakley II' and 'Cajun Delight Hybrid', which mature about 50 days from seeding.

'Little Lucy' is a small variety that has burgundy-colored leaves, pods, and stems and only grows 2 feet tall. The yellow flowers have red throats, making them a beautiful contrast to the red foliage. Because of its size, 'Little Lucy' is a great container plant.

Okra needs heat! Don't direct seed or transplant okra until the soil temperature is at least 65 degrees, usually in early summer. Start seeds indoors 4 to 6 weeks before your average last frost date. In cold-winter areas, lay black plastic mulch to preheat the soil and choose quick-maturing varieties. Thin plants to 1 to 2 feet apart. Fertilize at planting, again when the first pods form, and then finally in midsummer with compost or a complete organic fertilizer such as 5-5-5.

Use a knife to harvest the pods just above the *cap* (where the base of the pod attaches to the stem) when pods are 2 to 3 inches long and still tender. Check the plants every few days. The more you harvest, the more the plants will produce. Because okra seed doesn't save well, buy fresh seed every year.

Okra stems and leaves have spines that can irritate your skin. Wear gloves and long-sleeved shirts when working and harvesting in the okra patch.

Pac choi

No Oriental stir-fry is complete without some juicy, crunchy stalks of pac choi (*Brassica rapa*) tossed in. If you see the words bok choy, pac choi, and pak choi, they're all referring to the same vegetable. These greens feature sturdy, white, crunchy stalks and lush, large, green, flat leaves. They produce their vase-shaped, very open heads about 40 to 50 days after transplanting and, like other greens, love cool weather. Judging from their sweet, almost nutty taste, it's difficult to imagine that these plants belong to the cabbage family.

Two great varieties are 'Mei Qing Choi', a baby-size head that only reaches 6 to 8 inches tall, and 'Joi Choi', a standard 12- to 15-inch-tall head that tolerates hot and cold weather without bolting. 'Violetta' and 'Red Choi' are two varieties with attractive red coloring on their leaves.

To try your hand at pac choi, see the growing instructions for Chinese cabbage earlier in this chapter. Because it matures so quickly, pac choi can be succession planted in spring, summer, or fall in most areas (see Chapter 16 for details). However, avoid summer planting in hot climates.

Parsnips

Parsnip (*Pastinaca sativa*) is the quintessential fall root crop. I love to grow these white, carrotlike roots because, like gardeners, parsnips get sweeter with age.

As with leeks (which I discuss earlier in this chapter), you plant parsnip roots in spring and forget about them until fall. Then, after a few hard frosts, you're ready to start digging. The cold weather helps the carbohydrates in the roots turn to sugar, and boy do they get sweet! But don't yank them all in fall. In all but the extremely cold areas of the United States, parsnips can be harvested all winter right into spring (as long as the ground hasn't frozen) for a sweet spring treat. Some standard varieties to try are 'Cobham Improved Marrow', 'Harris Model', and 'Andover'.

Parsnips take a long time to germinate and mature. Most varieties take 2 weeks or more to germinate and 100 to 120 days to produce roots. Luckily, they grow well in cold weather. Grow parsnips as you would carrots (see Chapter 6), but with one exception: When planting, place pairs of seeds in small holes that are ½ inch deep and spaced 1 inch apart, and then fill the holes with potting soil. Because parsnips may not germinate well, the second seed ensures a better germination rate. When the seedlings are 3 to 4 inches tall, thin them to one seedling per hole.

When growing root crops, especially parsnips, don't spread high-nitrogen fertilizer on the beds before planting. Soils rich in nitrogen produce hairy, forked roots.

Peanuts

The peanut is a crop you can grow that will taste good and amaze your kids (who may have thought that peanuts only grew in ball parks and circuses). The peanut (*Arachis hypogaea*), a warm-season crop, isn't really a nut; it's actually a legume similar to peas and beans. They grow where okra and sweet potatoes thrive. They like heat and a long growing season. However, even gardeners in cold areas can have some success with peanuts, provided they start early and choose short-season varieties such as 'Early Spanish'.

Unless you grow a field of peanuts, you probably won't get enough to make a year's supply of peanut butter, but boiled in salt water, roasted, or eaten green, fresh peanuts are a tasty and healthy snack food. (I still remember when my daughter Elena and I ate almost nothing but hot, boiled peanuts on a vacation in Georgia one winter.) Some other varieties that have big pods and more seeds per pod include 'Tennessee Red Valencia' and 'Virginia Jumbo'. They all need 100 to 120 days of warm weather to mature.

There are actually four different types of peanuts (runner, Virginia, Spanish, and Valencia). The first two are runner types with 2 large seeds per pod. The second two are bush types with 2 to 6 seeds per pod. Growing techniques are the same for each type.

Peanuts like well-drained soil and can tolerate some drought. Plant the seeds, with the shells removed, directly in the soil after all danger of frost has passed. Space plants 1 foot apart in rows 2 to 3 feet apart. The young plant looks like a bush clover plant. Fertilize and water the plants as you would beans (see Chapter 7), but side-dress with 5-5-5 organic fertilizer when flowers appear to help with the nut formation. Yellow flowers appear within 6 weeks after planting. Hill the plants to kill weeds (see Chapter 6 for more on hilling), mulch with straw, and then watch in amazement as the fun part begins.

After the flowers wither, stalklike pegs emerge from the flowers and curve downward, eventually drilling 3 inches into the soil (see Figure 11-3). At the ends of these pegs, peanut shells containing the peanuts form. When the plants start yellowing, the peanuts growing underground are mature and ready to harvest. Pull the whole plant up and dry it in a warm, airy place out of direct sun; then crack open the peanut shells for a tasty treat. Most kids are fascinated by things that grow underground, and peanuts are pretty amazing in their own right, so watch your kids get wide-eyed at this underground treasure.

Figure 11-3:
Peanut flowers produce stalklike pegs that curve under-ground.

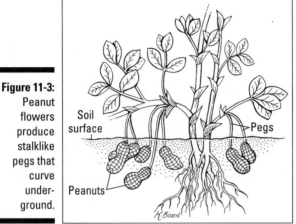

Radicchio

Radicchio (*Cichorum intybus*) is a type of leaf chicory that can be eaten as a lettuce or allowed to form a small, red, cabbagelike head. It's the latter form that people are most familiar with in salad bars and restaurants. The heads form white veins and grow to the size of grapefruits. Radicchio has a slightly bitter, tart, and tangy flavor and adds culinary and visual pizazz to salads.

For some home gardeners, radicchio isn't the easiest crop to grow, because it often doesn't form heads. Radicchio likes it cool, and it sometimes grows best in spring and sometimes in fall, depending on the variety. The following four modern varieties more consistently form heads than older varieties: 'Palla Rossa', 'Chioggia Red Preco No. 1', 'Early Treviso', and 'Indigo Hybrid'. The latter two varieties are good fall and winter selections. If you grow these four varieties at the right time, they should form heads.

In cold-winter climates, start radicchio indoors, similar to lettuce transplants, and grow it as a spring or fall crop. In mild-winter climates, it's best grown as a fall crop. Grow radicchio as you would lettuce (see Chapter 10). Most modern varieties, including those previously mentioned, form heads on their own (without being cut back) 80 to 90 days from seeding. Harvest the heads when they're solid, like small cabbages. The heads are crunchy, colorful, and good for cooking.

If plants don't start forming heads about 50 days after setting them out in the garden, cut the plants back to within 1 inch of the ground and enjoy the lettucelike greens. The new sprouts that grow will form heads.

Radishes

If you're looking for quick satisfaction, grow radishes (*Raphanus sativus*). The seeds germinate within days of planting, and most varieties mature their tasty roots within 30 days. Daikon, Spanish, Chinese, and rat-tail radishes take 50 days to mature. When grown in cool weather and not stressed, radishes will have a juicy, slightly hot flavor. Of course, anyone who's grown radishes knows that if radishes are stressed by lack of water, too much heat, or competition from weeds or each other, you end up with a fire-breathing dragon that people won't tolerate. I list some popular varieties and provide tips for growing radishes in the following sections.

Varieties

Most gardeners are familiar with the spring-planted red globes or white elongated roots found in grocery stores, but exotic-looking international radishes are now showing up in specialty food stores and restaurants. These radishes require a longer season and are often planted to mature in fall or winter. (They're often called *winter radishes* for that reason.) Here are some you can try:

- ✔ Japanese radishes called *daikons* can grow up to 2-foot-long white roots.
- ✔ Spicy-hot Spanish black radishes look like round black balls or cylinders and can be kept in a root cellar for 6 months.
- ✔ Chinese radishes look like turnips but are red, green, or white on the inside. They taste similar to the Japanese radishes.
- ✔ Rat-tail radishes are grown for the spicy-tasting seed pods that form after flowering.

The following varieties work well for the beginning gardener:

- ✔ For the classic red or white round radishes, try 'Cherriette Hybrid', 'Easter Egg II' (a mix of red and white), and 'Amethyst' (purple skin, white flesh).

- ✔ For the elongated white or red roots, try 'French Breakfast' (a mix of red and white), 'White Icicle', or 'D'Avignon' (the top of the root is red and the bottom is white).

- ✔ For daikons, try 'Minowase Summer Cross #3', 'Miyashige', and 'April Cross'.

- ✔ Some good black Spanish radish varieties are 'Nero Tondo' (round shape) and 'Long Black Spanish'.

- ✔ Some Chinese varieties are 'Red Meat' (green outside, red inside), 'China Rose' (red outside and red inside), and 'Misato Green' (green all the way through).

Growing guidelines

The round or elongated "traditional" radishes are normally planted in early spring to mature while the temperatures are still cool. Daikons can be planted in spring or summer, depending on the variety. Chinese and black radishes, however, are best planted in late summer or early fall for a fall or winter harvest. Rat-tail radishes are planted in spring.

For all types of radishes, form raised beds, fertilize, and sow both spring and fall plantings as you would carrots (see Chapter 6). The keys to success with any radish crop are loosening the soil well, weeding, thinning the plants to give the roots enough room to expand (usually 6 inches apart), keeping the plants well watered, and growing them when it's cool.

You can harvest spring-planted radish roots as soon as they start to form. Harvest daikon, Chinese, and black radishes when you need them (although they're most tender when eaten on the small side); they can withstand light frosts in the fall. Harvest rat-tail radish pods once they form.

Rhubarb

Rhubarb (*Rheum rhubarbarum*), like asparagus and horseradish, is an exception in the vegetable world. It's a perennial plant (except in zones 8 and warmer, where it's treated as an annual), so once established, it will come back faithfully year after year. It will even spread, allowing you to dig, divide, and share plants with friends. Hopefully, you have many friends, because you'll only need a few healthy rhubarb plants to produce plenty for pies, jams, and jellies.

Nothing tastes better than a fresh heirloom tomato picked from a plant you've grown yourself. Chapter 4 has information on growing your own tomatoes.

Many hot pepper varieties are as beautiful as they are tasty. They produce a range of colorful fruits that pack a spicy punch. See Chapter 5 for more on hot peppers.

Eggplant varieties come in a number of different colors, such as this striped heirloom. Check out Chapter 5 for more information on eggplants.

Carrots aren't always orange. You can grow carrots in a rainbow of colors such as purple, yellow, and red. Chapter 6 has details on growing carrots.

When your onions' tops fall over, it's time to harvest! See Chapter 6 for more on growing onions.

You can grow more than just white potatoes. Varieties with red, yellow, and purple flesh make for a colorful potato salad. Flip to Chapter 6 for more on potato varieties.

Three different types of peas exist: English, snap, and snow. All of them grow well in cool temperatures. See Chapter 7 for more on growing peas.

Pole beans need support to grow their best; bamboo poles formed into teepees work well. Chapter 7 has the scoop on all kinds of beans.

Most cucumber varieties have separate male and female flowers; bees need to pollinate the flowers in order for cucumbers to grow. Find out more about cucumbers in Chapter 8.

Watermelons have vigorous vines. One way to grow them in a small garden is to trellis the vines and support the hanging fruits. Check out Chapter 8 to discover different ways to grow watermelons.

Winter squash and pumpkins (which are actually a type of winter squash) can be stored indoors into the winter. Chapter 8 has information on growing winter squash and pumpkins.

Summer squash plants are naturally prolific. Usually you need only a few plants to have plenty of squash all summer long for a family of four. See Chapter 8 for tips on growing squash.

The heads of some cauliflower varieties need to be covered to keep them white. Chapter 9 describes how to grow cauliflower.

Ornamental cabbages make an attractive display in fall, and yes, they're edible too. See Chapter 9 for information on cabbages.

Broccoli is a cool-season crop that produces one main head and multiple side shoots throughout the summer. Flip to Chapter 9 for more information on growing broccoli.

Although they look odd, Brussels sprouts are a tasty fall crop. The small sprouts form along the stem and can be harvested right into winter. See Chapter 9 for more on growing Brussels sprouts.

Swiss chard, kale, and other greens are some of the easiest vegetables to grow in your garden. Plus, they're loaded with nutrients. See Chapter 10 for ways to grow greens.

Many different varieties of sweet corn are available for the home gardener. By planting early-season, mid-season, and late-season varieties, you can harvest sweet corn from your garden for weeks. See Chapter 11 for more on growing sweet corn and a variety of unusual vegetables.

...sil is not only a great ... to grow for making ...sto and cooking, but ...me varieties are also ...beautiful, producing ...le-tinged leaves and ...s. See Chapter 12 for ...re on growing herbs.

Plant blueberries rather than traditional ornamental shrubs around your home. The bushes have beautiful summer and fall foliage, and they produce an abundance of tasty fruits. See Chapter 12 for more on growing berries in your yard.

...vender is an edible flower and a ...example of an edible landscape ...t. See Chapter 12 for information on edible landscaping.

Soil in raised beds warms up and dries out faster in the spring. It also stays less compacted so plant roots can grow more freely. See Chapter 3 for more on raised beds.

Pathways in a vegetable garden can be made from materials as simple as hay, bark mulch, or straw, or as elaborate as bricks and pavers. See Chapter 3 for more on garden pathways.

A self-watering container has a reservoir in the bottom of the pot; the water naturally wicks into dry soil so you don't have to water as often. See Chapter 18 for more on container gardening.

The part of the rhubarb plant you eat is the leaf stalk that grows from the crown of the plant. Don't eat the leaf itself, unless you want an upset stomach.

Depending on the variety, the stalks are green or red and taste sour. The most tender varieties have leaf stalks that are red all the way through, such as 'Chipman' and 'Valentine'. Because of its tart taste, rhubarb usually isn't eaten raw (even though I have fond memories of eating rhubarb as a child by dipping the stalks in a bowl of sugar!). It's best used as an ingredient in cooking. Can't you just smell that strawberry-rhubarb pie fresh from the oven?

Rhubarb is one of those "plant and forget" crops. It's a perennial, like asparagus, so it comes back year after year. If it has full sun, well-drained soil, water, and lots of compost and manure mixed in, it will grow like a weed. Rhubarb does best in cool climates, so gardeners in Florida and Arizona may have to rely on their northern friends for fresh rhubarb. You also can buy plants from a local garden center or online.

For best quality, harvest the leaf stalks as soon as the leaves completely unfold to a flat surface. Always leave at least two leaf stalks per plant so the plant can rejuvenate itself. If a seed stalk forms (usually from the center of the plant), cut it off to extend the leaf-stalk harvesting season. The plants die back in fall, but they reemerge in spring from the roots.

Rhubarb is easy to dig and divide. In spring, just as the new shoots are starting to emerge, dig up the whole plant with a sharp spade and divide the main crown into many 3- to 4-inch-diameter sections. Plant these sections; within 2 to 3 years, you can harvest from these new plants.

Rutabagas

Probably the only time anyone thinks of rutabagas (*Brassica napus*), if at all, is Thanksgiving, when they're traditionally served with turkey, stuffing, and all the trimmings. They also can be boiled, mashed, or used in hearty winter soups.

This Old World root crop is easy to grow, and any gardener can have a small patch to satisfy all her fall and winter rutabaga desires (once she knows enough about rutabagas to desire them). The flavor and growth are similar to those of turnips (which I cover later in this chapter). In fact, another name for the rutabaga is Swedish turnip, or "Swede" for short. Because the rutabaga is actually a cross between a cabbage and a turnip, if you like either of those vegetables, you may want to give rutabaga a try. The roots have either yellow or white flesh, depending on the variety.

Like turnips, rutabagas love cool weather, and you can eat the lush greens as well as the root. A few varieties to try are 'American Purple Top' (yellow flesh), 'Laurentian' (yellow flesh), and 'Gilfeather' (white flesh).

Grow rutabagas the same way that you grow turnips, except rutabagas need about 100 days to mature from direct sowing; turnips mature in half that time. Rutabagas love the cold, and the roots can get as large as softballs and still remain tender. Leave them in the ground until just before the ground freezes; then harvest them as you need them. The longer rutabagas are in the ground, the sweeter they'll taste.

Shallots

If you like the taste of onions or garlic but have a hard time getting them to grow, consider growing shallots (*Allium cepa*). They look like small onions, but their flavor is milder than any of their *allium* cousins — and growing them is a snap.

Shallots are an indispensable part of many French dishes. Substitute three to four shallots for each onion in recipes. Minced, they can be sautéed in wine and herb butter or used in a béarnaise sauce (ooh-la-la). A little candlelight, a little champagne, and voilà: Shallots become romantic.

Varieties include the traditional 'Gray' shallots with a yellow/gray skin and white, creamy-colored flesh, and red shallots such as 'French Red' with red skin and pink flesh. Shallots are usually purchased as sets (similar to onion sets), but recently shallot seeds have become available in many varieties such as 'Pikant' and 'Ambition', allowing you to grow more shallots at a lower cost.

Plant shallot seed or sets as you would onion seed or sets (Chapter 6). They can be grown in spring or fall and will overwinter in all but the coldest winter climates. They require the same fertility and growing conditions as onions. About 90 days after planting in the garden, the tops will brown and die. Notice that 1 bulb sprouts 4 to 5 side bulbs around it. Separate the side bulbs and dry and store these as you would onions.

Save some of the largest shallots for a fall or spring planting, and you'll never have to buy shallots again — that is, if you can resist eating them all.

Sunflowers

Sunflowers (*Helianthus annuus*) are all the rage as cut flowers in floral shops. To meet the need, breeders have created varieties with colored heads ranging from red to white and plants that are 2 feet tall to 10 feet tall. Because this book is concerned with things you eat, I focus on the giant snack varieties of sunflowers. Technically, all sunflowers can be eaten, but the snack varieties produce the largest heads containing the meatiest seeds.

Not only are the seeds good human food, but the birds love them, too. Why not store some seeds for your feathered friends this winter? Some of the best snacking varieties for both people and birds are 'Mammoth' and 'Grey Striped'.

This may sound obvious, but sunflowers really do like the sun. As a matter of fact, the more sun, the better. Plant seeds in well-drained soil, 10 to 18 inches apart in rows, after all danger of frost has passed. To get a jump on the season, you can start them indoors 4 to 6 weeks before your last frost date. The eating varieties tend to produce a large, yellow-petaled head on a thick stalk with large, hairy leaves. Many of these plants can be huge (sometimes as tall as 15 feet), so the plant needs adequate fertility to grow and produce the best seeds. Before planting, amend the soil with plenty of compost or manure, and side-dress monthly with a complete organic fertilizer such as 5-5-5 (see Chapter 15 for details on side-dressing). In about 80 days, the heads will open.

Sunflowers don't like company. Their roots exude a chemical into the soil that inhibits the growth of other plants in the area. Therefore, plant sunflowers in their own section, against a fence, or as a background in your garden.

Once the sunflower head opens, you'll have to be quick to get the seeds before the birds do. A simple technique is to cover the heads with a paper bag until the petals naturally wilt and the seeds mature. When you can rub off the seeds with your hand, cut off the head, remove the seeds, and dry them. Lightly roasted, sunflower seeds are a great snack food for kids and grown-ups, and you can save some raw seeds for your bird feeder.

Most people are familiar with eating sunflower seeds, but did you know that you can actually eat the unopened flower bud? To do so, cut the flower bud a few inches from the head with a sharp knife. When steamed and dipped in butter, it tastes like a globe artichoke. Who would've thunk it!

Turnips

All right, turnips (*Brassica rapa*) aren't exactly America's favorite vegetable, but I think they've been given a bad rap. Turnips are easy to grow, and you can eat the greens as well as the roots. If grown in cool weather, they have a slightly sweet flavor.

Like rutabagas (which I describe earlier in this chapter), turnips can be eaten boiled, mashed, or added to soups and stews. I've even eaten young roots raw like an apple. Just peel away the outer skin and crunch down. It's juicy and refreshing!

The white or white-and-purple roots are smaller than rutabagas (tennis-ball size) and mature quicker (in less than 50 days from seeding). The greens are great steamed, and they walk hand in hand with collard greens as the favorite Southern leafy crop. Some varieties to try are 'Purple Top White Globe', 'Shogoin', and 'Tokyo Cross'. The latter two produce excellent, mild-tasting greens.

Turnips love cool weather. In most areas, you can grow spring and fall crops. Here's how:

- ✔ Start in spring a few weeks before your last frost date.
- ✔ In early fall, wait until the hot summer weather has passed before planting.

Turnips are best directly seeded in the garden. Prepare the soil and fertilize as you would for any root crop (see Chapter 6). If you want roots, thin the young seedlings to 4 inches apart. If you're growing them for greens only, don't bother thinning them; just start clipping when the greens are 4 to 6 inches tall. Keep the plants well watered and mulched with hay or straw, which, in addition to holding in moisture and controlling weeds, helps prevent the roots from developing a strong flavor. Begin harvesting when the roots are 3 to 4 inches in diameter. Turnips can take a frost, so you can harvest right into winter until the ground freezes.

Chapter 12

Growing Berries and Herbs for an Edible Landscape

In This Chapter

▶ Growing berries and other fruits in your edible landscape

▶ Planting, harvesting, and preserving herbs

▶ Discovering flowers that you can eat

*I*n previous chapters, I mostly talk about your vegetable garden as a separate entity in the yard. That setup is great, especially if you're trying to grow lots of vegetables to reduce your food costs. However, another way to grow vegetables, and any other food crops for that matter, is to integrate them into your existing landscape. This is called *edible landscaping*. The concept is simple: Instead of planting an ornamental shrub, tree, or flower, why not grow a similar, attractive vegetable, fruit, or herb that can double as a food crop?

With concerns about carbon footprints, pollution, food safety, and energy consumption, many gardeners across the country are ripping out their lawns and creating edible landscapes that are both beautiful and functional. My front yard is made up of all fruits, veggies, and herbs. I love to look at it *and* eat from it.

Many vegetables such as kale, Swiss chard, eggplant, and okra are beautiful plants in their own right. They deserve places in both the flower garden as well as the vegetable garden. Start looking at your vegetables from a different viewpoint, and you'll see the beauty of their flowers, leaves, and shapes. But why stop with veggies in an edible landscape? You may want to grow other foods as well. For example, in this chapter, I describe some favorite fruits, herbs, and edible flowers that you can grow in place of ornamentals in your yard; see Chapter 3 for a sample edible landscape design.

When substituting an edible for an ornamental, the rules of selection remain the same as with any plant: Pick an edible plant that suits the growing conditions in the yard with respect to sun, soil, and climate (see Chapter 3 for details). Also, select an edible plant that grows to the proper size for the spot. For example, instead of a burning bush grow a blueberry bush. The size and shape of the shrub are similar, and it has great fall foliage color like a burning bush. However, the blueberry yields mouthwatering fruits, too.

Sweetening Your Landscape with Berries and Fruits

Many gardeners avoid planting fruits in the yard because they think that growing them is complicated. Actually, it isn't difficult at all. If you select the right fruits and varieties for your location and climate, these plants can be low maintenance and very rewarding to grow. In the following sections, I describe several popular berry types and other unusual fruits that work well in edible landscapes.

Strawberries

Strawberry plants have a nice compact habit that fits perfectly into a raised bed like you use for vegetables. You can grow these perennials in a bed along the house, in the front of a flower garden, or in a container. They're also a fast crop that provides a delicious harvest within a year of planting. And because you should replant the plantings every few years (they develop diseases or become unproductive if you don't), you can move strawberry plants around if you want.

Space the plants 12 to 18 inches apart in full sun and keep them well watered. Strawberries spread by sending out little runners that end with new baby plants. After these young plants have formed obvious roots, usually in a few weeks, cut the runners and move these young plants around to start new beds. It's important to thin the plants so the young plants don't fill in around the older plants and crowd them (refer to Chapter 13 for details on thinning). Make sure to plant varieties adapted to your area, and mulch heavily in cold-winter areas.

While most strawberry varieties are called *June-bearing* because they bear fruit in early summer, some newer varieties are *day-neutral* or *everbearing* (they produce fruit throughout the summer). One of my favorite everbearing varieties is the alpine strawberry. These berries don't produce runners; they stay compact and bushy and produce small, sweet berries from summer until frost. They're great for eating out of hand or tossing on cereal in the morning. These small plants make excellent container plants and often are planted in a *strawberry barrel* (a container with holes on the side for growing strawberry plants).

Blueberries

I don't know why more people don't grow blueberries. What's not to like? They thrive in full sun and grow on handsome, perennial shrubs that range in height from 2 to 6 feet, depending on the type that you grow. You can choose from *low-bush* (1 to 2 feet tall), *half-high* (2 to 4 feet tall), and *high-bush* varieties (5 to 6 feet tall) that can fit into many locations in your yard. They have pretty white flowers followed by large clusters of tasty, blue fruit. Berries appear the second year after planting. The attractive green leaves turn bright shades of red, orange, and yellow before dropping in the fall. Blueberries make an excellent foundation plant grown up against the house or grouped to form a hedge between properties.

Blueberries must be grown in acidic soil (with a pH level between 4.5 and 5.5), so if you don't have that kind of soil, you need to make some adjustments. Amending your soil with a lot of peat moss and some sulfur is one easy way to lower the soil pH; see Chapter 14 for more on soil pH and amending your soil.

Plant at least two different blueberry varieties to ensure good pollination and fruit set. Variety selection is the key to success. Blueberries grow best in areas with cold winters and mild summers. In hot-summer areas of the South, grow blueberry types that are adapted to the heat, such as Southern blueberries or rabbit-eye blueberries. In cooler climates, all other blueberry types are fine to plant.

Blackberries and raspberries

If you're looking for an edible plant to double as a barrier for animals and people, grow some blackberry or raspberry brambles. Both are fast–growing, thorny plants. They grow to 6 feet tall and spread wildly from *suckers* (new shoots) off their roots. If you don't watch out, the plants can easily get out of control. However, if you train them to a sturdy trellis and are diligent about pruning them, blackberries and raspberries can be very productive, hedgelike plantings.

In the first year, most blackberry and raspberry canes (shoots) produce only leaves; they bear fruit in the second year (see Figure 12-1). Plant brambles in spring, spacing the plants 1 foot apart in rows in well-drained soil in a partly-to-mostly-sunny location. Amend the soil with compost and mulch yearly with hay or straw. Bramble roots love it cool and moist, but not too wet.

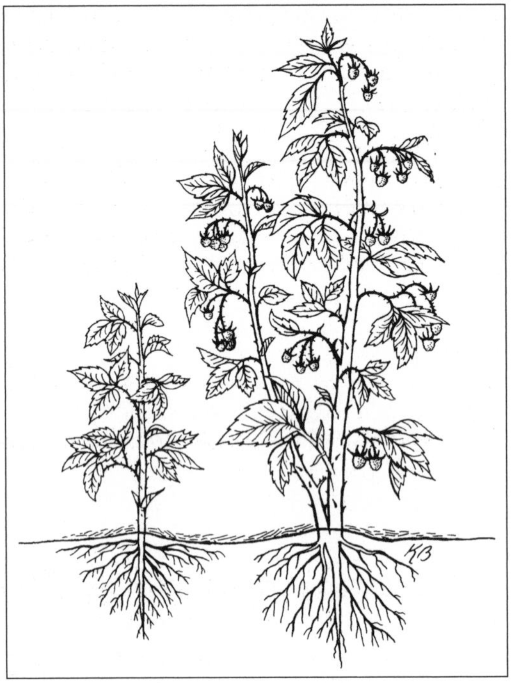

Figure 12-1:
For most varieties, first-year blackberry and rasp-berry canes produce just leaves, while second-year canes produce fruit.

Even though most blackberry and raspberry varieties produce only one crop a year like strawberries, everbearing varieties produce a summer and fall crop of delicious fruits. Choose varieties that are adapted to your area and that produce the colored berries you want. Raspberries come in varieties that produce red-, yellow-, black-, and purple-colored fruits. Blackberries come in black-colored fruit only, but you also can find varieties without thorns.

Unusual fruits

The berries in the previous sections are the most popular fruits grown in edible landscapes, but you also can get a little wild and try other unusual fruits, too. You can experiment with a wealth of exotic fruits from around the world that may grow well in your edible landscape. Expand your taste horizons and try some exotic-flavored fruits. At the very least, they'll be a conversation piece! Here are a few examples:

- **Gooseberries:** These woody shrubs grow 2- to 4-feet tall and wide. They're widely adapted and produce green or red, round juicy fruits that are great eaten fresh or made into pies and preserves.

- **Currants:** These bushes, which are a size similar to gooseberry bushes, produce small red, white, or black berries depending on the variety.

The fruits are juicy and tart, so they're primarily used for preserves, pies, and juices. In fact, currant juice is touted as an elixir that's high in health-promoting antioxidants. (Chapter 2 has more on the health benefits of fruits and vegetables.) Like blueberries, these shrubs bear fruit the second year after planting.

✔ **Dwarf fruit trees:** While berry crops are the easiest to grow, don't shy away from trying a dwarf apple or cherry tree, too. Tree fruits definitely require more study, but many new varieties are disease resistant and dwarf, making them perfect additions to an edible landscape. Fruit trees generally produce fruit a few years after planting, depending on the type you're growing.

Some other unusual fruits to try depending on your sense of adventure and climate are figs, citrus, cranberry, elderberry, lingonberry, kiwi, and banana. For more information on where to find some unusual fruits for your landscape, flip to the appendix.

Spicing Up Your Landscape with Herbs

How could you plant a vegetable garden without herbs? My mamma's pasta sauce wouldn't taste half as good without fresh basil, oregano, and thyme from the garden; my burritos wouldn't pop with flavor without fresh cilantro. Herbs are easy to grow and take up little space, and many have attractive foliage and flowers — the perfect edible landscape plant. Even if you don't use all the herbs fresh, you can add them to vinegar and oils, or dry them for future use (see the nearby sidebar for details).

I like to plant herbs close to the house for easy access when I'm cooking. The best place for herbs that you often need for cooking is in a container on a deck or patio. Most herbs are compact enough to grow well in containers, yet still give you the yields for fresh eating.

Many herbs produce attractive flowers that bees and other pollinating insects love. A healthy garden should be a-buzz with bee activity, and herbs help keep our insect friends happy. I mix herbs in the vegetable garden, around flowers, and in containers. Creeping herbs, like thyme and oregano, grow great in windowboxes and containers. Taller herbs, like rosemary and basil, make beautiful additions to a flower garden.

While herbs vary in their flavors, smells, and growth habits, most require the same growing conditions: a minimum of 6 hours of sunlight per day, excellent soil drainage, and moderately rich, loose soil. If you don't have fertile soil, a simple addition of compost in spring is probably enough in most cases. Too much fertilizer makes for a bushy plant that doesn't produce the proper amount of essential oils and flavor. And that's what you want from your herbs — great flavor.

Harvesting and drying herbs

Most plants benefit from being cut back, so I suggest that you harvest herbs throughout the growing season. The best time to harvest herb leaves is just as the plants begin to set flower buds — the time when they have their maximum flavor and fragrance.

Cut herbs in the morning when the dew has dried but before the sun is very bright, because many herb oils in the leaves *volatilize* (evaporate) into the air in the heat of the day. After cutting them, wash the herbs, pat them dry, and hang or lay them in a warm, well-ventilated place that's out of direct sunlight until they're dried (about 1 week). Label and store the herbs in sealed glass or plastic containers out of direct sunlight.

To freeze herbs, wash and pat them dry, and then chop them by hand or in a food processor. Place the chopped herbs in labeled plastic containers and then freeze them. A quick and easy way to freeze herbs is to add a bit of water (enough to make the mixture soupy) to the herbs in the food processor and then pour the mixture into ice cube trays and freeze. When you need herbs for stew, soups, or sauces, just pop in an herb cube.

The following sections take an alphabetical look at my favorite herbs.

Basil

My mother would kick me out of the family if I didn't talk about one of the classic Italian herbs: basil (*Ocimum basilicum* and other species). She's 85 years old and doesn't vegetable garden any longer, except for the pot of basil on the back deck. She and I can't live without it!

While the 'Genovese' or Italian basil is essential for tomato sauces and pesto, you also can choose from varieties with different tastes for Greek, Thai, Indian, and Chinese cooking (among other cuisines). You can grow basil with flavors such as licorice, lemon, lime, and cinnamon. Plus, these annual plants grow 6 to 18 inches tall depending on the variety, making them perfect container plants. Some varieties have gorgeous all-purple leaves or purple and green leaves with ruffles, making this an attractive plant in the garden.

Even though you can't plant basil until after the last frost date (check the appendix for the last date in your area), it produces abundantly in the heat of the summer. Start basil seeds indoors about 6 weeks before the last frost date or sow the seeds directly in your garden (¼-inch deep) after the last frost date when the soil is at least 60 degrees Fahrenheit. In addition to seeds, most nurseries also carry basil transplants. Set transplants or thin seedlings to stand at least 10 to 12 inches apart; more room (16 to 24 inches) is even better because it encourages low, bushy plants to develop. Plant in full sun.

After the plants have grown for 6 weeks, pinch the center stalks of the basil to force side growth and prevent early flowering — flowers take energy away from the leaves that you eat. If flower stalks do develop, cut or pinch them off early. Mulch the soil and maintain consistent moisture levels. Basil is generally pest-free.

Basil makes an excellent container plant. Some tall varieties, such as 'Siam Queen' Thai basil, have attractive purple coloring on the leaves and stems. 'Spicy Globe' basil forms a small, compact, 8- to 12-inch-tall and round plant that fits easily in a small container.

The best time to harvest basil is just before the formed flower buds open. In the morning, snip the leaves and branches and pinch off the flower buds to keep the plant productive. You also can cut the entire plant about 6 to 8 inches above the ground, leaving at least one node (where a leaf was) with two young shoots attached. The plant should produce a second, smaller harvest a few weeks later. As the plants mature, early cold weather can ruin your crop, so be sure to harvest if temperatures dip into the 30s.

After you harvest your basil, you can

- **Store it fresh:** The best way to store fresh basil is to place the stem ends in water like a small bouquet. You can put the leaves in the refrigerator, but they won't last long.

- **Freeze it:** Because the leaves lose some of their flavor when dried, freezing is the best method for winter storage. To quick-freeze basil, clean and dry whole sprigs (stem pieces with 3 to 4 leaves) and pack them in plastic bags with the air pressed out.

- **Dry it:** To dry basil, pinch off the leaves at the stem, and dry them in a shady, well-ventilated area. Check the leaves in 3 or 4 days, and if they aren't totally dry, finish drying them in an oven; otherwise, the leaves may turn brown and black. Use the lowest heat setting possible with the oven door slightly open; turn the leaves for even drying and check them frequently until they're dry and crumbly. They should dry in 10 minutes.

Chives

Chives are one of the easiest plants to grow. After you plant chives in your garden, you always have them because they're a hardy perennial — one of the first harvests each year. You can easily dig the plants up, divide them, and move them as your garden evolves. And you need only a few plants to harvest all the chives you'll ever need.

Common chives (*Allium schoenoprasum*) grow to 1 foot tall and have narrow, hollow green leaves and spherical pink or purple flowers; the plants are quite pretty. You can use the leaves in all kinds of sauces and salads to lend a delicate onion flavor. And, of course, what would baked potatoes be without chives? The flowers, when added to white vinegar, impart a lovely pink or purple color. You also can add the flower buds to salads.

Garlic chives (*Allium tuberosum*) are close relatives of common chives, but they differ slightly in appearance and flavor. Garlic chives have flat leaves, and their white flowers, which are highly attractive to bees, appear in the summer. The seed heads are excellent for decorating wreaths, but be careful not to let the seeds fall; garlic chives can become a weedy nuisance. Sometimes called Oriental chives, you can use garlic chives in soups, salads, sauces, and meat dishes to impart their garlicky flavor.

You can start chive plants from seed, purchase a plant or two, or dig up part of a clump from a neighbor's garden (with her permission, of course). If you're seeding, plant in mid to late spring in a sunny or slightly shady area. Chives prefer rich soil, and after they're established, they'll tolerate either moist or dry conditions. Sow the seeds in clusters that are 1 to 1½ feet apart. Remove the flower stalks after they bloom in early summer. Divide the plants (dig up and separate the small plants) every 3 to 4 years.

Small clumps of chives planted in pots will grow in a sunny spot outdoors. These pots can be brought indoors in fall, and the chives will continue to grow as a windowsill plant into the winter.

You can begin harvesting chives 6 weeks after planting or as soon as the established plants resume growth in the spring. As you need leaves, cut the outer ones near the base. New leaves will keep forming all summer. Use the leaves fresh or frozen in soups, on baked potatoes, or in salads. Chives also retain their flavor well when dried using the technique for drying basil.

Cilantro

Now considered one of the top culinary herbs in the United States, cilantro (*Coriandrum sativum*) has gained in popularity due to the influx of Mexican and Asian cooking. This annual herb is actually two herbs in one. When the green, ferny foliage is eaten fresh it's called *cilantro*. If allowed to go to seed, the seeds are called *coriander*. Both are essential for ethnic cooking.

Cilantro is a cool-season herb that can quickly *bolt* (go to flower and seed) when the weather becomes hot. After the plant has bolted, the foliage becomes tough and the flavor less pronounced. Select varieties that are slow to bolt, such as 'Slo Bolt,' and grow cilantro in spring and fall while the weather is cool.

Direct sow seeds after the last frost and thin plants to 2 to 4 inches apart. Most varieties grow 12 to 18 inches tall. Sow successive crops every 3 weeks to have a continuous supply of cilantro throughout the season. To harvest, pinch the leaves about 2 months after seeding or as needed. Snip off the flower stalk as it forms to prolong the leaf growth. If interested in harvesting coriander seeds, allow the plant to bolt and form seeds (after you let the plants go to seed, you'll have cilantro seedlings for years to come). Cilantro is best used fresh; the leaves aren't as tasty dried or frozen. You can harvest fresh cilantro and keep stems in water for a few days using it as needed.

Dill

Common dill (*Anethum graveolens*) grows to a height of about 3 to 5 feet. It grows best toward the back of your garden where it has plenty of room. It also looks beautiful mixed with annual flowers such as salvia. 'Dukat' is an improved new variety with high oil content and, therefore, more flavor.

Dill does poorly when transplanted, so start from seed sown directly into your garden. The annual plants thrive in rich, loose soil in a sunny location. Plant the seeds 1 to 2 weeks before the last spring frost date if you want the crop to mature when you do your first cucumber pickling. Sow seeds ¼-inch-deep in rows that are 18 to 24 inches part; or broadcast seeds over a 2-square-foot bed and gently rake the seeds into the soil. Plants should emerge in 10 to 14 days; let them grow for another 10 to 14 days and then thin them to 12 to 18 inches apart. Make small sowings a few weeks apart in different 2-square-foot areas in your garden until midsummer to get a supply of fresh leaves throughout the season.

Let a few plants mature their seed (let the seed form and drop from the flower naturally); if left undisturbed, they'll provide many new plants next season.

'Fernleaf' is a dwarf variety of dill that reaches only 18 inches tall, is slow to go to seed, and is great in containers. Taller varieties tend to flop over in a pot, so low-growing varieties like 'Fernleaf' are better choices for a container.

You can start harvesting the fernlike leaves about 8 weeks after planting by pinching the outer leaves close to the stem. The leaves have the strongest flavor just when the flower heads are opening. Store fresh dill by wrapping the cut ends with a moistened paper towel and placing the dill in a plastic bag in the refrigerator. To dry the leaves, place them in a dark place on a window screen; after they're dry, seal them in an airtight jar. Freezing the leaves in bunches in freezer bags retains even more of their flavor.

For pickling, cut off the seed heads when they're light brown. Dry them for a few days in paper bags with air holes in the sides, and then shake the seeds loose in the bottom of the bags. You can use then use these seeds for cooking. Dill seeds are great not only for pickles but also for beans and fish.

French tarragon

French tarragon (*Artemisia dracunculus sativa*) is an essential herb for many cooks, but it can cause some confusion for the first-time grower. You must know exactly what you're buying when you purchase a French tarragon plant because it's often confused with similar-looking Russian tarragon, a weedy plant that has little value in cooking. French tarragon is a hardy perennial that can be grown only from root cuttings, divisions, or tip cuttings of new growth.

If you find tarragon seed for sale, it's probably Russian tarragon. If you're buying plants at a nursery, rub some of the leaves together and then smell them to determine the variety; the French variety will have the strong licorice scent that you want.

Because seeds can be difficult to find, I suggest that you purchase plants. Or if you have a friend with an established tarragon bed, ask if he can divide his plants in early spring. You want to divide each established plant into two or three plants. You divide by digging up the entire plant, cutting it evenly into two or three smaller plants, and then replanting one plant and giving away the rest. Space tarragon plants 2 to 3 feet apart and give them room to spread. Divide the plants every 2 to 3 years to keep them vigorous and healthy. Tarragon does best in full sun or partial shade, and it needs well-drained soil.

Cut back plants to 2 feet when flower buds start to form (midsummer) to prevent flowering and to keep the plants from getting floppy. In cold-winter climates, apply a layer of thick organic mulch — such as straw — over the roots in the winter.

Tarragon's aniselike flavor makes it a wonderful addition to salads, fish, chicken, sauces, and vinegar. Tarragon leaves have the best flavor if you use them fresh in early summer or freeze them for later use. Store fresh tarragon in the refrigerator in a plastic bag with a moist paper towel wrapped around the base. Freeze stems with leaves attached in small plastic bags. Drying some of the harvest is also an option, but the leaves can lose a lot of their flavor if you let them dry too long. To dry, hang in bunches in a warm, well-ventilated room out of direct sunlight. They should dry within a week. Pack them in an airtight container as soon as they're dry.

Mint

The mint family offers a tremendous diversity of refreshing scents and tastes for cooking, beverages, and potpourris. Consider these varieties:

✔ Spearmint (*Menthe spicata*) is most commonly used in the kitchen for mint juleps, sauces, jellies, and teas, or to highlight flavor in a fruit salad. It's very fragrant and grows 2 to 3 feet tall with pale violet blooms in mid to late summer.

✔ Peppermint (*M. piperita*) is another popular mint with a strong aroma; it grows 3 feet tall with smooth, 1- to 3-inch-long leaves and blooms in mid-summer.

✔ Another dozen or so mint varieties include some interesting types such as orange, ginger, chocolate, and apple mint. They're available from garden centers or mail-order herb suppliers (see the appendix for addresses).

Start with one or two plants and set them 2 feet apart in a sunny or shady location with rich, moist soil. These perennial plants will quickly fill in the open area between them. Use a light mulch to maintain soil moisture and to keep the leaves dry and off the ground. You can easily propagate mint plants by dividing the clumps, so you can share your plants with friends.

Many types of mint are very invasive, growing into other garden space, especially in rich, moist soil. So unless you grow them in pots or with some kind of confinement, such as metal or plastic (to a depth of 14 inches), they can become a very troublesome weed. I once had mint take over my herb garden in just a year, crowding out all the other herbs. So beware! Figure 12-2 shows you how to plant mint in pots buried in the ground; make sure that the lip of each pot is above the soil line. And remember: Don't let the plants get too thick. Cut them back frequently to promote fresh growth.

Figure 12-2: Plant mint plants in pots buried in the ground if you want to stop them from spreading.

Lip of pot is above soil line

Pick young or old mint leaves as soon as you need them throughout the growing season. You can easily dry mint leaves on trays or by hanging bunched branches upside down in a dark, warm, well-ventilated area. The leaves are easy to freeze too; just place the leaves in plastic bags. Store fresh mint in the refrigerator similar to how you would dill.

Oregano

You can grow several types of oregano; I recommend only one for kitchen use. Others do have a mild oregano flavor, but they taste like hay; they're best used as border plantings or for wreathmaking.

The oregano most often used in cooking is *Oreganum heracleoticum,* and it goes by the common names Greek oregano, winter sweet marjoram, and Italian oregano. It's a hardy, perennial plant that establishes quickly, getting no taller than 6 to 8 inches, making it perfect for container growing. I prefer it over common oregano (*O. vulgare*), which isn't as flavorful. However, common oregano is lovely; it's covered with ornamental lavender-colored flowers in summer that dry well, are often used in wreaths, and are irresistible to bees.

You can start oregano from seed planted after the last spring frost, divide established beds to get new plants, or buy transplants at a garden center. Planting in rich, fertile soil and full sun is best. When the plants are 3 to 4 inches tall and wide (a few weeks after planting), thin them to stand 8 to 10 inches apart. Trim back or prune the plants before they flower (about 5 to 6 weeks after planting).

Harvest oregano leaves as you need them, but remember that you'll get optimal flavor just before the flowers bloom. Use the trimmings in your cooking. After trimming, wait for new growth and use as needed. Oregano leaves dry easily and store well, and you also can freeze them. Dry and freeze the leaves similar to how you would mint.

Parsley

Parsley deserves recognition for more than just its role as a garnish. It's also a good breath freshener that's rich in iron and vitamin C. The curly leafed parsley (*Petroselinum crispum*), which comes in many varieties, is the most common type because it makes such an attractive garnish. For cooking, the flat-leafed parsley or Italian parsley (*P. crispum neapolitanum*) is preferable; it's easier to work with and has better flavor than curly leafed parsley. I use both to make a delicious and healthful green shake consisting of parsley, bananas, and water! It's not for everyone, but I love it. You also can use parsley as a substitution for basil when making pesto.

Although parsley is a *biennial* (it grows leaves the first year and goes to flower and seed the second), it grows best if you sow seeds every year because the flavor is diminished in the second season. Growing parsley from seed, however, requires patience because the seedlings can take up to 4 weeks to emerge from the soil. Soaking seeds overnight in warm water before planting speeds germination.

Sow seeds in individual pots indoors, plant seeds outside in your garden after the first frost, or purchase transplants from a local garden center (the easiest way to go). Plants do well in sun or partial shade, and they prefer rich, moist soil. Choose a weed-free area when sowing seeds in your garden — you don't want a jungle to grow while you wait for your seeds to germinate. Parsley can handle cold weather, so start seeding 3 to 4 weeks before the last spring frost. In mild-winter areas, you can plant seeds in fall for a winter harvest, but plants will go to seed early the next spring. When the plants have four leaves, thin them to stand 6 to 10 inches apart. Provide the plants an even supply of water throughout the summer.

To harvest parsley, cut the outer leaves from the plant as you need them. To dry parsley, cut the plant at the soil level (you can cut as much of the plant as you want to dry; it will grow back from a complete cutting) and hang it in a shady, warm, well-ventilated area. After it's thoroughly dried, crumble the parsley and store it in an airtight container. I also like to freeze the fresh leaves to use in the winter, adding them to soups and stews. To keep parsley fresh as long as possible, store it in the refrigerator, with the leaf stalks in water.

Rosemary

Rosemary (*Rosmarinus officinalis*) is a perennial herb that can be low-growing and spreading or 3 to 5 feet tall and wide, depending on the selection. Most varieties are only reliably hardy to USDA zone 9 (see the appendix for more on zones), so gardeners in cold climates need to grow the plant in a pot and move it to a protected spot in winter (and replant in spring) or grow it like an annual herb. 'Arp' is a cold-tolerant variety that can be grown in USDA zone 6 if protected in the winter with light mulch. Where rosemary plants are kept as perennials year-round, they can be trimmed into hedges or made into topiaries.

The blue-green rosemary leaves are highly aromatic and great roasted with potatoes and used in soups, stews, and casseroles. I've even used the branches as shish kebab skewers, giving the vegetables a super rosemary flavor. The attractive plant also produces beautiful blue flowers in summer that bees adore.

Purchase rosemary transplants at your local garden center; seeds germinate slowly and erratically. Usually one or two plants are plenty for typical family use. Drought-tolerant rosemary thrives in full sun on well-drained soil. Plant rosemary in spring about 1 to 2 feet apart depending on the variety. Amend the soil lightly with compost. Periodically pinch back any errant branches in summer to keep the plant bushy. Leaves can be dried and stems frozen for winter use similar to French tarragon.

Rosemary makes an excellent container plant — especially the low-growing prostrate varieties, such as 'Collingwood Ingram'. Keep the soil moist but not wet. In cold areas in fall, bring the plant indoors to a sunny, well-ventilated location. Cut back on watering, but mist weekly with tepid water; the plant should survive the winter to be planted in spring.

Sage

Sage encompasses a large group of plants, although only a few are really considered good culinary herbs. Most types of sage are perennials in all but the coldest winter areas. First and foremost among the culinary herbs is garden sage (*Salvia officinalis*), a hardy perennial recognized by its gray-green foliage and beautiful blue flowers in the spring. Plants can get quite tall (more than 2 feet) and leggy, so the dwarf type (such as *S. o.* 'Nana') is a better, more compact form. The dwarf type has equally good flavor but isn't quite as hardy as its garden counterpart.

Several varieties of garden sage have ornamental leaf color. Purple sage (*S. o.* 'Purpurescens'), golden sage (*S. o.* 'Aurea'), and tricolor sage (*S. o.* 'Tricolor') can add beautiful color to your garden and your dishes.

You can easily start sage plants indoors from seed or in your garden in early spring. However, plants grown from seed may not have the same leaf shape and color as their parent. A better way to grow true-to-form, high-quality sage is to grow cuttings from a friend's best-looking plants. Or opt to purchase plants from a nursery.

Set plants or thin seedlings to stand 24 to 30 inches apart. Sage thrives in full sun and well-drained soil. After the plants are established (a few weeks), they prefer the soil to be on the dry side. Each spring prune the heavier, woody stems from the plants. The leaf production and vigor of the plants drop off after 4 or 5 years, so dig up older plants and replace them with new ones every couple of years.

You can harvest the leaves at any time and use them in a variety of meat-based dishes, such as chicken marsala and veal scaloppini. The leaves keep well dried or frozen. Dry and freeze sage leaves similar to French tarragon. Sage leaves intensify in flavor when frozen.

Don't harvest sage plants too heavily the first year; leave at least half of each plant intact to give the plants time to get established.

Thyme

The thyme family of herbs is aromatic, versatile, and plentiful — more than 50 varieties are grown for culinary or ornamental use. Creeping varieties of thyme are good as edging plants and in rock gardens. Most thymes are perennial and reliably hardy, except in cold-winter areas. Here are a few common varieties:

✔ **Cooking thyme:** The thyme most often used in cooking is known as English thyme (*Thymus vulgaris*). Like the other thymes, English thyme has woody stems with small oval leaves. It grows only 8 to 12 inches high (many other thymes are even shorter). Thyme is used in many dishes including fish and meats.

✔ **Lemon thyme:** Loved for its lemony scent, lemon thyme (*T. citriodorus*) is a delightful plant for both your garden and kitchen. Some varieties have both silver and yellow *variegated* leaves (leaves that sport two or more colors). Lemon thyme is a wonderful ground cover and an excellent container plant.

✔ **Caraway thyme:** Caraway thyme (*T. herba-barona*) is a low-growing plant that combines the fragrance of caraway and thyme; it has dark green leaves.

Thyme seeds are troublesome to start because they germinate slowly and unevenly. Instead of starting from seed, buy a plant or two from a nursery, and plant them in the spring in light, well-drained soil that receives full sun. You also can start plants from cuttings if a friend is willing to part with some. Space plants 9 inches apart. Where winters are cold, mulch the thyme plants after the ground freezes with a light mulch, such as pine needles. Trim the plants back a bit in the spring and summer to contain them and prevent the buildup of woody growth.

Like oregano, thyme makes an excellent container plant. Creeping varieties grow well in windowboxes and hanging pots. Taller varieties look great combined with annual flowers such as lobelia. You can harvest thyme leaves and sprigs all summer. In early fall, cut the sprigs, tie them together, and hang them upside down in a warm, dark, well-ventilated place to dry. You also can dry stemless leaves on a tray or freeze them. Freeze stems of thyme in plastic bags. Store fresh thyme in the refrigerator as you would dill.

Making Your Landscape Blossom with Edible Flowers

With your edible landscape it seems that you could be eating almost anything in your yard, so why not the flowers? That's right, many flowers are edible. Now I'm not saying that all edible flowers pack a huge flavor punch, but putting a few in a salad adds pizazz and color.

Plant edible flowers anywhere you'd naturally plant other flowers. They look great in containers, in the vegetable garden, along a walkway, or mixed with other annual flowers. Even though you'll be picking some of the flowers, the beauty of these plants is that they produce an abundance of flowers so they'll still look good even after a harvest.

Here are some edible flowers to munch on. Remember that flowers should be washed before eating, and don't harvest flowers that have been sprayed with pesticides. Some people may be allergic to the pollen-bearing parts of a flower so eat only the flower petals.

✔ Apples	✔ Lilacs
✔ Bee balm	✔ Signet marigolds
✔ Calendulas	✔ Nasturtium
✔ Borage	✔ Pansies
✔ Dandelions	✔ Red clover
✔ Daylilies	✔ Roses
✔ Hibiscus	✔ Tulips
✔ Lavender	✔ Violets

Although some flowers are edible, many others are poisonous. Make sure that you know what you're picking before you eat it. And don't let young children or pets eat flowers unattended.

For more information on edible flowers, check out the book *Edible Flowers: From Garden to Kitchen* by Kathy Brown (Aquamarine Publishers, 2008). A good publication on edible flowers and poisonous plants can be found at attra.ncat.org/attra-pub/PDF/edibleflowers.pdf.

Part III
Getting Down and Dirty in Your Vegetable Garden

The 5th Wave   By Rich Tennant

"You know, vegetable gardening does require some measure of patience."

In this part . . .

This part has all you need to know about seeds, soil, fertilizers, watering, pest controls, and harvesting. I also talk about some cool farmer techniques, such as succession cropping and interplanting. And for those with less space, I show you how to successfully grow vegetables in containers.

Chapter 13

On Your Mark, Get Set . . . Grow!

*A*re you ready to plant some vegetables? Now the fun really starts. You can plant vegetables two different ways — from seed or by transplant:

✔ When planting seeds, you either sow the seeds indoors and then transplant the young seedlings in your garden (when the time is right, of course), or you sow the seeds directly in your garden.

✔ To skip the whole seed process altogether, you purchase young *transplants* (seedlings ready to be transplanted) at your local nursery or through the mail and then plant them directly into your garden.

Both methods have their advantages, and timing is critical to success. You can plant seeds quickly and without much thought. But working deliberately and carefully — whether planting indoors or out — pays off in sturdier, more vigorous plants. In this chapter, I guide you through the planting process, giving you information about correct seed spacing, planting depth, soil and germinating conditions, and fertilizing so you produce strong-growing, vigorous plants. I also show you how to plant transplants, whether you grow them yourself or buy them.

As I say throughout this book (maybe because my dad used to say it in all situations): Timing is everything when you plant vegetables. If you really want to be successful, you need to find out the planting dates for your area. Each vegetable has its own optimum growing conditions — a right soil temperature, daytime temperature, length of day, and so on — but all these factors vary greatly, depending on where you live. So make sure you check out Chapter 3 for important climate-specific information. Okay, I've made my point — on to the planting.

Choosing Seeds or Transplants

Whether you choose to grow vegetables from seeds or transplants, each planting method has its own advantages. Here are some advantages to starting from seed:

- ✔ **A wider choice of varieties:** Your local garden store or nursery may carry only three or four varieties of tomato transplants but offer a great selection of seeds. And mail-order seed catalogs (see the appendix for addresses) offer hundreds of varieties of seeds and specialty types, such as organically grown seed.

- ✔ **Healthy plants:** You don't have to settle for plants that are *leggy* (tall, weak, spindly stems) or *root-bound* (roots crammed into a small pot) and that may have been hanging out at the nursery too long. Such plants usually don't get off to a fast start when you plant them in the ground. Also, when you start from seed, you don't have to worry about introducing any insects or diseases into your garden that may be lurking on nursery-grown transplants.

- ✔ **Reduced cost:** Especially if you have a large garden, starting from seed can save you some dough. A six-pack of seedlings may cost you $3.00, whereas for the same price you can buy a seed packet with 100 seeds.

- ✔ **A lot of fun:** The excitement of seeing those first seedlings push through the soil is something special. Two feet of snow may be on the ground outside, but by sowing seeds indoors, you can enjoy a little spring.

The advantages to growing seeds stack up pretty impressively. But planting nursery-grown transplants has a major benefit as well — convenience and immediate gratification. Growing plants from seeds takes time and diligence, but going with nursery transplants gives you an instant garden. And if you have problems with transplants, you can always buy more. If you have problems with the special seed varieties you started, it's usually too late to start them again indoors, so you're out of luck growing that variety that year.

Growing seeds is like taking care of a new pet. You have to check on seeds everyday, maybe several times a day, to make sure they're happy. Unless a reliable neighbor or friend can care for your seedlings, say goodbye to your winter trip to the Caribbean. Also, you have to think in advance of what you'll be growing and need to start indoors. In this harried world, it's often easier to decide a week or so before planting what vegetable varieties you need and to buy transplants than to plan months in advance to start seeds. Plus, you have to store unused seeds somewhere where you won't forget them next winter. A metal tin in a cool, dark part of the house is best.

After you consider the advantages of each planting method, you need to make sure that you time your planting for the most productive results. Keep reading for full details on starting veggies from seeds and growing veggies from transplants.

Deciding on Your Seeding Method and Decoding a Seed Packet

Suppose you decide to grow your veggies from seeds. Now what? You have another choice to make: Will you start your seeds indoors or outdoors? If you plant seeds indoors, you have to transplant them into your garden later. With *direct seeding,* you skip the indoor step and sow the seeds directly into your garden. Which option should you choose? Probably both, if you're serious about growing vegetables. But consider these points when making your choice:

- **Starting indoors gives you a jump on the growing season.** If you start at the right time (remember, timing is everything), you can have vigorous seedlings that are ready to go into the ground at the ideal time. In areas with short growing seasons, starting seedlings indoors really gives you a head start.

   The best candidates for an early start are plants that tolerate root disturbance and benefit from a jump on the season. These veggies include broccoli, Brussels sprouts, cabbage, cauliflower, celery, eggplant, leeks, lettuce, onions, peppers, and tomatoes. Another group of vegetables that have to be transplanted carefully but do benefit from an early start include cucumbers, melons, and squash.

- **Seeds are easier to start indoors.** You have more control indoors, enabling you to more easily provide the perfect conditions for hard-to-germinate or very small seeds. You can provide the ideal temperature, moisture, and fertility so your seedlings grow strong and sturdy.

- **Some vegetables don't like to be transplanted and are better sown directly in the ground.** These vegetables include many of the root crops, such as carrots, beets, turnips, and parsnips. They're cold-hardy vegetables, so you can direct seed them pretty early anyway. Crops such as corn, beans, and peas also are pretty finicky about transplanting and grow better when you sow them directly in the ground. (I discuss sowing seeds outdoors in detail later in this chapter.)

No matter your decision, the seed packet you buy to start your vegetables indoors or to plant directly in the ground is loaded with useful information. You still want to use a good book (like this one!) to get all the nitty-gritty details, but much of the information you need to plant your seeds is right on the packet. Consider some things your seed packet can tell you:

- ✔ The name or description should indicate whether it's a hybrid or open-pollinated variety (see Chapter 3) and whether the seed is treated with a fungicide.

- ✔ The description tells you the high points about the variety, including yields, disease resistance, and suggestions for use. Remember to read with a critical eye, because companies can make all varieties sound fabulous.

- ✔ Cultural information tells you information such as when to plant, days to germination, mature plant size, days to maturity, and plant spacing.

- ✔ The packing date tells you the year in which the seeds were packed. Always buy this year's seeds for best germination. Even though 1- to 2-year-old seeds will still grow well, you shouldn't be paying full price for them.

Starting Seeds Indoors

To start seeds indoors, all you need is a container, soil, seeds, moisture, warmth, and light. Oh, if only everything in life were this simple. Check out Part II to find out when to start specific vegetables indoors — remember, timing is everything. Here are the basic steps for planting seeds indoors:

1. **Sow the seeds in containers filled with sterile soil (which garden centers call a *germinating mix*).**

   Keep the seeds in a warm place until *germination* (when the first shoots start to push through the soil).

2. **After the seeds germinate, move the seedlings to a well-lit location (preferably under lights).**

   While your seedlings are growing in their well-lit location, be sure to keep them moist.

3. **Thin crowded seedlings.**

   When the seedlings' heights are three times the diameter of your pot, transplant the seedlings to a larger container.

4. **Acclimate the seedlings to outdoor conditions.**

Adapting your seedlings to the weather conditions in the great outdoors is called *hardening off.*

5. **Plant the seedlings in your garden.**

Piece of cake; go have a drink. Now on to the details, which I cover in the following sections. (Be sure to check out the later section "Transplanting Indoor Seedlings and Starter Plants" as well.)

Picking a pot to plant in

Any container that holds several inches of soil and that you can punch drainage holes in is suitable for growing seedlings. Several low-cost possibilities include milk cartons, paper or Styrofoam cups, cottage-cheese containers, and homemade wooden *flats,* which are shallow, wide, seedling trays. Flats enable you to start many seedlings in a small space, which is helpful when you water or move the plants. After you plant the seeds in the flats, the seedlings stay there until planting time.

Garden stores and most mail-order garden catalogs sell a wide variety of plastic, fiber, peat, and Styrofoam flats and containers that satisfy just about any budget. You can even purchase pots made out of cow manure. Yum. Figure 13-1 shows you some flats that you can buy, along with the appropriate lights (which I discuss later in this chapter).

Figure 13-1: Seed-starting flats and lighting that plants love.

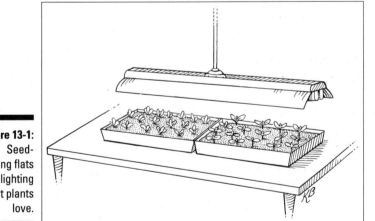

You can use individual peat pots for plants like cucumbers, which don't like to have their roots disturbed during transplanting. Similarly, for gardeners who put a premium on convenience, premade growing cubes are a good idea. But I have to be honest; I'm not a huge fan of peat pots or peat cubes (compressed peat pots that expand when soaked in water). The idea behind a peat pot is that once planted (pot and all) in the garden, the plants' roots grow through the sides of the wet pot, and as the season progresses, the peat naturally breaks down and disappears. But sometimes when I've used them, the peat didn't break down. In the fall when I pulled up my plants, the peat pots were still intact and some roots were constricted in the pots. If you still want to give peat pots and cubes a try, follow the guidelines in the later section "Making the big move to the ground."

Before you sow any seeds, sterilize your flats and pots (especially ones that you've used before) to prevent the fungus called *damping off* from killing your seedlings. (See the later sidebar "Dealing with damping off" for more on this soil-borne disease.) Dip the containers in a solution of 9 parts water to 1 part household bleach and then rinse them in clear running water.

Using a mix that doesn't include soil

The most practical seed-starting mediums for gardeners are the commercially prepared soilless or peatlite mixes that are sold in most garden stores as *potting soil* or *germinating mix*. As the name implies, the mix doesn't contain any true soil. Instead, it's usually a combination of peat moss, vermiculite or perlite, ground limestone (which brings the pH to proper levels, as I discuss in Chapter 14), fertilizer, and sometimes compost, which is good for plant growth. Potting soil is lightweight, is free of disease organisms that may be present in true garden soil, and holds moisture well but at the same time offers good aeration and drainage.

Don't use garden soil to start seeds indoors. Garden soil isn't light enough (that is, it doesn't have enough air spaces) and may contain insects or diseases that can kill your tender seedlings.

Sowing your seeds

After you've chosen the proper container and soilless soil (or *growing medium*), follow these steps to sow your seeds:

1. **Fill a container with moistened growing medium to within ½ inch of the top of the container.**

Soilless mixes are dusty and difficult to wet initially. Pour the mix into a plastic bag, and then add enough warm water to moisten the mix but not turn it into a drippy mud pie. Mix the water and growing medium with your hands or a strong wooden spoon, closing off the opening of the bag as much as possible to keep the dust in. Remove the soil from the bag and place it in the container. Gently firm down the medium with a flat piece of wood, such as a ruler.

2a. **If you're planting seeds in a flat, follow these directions to sow your seeds:**

Make shallow *furrows* (rowlike impressions) with a blunt stick or by pressing the narrow edge of a ruler into the medium. Then sow the seeds according to these guidelines:

- Sow small seeds, such as lettuce, at about five to eight seeds per inch if you intend to transplant them into different containers soon after they come up. Sow larger seeds, such as melons, at three to four seeds per inch.

- Sow seeds more sparingly, at three to four seeds per inch, if you intend to thin and leave them in the same container (rather than transplant into a larger container).

Either method — transplanting the seeds into a new container or leaving them in the same container — works fine; it's just a matter of what pots and room you have. Transplanting into individual pots takes up more room but allows larger plants such as tomatoes more room for their roots to grow. Smaller plants, such as lettuce, grow fine when thinned and left in their original containers.

You can *broadcast* (randomly spread) seeds rather than plant them in rowlike trenches, but row planting and thinning are easier.

2b. **If you're planting seeds in individual containers, here's how you sow:**

- Put two to four seeds in each container.

- Later, thin the seedlings, leaving the strongest one.

3. **After sowing the seeds at the correct depth (see the appendix), cover them with fine potting soil or vermiculite.**

TIP

Label each row or container because many seedlings look alike. You can purchase labels from a nursery or through a mail-order catalog, or you can use old ones from previously purchased nursery transplants. Using a waterproof pen, record the type of vegetable, the variety, and the date that the seed was planted.

4. **Water the seeds gently with a mister or spray bottle.**

A stronger stream of water can wash seeds into one section of the container or move them too deeply into the soil.

5. **Cover the container with a sheet of clear plastic or a plastic bag to hold in the moisture.**

   If necessary, use small stakes to prop up the plastic so it doesn't rest on top of the soil.

6. **Place the planted containers in a warm spot.**

   The cooler the temperature, the longer it takes for the plants to emerge, so keep 'em warm and toasty! Some warm spots include the top of your refrigerator or near your furnace. But be careful how you water around electrical appliances. You also can buy heating cables or mats that keep the soil warm from below. Follow the package instructions carefully.

   Never put containers in direct sun; the plastic cover holds in the heat, cooking your seeds to death.

7. **Check the containers daily to make sure they're still moist but not so wet that they mold.**

   If you see signs of mold, loosen the cover and let air in; the mold should disappear. You also can hook up a small fan to gently blow across the seedlings (without the plastic cover on), keeping the soil on the dry side. However, be careful not to dry out the seedlings.

8. **As soon as you see the first green shoots emerge, remove the plastic cover and move your seedlings to a spot that provides plenty of light and the proper growing conditions for that vegetable.**

   Refer to the chapter covering that vegetable for information about the proper growing conditions. Until seedlings emerge from the soil, light is unnecessary, with the exception of lettuce and celery seeds. Sow these seeds by lightly pressing them into the soil or covering them very lightly with ⅛ inch of fine potting soil, and then place the containers in a bright spot or position them under a 40-watt incandescent light.

Providing the right amount of light and heat

The light that your young seedlings receive is one of the most important factors in good growth. Placing the seedlings in a south-facing window is one option but not always the best one. Even in a sunny window, plants get only a fraction of the light that they would get outside. Windowsill plants often get tall and spindly because they get too warm in relation to the light they receive.

Try to keep your seedlings on the cool side — 60 to 65 degrees Fahrenheit (75 degrees maximum) — to encourage slower growth; cooler temperatures give you sturdy, stocky plants that transplant well. Although a 10- to 15-degree drop in temperature at night is beneficial, a windowsill can get pretty chilly at night when it's wintry outside. Place a blanket between the plants and the glass to keep windowsill seedlings warm on frosty nights, or move plants away from the window at night.

Growing seedlings under fluorescent lights is a good way to keep light-hungry plants happy. Ordinary cool-white, 40-watt fluorescent bulbs are fine for starting seedlings. If possible, set up your lights near a window so the plants can receive both natural and artificial light. The more expensive grow lights that you can purchase at a nursery or through a mail-order seed catalog produce the broader spectrum light that plants need for flowering and fruiting (although your seedlings will be in the garden before they're ready to flower).

No matter what kind of light you have, use one set of lights (usually 2 bulbs to a set) for every 1-foot-width of seedling-growing area and keep the bulbs 2 to 4 inches from the tops of the seedlings at all times. Keep the lights on for no more than 16 hours per day so the plants can get their natural rest period. Inexpensive timers that turn the lights on and off automatically are available at nurseries and hardware stores.

Watering your seedlings

Water fragile seedlings carefully, or you risk uprooting them. Mist them with a gentle spray, or water them from the bottom by setting your container in a pan of water just long enough for the soil surface to wet (keeping them in water longer than this can damage the plants' roots). After the surface is wet, remove the container from the water and let it drain. Keep the soil surface lightly moist but not soggy. Always water with lukewarm water, and try to do so early in the morning, if possible. This way the foliage can dry off quickly during the day to avoid disease problems.

As your plants get sturdier, you can water with a sprinkling can that has a *rose,* a nozzle that breaks the water into many fine streams. After the plants grow their first set of true leaves (the first leaves to open as the seed germinates are called *seedling leaves,* and the next set are *true leaves*) and have a bigger root system, let the soil dry out slightly between waterings.

Give the plants enough water at one time so that some of it runs out the drainage holes in the bottom of the container, but never leave the container sitting in water. Overwatering promotes damping-off disease (see the sidebar "Dealing with damping off") and decreases the amount of air in the soil, resulting in a weaker root system.

With soilless mixes, you may have a difficult time deciding when to water, because the soil looks dry on the surface even though plenty of moisture is still present. To check whether the soil has moisture, take a small amount of soil off the top ½ inch of mix and squeeze it between your fingers. If you can squeeze out any water, hold off watering. The difference in a container's weight when the soil is moist compared to when it's dry can also indicate when to water. Dry soil is very light. Finally, wilted seedlings also are a sure sign that you've waited too long to water (unless, of course, your plants have damping off).

Certain types of containers require more frequent watering. For example, soil in clay pots dries out faster than soil in plastic pots. Peat pots dry out fast and are difficult to rewet. Try putting your peat pots or growing-cubes in a tray and packing moist peat moss between them to keep them from drying out too quickly.

Self-watering seed starting kits that reduce the need for checking your seedlings daily for dryness are now available. These kits have a reservoir of water in the bottom of the tray that wicks into the pots when the soil is dry. See the appendix for companies carrying seed starting supplies.

Thinning and transplanting indoors

After seedlings develop their first set of true leaves (or when onions or leeks, which send up a single blade, are 2 inches tall), you need to thin them or move them from shallow flats to larger quarters. Thinning is an important step, and timing is crucial. If you let your seedlings grow too large in a small container, their growth is stunted. And if you don't space them out at all, you end up with weak plants.

To thin plants that will continue growing in the same container, snip out extra seedlings at the soil line with a pair of scissors, as shown in Figure 13-2. If you try to pull these seedlings out, you may disturb the roots of the plants that are staying. Also be sure to snip out any weak or misshapen plants. The appendix explains how much space to leave between different types of vegetable seedlings.

To move seedlings to a new container, first fill a larger container (plastic six-packs, 4-inch pots, or peat pots) with moist potting soil. Poke holes in the soil large enough to put the seedling roots in — the eraser end of a pencil is a good tool for this. Dig around the plants carefully by using the blade of a table knife or a small stick, such as a plant label, and then lift the seedlings out of the soil. Always hold the seedlings by the tips of their leaves; otherwise, you can easily crush their delicate stems or injure their growing tips. Set the plants in the new container, slightly deeper than they were growing before. Firm the soil gently around the roots, water well, and keep the plants out of direct sun for a day or two until they adjust to their new pots.

Figure 13-2: Thin seedlings at the soil line with scissors.

Feeding your seedlings

Regular fertilizing helps produce strong, healthy plants. Some potting soils already have fertilizer mixed in, and in that case you don't have to add more. For other types, use a diluted water-soluble fertilizer to one-third strength (usually 1 teaspoon of fertilizer per gallon of water) to water your seedlings. Water with the solution once a week. For more on fertilizers, see Chapter 15.

Dealing with damping off

One day you're admiring your strong, healthy seedlings, and the next day you're gaping in dismay at the sight of them toppled over and dying. The attacker is called *damping off,* which is a fungus that infects young seedlings, sometimes even before they have a chance to emerge from the soil. If you examine infected seedlings closely, you usually can see that part of the stem near the soil line is sunken, shriveled, and water soaked. Sometimes a white mold also forms on the stem.

Damping off is one of the most common problems that seed-starters face, but fortunately you can control it with good sanitation and cultural practices (proper watering, fertilizing, and lighting). Sterilizing containers with a bleach solution and using sterile potting soil go a long way toward preventing problems. Wet potting soil and high nitrogen encourage this fungus, so avoid overwatering, and use a well-drained germinating mix that's low in nitrogen. Or consider using fertilizer only after the seedlings develop their first true leaves. Sowing seeds thinly to allow good air circulation also can help. Many seeds come coated with a fungicide that helps prevent damping off.

If you notice seedlings in one portion of a container beginning to wither, cut them off and remove the soil around them as quickly as possible. Then do whatever you can to make conditions less favorable for the fungus (basically, let the soil dry more). With luck, you'll be able to save the rest of the batch.

Transplanting Indoor Seedlings and Starter Plants

After you nurture your seedlings indoors for a good 4 to 8 weeks, and when the weather's right for planting (see Chapter 3 to find out when to plant in your area), you're ready to transplant the seedlings outdoors. Or maybe you haven't grown seedlings at all, but you want to buy some starter plants at a nursery and get them in the ground. I discuss both scenarios in the following sections.

Buying starter plants

If you don't start your transplants from seeds at home, you can buy them at a nursery or garden center. You can find seedlings of almost every type and size around planting time. However, the range of varieties available will be greater if you start your own transplants from seed.

Follow these tips when buying starter plants:

- ✔ **Choose healthy-looking plants.** Tomatoes, for example, should have a stocky stem, be about 4- to 6-inches tall, and sport dark-green foliage. Read the Part II chapters that discuss the vegetable you want to find out what makes a healthy-looking plant.

- ✔ **Avoid large, crowded, spindly plants in small containers.** The roots of these types of plants are often bound up and have no room to grow. You can check the roots for yourself by gently removing the transplants from their containers (if you aren't sure how to do this, see "Making the big move to the ground," later in this chapter). If you see a dense mat of roots around the outside of the *root ball* (the soil with roots growing in it), the plants probably have been in the pot too long.

- ✔ **Buy plants at the optimum size.** Plants with four to six leaves and short, stocky stems are usually best. In general, younger plants are better than tall, older plants that most likely were stressed at one point or another.

- ✔ **Avoid plants that are already flowering and have fruit on them.** Plants with flowers and fruits never produce well.

You can sometimes buy large tomato plants in 1-gallon or larger pots — sometimes they even have tomatoes on them. In my experience, these large plants rarely grow well after you get them home. I prefer smaller transplants that can get off to a running start.

You can buy vegetable transplants locally, but many mail-order seed companies now also offer a wide range of vegetable varieties as small plants or plugs. The plants usually are in good shape. They offer a wider selection than you can find in garden centers, you don't have to drive around to find the best transplants, and they ship plants to you at the appropriate planting time for your region. See the appendix for the addresses of various mail-order companies.

Toughening up all types of transplants

Vegetable seedlings that are grown indoors at home or purchased from a greenhouse or nursery in spring need to acclimate gradually to the brighter light and cooler temperatures of the outside world. This process, called *hardening off,* slows plant growth, causing the plants to store more food internally and increase the thickness of their outer leaf layers. Basically, hardening off toughens up transplants for the cold, cruel, outside world.

To harden off your transplants, follow these steps:

1. **A week or two before you intend to set plants out in your garden, stop fertilizing and reduce the amount of water you give them.**

   Give plants just enough water so they don't wilt.

2. **Take your plants outside for a short time.**

   Give the plants a half hour of filtered sunlight — setting them under an arbor or open-branched tree — during the warmest part of the day. If the weather is windy, put the plants in a spot where they're sheltered, or construct a windbreak out of pieces of wood.

3. **Gradually increase the amount of time that the plants spend outside and the intensity of the light that they're exposed to.**

   You want to increase the amount of time your plants are outside so that by day seven, they're out all day. Move them into progressively sunnier locations during the week so they get used to their future condition in the ground. However, make sure that you bring the plants in every night.

Another option is to move your plants to a cold frame (see Chapter 21), and then you can open the cold frame more each day and close it at night. Plants that are raised in a cold frame from the time that they're young seedlings will need much less hardening off.

Don't overharden your plants. Certain crops, such as cabbage and broccoli, can quickly *bolt* (flower before they're supposed to) if seedlings older than 3 weeks are repeatedly exposed to temperatures lower than 40 degrees for a couple of weeks.

Making the big move to the ground

Before transplanting your homegrown seedlings or nursery-bought transplants, you need to prepare your soil and sculpt beds or rows (as described in Chapter 14), and your garden must be ready to plant. If you're worried about keeping the rows straight, use string and stakes as described in the later section "Row planting."

Choose a calm, cloudy day to transplant, if possible. Late afternoon is a good time because plants can recover from the shock of transplanting without sitting in the midday heat and sun. Your garden soil should be moist, but not soggy. If the weather has been dry, water the planting area the day before you plant. Moisten the soil in your flats or pots so it holds together around the plants' roots when you remove the plants from their containers.

When setting out plants in biodegradable peat pots, make slits down the sides of the pots or gently tear the sides to enable the roots to push through. Also, tear off the lip (top) of the pot so it doesn't stick up above the soil surface and pull moisture out of the soil. If you're using premade growing blocks encased in netting, cut off the netting before planting.

To transplant seedlings, follow these steps:

1. **Use a hoe, spade, or trowel to make a small hole in your garden for each seedling.**

   The hole should be deep enough so the transplant is at the same depth in the ground as it was in the pot (except for tomatoes). Make the hole twice as wide as the root ball.

2. **Unpot a seedling (unless it's in a peat pot) by turning its pot upside down and cupping the seedling with your hand.**

   Be sure to keep the root mass and soil intact. If the seedling doesn't come out easily, gently tap on the edge of the pot or gently press on the bottom of each cell of the flat with your fingers. Whatever you do, don't yank out a plant by its stem.

3. **Check the root ball's condition.**

   If the roots are wound around the outside of the pot, work them loose with your fingers so they can grow out into the soil. Unwind larger roots and break smaller ones (this won't hurt them) so they all point outward. Try to keep as much of the original soil intact as possible.

4. **Mix a diluted liquid fertilizer into the soil of the planting hole to help the plants get off to a fast start.**

   Reduce the recommended strength on the fertilizer container by half. For example, if it says apply 1 tablespoon per gallon of water, use only ½ tablespoon. (See Chapter 15 for more on fertilizers.)

5. **Put each prepared seedling into the holes that you made.**

Most young vegetables should be planted at the same soil level as they were in the pot, as shown in Figure 13-3. For some vegetables, such as tomatoes, you can sink the seedling a little deeper. They grow extra roots along the lower portion of their stems and thrive with this treatment.

6. **After firming the soil around the roots with your hands, form a shallow soil basin around the base of the transplant.**

The soil basin serves as a moat around the seedling to hold water. When you water or it rains, the moisture stays in the moat and drains to where the roots are located. Chapter 15 provides more information on soil basins.

7. **Depending on the conditions, water the bed that day or the next.**

If the weather has been dry or if the soil is sandy, you may want to water the entire bed; if it's rainy or the soil is already very wet, wait until tomorrow to water.

8. **Keep the bed moist while the seedlings get established and begin to grow strongly.**

In extreme hot, dry weather, provide temporary shade for transplants with paper tents or wooden shingles pushed into the ground on the south or west side of the plants.

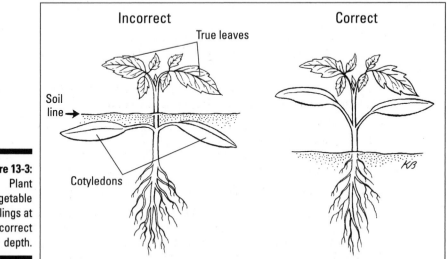

Figure 13-3: Plant vegetable seedlings at the correct depth.

If you don't get an ideal transplanting day and the weather is hot and sunny, shade the plants until the sun goes down. And don't be alarmed if your plants look a little droopy after you set them out; they'll soon recover. Cabbage seedlings can droop and look almost dead, for example, and be up and growing in a day or two.

Sowing Seeds Directly in Your Garden

Unless you live in an area where summers are really short, some vegetables are better off sown directly in a garden rather than as transplants. Large-seeded, fast-growing vegetables — such as corn, melons, squash, beans, and peas — usually languish if they're grown in containers for even a day or two too long. Plants sown directly in the ground usually surpass these seedlings if both are planted at the same time. (Even if you live in a short-season area, you can help speed new plants along. See Chapter 21 for information on extending your growing season.)

In the following sections, I describe different methods for planting seeds right into your garden and show you how to thin seedlings carefully.

Deciding on a seed-planting method

You can plant seeds in a variety of patterns: single rows, wide rows, beds, raised beds, or hills. The method you choose depends on your climate, your tools, and your taste. You can find out more about these planting methods in Chapter 3. Whichever method you choose, here are a few basic principles to keep in mind when planting seeds:

- **Make sure that the soil has dried out sufficiently before you work it, and be sure that the soil is warm enough for the seeds that you want to plant.** Pea seeds, for example, germinate in soil as cool as 40 degrees, and you can plant them as soon as you can work the soil in spring. Squash seeds, on the other hand, need warmth. If your soil temperature is much below 65 degrees, the seeds are likely to rot in the ground before they sprout. (See the appendix for a list of appropriate soil temperatures for different kinds of seeds.) The best way to determine the temperature of your soil is to use a soil thermometer, which you can buy at a garden store. Chapter 14 provides more information on preparing your soil for sowing.

- **Immediately before planting seeds, loosen your garden soil with a hoe or shovel to a depth of 6 inches.** Rake over the area to create a smooth planting surface. Don't walk over areas where you'll be sowing seeds; stay in the pathways. Compacting the soil makes it difficult for seedlings to emerge and send down their roots.

- **Sow seeds at the proper planting depth.** A seed planted too deeply uses up its supply of stored nutrients before the seedling can push its way to the surface; a seed planted too shallow may dry out. A general rule is to plant seeds to depths that are two to three times their diameters, but the appendix gives recommended planting depths for different kinds of seeds. Also try to sow at a uniform depth because seedlings are more likely to emerge at the same time, enabling you to see where your plants are when you do your first weeding.

✔ **Water newly planted seeds carefully.** Use a watering can with a rose (nozzle with multiple holes) or a hose with a *breaker attachment* (a nozzle that breaks the stream into a gentle spray). A strong stream of water can wash seeds out of a bed or too deeply into the ground. Keep the seeds moist but not soggy until the seeds germinate. Heavy soils often form a crust as they dry out, making it difficult for the seedlings to break through. A moist surface helps prevent crusting, as does covering seeds with vermiculite or sand, instead of soil alone. If the weather is dry after you sow the seeds, gently water the seeded area every 2 days or so.

The following sections explain the basic methods for planting your seeds.

Row planting

The first step when row planting is to mark the placement of a row within your garden. A planting line consisting of a simple string and stakes enables you to easily lay out rows. Make a *furrow,* or trench, at the correct depth along the row. To make a shallow furrow, lay a rake or hoe underneath your string marker, and press the handle into the soil. You can make deeper furrows (ones that can be used for watering, too) by dragging the corner of your hoe across the soil surface, using the string as your guideline.

Sow seeds more thickly than you want the final spacing of the crops to be to ensure an adequate number of plants; some seeds may fail to sprout. Thinning rows is less of a chore if you space seeds as evenly as possible. Large seeds like peas and beans are easy to space at precise intervals, but evenly spacing small seeds can be a real challenge.

Cover the seeds with fine soil and then firm them in with the back of a hoe to make sure that all the seeds are in contact with the soil. Water gently.

If you're planting long rows of corn, beans, or peas that will be furrow-irrigated (see Chapter 15), fill the furrows with water first and then push the large seeds into the top of raised beds.

Wide row planting

You can plant more seeds in less space and get higher yields by using the wide row planting method. (Figure 13-4 compares wide rows and straight single rows.) This method not only saves space but also allows you to concentrate watering, weeding, and fertilizing in a smaller area. Follow these steps for wide row planting:

1. **Choose the location and width of your row, usually 10 to 16 inches wide, and then smooth the soil until it's level.**

   You may want to run strings along the outside edges of the row to clearly designate the planting area.

2. **Sprinkle seeds over the entire row — with most crops, try to land the seeds about ½ to 1 inch apart (for peas and beans, 1½ to 2 inches).**

   Pat the seeds down with the back of a hoe.

3. **Use a rake to lift soil from the side of the row to cover the seeds, and gently smooth the soil covering the seeds to the same depth throughout the row.**

   With small seeds like carrots and lettuce, cover the seeds with a thin layer of potting soil. Then pat the potting soil down again to bring the added soil into firm contact with the seeds.

4. **Water the seeds gently.**

   Keep the soil moist by gently watering a few times a week or when you see that the top layer of soil is drying out.

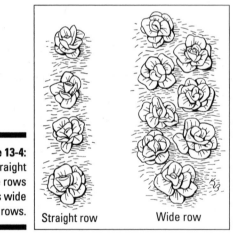

Figure 13-4:
Straight single rows versus wide rows.

Straight row   Wide row

Raised bed planting

Planting raised beds is essentially the same as planting wide rows. To prepare your beds, see Chapter 14. If you don't have permanent beds, mark the dimensions and smooth out the soil. You can broadcast sow (sprinkle by hand) in single rows with a few inches between rows, as shown in Figure 13-5, or you can plant individual seeds at the proper distance apart.

Figure 13-5:
Broadcasting
seeds in a
raised bed.

Hill planting

Plant seeds for vining crops that spread out — such as squash, melons, or cucumbers — in hills or circular groups, as shown in Figure 13-6. Loosen and level the soil in a 1-foot-diameter area, and then plant five to six seeds close together. After the second set of true leaves form, keep the two strongest seedlings (the ones that are the biggest and sport the most leaves) and thin out the remaining seedlings by cutting them with scissors (see the next section for details).

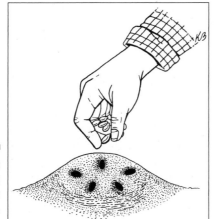

Figure 13-6:
Sow vining
crop seeds
in hills.

If your soil is heavy, you may want to plant in a *raised hill* (also called a *mound*). The raised soil warms up more quickly than the surrounding soil and drains better. But be careful in midsummer not to let the mound dry out. You can easily construct a soil basin around the mound for watering (see Chapter 15).

Thinning seedlings in your garden

Soon after seedlings grow their second set of true leaves, you need to thin them out. Don't neglect this important step; crowded seedlings turn into weak, spindly plants that don't produce well. Separate the plants by hand or with a narrow hoe according to the distances in Chapter 3.

When you thin plants, either discard the extra seedlings or move them to another part of your garden. Newly transplanted seedlings need extra attention until they get established. Shade them from the hot sun for a day or two and be sure to keep them well watered. Lettuce is one of the easiest vegetables to move when it's small. Root crops such as beets and carrots transplant poorly, as do beans and peas.

You can thin some crops in stages, with delicious results. Carrots, lettuce, and beets are all good candidates for gradual thinning. If you've ever tasted beet greens cooked up with tender, marble-sized beets still attached, you know what a real treat they are. Start thinning carrot, lettuce, and beet seedlings when they're 1 to 2 inches apart. After the plants grow to 6 to 8 inches tall, pull up every other one and enjoy them. Leave a final 4- to 6-inch spacing for larger plants to develop.

Chapter 14

Workin' the Dirt

· ·

In This Chapter

▶ Clearing your garden plot

▶ Adding the right nutrients and other stuff to your soil

▶ Mixing your amendments into the soil

▶ Forming a compost pile

· ·

*P*roperly preparing the soil before planting is an all-important first step toward a bountiful harvest. Don't take shortcuts with your soil. You'll be cheating your plants at their roots, and they won't like it.

In this chapter, I tell you how to take care of your soil — clean it up, straighten it out, and make it an all-around better place for roots. Remember, good soil makes happy roots, and happy roots mean a healthy garden.

Razing Your Garden Spot

After you choose a good sunny spot for your vegetable garden and draw a plan on paper (see Chapter 3 if you haven't done this preparatory work), you need to clean up the area so the soil will be easier to work. You can clear your garden area any time during the year, but the season before planting works best — clear in the fall for spring planting, clear in the spring for summer or fall planting. You can clear the area the day before you plant, but you may have more weed problems later.

If you already have an established garden, clean up any debris in fall or winter, depending on where you live, and till the ground before planting.

Here are the basics of initially clearing your garden spot, which I explain in more detail in the sections that follow:

1. **Outline the areas of your garden plot that you want to clear.**

   You outline the areas depending on how you want the plots to be shaped. Follow these guidelines:

   - To get your edges straight for a square or rectangular vegetable plot, stretch a string between sticks and mark the line with a trickle of ground white limestone, which is available at garden centers.

   - For a round garden, use a hose or rope to lay out the area, adjusting the position to create a smooth curve.

   - If you want several individual beds separated by permanent paths, outline each bed independently with string, sticks, and limestone so you don't waste time improving soil that you'll never use. But if you think that you may change your garden layout from season to season or year to year, work the entire area within the outline.

2. **Clear the surface by first removing plants, weeds, brush, and rock. If necessary, mow the site to cut back the grass and weeds close to the surface of the soil.**

   See the section "Killing weeds and aggressive grasses," for details on removing weeds.

3. **Dig out the roots of small trees and tough weeds with a hoe, shovel, or pick ax.**

4. **After the vegetation is manageable, remove any sod.**

   See the section "Stripping sod" for details on how to do this.

Killing weeds and aggressive grasses

If your garden area contains a lot of perennial weeds — weeds, like quack grass, that come back year after year — or if you need to clear an area of a warm-season lawn composed of vigorous grasses (like Bermuda grass), make sure that you first kill these weeds or grasses. You can pull out or mulch out seedlings (see Chapter 15 for more on mulches and weeding), but many aggressive weeds and turf spread by underground roots as well as seeds; these underground roots can haunt you for eons.

If you have an existing garden, you have to be diligent about weeding, or you may need to start all over again with tilling and removing as much of the weed's root system as you can.

You can kill weeds and aggressive grasses two ways:

✔ **Hand dig and sift:** For a small garden dig up the earth and carefully sift the soil, removing sod and root parts that may come back next year as weeds (see the tip on sifting compost at the end of this chapter).

✔ **Apply a covering:** An easy, chemical-free way to clear your garden is to cover it with clear or black plastic, cardboard, or even old rugs. After a month under these impermeable coverings, existing plants die from the lack of sunlight. You must plan ahead to use this method, and it may not look pretty, but it works like a charm — especially on annual weeds. For perennial weeds, you may need to dig out their roots, too, after applying the plastic.

You can buy plastic in rolls at hardware stores or home improvement centers; check department stores for old pieces of cardboard and carpet stores for old rugs. Use the thickest plastic or cardboard you can find — it should be at least 2 millimeters, but 4 millimeters is even better.

Controlling weeds and grasses by applying a covering to your garden area is easy. Just follow these steps:

1. **Spread the covering over your entire garden area, securing the edges with spare rocks, bricks, or boards.**

   Let neighboring pieces overlap by several inches so no light can penetrate. If you're using old rugs, place them nap side down.

2. **After a month, remove the covering and strip off any grass or weeds.**

   Use a shovel to cut off any grass or weeds at the root level (just below the soil surface). If they aren't too thick, rototill them into the ground.

3. **Wet the area and wait about 10 days for weeds to sprout.**

   Leave the covering off; you want weeds to sprout. You should get some growth because you haven't removed weed seeds.

4. **Use a hoe to kill the weeds.**

   Hoeing the weeds down is sufficient to kill annual weeds, but if you have perennial weeds, you need to dig out the roots. Check out the National Gardening Association's Weed Library (www.garden.org/weed library) for help identifying the weeds in your garden.

For an organic approach to killing weeds and building your garden soil, try a no-till layered garden technique (see Figure 14-1). It's like making lasagna. The season before planting, lay down a 3- to 4-sheet-thick layer of black and white newspaper over the garden area. Water the paper to keep it in place. Cover the newspaper with a 6-inch-thick layer of hay or straw. Top that with a 1- to 2-inch-thick layer of compost. By the next planting season, the layers will have killed the grass and most of the annual and perennial weeds in your garden.

You can hand pull any tenacious perennial weeds that survived. Earthworms will have munched up much of the newspaper turning it into valuable compost. You can plant your seedlings right into the mulched layers, and they'll grow like weeds (even better).

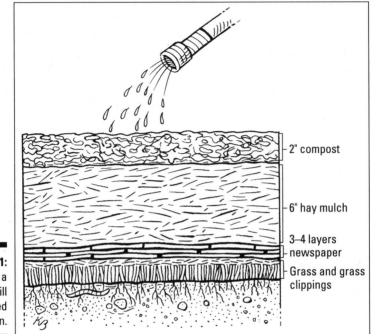

- 2" compost

- 6" hay mulch

- 3–4 layers newspaper

- Grass and grass clippings

Figure 14-1:
Creating a no-till layered garden.

Stripping sod

If you don't want to try the techniques in the preceding section, you can immediately remove the lawn grass by stripping the *sod* (grass and roots) before planting. I show you how to clear it away in this section. If your lawn consists of bluegrass and other less-spreading grasses, you can strip the sod without first killing the grass; most lawns in the northern United States consist of these types of grasses. But you should kill weedier grasses, like Bermuda grass, before you strip the sod (see the preceding section for details on killing weedier grass). Stripping sod takes a lot of effort, but it works. Just follow these steps, and have your wheelbarrow or garden cart handy:

1. **Water the area that you want to clear for 15 minutes for each of the 2 days prior to digging up your sod.**

   I suggest watering this way because stripping sod is easier when the ground is slightly moist.

2. **Starting at one end of your plot, slip a spade under the grass and slide it under the sod.**

   An easier method is to precut the sod into square or rectangular sections and then loosen each section with a spade. Either way, don't dig too deep; you just want to remove the sod and 1 to 2 inches of roots. You also can use a rented sod stripper to cut the sod into rows that you roll up and remove.

3. **Pivot your spade up and let the sod flip off the spade and back onto the ground. Use your spade to slice off the sod section, toss the sod into a wheelbarrow or garden cart, and take it to a compost pile.**

   If your sod has healthy grass with few weeds, and you don't want to compost it, use it to patch bare spots in your lawn. Keep it well watered, and it should root and blend in with the existing grasses.

4. **Repeat Steps 2 and 3 until your garden is cleared of sod.**

These steps should clear all the grass in your garden. You'll get new growth only if you have an aggressive grass like Bermuda and don't kill all the roots.

Analyzing and Improving Your Soil

After clearing your garden area, you need to take a close look at your soil — give it a good squeeze, have it tested, amend it, and then work it out to make sure it's in shipshape. Good soil gives vegetable roots a balance of all the things they need: moisture, nutrients, and air. And knowing your soil type enables you to counteract problems that you may face when gardening on that piece of land. I explain the basics in the following sections.

Distinguishing different types of soil

Three main types of soil exist, with a lot of variations in between. Hard clay is at one end of the spectrum; soft, sandy soil is at the other end; and loam is in the middle. Being familiar with your soil helps you know what to expect when gardening. Clay soil tends to have a lot of natural fertility but is heavy to work with and doesn't drain water well. Sandy soil, on the other hand, drains water well (maybe too well) but doesn't have a lot of natural fertility. Loam, the ideal soil, is somewhere in between the two.

Here are general characteristics of the three basic types of soil:

✔ **Sandy soil** is composed of mostly large mineral particles. Water moves through this soil quickly, taking nutrients with it. Sandy soil is well aerated, quick to dry out and warm up, and often lacks the nutrients that vegetables need.

✔ **Clay soil** consists of mainly small particles that cling tightly together and hold water and nutrients. It's slow to dry out and warm up, and has poor aeration, but it's fertile when it can be worked.

✔ **Loam soil** is a happy mixture of large and small particles. It's well aerated and drains properly, but it can still hold water and nutrients. This is *the* soil to have for a great vegetable garden.

To find out what type of soil you have, grab a handful of moist soil and squeeze it, as shown in Figure 14-2. Then use these guidelines to determine what type of soil you're working with:

✔ **Sandy soil** falls apart and doesn't hold together in a ball when you let go. It feels gritty when you rub it between your fingers.

✔ **Clay soil** oozes through your fingers as you squeeze it and stays in a slippery wad when you let go. Rubbing clay soil between your fingers feels slippery.

✔ **Loam soil** usually stays together after you squeeze it, but it falls apart easily when you poke it with your finger.

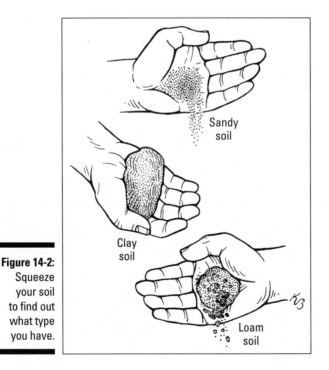

Figure 14-2:
Squeeze your soil to find out what type you have.

If you have sandy or clay soil, don't despair; you can improve your soil and make it more like loam. Check out the section "Adding organic matter (aka the dead stuff)," later in this chapter, for details.

Testing your soil

Vegetables are kind of picky about soil chemistry. Too much of this nutrient or too little of that nutrient, and you have problems. If you don't believe me, check out Chapter 4 to see what happens when tomatoes grow in soil that's deficient in calcium; they develop blossom-end rot. Yuck. Sometimes too much of a nutrient, such as nitrogen, causes lots of leaf growth on plants (such as peppers) but few fruits. Getting the levels just right is important for the best harvest.

In addition to nutrient levels, soil pH also is an important factor in plant growth. The right pH enables vegetables to use nutrients from the soil. Soil is rated on a pH scale, with a pH of 1 being most acidic and a pH of 14 being most alkaline. If your soil's pH isn't within a suitable range, plants can't take up nutrients — like phosphorus and potassium — even if they're present in the soil in high amounts. On the other hand, if the pH is too low, the solubility of certain minerals, such as manganese, may increase to toxic levels.

Most vegetables grow well in a slightly acidic soil with a pH between 6 and 7. Potatoes, including sweet potatoes, prefer a slightly more acidic soil, in the 5 to 6 range. But in general, if you aim for a soil pH between 6 and 7, your vegetables should grow well.

The only way to find out whether your soil will be to your vegetables' liking is to test it. Don't worry; analyzing your soil isn't complicated, and you don't need a lab coat. Here are two ways that you can test your soil:

- **Use a do-it-yourself kit.** This basic pH test measures your soil's acidity and alkalinity and sometimes major nutrient content. Buy a kit at a nursery, follow the instructions, and voilà — you know your soil's pH. However, the test gives you only a rough picture of the pH and nutrient levels in your soil. You may want to know more about your soil.

- **Have a soil lab do a test for you.** A complete soil test is a good investment because a soil lab can thoroughly analyze your soil. Here's what you can find out from a soil lab's test in addition to the pH level:

  - **Your soil's nutrient content.** If you know your soil's nutrient content, you can determine how much and what kind of fertilizer to use. In fact, many soil tests tell you exactly how much fertilizer to add; see Chapter 15 for more on fertilizer.

- **Soil problems that are specific to your geographic region.** A soil test may help you identify local problems. The soil lab should then give you a recommendation for a type and amount of fertilizer to add to your soil. For example, in dry-summer areas, you may have salty soil; the remedy is to add *gypsum,* a readily available mineral soil additive.

Of course, soil labs charge around $20 to $30 for their basic services. Your local Cooperative Extension Service office or a private soil lab can conduct a complete and reliable soil test. To locate a private lab, look in the phone book under *soil testing* (or search the Internet for soil test labs around the country). You also can ask your Cooperative Extension Service office for recommendations.

Fall is a good time to test soil because labs aren't as busy. It's also a good time to add many *amendments* (materials that improve your soil's fertility and workability) to your soil because they break down slowly.

To prepare a soil sample to use with a do-it-yourself kit or to send to a soil lab, follow these steps:

1. **Fill a cup with soil from the top 4 to 6 inches of soil from your vegetable garden, and then place the soil in a plastic bag.**

2. **Dig six to eight similar samples from different parts of your plot.**

3. **Mix all the cups of soil together; place two cups of the combined soil in a plastic bag — that's your soil sample.**

After you've collected your sample, consult the instructions from your soil test kit or the testing lab.

If you're testing a soil imbalance — a known problem that you've identified in either pH or nutrients — you may want to test your soil every year because changes in pH and most nutrients are gradual. A home testing kit is a good way to test a pH imbalance. For nutrients, you may want to do a yearly test at a lab until the imbalance (high or low levels of a nutrient) is fixed. To maintain balanced soil, test it every 3 to 5 years.

Adjusting soil pH

Most garden soils have a pH between 5.5 and 8.0. This number helps you determine when and how to adjust your soil's pH level. The following guidelines help you interpret this number:

✔ If the number is below 6, the soil is too acidic, and you need to add ground limestone.

✔ If the measurement is above 7.5, the soil is too alkaline for most vegetables, and you need to add soil sulfur.

In the following sections, I explain how to figure out how much lime or sulfur you need to add to your soil and how to apply the materials.

Calculating how much lime or sulfur you need

All Cooperative Extension Service offices, any soil lab, and many lawn and garden centers have charts showing how much lime or sulfur to add to correct a pH imbalance. The charts tell you how many pounds of material to add per 1,000 square feet, so you need to measure the size of your vegetable garden first. Then use Tables 14-1 and 14-2 to figure out how much lime or sulfur you need to add to your soil.

Table 14-1	Pounds of Limestone Needed to Raise pH (per 1,000 Square Feet)		
pH	*Number of Pounds for:*		
	Sandy Soil	*Loam Soil*	*Clay Soil*
4.0–6.5	60	161	230
4.5–6.5	50	130	190
5.0–6.5	40	100	150
5.5–6.5	30	80	100
6.0–6.5	15	40	60

Table 14-2	Pounds of Sulfur Needed to Lower pH (per 1,000 Square Feet)		
pH	*Number of Pounds for:*		
	Sandy Soil	*Loam Soil*	*Clay Soil*
8.5–6.5	45	60	70
8.0–6.5	30	35	45
7.5–6.5	10	20	25
7.0–6.5	2	4	7

In general, soils in climates with high rainfall — such as east of the Mississippi River (particularly east of the Appalachian Mountains) or in the Pacific Northwest — tend to be acidic. West of the Mississippi, where less rainfall occurs, soils are more alkaline. But regardless of where you live in the United States, you should easily be able to find the lime or sulfur that you need at your local garden center.

Applying lime or sulfur to your soil

The best way to apply sulfur and limestone to your soil is to use a *drop spreader* (the same machine you may use to apply lawn fertilizer). This simple machine doesn't cost very much, and it helps you spread the material more evenly. Some nurseries may even loan you a spreader or allow you to rent one inexpensively. You also can spread these materials by hand if you're careful and wear gloves. No matter how you spread the materials, make sure that you work the soil well afterward.

You can purchase and apply different types of limestone to your soil. The type you use may depend on the type of nutrients your soil needs:

- **Dolomitic limestone** contains magnesium as well as calcium. Magnesium is one of the nutrients that a soil lab may test for, and even though it isn't in the top three (nitrogen, phosphorus, and potassium), it's as important as calcium for plant growth. Use dolomitic limestone to adjust the pH if your soil test shows that your soil is low in magnesium.

- **Pulverized limestone** is the most common and inexpensive acid neutralizer. Use this limestone if you don't need to add magnesium to your soil.

- **Pelletized pulverized limestone** is a little more expensive than ordinary pulverized limestone, but it's cleaner, less dusty, and easier to use than both dolomitic and powdered limestone.

Sulfur usually only comes in powdered form or mixed with other nutrients such as ammonium sulfate.

Your soil uses limestone and sulfur most efficiently when it's tilled into the soil to a depth of 4 to 6 inches.

Adding organic matter (aka the dead stuff)

If you're like most people, your garden doesn't have perfect loam soil. So to fix that mucky clay or loose sand, you need to add *organic matter* — once-living stuff like compost, sawdust, animal manure, ground bark, grass clippings, and *leaf mold* (composted tree leaves). You can't change the type of soil (clay, sand, or loam) you have, but adding organic matter makes your soil more like loam, which is perfect for vegetable roots. Even if you have loam soil, you still should add organic matter to your soil every year.

What is organic gardening?

Organic gardening has become a household term in the past 10 years. Many people are choosing organically grown produce from the grocery store because they feel it's safer and healthier. Because organic produce costs more than conventionally grown produce, it's a good idea to grow your own. And you're in luck, because throughout this book, I suggest ways to grow your vegetables organically.

Organic gardening, in many ways, is just good, simple gardening practices and common sense. Some of the basic facets of organic gardening include the following:

- ✔ Feeding the soil — not just the plants — with organic fertilizers, manure, and organic matter (Chapter 15)

- ✔ Rotating crops (Chapter 16)

- ✔ Planting a diverse group of crops

- ✔ Solving pest problems by planting disease-resistant varieties

- ✔ Using barriers (covers that keep bugs away from plants)

- ✔ Releasing beneficial insects

- ✔ Using the least harmful biological and plant-based sprays (Chapter 17)

The USDA now has a certification program for organic farms, and the fertilizers and pesticides that can be used on these certified farms are widely available at local garden centers and through the mail. But you don't have to be certified to grow plants organically. My philosophy in this book is to emphasize compost and soil-building practices and to suggest the use of sprays only as a last resort (and even then you should use only organic ones).

Organic matter improves garden soil in the following ways:

- ✔ It helps loosen and aerate clay soil.

- ✔ It improves the water- and nutrient-holding capacity of sandy soil.

- ✔ It provides the once-living material that attracts microorganisms, beneficial fungi, worms, and other soil-borne critters that improve the health of your vegetables.

Work some organic matter into your soil before you plant each season. If you're using unfinished (raw) organic matter like leaves or undecomposed manure, add it to your soil at least 1 month before planting. That way it will break down before you plant. Add finished compost and manures just before planting.

Follow these steps to add organic matter to your garden soil (for information on the best kinds of organic matter, see the following sections):

1. **Add a 1- to 2-inch layer of organic matter to the area where you intend to plant your vegetables.**

   Go for the higher end (2 inches) if your garden is new or if your soil is heavy clay or very sandy. Use less if you've grown there for years or if your soil is loamy and fertile.

   You need 3 cubic yards of compost to spread a 1-inch-thick layer over 1,000 square feet.

2. **Work in the organic matter to a depth of at least 6 inches.**

   There's nothing glamorous about spreading manure. The best way to spread organic matter is with a wheelbarrow and a shovel. Work it into the soil with a shovel, iron fork, or rototiller.

Another way to add organic matter to your soil is to grow your own. You can find out more about growing green manure and cover crops in Chapter 16.

The best choice: Compost

The best organic material to add to your soil is compost. Composting breaks down yard waste, agricultural waste, wood scraps, and even sludge into a crumbly soil-like material called *humus*.

Compost is usually clean, easy to use, and available. You can buy it in bags or have it delivered by the truckload. Most waste disposal sites make compost and sell it relatively cheap. You also can make your own compost; see the later section "Making Your Own Compost" for details.

Before you buy compost, ask whether the compost contains any heavy metals, such as lead, and whether the compost is safe to use in a vegetable garden. Your local health department should be able to tell you what levels of lead and heavy metals are unsafe. The folks at the waste disposal site also may even be able to give you a precise nutrient content if they've performed any tests on the compost.

Other organic materials, such as sawdust and manure

Using organic materials other than compost — such as sawdust and manure — is fine, but these materials present a few problems that compost doesn't. Here are some advantages and disadvantages:

 ✔ Sawdust adds organic matter to your soil, which eventually breaks down and forms humus. However, the sawdust also robs the soil of nitrogen when it decomposes, so you have to add more fertilizer to compensate (see Chapter 15).

✔ Livestock manure improves your soil's nitrogen level (see Chapter 15 for more information on manure). However, livestock diets often include lots of hay that's full of weed seeds, which may germinate in your vegetable garden. Some manures (such as horse manure) add organic matter and some nutrients to your soil, but they're also loaded with bedding materials (like dried hay) that cause the same problem that adding sawdust causes.

If you use manure, make sure it's *fully composted* — that is, it has been sitting around for a year or two, so it's decomposed, and the salts have been leached out. Too much salt in the soil can be harmful to plants. Good quality compost or fully decomposed manure should have a dark brown color, earthy smell, and have little original material visible.

Turning Your Soil

After adding nutrients and amendments to your soil, you need to mix them up. Turning your soil to mix the amendments enables them to break down faster and be available where the roots can use them.

If your soil is dry, water well, and let it sit for a few days before digging. Then, to determine whether your soil is ready to turn, take a handful of soil and squeeze it. The soil should crumble easily in your hand with a flick of your finger; if water drips out, it's too wet.

Don't work soil that's too wet. Working soil that's too wet ruins the soil structure — after it dries, the soil is hard to work and even harder to grow roots in.

The easiest way to turn your soil, especially in large plots, is with a *rototiller* (or *tiller,* for short). You can rent or borrow a tiller, or if you're serious about this vegetable-garden business, buy one. I prefer tillers with rear tines and power-driven wheels because you can really lean into the machines and use your weight to till deeper. If you have a small (less than 100 square feet) vegetable plot, consider using a minitiller (see Chapter 20 for more details on this tool) or hand dig it if you're up for a little exercise.

If you use a rototiller, adjust the tines so the initial pass over your soil is fairly shallow (a few inches deep). As the soil loosens, set the tines deeper with successive passes (crisscrossing at 90-degree angles) until the top 8 to 12 inches of soil are loosened.

To turn your soil by hand, use a straight spade and a digging fork. You can either dig your garden to one spade's depth, about 1 foot, or *double dig* (that is, work your soil to a greater depth), going down 20 to 24 inches. After turning the soil, level the area with a steel rake, breaking up clods and discarding any rocks. Although double digging takes more effort, it enables roots to penetrate deeper to find water and nutrients. If you're double digging, dig the upper part of the soil with a straight spade to remove the sod and loosen the *subsoil* (usually any soil below 8 to 12 inches) with a spade. Replace the original topsoil often when you loosen the subsoil.

Don't overtill your soil. Tilling to mix amendments or loosen the soil in spring or fall is fine, but using the tiller repeatedly in summer to weed or turn beds ruins the soil structure and causes the organic matter (the good stuff) to break down too fast.

Making Your Own Compost

Making your own compost is a way to turn a wide array of readily available organic materials — such as grass clippings, household garbage, and plant residue — into a uniform, easy-to-handle source of organic matter for your garden. Even though finished compost is usually low in plant nutrients, composting enables you to enrich your soil in an efficient, inexpensive way. You can add organic matter that isn't decomposed to your soil and get a similar result, but most people find that dark, crumbly compost is easier to handle than half-rotten household garbage — yuck.

A *compost pile* (a pile of organic matter constructed to decompose) can be free standing or enclosed and can be made any time of year. However, you'll have the most organic matter in summer and fall when decomposition occurs faster due to the warm weather.

Wire fencing makes a good container because it lets in plenty of air. You also can purchase easy-to-use composters at garden centers or through mail-order catalogs (see Figure 14-3). Some composters simplify the turning process (see "Moistening and turning your compost pile" later in this chapter), because they rotate on swivels or come apart in sections or pieces. They're easy to use, but usually aren't large enough for the amount of material produced in a large garden. You can build your own composter as well.

In the following sections, I show you how to build, moisten, and turn a compost pile; I also warn you about materials that should never, ever go into a compost pile.

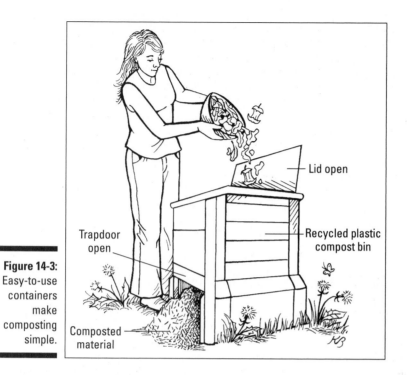

Lid open

Trapdoor
open

Recycled plastic
compost bin

Figure 14-3:
Easy-to-use
containers
make
composting
simple.

Composted
material

Building a compost pile

Building a good compost pile involves much more than just tossing organic
materials in a pile in the corner of your yard, though many people (including
me at times) use this technique with varied success. Because, you know,
everything does eventually rot. But to compost correctly, you need to have a
good size for your pile, add the right types and amount of materials, and
provide the correct amount of moisture.

Here are the characteristics of a well-made pile:

  ✔ It heats up quickly — a sign that the decay organisms are at work.

  ✔ Decomposition proceeds at a rapid rate.

  ✔ The pile doesn't give off any bad odors.

  ✔ The organisms that do all the decay work take up carbon and nitrogen
  (the stuff they feed on and break down) in proportion to their needs.

You can easily come up with the correct amounts of materials for a compost pile by building the pile in layers. Just follow these steps:

1. **Choose a well-drained spot in your yard.**

   If you build your compost pile on a naturally wet spot, the layers will become too wet and inhibit the decomposition process.

2. **Create a 4- to 6-inch layer of "brown" materials that are rich in carbon.**

   These brown materials include roots and stalks of old plants, old grass clippings, dried hay, leaves, and so on. The more finely chopped these materials are, the more surface area that decay organisms can attack, and the faster the materials decompose.

3. **Add a thin layer of "green" materials that are high in nitrogen.**

   Green materials include green grass clippings, kitchen vegetable scraps, a 2- to 4-inch layer of manure, or a light, even coating of blood meal, cottonseed meal, or organic fertilizer high in nitrogen (see Chapter 15 for more on fertilizers).

4. **Repeat these green and brown layers (Steps 2 through 3) until the pile is no more than 5 feet high.**

   If a pile is higher than 5 feet, too little oxygen reaches the center of the pile, enabling some nasty anaerobic decay organisms to take over and produce bad odors; I hate that. Five feet is a good maximum width for the pile as well.

Here are a few additional ways to ensure success in your compost pile:

- **Moisten each layer of your compost pile lightly with a watering can as you build it.** However, don't let the pile get soggy.

- **Cover each layer with a few inches of garden soil.** The soil covers any material in the nitrogen layer that may attract flies, such as household garbage.

- **Add a dusting of ground limestone or wood ashes on the carbon layer.** This dusting keeps the compost's pH around the 6 to 7 mark that your plants like.

Avoiding materials that don't belong in a compost pile

A well-made pile heats up enough to kill off many insects and disease organisms, but the heating isn't uniform enough to be relied on to kill everything that you want it to. So don't add the following materials to your pile:

- ✔ **Diseased or infected plant material:** Disease organisms may survive the composting process and stick around to reinfect your plants when you apply the finished compost.

- ✔ **Weeds that have gone to seed:** The heat may not be high enough to kill the weed seeds. And then those weeds will show up in your garden.

- ✔ **Pieces of aggressive weeds like quack grass or Bermuda grass:** Even a small piece of a root can produce a new plant.

- ✔ **Grass clippings from lawns treated with herbicides:** Some herbicides may not break down during the composting process.

- ✔ **Meat scraps and fats:** They break down slowly and may attract animals to the pile.

- ✔ **Dog or cat feces:** They may carry diseases that can be transmitted to humans.

Moistening and turning your compost pile

After you build your compost pile, the decay process begins, causing the center of the pile to heat up. Proper moisture helps decay organisms to work properly. Following are some ways to keep your compost pile moist:

- ✔ Water the pile as needed. To determine whether you need to water, dig about 1 foot into the pile and see if it's moist.

  Be careful not to overwater your pile. It's easy to do. The water seeps in and tends not to evaporate readily, so people think the pile is dry when it's not.

- ✔ If there's a long dry spell or if you live in a dry-summer area, water the entire pile to keep it lightly moist.

- ✔ Make a depression in the top of the pile to collect rainfall.

You also must turn the pile periodically to aerate it, prevent it from overheating, and ensure that all the material decomposes uniformly. You can turn your compost pile by forking the material from the outside of the pile to the center or by moving the pile from one area to another. If you made a pile out of wire fencing, simply unhook the ends, pull the fencing apart, and move the cylinder a few feet away from the pile. Then fork the materials from the pile into the empty wire cylinder.

How often you turn the pile and how quickly the compost is done depend on how quickly decay takes place. For example, green, succulent organic material — like fresh grass clippings — decays faster than dried plant material; cool fall temperatures or a spell of rainy days that turn the pile soggy slow things down. Follow these guidelines for deciding when to turn your pile:

✔ If you added only shredded material, the pile may be ready for turning in a week.

✔ If the pile contains a lot of big pieces of organic material, wait several weeks before turning.

✔ If the pile heats up and then cools, turn it.

✔ Turning the pile two to three times throughout the process is plenty.

You can tell that decay has set in if your pile starts to smell bad. If smells occur, hold your nose and fix things by spreading out the pile and reconstructing it.

Your compost is ready for use when the interior of the pile is no longer hot and all the material in the pile has broken down into a uniform, dark crumbly substance; this process takes about 1 to 2 months. To determine whether the pile is no longer hot, feel the interior of the pile with your hand. If you're squeamish, use a compost thermometer (which is available at garden centers).

Chapter 15

Maintaining Your Vegetable Garden

*A*fter planting your garden, you need to keep your vegetables growing vigorously until harvest. Maintaining your vegetable garden is similar to running a long-distance road race. After you're off and running, the key is to pace yourself for the whole race and not burn out in the beginning. Gardeners face a similar situation. You not only have to have lots of enthusiasm to prepare the soil and plant, but you also have to be consistent about checking plants, watering, weeding, fertilizing, and harvesting (among other tasks) to get the best results. If you lose interest in your garden halfway through the growing season, your harvest may be small or poor. Don't worry though; your garden won't require all your time — just some of it each week.

In this chapter, I tell you everything you need to know to keep your vegetables happy — including keeping your soil moist and fertile, adding mulch, supporting your plants, and keeping weeds at bay.

Introducing Your Inner Gardener to the Watering Basics

Even though Mother Nature is often very generous with rain, she still sometimes leaves gardens with a dry spell. Flooding isn't good for your garden, but neither is drought. If your plants don't have adequate water at the right times, they can easily die.

Different crops have different water needs. Some vegetables, like celery, are real water lovers and prefer to have moist soil around their roots at all times. Shallow-rooted crops (like onions and cabbage) need more careful watering during dry spells than deeper-rooted crops (like tomatoes) that can pull water from greater depths. Part II provides specific watering information for all the different vegetables.

You also need to keep in mind a plant's growth stage when watering. Here are some general watering guidelines for different growth stages:

- ✔ **Seedlings and germinating seeds:** Seedlings with small root systems near the soil surface and germinating seeds benefit from frequent, gentle watering, which enables them to sprout and emerge quickly. Water once a day to a few inches deep if it doesn't rain. (Chapter 13 has more details on seedlings and transplants.)

- ✔ **Transplants:** Water transplants when they're first planted in the garden and then every few days after that to 6 inches deep or so. Watering frequently helps the roots recover from transplant shock.

- ✔ **Established plants:** Plants that have been in your garden for a few weeks and that are beyond transplant shock need to be watered deeply. Try to wet the soil at least 6 inches deep. Watering to this depth encourages roots to penetrate deeply, where they're less susceptible to drought. Give the soil a chance to dry out slightly (3 to 6 days if it doesn't rain) before watering thoroughly again.

When I tell you to water to a certain number of inches, don't feel like you have to guess when you've hit the mark; you can dig into the soil with a trowel to see how far the water has penetrated.

In the following sections, I explain when to quench your veggies' thirst and provide information on different watering methods. I also give you tips on how to conserve water.

Knowing when your veggies need a drink

In general, most vegetables use about 1 inch of water per week (1 to 2 inches in hot, windy, dry climates). If you don't get water from rainfall, you have to supply it. Here are some general guidelines for determining when your plants need water:

- ✔ **Your finger is the best indicator of when the soil has dried sufficiently to rewater.** Dig down several inches into the soil; if the soil is dry to your touch 3 to 4 inches down, it's time to water.

- ✔ **Wilting plants can be a sign that your soil needs water.** *Wilting* is when the leaves or stems of a plant droop, bend over, and look limp. These symptoms, however, can be misleading at times. Some plants, like tomatoes, peppers, and eggplants, tend to droop slightly during the heat of the day, even if the soil has enough moisture. If your plants don't stand tall and proud and the soil feels dry, add water and watch them perk up fast.

  Overwatering also causes plants to wilt, so check the soil before watering. If the soil is waterlogged, roots die from lack of air. With fewer roots, plants can no longer take up the water they need from the soil, and so they wilt. Damage from insects and disease also cause wilting.

- ✔ **Each vegetable has a critical period when you need to be especially careful about watering.** If you slack off during these times, your crop may be ruined. Table 15-1 shows the important watering periods for different types of vegetables.

Table 15-1	Critical Watering Periods for Vegetables
Vegetable	**Important Watering Stage**
Bean, lima	When flowering and forming pods
Bean, snap	When flowering and forming pods
Broccoli	When forming a head
Brussels sprouts	When forming sprouts
Cabbage	When forming a head
Carrots	When forming roots
Cauliflower	When forming a head
Corn, sweet	When silking, tasseling, and forming ears

(continued)

Table 15-1 *(continued)*

Vegetable	Important Watering Stage
Cucumber	When flowering and developing fruit
Eggplant	Give uniform supply of water from flowering through harvest
Lettuce	When true leaves form
Melon	During fruit set and early development
Onion, dry	During bulb enlargement
Pea	When flowering and during seed enlargement
Pepper	Give uniform supply of water from flowering through harvest
Potato	When tubers set and enlarge
Pumpkin	When fruits form
Radish	When forming roots
Spinach	When true leaves form
Squash, summer	When forming buds and flowering
Swiss chard	When true leaves form
Tomato	Give uniform supply of water from flowering through harvest
Turnip	When forming roots

Discovering ways to water your vegetable garden

You can water your vegetable garden several different ways. This section discusses some of the basic techniques, from the simplest — furrows — to the most complicated — drip irrigation systems.

You can measure water flow by attaching an inexpensive *flowmeter* (available at hardware and garden supply stores) to your outdoor spigot. To figure out the flow rate at the spigot, turn off all the spigots and read your water meter. Then turn on the spigot serving the hose line for 1 minute. Reread the meter to find out how much water flows through the hose in 1 minute. You need about 60 gallons per 100 square feet of garden to get 1 inch of water.

Furrows

Furrows are shallow trenches between raised beds that channel water to plant roots. This watering method is based on an old farmer technique of planting on narrow raised mounds or beds and then using furrows to water. The beds can be 1 to 3 feet apart — the wider apart they are, however, the more water you need to add. You can use a hoe to dig a furrow at planting time and then plant the seeds or transplants on top of the raised beds, in between the furrows.

When you're ready to water, fill the furrows completely with water and then wait a while, or fill them more than once so the water penetrates down as well as sideways into the raised soil. Poke around with your finger to make sure the water has penetrated the bed.

Furrows work best on level or slightly sloping ground; otherwise, the water moves too fast down the furrows without sinking in. This watering technique traditionally has been used in arid areas with clay soil, such as the Southwest, where little natural rain falls during the growing season and streams or ground water can be used in the garden. Furrows don't work well in sandy soil because the water soaks in before it can reach the end of the furrow.

Furrows aren't the most efficient way to water. Here are a few reasons:

✔ It takes time for the water to run from one end of a mound or bed to the other.

✔ The beginning of a row always gets more water than the end.

✔ You have to move your hose around a lot to fill each furrow.

✔ Water is wasted through evaporation as it's sitting in the furrow.

Basins

A *basin* is a donutlike depression around a vegetable plant that you fill with water — almost like a circular furrow. You make a basin in a 2-foot-diameter circle around the plant. Plastic basins that fit underneath plants such as tomatoes and eggplants are sold commercially. These basins concentrate the water around the roots of the plant.

Homemade basins work particularly well for watering sprawling plants like melons and squash early in the season. After the plants mature, however, their roots grow out of the diameter of the basin, and the method is no longer effective.

Hoses

Watering with a hose is probably the most common way that gardeners water. It's simple, and some might say therapeutic. Who hasn't seen a gardener after a long day at work come home and take some time to hose down the garden with a cup of coffee or drink in hand?

However, watering with a hose isn't the ideal watering system and probably is best for watering containers; for watering individual, large plants such as tomatoes; and when used in conjunction with the basin method (explained in the preceding section). In these situations, you can be sure that you're applying the right amount of water to your plants.

Unless you check the amount of water you're applying by digging the soil after watering, you may not water your garden evenly with a hose. Some areas may have lots of water, whereas other areas may just have water on the surface. Also, like overhead sprinklers (described in the next section), using a hose is a more wasteful way of watering because much of the water falls in pathways or on the lawn around your garden.

The best way to water your vegetable garden with a hose is to leave the hose running at a trickle in a basin near each plant until the water has soaked down at least 6 inches deep.

Sprinklers

A sprinkler, shown in Figure 15-1, is effective for watering vegetables planted in sandy soil that absorbs water quickly. It's also an effective way to water a large garden when you're pressed for time. Just set up the sprinkler, and based on the amount of time it takes to water to 6 inches deep (see the earlier section "Knowing when your veggies need a drink"), you can set a timer and go about other business. However, if you have heavy clay soil that absorbs water slowly or if your garden is on a slope, the water may run off and not sink into the soil where the plants need it. Instead, it's best to use drip irrigation (see the next section) so the water soaks into the ground.

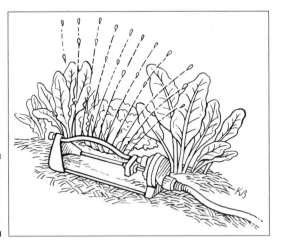

Figure 15-1:
Watering
with a
sprinkler.

For vegetable gardens, portable-type sprinklers (versus in-ground permanent sprinklers used in lawns) are best. You can move them around in your garden to cover a certain area or the whole garden. Some sprinklers throw water back and forth, whereas others send it in a circular direction. Choose the type that best suits your garden design.

Constantly wetting the foliage of vegetable plants can encourage disease problems. So when you use a sprinkler, water in the morning so the foliage can dry before nightfall and so you lose less water to evaporation.

As taller plants such as corn and tomatoes grow, sprinklers tend to be less effective because the water hits the foliage, damaging it and not thoroughly watering the rest of the garden. Some gardeners use watering towers that have an overhead sprinkler attached to the top. You position the sprinkler a few feet above the plants, hook it up to a hose, and sprinkle the garden. However, even these sprinklers prove to be less effective when plants reach above 4 to 5 feet tall. For these taller plants, it's best to choose one of the other watering methods described in this chapter.

Soaker-hose irrigation

A *soaker-hose irrigation system* consists of a rubber hose perforated with tiny pores that leak water, as shown in Figure 15-2. You can lay the hose between rows or curve it around plants, similar to how you use a drip irrigation system (described in the following section). Water leaks out of the hose and onto the soil, leaving your plant foliage dry and reducing evaporation.

Figure 15-2:
Watering
with a
soaker
hose.

Using a soaker-hose system is easier than using a drip irrigation system because it involves fewer parts and no nozzles. Its primary limitation is that it works best on flat terrain, often delivering water unevenly on sloped or bumpy gardens. It also may clog over time and not deliver water evenly along the hose.

Drip irrigation

A *drip irrigation system* provides water slowly through holes, or *emitters,* in flexible plastic pipes. Many different drip irrigation systems are available; they can consist of a single pipe with flexible lines running off it, or a series of pipes. You weave these pipes — which are connected to a water supply, a filter, and often a pressure regulator — along rows of plants so the water flows directly to the roots of your vegetables, as shown in Figure 15-3.

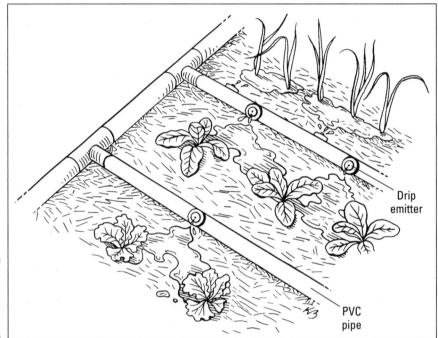

Drip emitter

PVC pipe

Figure 15-3:
Watering with drip irrigation.

This watering technique is the most effective and efficient way to water vegetables because water drips right to the roots of the plants and little water is wasted on pathways, in between plants, and in between rows. Drip irrigation works well even if your garden is on a slope, which poses problems for most other systems.

The downside to drip irrigation is that it's more costly than the other methods listed in this chapter; it's also more involved to set up and take down at the end of the season. Drip irrigation is best for those gardeners who are into technology, who don't have lots of time to water, and who live in water-restricted areas.

You can wet an entire bed from one end to the other at each watering with drip emitters. You snap the emitters in the pipes wherever you want them, or you can buy a pipe with emitters already evenly spaced along the length of the pipe. The moisture radiates sideways underground and wets the soil between emitters.

As an alternative to emitters, you may want to use *microsprinklers,* which are tiny sprinklers that hook to plastic pipes like drip emitters. They're usually supported by 12- to 24-inch stakes and cover various-sized areas of soil with a fine spray of water. They're particularly useful for watering closely spaced vegetables like lettuce and root crops, or for watering germinating seeds.

Most nurseries sell drip irrigation systems, but you also can purchase them through the mail (see the appendix for details). Emitters and microsprinklers are available with different application rates, varying by the number of gallons applied per hour. Pressure-compensating emitters apply water consistently from one end of the line to the other, regardless of pressure changes due to uneven ground.

Follow these steps to set up a drip irrigation system in your garden:

1. **Lay the pipe (or pipes — depending on the system) on top of the soil and cover the pipe with plastic mulch, or bury the pipe a few inches below the surface of the soil.**

   Most people like to keep the pipe close to the surface so they can check it for clogs and fix breaks.

2. **If your pipe doesn't already have emitters in it, snap emitters in the pipe wherever you want them.**

   Position the emitters so they're close to the bases of your plants.

3. **Run the drip system for at least several hours a day (2 to 4 hours).**

   Watch the system carefully the first few times that you water. Dig around in your garden to see how far the water travels over a given time period, and then adjust your watering schedule in the future.

If you live in an area where the soil freezes, don't leave your drip irrigation system or soaker hoses outside in the winter because they may burst. Instead, drain the water out, roll up the tubing, and store it in your garage.

Conserving water with a few handy tips

In many areas of the country, restrictions limit the amount of water you can use to grow your plants. If you're in one of these areas, it's especially important that you water smartly (though watering efficiently should be everyone's goal!). Sensible watering will save this precious resource and save you money.

Keep these water-saving pointers in mind when tending to your crops:

- ✔ **Grow plants that perform better under low water conditions.** Some drought-resistant food crops you might try include herbs and hot peppers.

- ✔ **Plant veggies closer together.** Doing so allows you to conserve soil moisture and shade the ground, keeping it cool and moist.

- ✔ **Consider the time of day that you water, especially if you use a sprinkler.** You lose less water to evaporation (an important consideration in hot, dry climates) if sprinklers operate in the cool of the morning rather than during the heat of the afternoon. Watering in the morning also gives leaves a chance to dry off before evening; wet foliage is an ideal fungus-growing medium.

- ✔ **Frequent, shallow waterings do more harm than good.** They cause roots to develop mainly in the upper few inches of the soil, where they're susceptible to drying out. Instead, go for occasional, deep waterings. Deep waterings allow moisture to penetrate deeply into the soil. The roots will follow the water, and the plant will be deep rooted and less likely to be effected by dry conditions. You'll water less frequently; maybe deeply once per week.

- ✔ **If your garden has heavy clay soil or is on a slope, and you find that water begins to run off before it penetrates 6 inches deep in the soil, try watering at intervals.** Water for 10 to 15 minutes, let the water soak in for 15 to 20 minutes, and then water again.

- ✔ **Try to use soaker hoses and drip irrigation to direct water to the plants and not waste it on pathways.** Use a timer to turn on the system during cool parts of the day for only as long as needed.

- ✔ **Collect rainwater from roofs and store it to be used in the garden.** In some areas you can even use gray waste water from your home in your yards. Check with your local water municipality for regulations on using gray water.

For more ways to save water while maintaining your gardens and flower beds, check out *Sustainable Landscaping For Dummies* by Owen Dell (Wiley).

Keeping Your Plants Cozy and Weed Free with Mulch

Mulch is any material, organic or inorganic, that you place over the surface of soil, usually directly over the root zone of growing plants. It has many benefits depending on the type used. Mulch suppresses weeds, holds in moisture, modifies soil temperature, lessens the chances of certain diseases attacking your plants, and adds an attractive look to your garden.

Some people use compost as a mulch, but you have to remember that compost has a different purpose than mulch. Compost is added and mixed into the soil to add nutrients and increase the workability of soil (water-holding capacity, aeration, and so on). Mulch generally doesn't add nutrients, but it helps hold in the ones already in the soil and prevents undesirables from attacking your growing plants. (You can read more about compost in Chapter 14.)

You can choose from two basic types of mulch: organic and inorganic. For vegetable growers, each type of mulch has a unique purpose, as described in the following sections.

Spreading organic mulch

Organic mulch includes grass clippings, compost, leaf mold, pine needles, shredded bark, nut shells, cotton gin waste, straw hay, grain and fruit byproducts, composted manure, mushroom compost, peat moss, and sawdust. Some of these mulches are easier to find in different parts of the country. You can even use newspaper as an organic mulch; black-and-white newspaper print is perfectly safe to use in your garden, and most colored inks are soybean based and biodegradable (see Chapter 14 for more on using newspaper as mulch).

Generally, a 2- to 4-inch layer of organic mulch, spread evenly on the ground beneath your plants, is sufficient. However, you may have to replenish the mulch during the growing season, especially in hot summer areas, because many organic mulches break down quickly.

Using organic mulch in your vegetable garden has many benefits:

✔ It conserves water by reducing the soil temperature and evaporation. It also keeps the soil cool by buffering direct sunlight.

✔ It prevents wild fluctuations in soil moisture levels that can really spell disaster in hot weather.

✔ It smothers weed seeds and prevents them from germinating. Any weeds that do come up in loose mulch are easy to pull.

✔ As the mulch breaks down, it adds nutrients and improves the texture of the soil that it covers.

✔ Organic mulch looks good and makes the ground tidy and clean.

The following list includes some of the downsides of organic mulches. As minor as they are, they may lead you to choose one type of organic mulch over another:

✔ **Bark mulches, such as pine, are quite acidic.** So if you use them, keep a close eye on the pH level of your soil and correct it accordingly. (Chapter 14 tells you how to test soil pH.) Also, the latest trend is artificially colored mulches. I'd avoid these brightly colored mulches for your veggies, because they may contain potentially harmful chemicals that can leach into your soil. Choose natural bark mulches instead.

✔ **Grass clippings decay quickly and must be replenished often.** Fortunately, grass clippings are usually pretty abundant. But if the grass goes to seed before you cut it, you may end up with grass growing in your vegetable garden. Also, make sure that no *herbicides* (weed killers) have been used on your lawn because the residue can damage or kill vegetables; if you have your lawn treated regularly, use another type of mulch. Likewise, hay mulch often has weed seeds in it, so use cleaner straw mulch if available.

✔ **Some organic mulches — such as fresh sawdust — rob nitrogen from the soil as they break down.** You may have to add supplemental nitrogen to your vegetables if they grow mysteriously slow or start to turn yellow. (I discuss fertilizers in detail later in this chapter.)

✔ **Some organic mulches, such as peat moss or leaves, can pack down or get hard and crusty when exposed to weather.** Water may not penetrate these mulches, running off the soil instead of soaking into the roots. My suggestion is to avoid peat moss; or at least mix it with another organic mulch such as sawdust. Don't forget that peat is also darn expensive.

✔ **Some lightweight mulches, like straw or cocoa hulls, can blow around in the wind.** You may want to avoid them if you live in a windy area.

✔ **Organic mulch, which keeps the soil cool, may slow the growth and maturity of warm-season crops such as tomatoes and melons.** This cooling can be especially problematic in areas with cool summers. However in very hot-summer areas of the country, organic mulches work to keep the roots of even warm-season crops cool and healthy.

> ✔ **Composted manures may burn young vegetables if used as mulch because the manures vary in the amount of nitrogen they contain.** If you want to use composted manure, mix it with three times the volume of another organic mulch before applying it.

You can purchase organic mulches like shredded bark, compost, and leaf mold in bags or sometimes in bulk from nurseries and garden centers. Grass clippings, compost, and wood chips come free from your yard or garden.

Laying inorganic mulch

Inorganic mulch includes things like plastic, landscape fabric, and believe it or not, old carpet. I explain how to use all types of inorganic mulches in the following sections.

Plastic

Plastic is the most-used inorganic mulch for vegetable gardens. Mulching with plastic (see Figure 15-4) works best when you install drip irrigation or a soaker hose underneath the plastic before planting. Otherwise, watering is difficult. (You can place the irrigation on top of the plastic, which enables you to more easily check for clogs, but you have to run individual emitters to each plant.) Plastic doesn't work well with vegetables planted very close together, such as root crops.

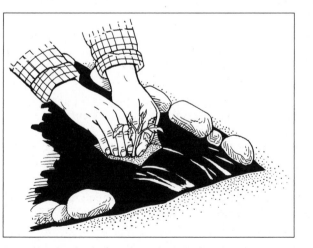

Figure 15-4:
Planting in black plastic mulch.

The color of plastic mulch you use depends on what you're growing. Some vegetables grow better with certain colored plastics. For example:

- ✔ Tomatoes, eggplants, and strawberries grow best with red plastic mulch.
- ✔ Melons grow well with dark green or IRT (infrared transmitting) plastic mulch.
- ✔ Peppers like a silver-colored mulch.
- ✔ White plastic is good for hot climates where you want to stop weeds from growing but not heat up the soil.
- ✔ Black plastic is good for weed control and warming soils. It can be used on many vegetables including cucumbers and squash.

To mulch with plastic, follow these steps:

1. **Purchase rolls or sheets of 2- to 4-millimeter plastic (the thicker the better).**

   You can find the thickness of the plastic on its label. Purchase plastic at garden centers or hardware stores, or check the appendix for sources of various colored mulches.

2. **If you're using irrigation under the plastic, lay down your drip irrigation and turn it on for several hours.**

   Note where the wet spots are in the soil. Adjust the drip hose so water doesn't pool in certain areas, but is evenly distributed. See the earlier section on drip irrigation for more details on installing this type of watering system.

3. **A week or two before planting, water the entire area with a hose or sprinkler so it's wet to 6 inches deep.**

   Roll out the plastic over the planting area and cover the edges of the plastic with soil.

4. **Cut holes in the plastic where you want to plant your transplants.**

   You can sow seed this way as well; just make sure that the seed can get through the holes in the plastic after it germinates.

5. **Plant your seeds or transplants in the holes.**

   Make sure you plant in wet spots; otherwise, the plants may not get enough water.

If you live in a climate that gets very hot in the summer (Texas, for example), after the weather starts to warm, you may want to cover black plastic with an organic mulch to prevent the soil from getting too warm. Or consider using white plastic instead.

Unless you have a problem with the irrigation system, you usually don't have to remove the plastic until the end of the season.

Other inorganic mulches

Beside plastics, you also can use the following inorganic mulches in your vegetable garden:

- **Cardboard:** Even though it's biodegradable, cardboard takes so long to decompose that I treat it as an inorganic mulch. You can cut cardboard boxes to fit in pathways. If you don't like their look, cover them with hay or straw.

- **Landscape fabric:** This inorganic mulch doesn't warm the soil as much as black plastic, but it's permeable, enabling you to water through it. It also does a good job of keeping down weeds. You can find landscape fabric at your local nursery. You apply landscape fabric the same way that you do plastic (see the preceding section).

- **Rug strips:** Roll out 3-foot rug strips and place them nap side down, leaving about 6 inches of open soil between strips for irrigation and planting. Even though rug strips look pretty weird in a garden, they keep the weeds down and make a nice path.

Deciding which mulch to use

Choosing a mulch and deciding when to use it in your vegetable garden depends on the type of vegetables that you grow and when you plant them. Check out these mulching tips for different types of vegetables:

- **Cool-season vegetables planted in early spring:** You want the sun to warm your soil in the spring because lots of sun helps young plants get off to a fast start. Here are a few mulching pointers for these vegetables:

  - Lay down organic mulch when the soil starts to warm and when the plants need regular water. If you mulch too early, the soil stays too cold and wet for proper root growth.

  - In areas with short growing seasons, you can plant broccoli, cauliflower, and cool-season plants through plastic. Cover the plastic with organic matter when the weather warms to keep the soil cool.

- **Cool-season vegetables planted in late summer or early fall:** With these vegetables, you want the cooling effect, so put down an organic mulch right after planting. Here are a few other things to keep in mind:

  - When the weather starts to cool, rake off or remove the organic mulch so the soil warms.

  - You can plant through plastic late in the year, but you should cover it with an organic mulch immediately so the soil doesn't get too hot. Then remove the organic mulch when the weather cools and let the plastic warm the soil through harvest.

- Many root crops can be stored in the ground well into winter if you cover them with a thick organic mulch like straw. Applied before the ground freezes, the mulch keeps the soil loose and unfrozen so you can dig the vegetables later into winter.

✔ **Warm-season vegetables planted in spring:** With these vegetables, keep the ground clear if you're planting really early — the more heat the better. Planting through plastic works in early spring. In hot climates, apply an organic mulch when the weather starts to get really warm in summer.

Determining Important Nutrients Your Soil Needs

Sixteen elements are essential for healthy plant growth. Of these elements, plants especially need carbon, hydrogen, and oxygen in large quantities. They also need energy from sunlight for *photosynthesis,* the process by which plants use carbon dioxide from the air and water from the soil to produce sugars that enable them to grow. Nature — and your conscientious watering — supply these elements.

Plants also need nitrogen, phosphorus, and potassium in relatively large quantities. Plants take up these three nutrients — often called *macronutrients* — from the soil. If your soil doesn't contain enough of these nutrients, you can supply them by fertilizing, which I discuss in detail later in this chapter.

The following sections list important nutrients that your plants need, along with information to help you determine when you need to add nutrients to your soil. To find out what quantities to add, refer to the chapters on individual vegetables in Part II. (Chapter 14 has details on soil pH and pointers on performing soil tests.)

Macronutrients

Nitrogen (N), a key component of proteins and *chlorophyll* (the plant pigment that plays a vital role in photosynthesis), is responsible for the healthy, green color of your plants. Nitrogen is a volatile creature; it easily moves around in the soil and can leach away from plant roots as a result of rain or watering. Therefore, you need to be sure that your plants receive a steady supply of nitrogen all season long.

✔ **How to detect too little:** Plants with a nitrogen deficiency usually show yellowing (in older leaves first) and slowed growth. However, with plants like tomatoes, a nitrogen deficiency may first appear as a reddening of the stems and the undersides of the leaves.

✔ **How to detect too much:** A plant with too much nitrogen has soft-textured, dark green foliage and an underdeveloped root system, and flowering and fruiting are delayed. Too much nitrogen fertilizer, especially when plants are young, can actually burn the roots and kill them. Because nitrogen leaches out of the soil quickly, if you have too much, stop fertilizing, wait, and eventually the problem will solve itself.

✔ **How to add it to your soil:** You can supplement soil nitrogen by adding organic fertilizers, decomposing organic matter, or composted manure.

Phosphorus (P) helps promote good root growth, increased disease resistance, and fruit and seed formation. It's less available in cooler soils, so adding a fertilizer containing phosphorus in spring is a good idea.

✔ **How to detect too little:** Plants lacking in phosphorus are stunted and sport dark green foliage and purplish stems and leaves (on the older leaves first). Soil pH affects the availability of phosphorus to plants; a pH of 6 to 7.5 keeps it available.

✔ **How to detect too much:** Too much phosphorous is a problem because it can cause zinc and iron deficiencies, and it can leach out of the soil and pollute streams and lakes. Signs of zinc or iron deficiencies appear as discolored or poorly formed leaves and reduced growth and production.

✔ **How to add it to your soil:** Sources of phosphorus include minerals, organic matter, inorganic fertilizers (such as rock phosphate), and organic fertilizers (such as bone meal).

Unlike nitrogen, phosphorus doesn't move quickly through soil. So, add a fertilizer containing phosphorus to the root zone before planting (instead of sprinkling it on the soil surface).

Potassium (K) promotes vigorous growth and disease resistance.

✔ **How to detect too little:** The first sign of a deficiency is slowed growth; brown leaf edges and deformed yellow leaves can indicate a severe deficiency.

✔ **How to detect too much:** Too much potassium can create nutrient imbalances in the plant and stunt its growth.

✔ **How to add to your soil:** Soil minerals provide potassium, as do organic matter and inorganic fertilizers, such as green sand and granite dust.

Secondary nutrients and micronutrients

Calcium, magnesium, and sulfur are known as *secondary nutrients*. Plants need them in substantial quantities, but not to the same extent that they need nitrogen, phosphorus, and potassium.

- ✔ **How to detect too little:** Most alkaline soils contain these secondary nutrients naturally, and few soils are deficient in sulfur. Most home garden soils contain these nutrients. But if you've eliminated other possibilities and you suspect a problem, a soil lab can do tests on your plant leaves to detect any deficiencies.

- ✔ **How to add them to your soil:** In regions where the soil is acidic, liming to keep your soil's pH in a good growth range provides adequate calcium and magnesium (the latter if you use dolomitic limestone). See Chapter 14 for more on liming.

Micronutrients (iron, manganese, copper, boron, molybdenum, chlorine, and zinc) are elements that plants need in tiny amounts. Too much of one of these elements is often as harmful as too little.

- ✔ **How to detect too little or too much:** A micronutrient deficiency or excess may mean that your soil is too acidic or too alkaline, so you can correct the problem by changing the pH rather than by adding more nutrients. Deficiencies and excesses most often are noted on plants that are growing poorly and through soil tests.

- ✔ **How to add them to your soil:** Sometimes, changing the pH sufficiently to increase micronutrient levels isn't practical, or you may need to give a plant a micronutrient quickly while you try to change the soil pH. In such cases, micronutrients are applied as *chelates*. Chelates are added to other chemicals, in this case micronutrients, to keep them available to plants when soil conditions are unfavorable. Apply chelated micronutrients to your soil, or better yet, spray them on plant foliage.

Fertilizing Your Vegetable Garden

Even if you have the healthiest soil around, growing vegetables is an intensive process that strips many important nutrients from the soil. So you need to add some fertilizer to your soil to keep it in optimum shape to feed your plants.

How much fertilizer you add depends on the soil and the plants you're growing. So it's difficult to generalize across the board on what type of fertilizer to choose and how much to apply. Soil tests are a great way to know what to add. Refer to Chapter 14 for more on soil tests.

Examining a fertilizer label

Commercial fertilizers are labeled with three numbers that indicate the fertilizer's nutrient content (see Figure 15-5). The first number indicates the percentage of nitrogen (N), the second number shows the percentage of phosphate (the type of phosphorus, P_2O_5), and the third number represents the percentage of potash (the form of potassium used, K_2O). (I explain these nutrients in detail in the earlier section "Macronutrients.")

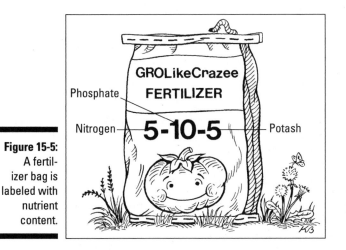

Figure 15-5:
A fertilizer bag is labeled with nutrient content.

For example, a 5-10-5 fertilizer contains 5 percent nitrogen, 10 percent phosphate, and 5 percent potash, and it's called a *complete fertilizer* because it contains some of each type of nutrient. In contrast, bone meal has an analysis of 4-12-0. It's a good source of phosphate but doesn't provide any potash. The other materials in a commercial fertilizer that the analysis numbers don't account for are generally filler — unimportant materials that add bulk to the bag so the fertilizer is easier to spread.

How much fertilizer do you use? Soil tests are the best way to correct deficiencies (see Chapter 14 for details), but fertilizer bags also give general dosage recommendations for gardens. Most fertilizer recommendations for maintenance fertilization (rather than to correct a deficiency) are made according to how much nitrogen a crop needs. So, for example, if you have a recommendation for 3 pounds of 5-10-10 fertilizer per 100 square feet, but the fertilizer that you have on hand is 5-5-5 fertilizer, apply 3 pounds of 5-5-5. Even though the 5-5-5 fertilizer's percentage of phosphate and potash is less than that of the 5-10-10, it offers the same recommended amount of nitrogen.

Choosing a fertilizer

Most home gardeners can grow a perfectly beautiful and productive garden using organic principles. In the last 20 years, an explosion of organic products (such as fertilizers) has hit the market, making gardening with this method much more accessible. I choose to garden with organic fertilizers, and I explain why in this section; I also warn you of the dangers of chemical fertilizers.

Organic fertilizers

Organic fertilizers — animal and green manure, blood meal, fish emulsion, cottonseed meal, granite dust, and rock phosphate — have several advantages:

✔ Many organic fertilizers contribute organic matter to your soil, improving its structure, feeding soil microbes, fighting fungal and bacterial diseases, and contributing micronutrients.

✔ Most organic fertilizers supply a slow but steady diet for plants.

✔ Some organic fertilizers, such as manure and compost, may be inexpensive — or free if you create them yourself.

✔ Complete organic fertilizers, such as 5-5-5, are now more widely available and have higher concentrations of nutrients than in the past, making them easy-to-use alternatives to chemical fertilizers.

However, it's not all sun and roses when using organic fertilizers. Here are some disadvantages:

✔ Some organic fertilizers, such as manures and compost, are bulky and difficult to store and transport.

✔ Their slow release of nutrients, in some cases dependent on the action of soil microorganisms, may take too long to remedy a dire situation when an adequate nutrient supply is needed.

✔ Many organic fertilizers are lower in nutrient content than their chemical equivalents, and the contents may vary depending on the weather and conditions where the fertilizers were produced. So you may not be exactly sure how much to put on your garden.

Chemical fertilizers

Chemical fertilizers are synthetically manufactured. They include elements such as sodium nitrate, potassium chloride, and superphosphate. Chemical fertilizers come in liquid, granular, powder, or pellet form. You can fertilize when you water with a watering can, using a liquid fertilizer. Or you can sprinkle some granular fertilizer around each plant.

Chemical fertilizers are widely available, less expensive than organic fertilizers, quick acting, and easy to use, but I believe that the disadvantages of using chemical fertilizers far outweigh the advantages. Here's why:

- ✔ **Chemical fertilizers add no organic matter to your soil and contribute nothing to improving soil structure.** In fact, some research suggests that chemical fertilizers actually harm the microorganisms in the soil, making the soil less able to support long-term plant growth.

- ✔ **Chemical fertilizers are concentrated and fast acting, but they have no long-term benefits for your soil.** It's like taking a vitamin for your health versus eating a good meal.

- ✔ **Manufacturing chemical fertilizers requires large amounts of energy, usually supplied by nonrenewable resources.** This massive use of energy increases pollution, global warming, and our carbon footprint. Even though some commercial organic fertilizers, such as rock phosphate and green sand, also are manufactured and require energy inputs, home gardeners can instead choose to use locally made compost and manures to get the nutrients they need for their gardens.

Side-dressing

Depending on the crops you grow and the type of soil you have, you may need to add repeat doses of fertilizer throughout the growing season — a practice called *side-dressing.* For example, because sandy soils don't hold nutrients well, giving plants small, regular fertilizer applications ensures a steady supply of nutrients.

In the following sections, I describe specific fertilizers and methods that are best for side-dressing and explain how frequently you should side-dress your veggies. For information on fertilizing vegetables growing in containers, see Chapter 18.

Fertilizers and techniques that work well for side-dressing

Granular organic fertilizers, such as 5-5-5, are a good choice for side-dressing most root and fruiting crops. Use 1 to 2 tablespoons per plant, or 1 to 2 pounds for every 25 feet in a row.

Depending on plant spacing, side-dress either in a narrow furrow down a row or around each individual plant (refer to Figure 15-6). In either case, spread granular fertilizer (which is easier to use than liquid fertilizer) at least 6 to 8 inches away from plant stems. Rake the fertilizer into the soil and then water.

Figure 15-6:
Ways to
fertilize
vegetable
plants.

For leafy green crops, fish emulsion is a quick-acting, highly soluble organic source of nitrogen that gives your greens a boost, especially if they're turning a pale green color. You can add micronutrients to this fertilizer by mixing it with seaweed. Add this liquid fertilizer to your watering can following the directions on the label. As you water, pour this solution around the bases of the plants and on the leaves.

Knowing when to side-dress

Too much fertilizer can be more harmful than too little. Excess fertilizer accumulates in the soil in the form of salts and damages plant roots. So be sure that growing conditions enable plants to use the fertilizer that you apply. For example, don't add fertilizer during a dry spell if you can't irrigate your garden, because without adequate soil moisture, roots can't take up nutrients. And if cool weather causes your plants to grow slowly and need less fertilizer, go easy on the fertilizer until the temperature warms up or you'll be wasting it.

The kind of plants that you grow makes a difference in how often you side-dress. Plants that take a long time to mature (such as tomatoes and eggplants) and heavy feeders (like corn) generally benefit more from side-dressing than quick-maturing crops that fix their own nitrogen — such as lettuce, or legumes like peas and beans. See Table 15-2 for some general side-dressing guidelines.

Table 15-2	Deciding When to Side-Dress Your Vegetables
Vegetable	**When to Side-Dress**
Beans, green	Not necessary
Beet greens	Two weeks after leaves appear
Beets	When tops are 4 to 5 inches high; go light on nitrogen, which encourages leaf growth
Broccoli	Three weeks after transplant; go light on nitrogen
Brussels sprouts	Three weeks after transplant; again when sprouts begin to appear
Cabbage	Four to six weeks after planting
Carrots	Three weeks after plants are well established and no longer seedlings
Cauliflower	Four to six weeks after planting
Celery	Three weeks after setting out; again six weeks later
Corn, sweet	Three weeks after planting; again when plants are 8 to 10 inches high; again when tassels appear
Cucumbers	When they first begin to *run* (form vines and sprawl); again when blossoms set
Eggplant	Three weeks after planting
Kale	When plants are 6 to 8 inches tall
Lettuce, head	Three weeks after transplant; again when heads form
Lettuce, leaf	Three weeks after germination
Melons	When they begin to run; again a week after blossom set; again three weeks later
Onions	Three weeks after planting; again when tops are 6 to 8 inches tall; again when bulbs start to swell
Peas, English	Not necessary
Peppers, sweet and hot	Three weeks after transplant; again after first fruit set
Potatoes	When plants bloom
Pumpkin	When plants start to run; again at blossom set
Radishes	Not necessary
Spinach	When plants are about 3 to 4 inches tall
Squash, summer	When plants are about 6 inches tall; again when they bloom
Squash, winter	When plants start to run; again at blossom set
Swiss chard	Three weeks after germination
Tomatoes	Two to three weeks after transplant; again before first picking; again two weeks after first picking; go light on nitrogen

Proceed carefully: Using wood ashes as a fertilizer

Wood ashes are a source of potash and phosphate, although the exact amounts of these nutrients depend on the type of wood burned (hardwoods generally contain more nutrients than softwoods), the degree of combustion, and where the wood was stored (for example, dry storage prevents nutrient leaching). A general analysis is usually in the range of 0 percent nitrogen, 1 to 2 percent phosphate, and 4 to 10 percent potash. But the major benefit of wood ashes is as a liming agent to raise the pH of the soil. Naturally, if you live in an area where soils are alkaline, don't use wood ashes as a soil amendment; they raise the pH even higher.

Apply wood ashes to your soil in moderation (no more than 10 to 20 pounds per 1,000 square feet of garden) because they may contain small amounts of heavy metals, such as cadmium and copper. *Remember:* These metals build up in plants if you add too much wood ash to the soil and can kill the plants — or harm you if you eat lots of those plants.

Give 'Em Something to Lean On: Supporting Your Vegetables

Some vegetables, like peas and beans, have climbing habits that require some type of support to grow on. Other vegetables — including tomatoes, cucumbers, and even melons — have sprawling habits that benefit from some type of staking or support. Staking plants, tying them to a trellis, or growing them inside wire cylinders reduces disease problems because it allows for better air circulation and keeps the fruits off the ground where they may be attacked by bugs or become sunburned. (Fruit skins get sunburned due to sudden exposure to strong sun and eventually rot.) Supported plants also are easier to harvest and require less space to grow (they go up instead of out).

Figure 15-7 shows some techniques for supporting vegetables, but you can find more in Chapter 16. In the following sections, I provide some suggestions for supporting different types of vegetables.

Beans and peas

Twining or clinging plants like beans and peas grow best when they're supported by some type of string trellis. I like to use an A-frame string trellis, which enables me to grow plants on both sides, but single poles are fine, too. Making an A-frame string trellis is easy; just follow these steps:

1. **Using at least six 2-by-2-inch redwood or cedar stakes, build two 6-by-6-foot squares.**

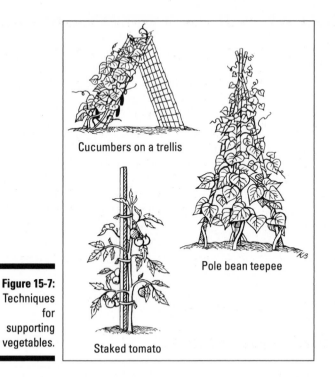

Cucumbers on a trellis

Pole bean teepee

Staked tomato

Figure 15-7:
Techniques
for
supporting
vegetables.

Redwood and cedar stakes are naturally rot resistant and good choices.

2. **Secure the corners of the squares with metal corner braces and connect the two squares on one side with sturdy hinges.**

   The hinges enable you to easily move or store the trellis.

3. **Hammer small nails at 2- to 4-inch intervals along the top and bottom of the trellis.**

   Don't pound the nails in all the way; leave about 1 inch sticking out.

4. **Weave some sturdy twine or string up and down the trellis, between the nails.**

   Bingo; you have an A-frame string trellis.

Handmade wooden teepees are a great way to support your beans, and kids love them because they're great places to hide. Here's how to construct your own teepee:

1. **Using four to six 2-by-2-inch redwood or cedar stakes that are 6 to 8 feet long, form a conelike teepee.**

2. **Tie the stakes together with twine at the top of the teepee.**

3. **Run some string or twine around the bottom of the teepee, securing the string or twine at each stake with a small nail.**

4. Run more string back and forth around the stakes, from the top of the teepee to the bottom, leaving several inches between each run.

Leave one side of the teepee open so your kids can get inside, and then plant beans around the base of the teepee. In time, the beans will cover the trellis, creating a great fort for your kids.

Melons and cucumbers

You can plant bush varieties of melons and cucumbers inside small (2- to 3-foot-high) wire cylinders similar to those used for tomatoes (see the next section). But for more vigorous varieties, I like to use a sturdier version of the A-frame trellis that's used for beans and peas (see the previous section). Instead of using string, I cut 6-foot-by-6-foot pieces of hog fencing (it has 6-inch squares) and nail them to each side of the trellis. The wire provides better support for heavy fruit (like melons) than string does, and the wide-open fencing doesn't constrict the growth of the fruit (so you get straighter cucumbers). You can purchase hog fencing at agricultural stores.

You also can grow melons on a trellis. Choose small-fruited varieties of watermelon or any variety of cantaloupe, and plant your seeds at the base of the trellis. Tie the vines to the trellis as they grow. After a fruit forms, slip the leg of an old nylon stocking over the fruit, tying the bottom of the stocking in a knot. Then tie the other end of the stocking to the wire trellis so that the fruit is supported. As the melon grows, the stocking expands and supports the fruit, which may break off otherwise. Flip to Chapter 8 to see how this support system looks.

Tomatoes

You can support tomato plants several different ways:

- ✔ Tie them to stakes, which you pound in the ground next to the plants.
- ✔ Grow them inside wire cages, which you can buy at nurseries or easily build yourself out of hog fencing.

  If you're growing *indeterminate* varieties, which keep growing and producing fruit all season, choose or build cages large enough to support the huge plants that will grow. Also be sure to secure them to the ground well so they don't blow over during a summer thunderstorm. (You can read more on indeterminate tomatoes in Chapter 4.)
- ✔ Construct string or wire trellises, like you do for beans and peas.

Fighting Weed Wars

A *weed* is any plant that's growing where you don't want it to. Some weeds are worse than others, but in general, you don't want any weeds in your vegetable garden because they compete with vegetables for light, water, and nutrients. If you have a lot of weeds, you'll have weaker plants and a less substantial harvest. Besides, weeds look terrible.

The key to battling weeds is to get to them early before they're firmly established. When they're young, weeds are easier to pull, easier to till under, and less likely to produce seeds that cause problems down the road. In the following sections, I show you how to fight weeds before and after you plant your veggies.

Making a preemptive strike on weeds

You can reduce weeds in your vegetable beds many different ways. Here are some things that you can do before planting your garden:

- **Presprout weed seeds.** *Presprouting* — forcing weed seeds to germinate before you plant so you can kill them early — really cuts down on the number of weeds in your beds. Follow these steps:

  1. **Prepare your planting bed several weeks before you're ready to plant.**

     Refer to Chapter 3 for details on planning and preparing your beds for planting.

  2. **Water the soil well and wait a few days.**

     Presto, young weeds begin popping up.

  3. **Kill the weeds.**

     You can choose to kill the weeds one of two ways: pull them out by hand, or rake the bed lightly to uproot the seedlings and then let them dry out to die.

     However you get rid of the young weeds, disturb the soil as little as possible when you do it; otherwise, you'll bring more seeds to the surface.

- **Plan for easy weeding.** Leave enough room between rows so you can weed the soil easily.

✔ **Solarize the soil.** When you *solarize* the soil, you use the power of the sun to kill weeds. This technique works best in the middle of summer in hot climates like Arizona and Florida. The only downside to solarizing is that it takes a while. Follow these steps to solarize your soil:

1. **Prepare your bed for planting and water it well.**

2. **Dig a 6-to-12-inch-deep trench around the perimeter of the bed.**

3. **Cover the entire bed with thick clear plastic (4 millimeters) and place the edges of the plastic in the trenches and fill the trenches with soil. Then wait.**

   The temperature gets so hot underneath the plastic that it kills insects, disease organisms, and weeds. It usually takes a few months of solarizing to get a beneficial effect.

✔ **Plant your vegetables at the proper time of year.** That way they get off to a fast start, and weeds have a harder time catching up with them. See Chapter 3 for details.

Battling weeds after planting

If you come across weeds after you plant your crops, you have several choices for eliminating them:

✔ **Mulch your beds.** Applying a layer of thick organic mulch is one of the best ways to battle weeds. Even if mulch doesn't smother the weeds and their seeds, the weeds that do come up are easy to pull. Planting through plastic is also an effective way to keep weeds from becoming a problem. See the earlier section "Keeping Your Plants Cozy and Weed Free with Mulch" for more information.

✔ **Pull the weeds by hand.** While they're young, weeds come out of the ground easily. Get 'em roots and all, whenever you see them. If you can't pull out the roots by hand, use a trowel.

✔ **Cultivate the soil.** Simply hoeing or lightly turning the soil between vegetables exposes the weeds' roots and kills many of them. Cultivating is most effective when it's done often (a few times a week in the first month or so of gardening) and early when the weeds are small. Some cultivating tools are designed especially for this purpose; see Chapter 20 for details.

✔ **Keep garden paths clean.** Try to keep your garden paths as weed free as possible; otherwise, weeds will creep into your planting beds. Try covering the paths with a thick mulch to keep weeds from becoming established.

✔ **Make sure the areas around the garden are weed free.** If you're growing vegetables near a field or weedy woodland edge, try to mow a wide strip between your garden and the field so the weed seeds can't blow in as easily. It won't stop all of them, but every little bit helps.

Chapter 16

Surveying Some Cool Farmer Techniques

In This Chapter

▶ Growing plants that improve the soil

▶ Planting schemes that increase harvest and reduce pests

▶ Using the phases of the moon to determine when to plant

*P*eople have been growing vegetables for eons — probably since the days of Adam and Eve, though you usually associate them with fruits, not vegetables.

Over the years, farmers, and even gardeners for that matter, have tried almost anything to get better, bigger, and earlier harvests. Some of these techniques, such as planting according to the cycles of the moon, are rooted more in mysticism than in hard science. Others, such as using cover crops and succession planting, are commonsense approaches to farming that are now established practices in modern agriculture. They're also useful techniques for home vegetable gardeners.

In this chapter, you can take a look at some cool farming techniques — some based on fact, some on fancy — and decide whether they'll work for you.

Adding Nutrients and Stability with Cover Crops and Green Manures

A *cover crop* is a general term for any plant grown to prevent erosion, improve soil structure, and maintain soil fertility. Sometimes, you'll hear cover crops referred to as *green manures*. Green manures are cover crops that are used primarily to add nutrients to the soil and are tilled into the soil when they're still green. Green manures are the most useful cover crop for vegetable gardeners.

The advantages of using cover crops are impressive:

- ✔ **They add organic matter to the soil.** By adding this matter to the soil, you improve water retention, aeration, and drainage.

- ✔ **They prevent erosion.** Cover crops prevent erosion by holding soil in place in windy or wet areas.

- ✔ **They loosen compacted soils.** Certain cover crops, such as oilseed radish and bell beans, have aggressive *taproots* (roots that grow deeply into the soil), sometimes reaching 3 feet deep, that help break up compacted soils.

- ✔ **They add nutrients to the soil.** Legume cover crops, such as hairy vetch and crimson clover, through a symbiotic relationship (I scratch your back, you scratch mine) with rhizobium bacteria on their roots, convert atmospheric nitrogen into a type that they can use to grow. The process is called *nitrogen fixing* (see Chapter 7 for more on this relationship). When the cover crop is tilled into the soil, the nitrogen is released for the next crop. Also, taprooted cover crops bring minerals to the surface from deep below the soil.

- ✔ **They help control weeds.** Cover crops control weeds by shading the weed seeds so they can't grow or by just being more aggressive than the weeds. Some crops, such as buckwheat, actually exude chemicals that inhibit weed growth.

- ✔ **They attract beneficial insects.** Many cover crops attract good bugs that prey on garden pests, reducing insect problems on your vegetables.

If you want a healthier, more productive garden, and you have room, include cover crops each year in different parts of your veggie garden. In the following sections, I explain how to select and plant the best cover crops for your garden.

Choosing cover crops

Cover crops can be *annual* (they die after flowering or overwinter) or *perennial* (they regrow each year). For home gardeners, the best crops to sow are annual cover crops. These are easy to maintain and won't turn your vegetable garden into a cover crop garden.

The most useful annual cover crops for home gardeners are listed here. All but the grasses and buckwheat are nitrogen fixing:

- ✔ **Annual ryegrass,** *Lolium multiflorum,* is a fast-growing, easy-to-establish grass that grows 2 to 3 feet high. It's hardy to –20 degrees Fahrenheit but can become weedy. Sow ½ to 2 pounds of seed per 1,000 square feet.

✔ **Berseem clover,** *Trifolium alexandrinum,* grows 1 to 2 feet high and is easy to mow and till under. It's hardy to 20 degrees. Sow 2 pounds of seed per 1,000 square feet. Crimson clover, *T. incarnatum,* is closely related, grows 18 inches high, and is hardy to 10 degrees. It has pretty red flowers that attract bees.

✔ **Buckwheat,** *Fagopyrum esculentum,* is fast growing, reaching 3 to 4 feet tall in about 40 days from seeding. It provides lots of organic matter, smothers weeds with its large leaves by shading them out, and exudes chemicals to prevent weeds from germinating. It breaks down quickly in the soil after tilling. Sow 3 pounds of seed per 1,000 square feet. Buckwheat doesn't fix nitrogen and is frost sensitive, so grow it in summer when the temperatures are warm.

✔ **Fava beans,** *Vicia faba,* grow 3 to 8 feet high and are hardy to 15 degrees. Bell beans are a shorter (3 feet) relative. Edible varieties include 'Sweet Loraine' and 'Windsor'. Sow 2 to 5 pounds of seed per 1,000 square feet.

✔ **Field peas,** *Pisum arvense* or *P. sativus,* come in several varieties that range in height from 6 inches to 5 feet high. They're hardy to 10 to 20 degrees. Sow 2 to 4 pounds of seed per 1,000 square feet.

✔ **Hairy vetch,** *Vicia villosa,* is the hardiest annual legume (–15 degrees) and grows about 2 feet high. Sow 1 to 2 pounds of seed per 1,000 square feet.

✔ **Winter rye,** *Secale cereale,* is a very hardy grass (–30 degrees) that grows 4 to 5 feet high. It's the best grass for cold areas with poor, acidic soils and produces lots of organic matter. Sow 2 to 3 pounds of seed per 1,000 square feet.

If you want a wide selection of cover crops plus a lot of helpful information, check out the Peaceful Valley Farm Supply Web site at www.groworganic. com (see the appendix for address information).

Planting cover crops

The best time to plant cover crops is late summer to early fall. What happens next depends on the climate where you live:

✔ **In mild-winter areas,** the plants will grow throughout winter and can be turned into the soil in spring.

✔ **In cold-winter climates,** plant hardy types that will grow for a while in fall, go dormant, and then grow again in spring before eventually dying. Some less hardy types, such as annual ryegrass, will die back in winter and be easier to till under in spring. You can work them into the ground in late spring or early summer and plant vegetables soon after.

An early spring planting of cover crops also works in cold-winter climates, but you won't be able to work the plants in until later in the summer.

Because beds planted with cover crops won't be available for planting vegetables until you turn them under, you have to plan ahead to use your garden efficiently. If you're short on space, consider alternating vegetables and cover crops so that each bed gets a cover crop every 2 or 3 years instead of each year.

If you plant cover crops in fall after your vegetables are done, you won't miss a beat and can plant vegetables again in spring. If you plant cover crops during the spring or summer, you'll have to sacrifice some space in your veggie garden. I'd opt for this route only if your soil is very poor and you need to build it up while growing vegetables at the same time. Just rotate where you plant the cover crops in your garden, and after a few years, your whole garden will get a cover cropping.

Plant cover crops by broadcasting seed (Chapter 13 has more info about this technique). To make sure the proper bacteria are present for nitrogen fixing in legume cover crops, use an inoculate. Most suppliers sell an inoculate that you mix with the seed. Till the soil, sow the seeds, and lightly cover the seeds with soil. If the weather is dry, water the seedbed to get the plants off to an early start and then keep the soil moist until it rains.

If you grow cover crops up to planting time (spring or fall) in your garden, the best time to work the cover crops into the ground is just before they start to bloom. With taller types, you may have to cut or mow the plants down before turning or tilling them in. After you work them in, wait about 2 weeks before planting vegetables.

Giving Your Plants Some Friends: Companion Planting

A *companion plant* is one that provides some sort of benefit to other plants growing nearby. It's sort of like how a good friend makes life easier for you. Well, plants have good friends, too. For example, the cover crops that I talk about earlier in this chapter can be considered companion plants.

Some plants are grown together because they seem to increase each other's yields. But what I want to talk about here are companion plants that repel pests. Is that really possible? Well, I'm not so sure. No clear-cut evidence says companion planting works against pests. But some people swear by it. (Louise Riotte's *Carrots Love Tomatoes* published by Storey Publishing is devoted to the subject.) It is true, however, that a variety of plants, herbs, and flowers provides a diverse ecosystem so that predatory insects are more likely to hang around and take care of the bad guys. Besides, trying some of these combinations certainly won't hurt your garden.

These plants are thought to repel specific pests; plant them near crops where these pests are a common problem:

- ✔ **Anise** planted among members of the cabbage family (cabbage, broccoli, cauliflower, kale, and so on) is said to repel imported cabbage worms.
- ✔ **Basil** is said to repel whiteflies, aphids, and spider mites; it's a good companion to tomatoes because these are insects that feed on tomato plants.
- ✔ **Catnip** is said to repel some types of aphids, flea beetles, squash bugs, and cucumber beetles.
- ✔ **Garlic** may repel nematodes and other soil insects.
- ✔ **Leeks** are thought to repel carrot flies.
- ✔ **Marigolds** planted around vegetables are said to repel root nematodes, Mexican bean beetles, and Colorado potato beetles.
- ✔ **Mustard greens** are supposed to repel aphids.
- ✔ **Nasturtiums** are said to repel Colorado potato beetles.
- ✔ **Radishes** may repel striped cucumber beetles.
- ✔ **Ryegrass** may repel root-knot nematodes.
- ✔ **Southernwood** may repel moths and flea beetles.
- ✔ **Tansy** is supposed to repel some aphids, squash bugs, and Colorado potato beetles as well as ants.
- ✔ **White clover** may repel cabbage root flies.
- ✔ **Wormwood** may repel flea beetles.

Many herbs, such as rosemary, oregano, and coriander, also are said to repel pests. Smaller companion plants, such as marigolds, can be interplanted with vegetables. Taller or more vigorous plants, such as ryegrass or wormwood, should be planted nearby — but not among — vegetables. You don't want them to overwhelm your veggie plants.

The research on companion planting may be thin, but hey, give it a try to see if it works!

Making Your Garden Work Double Time with Intercropping

Intercropping is a space-saving technique in which you grow fast-maturing, smaller crops among slower-growing, larger vegetables. By the time the bigger plants start to take over, you have already harvested the crops in between. Intercropping makes one bed as productive as two.

The best crops for intercropping include beets, carrots, lettuce, onions, radishes, spinach, and turnips. Use these examples to help you decide how to do it:

- Plant lettuce, carrots, or radishes among young tomatoes and broccoli. For that matter, plant carrots and radishes wherever you have open space.

- Plant turnips and other root crops among your cabbage.

- Plant spinach or lettuce under your bean trellis. As the weather warms, the beans will shade the spinach and keep it cool.

- Plant green onions between rows of corn.

Succession Planting for an Extended Harvest

Succession planting is a method of extending the harvest of vegetables, such as radishes and corn, that ripen all at once and lose quality if left in the garden instead of being harvested. Farmers use the technique to ensure a constant supply of vegetables to take to market; you can use it to produce a consistent supply of vegetables to take to your table. To succession plant, you simply make smaller plantings separated by 2 to 3 weeks instead of planting everything at once. Some great crops to succession plant are lettuce and greens, bush beans, beets, carrots, onions, radish, spinach, and sweet corn.

If you want to experiment with succession planting, use these steps:

1. **Figure out how much of a certain vegetable your family needs for a 2- to 3-week period and how much room it will take to grow it.**

   Figure 16-1 shows a sample garden plan for succession planting. Check out Chapter 3 for additional information on how to plan your garden.

2. **Break your planting beds into three or four appropriate-sized sections to grow your 2- to 3-week supply of the vegetable.**

3. **At the start of the planting season, plant the first bed; wait about 2 weeks and plant the second bed, and then plant the third bed about 2 weeks later.**

   Just about the time you finish harvesting the first bed, the second bed will be ready to harvest.

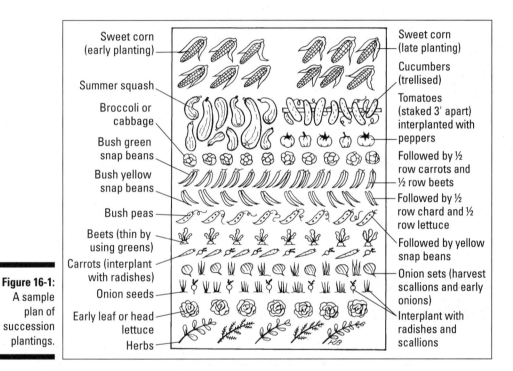

Figure 16-1: A sample plan of succession plantings.

Labels (left): Sweet corn (early planting) · Summer squash · Broccoli or cabbage · Bush green snap beans · Bush yellow snap beans · Bush peas · Beets (thin by using greens) · Carrots (interplant with radishes) · Onion seeds · Early leaf or head lettuce · Herbs

Labels (right): Sweet corn (late planting) · Cucumbers (trellised) · Tomatoes (staked 3' apart) interplanted with peppers · Followed by ½ row carrots and ½ row beets · Followed by ½ row chard and ½ row lettuce · Followed by yellow snap beans · Onion sets (harvest scallions and early onions) · Interplant with radishes and scallions

The length of your planting season will determine how many successive plantings you can make and how successful the later plantings are. Depending on the weather, some of your later plantings may not yield well, but that's another reason to plant a number of plantings through the season: you're sure to get some of every type of veggie.

Another way to use succession planting is to replace a crop that's finished producing with a new one in the same place. With this method, you can grow more and a wider variety of vegetables in a small space. Just make sure you're planting a cool-season veggie for spring or fall and a warm-season veggie for summer. Table 16-1 lists some good succession planting combinations to try. (Chapter 3 has more information on cool-season and warm-season veggies.) You can choose one veggie from each column to plant in succession.

Table 16-1	Succession Planting for Different Seasons	
Spring	*Summer*	*Fall*
Spinach	Bush beans	Kale
Mesclun greens	Cucumber	Lettuce
Peas	Sweet corn	Collards
Radish	Eggplant	Chinese cabbage

Yet another way to ensure a constant harvest of vegetables is to plant using the *square foot method.* This method is for the mathematically inclined (even though you don't need an A in calculus to use it). You select a 4-foot-by-4-foot section of your garden and divide it into 16 squares (each section is 1 square foot). Each square will have a different number of plants, depending on what you're growing:

- ✔ **1 plant per square:** Tomatoes, peppers, broccoli, cabbage, cauliflower, eggplant, corn, melon, squash

- ✔ **4 plants per square:** Lettuce, garlic, Swiss chard

- ✔ **8 plants per square:** Pole beans, peas, spinach

- ✔ **16 plants per square:** Beets, carrots, radishes, onions

By planting so few plants, you'll have many small harvests, and you can easily make more succession plantings and rotate plantings each year. (I talk about crop rotation later in this chapter.)

For more information about square foot gardening techniques, look for the book *All New Square Foot Gardening,* by Mel Bartholomew (published by Cool Springs Press), his videos, or visit this Web site: www.squarefootgardening. com.

Rotating Crops to Preserve Soil Nutrients and Maintain a Pest-Free Bed

If you plant the same vegetables in the same spot year after year, you're going to cause a number of problems, including these:

- ✔ Insects and diseases that spend part of their life cycle in the soil will build up there and be more difficult to control.

- ✔ Specific nutrients that the vegetables need will consistently be depleted and will be harder to replace.

The way around these problems is to rotate your crops from season to season. In other words, plant them in different beds, as far away as possible from where they were planted before. Crop rotation is easy if you keep a journal and make note of what was planted where. And if you keep things out of the same beds for 3 years, you'll probably be in good shape.

It's important to do more than rotate individual crops. You should rotate families of crops as well. In Part II, I talk about vegetables such as tomatoes, peppers, eggplant, and potatoes being in the same family. A disease or insect that attacks one plant in a family is likely to attack others. Blight on tomatoes and potatoes is an example. When rotating crops, make sure you don't plant a family member in the same spot 3 years in a row. For example, in one bed, plant beans (legume family), the next year plant potatoes (tomato family), and the third year plant cucumbers (squash family). After that, you can start over with another legume-family vegetable or start another rotation series. Keep the families apart for 3 years, and you'll have fewer problems in the veggie patch.

If you only have one sunny spot to garden, consider using containers as a way to rotate crops. For example, plant your tomatoes in a container one year and in the garden the next.

Planting by the Phases of the Moon

Planting by the phases of the moon isn't just a New Age technique. It actually has been used for eons by many ancient farmers and gardeners. They noticed that certain vegetables perform better when planted during different moon phases. The planting seasons don't really change, but planting dates during those seasons become very important.

Here's how moon gardening works: If you divide the 28-day moon cycle (from the new moon to the full moon and back to the new moon) into quarters, as any calendar does, certain quarters are thought to be better than others for planting specific vegetables. The following list gives you an idea of what to plant when, according to the moon cycle:

✔ **The first quarter,** when the moon goes from new moon (invisible) to a quarter visible, is thought to be best for planting asparagus, lettuce, broccoli, cabbage, cauliflower, and other vegetables that produce their seeds on parts of the plant that aren't eaten.

✔ **The second quarter,** when the moon goes from half to full, is best for planting vegetables in which the seeds are eaten, such as beans, tomatoes, peppers, and squash.

> ✔ **The third quarter,** as the moon moves from full back to half again, is best for planting root crops such as beets, carrots, potatoes, radishes, and turnips.
>
> ✔ **The last quarter,** when the moon goes from half to invisible, is not thought of as a good planting time. Instead, it's a time to prepare the soil and rid the garden of pests and weeds.

You can get even more complicated by factoring in astrological signs, planets, and how they influence plant growth, but I'll leave that up to you and your further research. I haven't tried factoring in these other elements, but I have a friend in India who swears by the results, as do many others. For more on moon gardening, check out this Web site: www.gardeningbythemoon.com.

Chapter 17

Keeping Your Plants Healthy

. . . .

In This Chapter

▶ Controlling insect pests

▶ Preventing plant diseases

▶ Keeping animals out of bounds

. . . .

Considering how tasty homegrown vegetables are, you shouldn't be too surprised to find that other creatures want to share in your harvest. And, no, I'm not talking about your neighbors. I'm talking about garden pests, insects that want to munch on your tomatoes, and animals, like deer, raccoons, and rabbits, that are just plain hungry. In addition, your plants face the threat of diseases, such as blight, which turns your potatoes to mush. With diseases, prevention is the key; once they take hold, they're almost impossible to eliminate.

Does the thought of all these potential problems make you want to run for cover? Well, you don't need to. It's true that insects, diseases, weeds, and animal pests can be very frustrating, but it's only really bad when the damage gets out of hand. The secret is to nurture a healthy, naturally balanced garden. Every garden can withstand some damage, and you have many weapons in your arsenal to prevent pest problems from getting out of control.

In this chapter, I tell you how to garden to prevent severe pest problems and how to identify the enemies. I also discuss safe ways to deal with these foes.

The Good, the Bad, and the Ugly: Controlling Pests

Most gardens are populated by a huge number of insects, most of which are neither good nor bad. They're just hanging out in your garden at no expense to your plants. But some insects are beneficial, waged in a constant battle with the bugs that are harming your plants. In the following sections, I describe both the good and the bad bugs and the safest methods of attack.

My approach to pest control is to have a maximum diversity of bugs in my garden. Despite what you may think, having some bad bugs around is important. Aphids are like hors d'oeuvres for some helpful insects, so it's okay to have a few in your garden. Otherwise, what will the good bugs eat? But accepting the bad bugs also means that you have to accept a little damage once in a while. So just try to manage the pests, not nuke them off the face of the earth. You want to keep them at acceptable levels without letting them get out of control.

In with the good bugs

As you know, some insects are beneficial to the success of your crops. Unfortunately, you won't always automatically attract these buggers to your plot, so sometimes you have to purchase them. Yes, that's right, you have to buy bugs. Following are some beneficial insects that you can buy inexpensively to help control pests that harm vegetables (see the appendix for companies that sell these beneficial insects):

- **Green lacewings:** These beneficial insects are some of the most effective insects for garden use. Their voracious larvae feed on aphids, mites, thrips, and various insect eggs. Release them into your garden in late spring, after the danger of frost has passed.

- **Lady beetles:** These insects are your basic ladybugs. Both the adults and the lizardlike larvae are especially good at feeding on small insects like aphids and mites. But releasing adults sometimes isn't very effective because Mother Nature has preprogrammed them to migrate down the road, so they leave your garden quickly.

  Try preconditioned lady beetles, which have been deprogrammed (don't worry — the procedure is safe); they're more likely to stick around. Release lady beetles just before sundown; that way, they'll at least spend the night. Release a few thousand of them in spring as soon as you notice the first aphid.

- **Parasitic nematodes:** These microscopic worms parasitize many types of soil-dwelling and burrowing insects, including cutworms and Japanese beetle grubs. Because grubs usually inhabit lawns, you have to apply these worms there, too, as well as around the bases of your plants. Mix the nematodes with water, and spray them on the soil around the bases of your plants in spring or fall.

- **Predatory mites:** These types of mites feed on spider mites and other small pests. Add predatory mites to your garden in the spring as soon as the danger of frost has passed.

- **Trichogramma wasps:** These tiny wasps (which are harmless to humans) attack moth eggs and butterfly larvae (that is, caterpillars). Release these garden good guys when air temperatures are above 72 degree Fahrenheit.

Good bugs are smart; they hang out in the gardens that offer the most diverse and reliable menu. That's why eliminating every last insect pest from your garden isn't a good idea. To get the good insects to stick around, follow these tips:

- ✔ **Avoid indiscriminately using broad-spectrum chemical or organic pesticides, which kill everything, the good bugs and the bad.** If you do spray, use a spray that specifically targets the pest that you want to eliminate and that has minimal effect on beneficial insects; the label on the spray usually gives you this information. (I discuss safe sprays in detail later in this chapter.)

- ✔ **Plant a diverse garden with many kinds and sizes of plants, including flowers and herbs.** Doing so gives the beneficials (beneficial insects) places to hide and reproduce. A garden with a variety of plants also can provide an alternative food source, because many beneficials like to eat pollen and flower nectar, too. Some plants that attract beneficials include Queen Anne's lace, parsley (especially if you let the flower develop), sweet alyssum, dill, fennel, and yarrow.

- ✔ **Provide a diverse habitat for beneficial insects.** Have a small bird bath and evergreen and deciduous shrubs to hide in nearby. These elements provide water and shelter for beneficial insects, making it more likely they'll hang around to munch on some insect pests.

The bad-bug roundup

It helps to know your enemy, and insect pests command the largest army of invaders. The following sections list the most common insect pests that are likely to infest your vegetables as well as the best ways to control them. You can find control measures for the pests that prey primarily on specific vegetables in the individual descriptions of those vegetables in Part II; I also provide general points for tackling bad bugs in the later section "Methods of attack."

If you need more help identifying garden pests and other plant problems, contact a full-service garden center with a variety of reference books that you can look through as well as employees who have personal experience with local problems. Also check with botanical gardens, libraries, Web sites, or a local Cooperative Extension Service office. You should be able to find your county office listed under county offices (these services are usually managed by area land-grant universities) or under *Cooperative Extension* or *Farm Advisor*. Often a well-trained home gardener called a Master Gardener is available by phone or in person to answer your gardening questions. (Check the appendix for state Master Gardener contacts.)

Aphids

Aphids are tiny, pear-shaped pests that come in many colors, including black, green, and red (see Figure 17-1). They congregate on new growth and flower buds, sucking plant sap through their needlelike noses. Heavy infestations can cause distorted growth and may weaken your plants. Aphids leave behind a sticky sap that may turn black with sooty mold and may carry diseases, such as viruses, that infect your plants. Many vegetables can be infested with this pest, including cabbage, cucumbers, and broccoli.

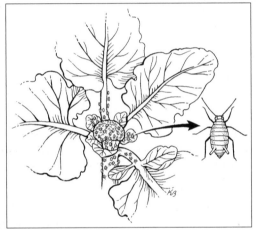

Figure 17-1:
Control aphids with insecticidal soap, neem oil, or hot pepper spray.

Aphids are easy to control. A strong jet of water from a hose can knock them off sturdy plants (they rarely climb back onto the plant to feed), or you can use insecticidal soap or neem oil. Insecticidal soap also helps wash off the sooty mold. (I talk more about insecticidal soap and neem oil in the later section "Methods of attack.") But if you have only a few aphids, wait a week for beneficial insects, especially lady beetles, to move into your garden; they usually take matters into their own hands before serious damage occurs.

Caterpillars and worms

Caterpillars and worms, moth and butterfly larvae, are avid eaters and can cause a lot of damage to a variety of plants. Some are hairy caterpillars; others are smooth skinned and more wormlike. Caterpillars include tomato hornworms and cabbageworms (see Figure 17-2), which are described in Chapters 4 and 9 respectively. You can handpick caterpillars and worms to reduce numbers, or you can release trichogramma wasps. But the most effective way to get rid of them is to spray with biological controls, such as Bt or spinosad. (You can read more about Bt and spinosad in the later section "Methods of attack.")

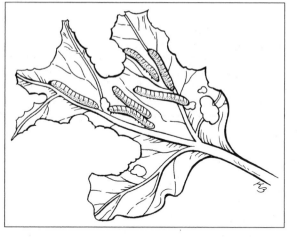

Corn earworms

Corn earworms are a common pest wherever corn is grown. These 1½-inch-long caterpillars with alternating light and dark stripes may be green, pink, or brown. In spring, night-flying moths lay yellow eggs on the undersides of leaves. The resulting first-generation caterpillars feed on the leaves. The eggs of later generations can be found on corn silks; the emerging caterpillars feed on the silks and the kernels at the tips of the corn ears, just inside the husks. The earworms, also called fruitworms, attack a variety of plants including tomatoes, beans, peas, peppers, potatoes, and squash.

The easiest way to deal with corn earworms on your corn plants is to just cut off the tip of the ear before you cook it. Or to prevent worms, you can spray Bt before the caterpillars enter the ears or fruit, but that doesn't always work. To prevent the worms from entering the ears, you also can place a few drops of mineral oil on the silks of each ear just as the silks wilt and start to turn from white or yellow to brown. (Don't do it too early or you'll interfere with pollination, but don't wait until the silks are all brown and shriveled either; you have about a week in which to work.)

Cutworms

Cutworms are ½-inch-long, grayish caterpillars. They emerge on spring and early summer nights to eat the stems of young seedlings, causing the seedlings to fall over like small timbers. Cutworms also climb up to older plants and feed on leaves and flowers.

To protect seedlings, surround their stems with barriers that prevent the cutworms from crawling close and feeding. These devices can be as simple as empty cardboard toilet paper rolls, Styrofoam cups with the bottoms cut out, or collars made from aluminum foil. Whatever you use, just make sure that the barriers encircle the stem completely and are set 1 inch deep in the soil. You also can trap cutworms by leaving boards around your garden; the worms hide under the boards during the day, enabling you to collect them. Parasitic nematodes also are effective against cutworms. (Flip to the earlier section "In with the good bugs" for more on these good pests.)

Flea beetles

Flea beetles are tiny ¹⁄₁₆-inch beetles that feed on vegetable leaves, riddling them with small holes. These beetles jump rapidly when disturbed, like fleas — hence their name. Various species feed on just about any plant in a garden, including eggplant, tomatoes, broccoli, cabbage, corn, potatoes, spinach, peppers, and sweet potatoes. Adult beetles can spread diseases — wilt in sweet corn, for example — and larvae feed on roots. Adults overwinter in the soil and on garden debris, emerging in early spring. Keep a close watch because these beetles can destroy young plants quickly.

To control flea beetles, make sure you clean up garden debris in the winter and till the soil. Use a floating row cover to exclude adults (I describe these covers later in this chapter), and release parasitic nematodes to attack the larvae. Pyrethrins and insecticidal soap also provide some control.

Japanese beetles

Japanese beetles can really be troublesome in many areas. These ½-inch-long beetles have coppery bodies and metallic green heads. They feed on the foliage of many vegetables, including corn, beans, and tomatoes.

Controlling Japanese beetles can be tough. Treating your lawn and garden soil with parasitic nematodes or with *milky spore* (a biological spray) may reduce the white C-shaped larvae, but more adults will probably fly in from your neighbor's yard. Floral-scented traps that attract adult beetles are available, but the traps may attract more beetles than you had before. If you try the traps, keep them at least 100 feet from your vegetables and encourage your neighbors to use them, too, to control the beetles community-wide.

Insecticidal soap and neem oil are effective against adult beetles. You also can handpick the beetles off your vegetables and stomp on them. Picking in early morning or evening is easiest because the beetles are sleepy then and tend not to fly away.

Nematodes

Nematodes are microscopic wormlike pests that can infect soil, especially in warm climates. They feed on the roots of plants and attack many vegetables, including carrots, tomatoes, and potatoes. Nematodes thrive in sandy, moist soil and can quickly stunt plants and cause roots to look hairy and knotted. Your best defense is to plant nematode-resistant varieties and to rotate your crops (see Chapter 16) to prevent a population from building.

These nematodes are different from the parasitic nematodes that I mention in the earlier section "In with the good bugs," which are actually beneficial for your garden.

Snails and slugs

Snails and *slugs* are soft-bodied mollusks that feed on tender leaves and flowers during the cool of night or during rainy weather. Snails have shells; slugs don't. Snails and slugs proliferate in damp areas, hiding under raised containers, boards, or garden debris.

To control these pests, roam through your garden at night with a flashlight and play pick-and-stomp, or trap them with saucers of beer, setting the rims at ground level. They'll jump in to drink the beer, not be able to climb out, and drown. What a way to go! Refill the saucers regularly. (These pests seem to like imported beers best, but why waste good beer on a slug?) Snails and slugs won't cross copper, so you can also surround raised beds or individual containers with a thin copper stripping, which is sold at most nurseries. In California, you can release decollate snails, which prey on pest snails; ask your Cooperative Extension Service office for information.

If all else fails, you can spread snail and slug bait containing iron phosphate. Sold as Sluggo and Escar-Go! this safe bait attracts and kills slugs and snails without being harmful to wildlife, pets, and kids.

Spider mites

Spider mites are tiny, spiderlike arachnids that you can barely see without a magnifying glass. If the population gets big enough, you can see their fine webbing beneath the leaves of your plants. As they suck a plant's juices, the leaves become yellowish with silvery *stippling* (small yellow dots on the leaves) or sheen. If things get really bad, the plant may start dropping leaves. Mites are most common in hot, dry summer climates and on plants with dusty (sooty) leaves. Tomatoes and beans are commonly infested.

A daily bath with a strong jet of water from a hose helps keep infestations down. You can control spider mites with insecticidal soap, which also helps clean off the plants' leaves. Applying summer oil or neem oil and releasing predatory mites also are effective.

Thrips

Thrips are almost-invisible troublemakers. They feed on leaves, giving them a stippled look and deforming them. You can distinguish thrips from spider mites by looking for the small fecal pellets that thrips leave behind. Thrips often pass on diseases as they feed. Beans, cabbage, onions, and eggplants are commonly infested. Many beneficials feed on thrips, especially lacewings. Insecticidal soaps and pyrethrins also are effective.

Whiteflies

Whiteflies look like small white gnats, but they suck plant juices and can proliferate in warm climates and greenhouses. They tend to congregate on the undersides of leaves, especially on tomatoes and beans. You can trap whiteflies with yellow sticky traps, which are sold in nurseries. In greenhouses, release Encarsia wasps, which prey on greenhouse whiteflies. Insecticidal soaps, summer oil, and neem oil are effective sprays.

Methods of attack

If the controls I mention in the previous sections aren't cutting it and you need to take further action, start with what I consider the first line of defense against pest outbreaks: physical barriers that keep the bugs away from your plants. The next step is to apply pesticides that are effective against a certain pest, are pretty safe to use, and have a mild impact on the rest of your garden's life-forms. In general, these products are short-lived after you use them in your garden — that's what makes them so good.

Physical controls

You can physically prevent pests from damaging your vegetables a number of ways. One of the best ways is to grab bugs by their tails, body slam them to the ground, and stomp on them. *Handpicking,* as it's usually called, works best with large bugs like tomato hornworms, Japanese beetles, snails, and slugs. The best time to handpick slugs is at night, using the light of a flashlight. If you have problems squashing bugs, drop them in a jar of soapy water instead.

Here are some other physical controls to try:

- ✔ **A strong jet of water** often dislodges insects like aphids and spider mites from the leaves of vegetables, and they rarely climb back onto the plant. This method also keeps the foliage clean.

- ✔ **Barriers** keep pests from reaching your vegetables. For example, place a small copper strip around the outside of raised beds or containers to keep snails from reaching your plants (snails won't cross the copper stripping). *Floating row covers* (see Figure 17-3), those lightweight, blanketlike materials described in more detail in Chapter 21, also keep pests away from plants. And if you have problems with cutworms, push a small cardboard collar (a paper cup with the bottom pushed out works well) into the ground around seedlings to keep bugs from reaching the stems.

- ✔ **Trapping** pests before they reach your vegetables is another way to reduce problems. Trapping works best with night feeders — such as slugs and earwigs — that seek shelter during the day and are attracted to dark, moist environments. You can trap snails and slugs under a slightly raised board at night, and then dispose of the board in the morning. Earwigs will collect in rolled-up newspapers.

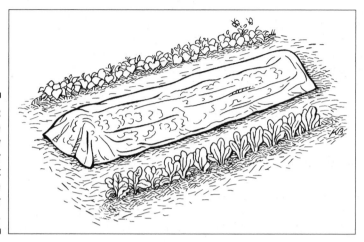

Figure 17-3:
Remove
floating row
covers for
crops that
require
bees for
pollination.

Safe pesticides

Here are my favorite safe spray methods of controlling harmful bugs:

- ✔ **Biological controls:** Using *biological controls* involves pitting one living thing against another. Releasing beneficial insects (as I suggest earlier in this chapter) is one example of biological control, but you also can use bacteria that, while harmless to humans, makes insect pests very sick and eventually very dead. The most common and useful biological controls are forms of *Bacillus thuringiensis,* or Bt, which kill the larvae of moths and butterflies (that is, caterpillars). Another variety of Bt, *B.t. tenebrionis* or *B.t. San Diego,* kills the larvae of Colorado potato beetles. *Bacillus popilliae* (milky spore disease) is an effective control of Japanese beetle grubs.

  Spinosad is a new biological control agent that has many uses. This soil-dwelling bacteria was discovered in Jamaica as a byproduct in the rum-making industry. It kills a broad range of insects, including caterpillars, thrips, spider mites, and leaf miners, but it isn't harmful to beneficial insects, animals, or pets. However, it is toxic to honey bees so spray it on cloudy days or late in the evening when the bees are less active. Like Bt, the insect must eat the toxin for it to work.

- ✔ **Botanical insecticides:** *Botanical insecticides* are derived from plants. The most useful insecticides against vegetable pests are *pyrethrins,* which are derived from the painted daisy, *Chrysanthemum cinerariifolium.* They're broad-spectrum insecticides, which means they kill a wide range of insects. Unfortunately, that means some of the good guys are killed, too. So to avoid killing bees, for example, spray pyrethrins late in the evening. I usually use this pesticide as a last resort. The advantage to using pyrethrins is that it kills pests like aphids and beetles quickly, and has low toxicity to mammals. However, always follow the label and never apply more than is recommended.

The terminology can be confusing. *Pyrethrum* is the ground-up flower of this type of daisy. *Pyrethrins* are the insecticide components of the flower. You also may see insecticides called *pyrethroids,* however. Pyrethroids, such as permethrin and resmethrin, are synthetic compounds that resemble pyrethrins but are more toxic and persistent. They shouldn't be used in organic gardens. Consequently, I avoid pyrethroids.

✔ **Home remedies:** Not all pesticides are exotic. Many gardeners have had great success using common household products to control insects in their gardens. One of my favorite home remedies is adding a clove or two of garlic and a few teaspoons of cayenne to a quart of water and then blending it all in a mixer. You then strain the solution to remove the chunks, and using a hand-held sprayer, spray your plants to control insects, such as aphids and whiteflies, and repel animals, such as rabbits and deer. Of course, after it rains, you have to reapply the mix. Commercial insecticide products, such as Hot Pepper Wax and Garlic Barrier, which are based on the common foods, also are available. Either type of product is effective, simple, safe, and fun to try.

✔ **Insecticidal soaps:** Derived from the salts of fatty acids, *insecticidal soaps* kill mostly soft-bodied pests like aphids, spider mites, and whiteflies. They also can be effective against Japanese beetles. They work fast, break down quickly, and are nontoxic to humans. Insecticidal soaps are most effective when mixed with soft water because soaps can sometimes burn tender foliage.

✔ **Neem oil:** *Neem oil* is extracted from the seed of the tropical neem tree. It has been used for centuries in India as an insecticide, to kill parasites in cattle, and even as a toothpaste for humans. Needless to say, it's very safe (except to unlucky pests). Home gardeners can purchase neem oil to repel and kill insects including aphids, whiteflies, leaf miners, caterpillars, and many others.

✔ **Summer or horticultural oil:** When sprayed on a plant, this highly refined oil smothers insect pests and their eggs. The words "highly refined" mean that the sulfur and other components of the oil that damage the plant are removed. This oil is relatively nontoxic and short lived. Use it to control aphids, mites, thrips, and certain caterpillars.

Make sure that you don't confuse summer oil with dormant oil. Dormant oil should be applied to leafless trees and shrubs during the winter. It isn't meant to be used on vegetables.

Double-check the oil's product label to make sure that you can use the oil on plants during the growing season. Then follow the mixing instructions carefully. Water your plants before and after applying the oil. But don't apply the oil if temperatures are likely to rise above 85 degrees Fahrenheit. When it's that hot, the oil can damage plant leaves.

Even organic pesticides that have relatively low impact on your garden environment can be dangerous to use as well as toxic to humans; this is true of several commonly used botanical insecticides, such as pyrethrin and rotenone. *Rotenone* is a botanical pesticide that was used heavily in the early days of organic growing, but now has lost favor with many gardeners because of research showing a potential link to cancer and Parkinson's disease. I don't recommend it.

Always follow the instructions on the product label exactly; in fact, not following these instructions is against the law. Also, wear gloves when mixing and spraying pesticides, and spray when the wind is calm. Store the chemicals in properly labeled containers well out of the reach of children (a locked cabinet is best). Dispose of empty containers as described on the label, or contact your local waste disposal company for appropriate disposal sites.

Gardening to Eliminate Diseases

Diseases differ from insects in that, with bugs, you can take action after you see them. With diseases, once you see symptoms, it's often difficult to stop the diseases from spreading. However, you can prevent or at least reduce most vegetable diseases by using good growing practices or by planting resistant varieties. Most vegetables have some varieties with disease resistance; see the chapters on individual vegetables in Part II for details. In the following sections, I provide useful methods for preventing and handling some common diseases.

Avoiding diseases with good habits

Here are some cultural practices that can help you avoid plant diseases:

✔ **Remove infected plants.** After you've identified a plant with a severe disease problem, yank out the entire plant. Even picking off infected leaves helps prevent a disease from spreading.

✔ **Avoid overhead watering.** Overhead watering can encourage foliage disease organisms to prosper. If you can't avoid this watering method, at least water early in the morning so plants have a chance to dry out before nightfall. Using drip irrigation or watering in furrows helps keep foliage dry (see Chapter 15).

✔ **Space plants properly.** Planting vegetables too close together reduces air circulation between them, a condition that favors disease and allows diseases to spread from plant to plant more readily. Keep your eyes open for developing problems.

✔ **Keep your garden clean and tidy.** Many diseases spread on plant debris, so rake up fallen leaves and remove dead plants. Also, keep the spaces under any containers clean. Removing diseased leaves can slow the spread of some organisms.

✔ **Rotate plants.** Don't plant the same vegetables in the same place year after year. Otherwise, you create a nursery for disease. Move things around as described in Chapter 16.

✔ **Mulch your beds.** A layer of mulch on the soil can act like a physical barrier, keeping disease spores in the soil and off the plants. See Chapter 15 for more on mulches.

Watching out for common diseases

The following list includes tips on how to prevent, identify, and treat (if possible) some common diseases that affect vegetables. Controls for diseases that are most troublesome for a specific vegetable are included with the description of that vegetable in Part II. Here are some diseases to keep an eye out for:

✔ **Damping off:** This disease attacks the bases of seedling stems, causing them to wilt and fall over. I discuss ways to prevent damping off in Chapter 13, which covers all aspects of growing vegetables from seed.

✔ **Powdery mildew:** This fungus coats leaves and flowers with a white powder. It's most common when days are warm but nights are cool. This disease is particularly troublesome to squash, cucumbers, melons, and peas. Controlling powdery mildew is difficult, but resistant varieties are available. The disease becomes less of a problem as the weather changes.

Some gardeners have had some success using a home remedy. Mix 1 tablespoon of summer oil and 1 to 2 teaspoons of baking soda in 1 gallon of water, and then spray the mixture often to protect new foliage. This mixture also is sold commercially under names such as Remedy. Some forms of neem oil also are registered for use on vegetables. A new biological spray called Serenade (*Bacillus subtilis*) contains a bacterium that attacks powdery mildew and other fungi.

✔ **Root rots:** A number of soilborne fungi cause plants to have basically the same damage — regardless of whether the soil is moist. Lettuce is notorious for dying like this. The best way to prevent root rot is to make sure that soil drainage is good and to avoid overwatering — let the soil dry partially between waterings. Otherwise, all you can do to control root rot is to remove the dead plants. Few other control measures are effective.

✔ **Southern blight:** This rather nasty disease that affects corn is common in the southeastern United States. Southern blight causes plants to rot at the base of their stems, wilt, turn yellow, and die. Unfortunately, this disease is difficult to control. Your best bet is to rotate your crops each year, get rid of all infected plant material, and turn your soil in the fall. You also can try soil solarization, as described in Chapter 15.

My outlook on fungicides: Avoid 'em if you can

Chemical *fungicides* (substances that kill fungus) are a nastier bunch of pesticides. I prefer not to use them on my vegetables. If you get a really stubborn disease in a prized planting, however, you may have no other choice. Here's a short list of some of the "safer" ones:

✔ Some mineral-based fungicides — such as copper for blight on tomatoes and sulfur for mildew on peas — are less toxic, but you should still use them only sparingly. They're most effective preventing the disease, so they need to be applied early.

✔ Neem oil also has been proven effective as a fungicide, making it another option. Like many fungicides, it's best used as a preventive spray or when the infection is just starting.

✔ *Bacillus subtilis* is a new biological fungicide that attacks many fungal diseases, such as mildew and blight. This bacteria is safe for bees, birds, wildlife, and beneficial insects.

As with any pesticide, follow the instructions on the label carefully and exactly.

✔ **Viruses:** These diseases affect many vegetables, including tomatoes, peppers, peas, beans, cucumbers, beets, potatoes, and squash. When infected with a virus, leaves and fruits often have mottled yellow spottings and are deformed. Plants are stunted and die young, often not producing usable fruit. Virus diseases are sometimes specific to certain vegetables and spread by insects such as cucumber beetles (see Chapter 8 for more on controlling this pest), aphids, and whiteflies; stopping these pests many times stops the disease. You also should destroy infected plants and try to plant disease-resistant varieties.

Keeping the Animal Kingdom at Bay

Besides insects and diseases, you also should keep an eye out for the 2- and 4-footed pests described in this section. If you have problems with critters, be sure to properly identify the culprit; identification may take some late-night work with a flashlight. What control you use will depend on who's doing the damage.

As you read the control suggestions in this section, you'll notice that fencing is one of my most common recommendations. But even a sturdy fence isn't a 100-percent guarantee, so live trapping and relocating may be the only solution to an especially persistent woodchuck or raccoon. (Check with your state Fish and Game Department to find out whether it has any regulations governing the trapping of the animal you have in mind.) You can buy live traps at most hardware stores; get the appropriate size for the animal that you want to catch. After you have the animal in the trap, release it in areas recommended by your local state Fish and Game Department officials.

Letting your family dog or cat prowl your grounds to ward off wild animals may sound like a good idea, but, in reality, keeping your pets indoors or restrained is the best idea, especially when large animals are around. Rabies is a problem with many wild animals, such as raccoons, and some wildlife, such as woodchucks, which are ferocious fighters.

The following list identifies animal pests that are common to vegetable gardens. It also provides some methods to control these critters:

- **Birds:** Starlings and crows have an uncanny sense of where you planted your corn seeds. To keep birds from eating seeds or pulling up newly sprouted plants, protect your seedbed with a bird tunnel (see Figure 17-4) or a floating row cover. By the time the plants outgrow the cover, they're no longer appetizing to birds.

Figure 17-4:
Covering seedlings with a portable bird tunnel is a sure way to keep birds away.

- **Cats and dogs:** Fences work best to keep four-legged friends — and your neighbors — out of your garden. Cats are a problem early in the season when they like to dig in newly tilled ground; laying chicken wire, pruned rose or raspberry canes, or hardware cloth over your seedbed until plants sprout encourages cats to dig elsewhere. Try spraying a pepper and garlic spray (see the earlier section "Methods of attack" for details) to deter these critters.

- **Deer:** A slanted fence can keep Bambi and her fawns out of your garden. Their instinct is to try to crawl under a fence before jumping it, and they're less likely to jump a wide fence. A slanted fence can be 4 to 5 feet high (see Figure 17-5); a vertical fence must be at least 8 feet high to keep deer from jumping over it.

- **Gophers:** Gophers can wreak havoc by eating plants' roots and underground parts. Trapping is the most practical solution in most cases. Probe the soil near a fresh mound of dirt with a crowbar, and set two traps in the runway, one facing each direction. Tie the traps together and cover them lightly with soil to keep out light.

Figure 17-5:
A slanted fence is the best design to keep deer out of your garden.

If your garden is small or organized into small beds, you may want to construct a gopher barrier, as shown in Figure 17-6. Dig the soil out of the bed to a depth of at least 12 inches and line the bottom and sides with 1-inch chicken wire. Then replace the soil.

✔ **Mice and small rodents:** A 12-inch-high fence made of ¼-inch mesh hardware cloth, with another 12 inches buried underground, keeps mice and other small rodents out of your garden.

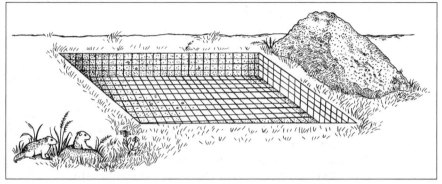

Figure 17-6:
Fencing is the safest and most effective way to deter digging animals like gophers.

TIP

✔ **Moles:** Moles don't feed on plants; they eat insects such as grubs and earthworms. However, their tunneling may damage the roots of your plants. The most effective way to control moles is to repel them. Moles don't like the smell of castor oil, so spray a mole repellent, such as Mole Med, that contains castor oil.

If the problem is severe, set traps in the tunnels. To find active tunnels, tamp down raised soil, which indicates tunneling. The tunnels that are raised the day after you tamp the soil are active.

✔ **Rabbits:** A 2-foot-high fence made of 1½-inch mesh should keep rabbits out of your garden. Make sure the bottom is tight to the ground or bury the bottom edge as recommended for woodchucks. You also can try a pepper and garlic spray designed to repel cats and dogs.

✔ **Raccoons:** A 4-foot-high fence similar to the one recommended for wood-chucks usually keeps raccoons out of your garden.

✔ **Woodchucks:** A fence at least 3 feet high with another 12 inches under-ground, curved away from the garden, is the best way to keep out wood-chucks, also known as groundhogs (see Figure 17-7). Leave the top 18 inches of the fence unattached to support posts. This way, as the wood-chuck attempts to climb over the fence, the fence will bend back down under the animal's weight. A strand of electric wire on top of a wire fence also discourages them.

Figure 17-7:
Build a
fence to
keep out
wood-
chucks and
raccoons,
making sure
to keep
the top 18
inches unat-
tached to
the stakes.

Chapter 18

Containing Your Veggies

. . . .

. . . .

You can grow almost any vegetable in a container; just fill a big pot with good soil, plant your chosen veggies, and then water and fertilize regularly. Why not just grow vegetables in your garden? Well, maybe you aren't a farmer with a big backyard and a 10-horsepower rototiller. Maybe your soil is more appropriate for raising worms than raising plants. Or maybe your garden is the balcony of your apartment or a tiny patio behind your condominium. You still have the right to fresh, homegrown tomatoes, don't you? You bet, and containers enable you to grow them.

Containers also enable you to grow vegetables that may not be able to grow successfully in your garden. For example: If you've tried to grow eggplant in a climate with cool summers, but it never matured before the first frost, try growing it in a container. Because containers heat up fast in spring, vegetables get a head start on the season.

Some people grow vegetables in containers simply because they like having their crops nearby — I certainly do. With containers, you can bring your crops close to your house where you can see and enjoy them (and eat them at the peak of freshness!). Because containers are so easy to move (or because you made them that way by putting them on wheels), containers are the great equalizer; if you need a little more or less sun, you simply move the containers. (It's a heck of a lot easier than moving the sun!) Similarly, if frost is threatening, you can move the containers to shelter.

Vegetables can be beautiful; I've seen pots of vegetables that are every bit as colorful as my favorite flowers. Whew, I'm getting excited about growing vegetables in containers! And that's what this chapter is all about: discovering how to get a bountiful and beautiful vegetable harvest from containers.

Considering a Few Container Characteristics

One trip to a nursery gives you an idea of just how many different styles and types of containers you can choose from. You can buy clay pots, glazed or not; plastic pots, pretty or ugly; or wood pots, big or small. And that's just the tip of the iceberg. Here are some things to keep in mind when choosing a pot for vegetables:

- **Size:** In most cases, pots that are bigger (in terms of width and volume) are better, especially for growing large plants like tomatoes. Lots of root space means that your vegetables are less likely to get cramped; they'll also be easier to water and fertilize. If you want to grow one head of lettuce in a small pot (8 inches in diameter), for example, you can do it, but you'll have to water and fertilize more frequently than if you had grown it in a larger pot. Although I've grown tomatoes in 5-gallon containers, I prefer at least the 15-gallon size.

  With some vegetables, the depth of a container is as important — if not more important — as its width. You can grow quite a few carrots or radishes in a narrow container, but the container must be deep enough to accommodate the length of the plant's mature roots. See the section "Knowing Which Vegetables Grow Well in Pots," later in this chapter, for more on size issues for specific vegetables.

  A half whiskey or wine barrel is a large, inexpensive container that can hold quite a few vegetables — ten heads of lettuce, ten bush bean plants, one or two small tomato plants, or four or five small cucumber varieties. You can purchase these containers at garden centers and nurseries.

- **Material:** What a pot is made of can affect how often you have to water and how long the container lasts. Pots made of porous materials like clay dry out faster than those made of plastic or wood, so you must water the plants in them more frequently, especially in hot or windy climates.

  If you want to use wood containers, make sure they're made of rot-resistant materials like cedar or redwood; otherwise, they won't last very long. I prefer not to use preservative-treated wood containers for growing vegetables or other edibles, because the chemicals may leach into the soil and then into my plants. If my redwood or cedar pots eventually rot after 10 years, I just replace them — the same goes for my half whiskey barrels.

✔ **Drainage:** All the pots you use for growing vegetables should have drainage holes; fortunately, almost all do. But because a wooden half barrel often doesn't, you have to drill your own holes in the bottom of the container (eight to ten evenly spaced, 1-inch holes should be fine). If pots don't have drainage holes, the soil becomes a swampy mess, the roots drown, and the plants die. Bummer.

You need to consider two other accessories when you shop for pots:

✔ **A saucer to place underneath your pot:** A saucer collects water that runs out of the holes in the bottom of a pot and prevents the pot from staining whatever it's sitting on. You can find saucers made of the same or similar material as your pot or ones made of clear plastic. Plastic saucers are least likely to stain.

Just make sure you don't let water stand more than a day in the saucer; water rots roots and wooden pots.

✔ **Wheels for mobility:** Most nurseries sell wheeled platforms that you place under large pots to move them easily. Otherwise, you have to lift the heavy pots or cart them around on a hand truck.

An especially useful type of pot is a *self-watering container* (see Figure 18-1). This type of pot is made of rubberized plastic and has a false bottom and reservoir under the soil that can be filled with water. You pour water into a pipe at the top of the pot or through a hole in the side of the pot to fill the reservoir. The water naturally wicks up from the reservoir and into the dry soil so you don't have to water as frequently. These pots allow you to get away during the heat of summer and not worry whether your plants are getting watered.

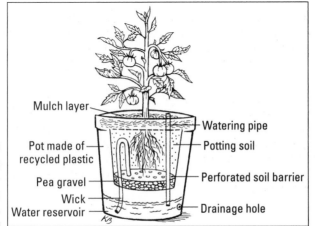

Figure 18-1:
A self-watering container.

Mulch layer

Pot made of recycled plastic

Pea gravel

Wick

Water reservoir

Watering pipe

Potting soil

Perforated soil barrier

Drainage hole

Filling Up Your Container: Potting Soil Made Simple

Don't fill your pot with soil from your garden — even if your garden has the very best soil on the planet. It's too heavy and too dirty (you know, weed seeds, bugs, bacteria — stuff that you don't want in your pots), and it may not drain properly in a pot.

Instead, use potting soil. I can tell you a lot about potting soil: how it's well aerated, sterile, lightweight, and made of a good balance of organic material and mineral particles like sand or perlite. I can even give you a recipe to make your own, but you'd nod off in a second. So just trust me on this one.

At your local nursery or garden center, buy a packaged, sterilized, soilless potting soil that's meant for container growing. If you need a large quantity, many nurseries sell potting soil in bulk. You may want to try different brands over time to see which ones are easiest to wet and which ones have the best moisture-holding capacity and drainage. But don't have a personal crisis over which brand of potting soil you buy; caring for your vegetables properly after you plant is more important than choosing the perfect potting soil.

If you're growing vegetables in large containers, you'll be shocked at how much potting soil you need to fill each container. However, you don't have to fill the whole container with soil. Most vegetable roots only penetrate 10 to 12 inches into the soil. Add more than that and you're simply wasting soil. A trick to use less soil is to put empty plastic soda and milk bottles in the bottom third of the container, and then throw the soil on top. The container will be lighter and easier to move, you'll be recycling to help the environment, and you won't have to buy as much soil. Talk about a win-win-win situation!

Don't use the same soil each year; it may have unwelcome diseases and insects in it. It's best to start fresh by replacing the potting soil in your containers each year.

Knowing Which Vegetables Grow Well in Pots

If you're persistent, you can grow any vegetable in a pot. However, some of the bigger plants, like squash and watermelon, are pretty tricky to contain and tend to get unruly. But don't worry, many other vegetables fit perfectly in pots. In the following sections, I describe popular container veggies you can begin with and provide some of my favorite veggie combinations.

Some common container veggies

Vegetable breeders have long had container gardeners in mind. They breed many small-space varieties (of even the most sprawling plants) that are ideal for growing in pots. So in the following list, I take a look at the most common vegetables to grow in containers. (For more information on varieties, see Part II.) If you can't find the dwarf varieties that I mention here, try anything with the words *compact, bush, baby, midget, dwarf, tiny,* or *teeny* in the name:

- ✔ **Beans:** Bush varieties like 'Provider' and 'Derby' are best; you can grow three to four plants in a 12-inch pot. You can grow pole types in a long narrow box, but you have to attach some type of trellis (see Chapter 15 for more on trellising).

- ✔ **Beets:** Any variety grows well in a pot, and smaller varieties like 'Red Ace' even grow well in smaller pots. However, make sure your pot is big and deep enough (at least 12 inches); beets don't like to be crowded. You should end up having about six plants in a 12-inch pot — more if you're growing them for greens or will pick them as baby beets.

- ✔ **Carrots:** Carrots are a perfect vegetable to grow in a pot. Start with baby varieties like 'Little Fingers', 'Short 'n Sweet', or 'Thumbelina'. If you water diligently, you can get a bumper harvest in pots as shallow as 6 to 8 inches deep. Longer varieties need deeper pots. After thinning, you should end up with 20 or so carrots per 12-inch pot.

- ✔ **Cole crops — broccoli, cabbage, cauliflower, and so on:** All the cole crops grow well in containers as long as your pots are big enough; try planting three or four plants in a half barrel.

- ✔ **Cucumbers:** You can't go wrong growing small cucumber types like 'Bush Pickle' and 'Salad Bush'. I've harvested cucumbers out of 12-inch-diameter hanging pots — planted with three seeds to a pot. Plants dangling over the edges of a hanging pot are something to behold. Plant large-growing varieties in bigger pots and slip a sturdy wire cylinder into the outside edge of the pot for the plants to climb on.

- ✔ **Eggplant:** An eggplant's purple foliage and compact habit are perfect for pots; any variety works as long the container is at least 5 gallons. Plant one eggplant per 5-gallon pot. If a plant gets floppy, push a small stake in the pot to support the plant.

- ✔ **Lettuce and other greens:** Lettuce and greens may be the ultimate container vegetables. The size of your pot doesn't really matter — just sprinkle some seeds in it, keep the soil moist, and then get out your salad bowl for a great harvest. You can harvest the whole plant or snip off just what you need. If you want a really pretty pot, plant some 'Bright Lights' Swiss chard.

- **Melons:** Melons aren't ideal container subjects; they're wild and unruly. But through the magic of modern science, some dwarf varieties, like 'Bush Sugar Baby' watermelon, grow well in containers. Plant one to two plants in a big pot (at least 5 gallons) and let the vines sprawl over the edges, supporting the fruit if necessary. And don't let up on water and fertilizer.

- **Onions:** Green onions — scallions or bunching onions if you prefer to call them that — grow well in containers. Just buy a bag of sets, plant them 2- to 3-inches deep, and you're in business. You can grow onions to full bulb size; just make sure that you use a big pot (preferably 5 gallons) and give them plenty of room to grow.

- **Peas:** Go with dwarf pea varieties like 'Green Arrow' and 'Maestro', English peas, 'Sugar Bon' snap pea, or 'Dwarf Grey Sugar' snow pea. Any variety larger than that needs a trellis. Planting six plants in a 12-inch pot should be fine.

- **Peppers:** You can grow any pepper variety in a pot, but the bigger the pot the better. I like to grow small-fruited varieties like 'Serrano' and 'Black Pearl' peppers; they produce so much colorful fruit that their containers become showpieces. A 5-gallon pot should hold one to two plants.

- **Potatoes:** Potatoes are fun vegetables to grow in a container. Just place 8 to 10 inches of potting soil in a big pot (at least a 5-gallon size). Plant two to three potato eyes 2 to 3 inches from the bottom of the pot, and then water them in. After the plants start to grow, cover the stems with more soil (leaving the very top exposed) until the pot is full. In a couple of months, you can harvest a pot full of spuds. Start harvesting earlier for new potatoes, later for larger ones. (For more on growing potatoes in small spaces using towers, see Chapter 6.)

- **Radishes:** Growing radishes is quick and easy even in the smallest container. Scatter some seeds in the top of a pot, keep the soil moist, and you'll have radishes in less than a month.

- **Squash:** I have to be honest; bush zucchini plants are too productive even in pots. Use a 5-gallon pot (or even larger) to grow space-saving winter squash varieties like 'Cornell Bush Delicata', 'Papaya Pear', or 'Table King'. Plant three seeds in each pot and thin to the healthiest plant.

- **Tomatoes:** Everyone deserves fresh tomatoes, and anyone can grow them in pots. Try your favorite dwarf indeterminate variety, such as 'Bush Big Boy' in a container that's at least 5 gallons (bigger is better), but be ready to stake or cage tall plants. Or you can grow dwarf varieties like 'Patio', 'Tiny Tim', and 'Window Box Roma', which fit perfectly in pots, even smaller sizes.

Most herbs grow well in containers; see Chapter 12 for details.

Some bee-u-tee-ful vegetable combos

I'm a firm believer that anything growing in a pot, including vegetables, should look good enough to place on a patio or deck. So I like to combine different vegetables that look good together, and sometimes I even throw in some flowers. Here are some of my favorite container vegetable combinations:

- **Mixed leaf-lettuce varieties:** All the different reds, greens, and purples form a soft, textured kaleidoscope of colors. You can sow premixed seeds, but I prefer to use transplants so that I can evenly space them for a more structured look.

- **Cool season masterpiece:** In a half barrel, place one or two red Swiss chard plants in the middle, and then surround them with red and green leaf lettuce, a few parsley plants, and some white pansies.

- **A salad bowl:** Plant some different lettuces or other greens with parsley, chives, green onions, and other herbs. (Are you starting to see how much I like to use lettuce as an ornamental?) If you really want to get fancy, add some edible flowers like pansies and violas. (For more on growing herbs, check out Chapter 12.)

- **Tomatoes and herbs:** Plant one of the smaller tomato varieties, like 'Patio', in the middle of a large pot. Surround it with basil or thyme, and mix in several dwarf yellow marigolds (which are edible flowers).

- **Cabbage and kale:** A large pot works best with these vegetables. Just mix red and green cabbage with some crinkly kale. Keep the older leaves trimmed so that the arrangement looks nice and clean. If you really want a knock-out display, plant some red tulip bulbs about 4 inches deep in the soil.

Well, I've given you five good combinations. Using your imagination, you should be able to come up with plenty more possibilities. But do you want one more for the road? Try planting rhubarb in a pot; the big leaves and colorful stems are stunning.

Planting Your Veggies in Pots

Planting in containers is very much like planting in open ground (see Chapter 13). But with containers, you can plant seedlings or seeds a little closer together because you're concentrating water and nutrients in a small space, so the seedlings and seeds, not the general soil, get more of what they need to grow. You also don't have to form berms or basins in the soil with container gardening.

Here's how to plant vegetables in a container:

1. **Fill your container with soil mix so that the soil reaches almost to the top of the container, and then wet the soil thoroughly.**

   Wetting the soil will probably take several passes with a hose. After the soil drains, it will have settled several inches.

2. **After the water settles, add more soil until the soil level is within 2 to 3 inches of the rim.**

   Level the top of the soil with your hands.

3. **Plant your seedlings or seeds.**

   If you're planting seedlings, make a small hole in the soil for each transplant. Place one seedling in each hole. The top of the *root ball* (the soil held together by the roots) should be level with or slightly below the surrounding soil. Use your finger to gently press down the soil around each seedling.

   If you're sowing seeds, plant them at the appropriate depth according to the information in Chapter 13.

4. **Water the container gently with a watering can or hose until the soil is thoroughly moist.**

   A watering can or a hose with a bubbler extension works best because it's less likely to wash soil out of the pot or dislodge seeds.

Care for your new plantings as described in Chapter 13, making sure to keep the soil moist until the seedlings are established or until the seeds germinate.

Caring for Container Veggies

Planting vegetables in containers is very much like planting them in the ground, but you must do a few things a bit differently when it comes to maintaining them. Here are some pointers for taking care of your container vegetables as compared to vegetables in your garden:

✔ **Water more frequently.** Because potting soil dries out faster than regular garden soil, container vegetables need more frequent watering (unless you're using self-watering containers, which I describe earlier in this chapter). In really hot weather, you may have to water more than once a day, especially if the plants are large and roots fill the pots. If you let your vegetables go dry just once, you may spoil your harvest, causing conditions such as blossom-end rot, which can affect tomatoes. (You can read about how this condition affects tomatoes in Chapter 4.)

Here are a couple ways to check whether your container is dry:

- **Stick your finger in the soil.** If the top few inches are bone dry, you should water.

- **Lift or tip the container on its side.** If the soil is dry, the container will be very light.

✔ **Water more thoroughly.** Wetting dry potting soil can be tricky. Sometimes, the root ball of the plant (or plants) shrinks a bit and pulls away from the side of the pot as the soil dries so that when you water, all the water rushes down the space on the side of the pot without wetting the soil. To overcome this problem, make sure you fill the top of the pot with water more than once so the root ball can absorb the water and expand. In fact, you should always water this way to make sure the root ball is thoroughly wet. It's also important, however, to avoid overwatering the soil; do the finger check before watering.

If you still have problems wetting the root ball, place your pot in a saucer and fill the saucer repeatedly with water. The water soaks up into the root ball and slowly wets all the soil.

If you have a lot of pots, you may want to hook a drip irrigation system to an automatic timer to water them; nurseries and garden centers sell special drip emitters designed for pots. You can find out more about drip irrigation and emitters in Chapter 15.

✔ **Fertilize more frequently.** Because nutrients are leached from the soil when you frequently water container vegetables, you need to fertilize your plants more often — at least every 2 weeks. Liquid or water-soluble fertilizers (you just add them to water) are easiest to use and get nutrients down to the roots of your plants. A complete organic fertilizer is best. (See Chapter 15 for more detailed fertilizer info.)

✔ **Watch for pests.** Worried about insects and diseases harming your container plants? Don't be too concerned. In general, vegetables in containers have fewer pest problems because they're isolated from other plants. Insects aren't waiting on nearby weeds to jump on your plants, and sterilized potting soil (which I recommend for container gardening) doesn't have any disease spores.

Even though container vegetables tend to have fewer pest problems, you should quickly deal with any problems that arise so your whole crop isn't wiped out. Solve your pest problems by using the same techniques that you use in your garden. Check out Chapter 17 to read about controls for specific diseases and insects.

Because container vegetables are often located on patios or decks that are close to the house, special care should be used in spraying them for pests. I know I said container vegetables don't get as many pests as in the garden, but you may have to spray occasionally; so, if possible, move the containers away from the doors and windows when you spray.

Experimenting with Greenhouses, Hoop Houses, and Hydroponics

You can grow cucumbers, tomatoes, and other vegetables in the dead of winter in a *greenhouse* (an enclosed, heated, controlled-atmosphere room). In fact, farmers throughout the world do it all the time. You don't even have to have a glass structure for a greenhouse. You can use plastic hoop houses instead. They're easy to build, inexpensive, and a great way to extend the growing season. (See Chapter 21 for more on hoop houses.) Either way, greenhouse growing is more involved — it's container gardening and vegetable growing at their highest levels; everything has to be just right to get a good crop. But maybe I've helped turn you into a really good gardener, so everything will be just right. After all, that was the point of this book.

You need to pay attention to many more conditions in a greenhouse, such as temperatures that are too hot and too cool, fertility, pests (once they get started, they're tough to stop in a greenhouse), pollination for crops like cucumbers and melons, and so on. You generally have to be more dedicated to vegetable gardening to grow good crops in a greenhouse. The easiest time to grow them is in the spring and fall to extend the season. Winter and summer are the toughest times to grow plants in a greenhouse because of the extremes in temperature and available light.

Another term that's associated with container vegetables is *hydroponics* (see the appendix for companies specializing in hydroponics). You may have bought hydroponic tomatoes at the grocery store, or you may have seen the amazing hydroponic lettuce at Disney World. When you grow hydroponic vegetables, you grow the plants in a soilless, liquid solution that provides all the plant's nutrient needs. You need special equipment and growing techniques, but you can grow any plant this way.

For more information on growing plants in greenhouses and hoop houses, visit growinggreenhouse.com. If you want to read more about growing plants hydroponically, check out www.hydroponics-at-home.com.

Chapter 19

Harvesting, Storing, and Preserving Vegetables

Suppose that you've done everything you need to do in your garden: You planted your veggies at the right time, watered and fertilized them as needed, and kept an eye out for pests. Way to go. Now for the best part: It's time to eat!

To get all the best flavor and highest nutritional value from your vegetables, you need to pick them at just the right time. Some vegetables taste terrible if you pick them too early; others are tough and stringy if you pick them too late.

And after you pick your vegetables, what if you can't eat them right away? When properly stored, most vegetables last a while without rotting or losing too much flavor (of course, eating them fresh picked is always best). In fact, you can store some vegetables, like potatoes and winter squash, for months.

So in this chapter, I discuss harvesting and storing your fresh vegetables. You put in too much work not to do the final steps just right.

Knowing When to Harvest

You should harvest most vegetables when they're young and tender, which often means harvesting the plants, roots, or fruits before they reach full size. A 15-inch zucchini is impressive, but it tastes better at 6 to 8 inches. Similarly, carrots and beets get *woody* (tough textured) and bland the longer they stay in the ground. Table 19-1 provides specific information on when to harvest a variety of veggies.

Other plants are continuously harvested to keep them productive. If you keep harvesting vegetables like snap beans, summer squash, snow and snap peas, broccoli, okra, spinach, and lettuce, they'll continue to produce pods, shoots, or leaves.

A good rule for many of your early crops is to start harvesting when you have enough of a vegetable for a one-meal serving. Spinach, Swiss chard, scallions, radishes, lettuce, and members of the cabbage family certainly fit the bill here. These veggies don't grow as well in warm weather, so pick these crops in the spring when temperatures are cooler.

After you start harvesting, visit your garden and pick something daily. Take along a good sharp knife and a few containers to hold your produce, such as paper bags, buckets, or baskets. Wire or wood buckets work well because you can easily wash vegetables in them.

Table 19-1	Harvesting Fresh Vegetables
Vegetable	*When to Harvest*
Asparagus	When spears are 6 to 9 inches long
Beans, snap	Start about 2 to 3 weeks after bloom, before seeds mature
Beans, dried	When the pods are dry and crack open easily
Beets	When 1 to 3 inches wide
Broccoli	When flower heads are tight and green
Brussels sprouts	When sprouts reach 1 inch wide
Cabbage	When heads are compact and firm
Carrots	When tops are 1 inch wide
Cauliflower	While heads are still white but not *ricey* (the florets are splitting apart)
Celery	When stalks are large enough to eat
Corn	When silks are dry and brown; kernels should be milky when cut
Cucumbers	For slicing, when 6 inches long; for picklers, when at least 2 inches long
Eggplant	Before color dulls; flesh should bounce back when pressed lightly
Garlic	Pull up stalks when the bottom leaves yellow
Kohlrabi	When 2 to 3 inches wide
Leeks	When the stalks are at least 1½ inches in diameter
Lettuce and other greens	While leaves are tender

Vegetable	When to Harvest
Muskmelons	When fruit slips off vine easily; while *netting* (raised area on skin) is even; when fruit is firm
Okra	When pods are soft and 2 to 3 inches long
Onions	When necks are tight and scales are dry
Parsnips	When roots reach desired size, possibly after light frost
Peanuts	When leaves turn yellow
Peas	While pods are still tender
Peppers	When fruits reach desired size and color
Potatoes	When vines die back
Pumpkins	When shells harden, before frost
Radishes	When roots are up to 1¼ inches wide
Rhubarb	When it shows red streaks on the stalks
Rutabagas	When roots reach desired size
Shallots	Harvest mature bulbs when tops wither and turn brown
Spinach	When leaves are still tender
Squash, summer	When 6 to 8 inches long
Squash, winter	When shells harden, before frost
Sweet potatoes	When they reach adequate size
Tomatoes	When uniformly colored
Turnips	When 2 to 3 inches wide
Watermelons	When undersides turn yellow and produce a dull sound when thumped

The harvesting information in Table 19-1 is based on picking mature or slightly immature vegetables. But many vegetables can be picked smaller and still have excellent flavor. Pick baby vegetables whenever they reach the size that you want. The following vegetables can be picked small: beets, broccoli, carrots, cauliflower, cucumbers, lettuce and other greens, onions, peas, potatoes, radishes, snap beans, summer squash, Swiss chard, and turnips. In addition, some small varieties of corn and tomatoes fit the baby-vegetable mold.

Be sure to avoid harvesting at the following times:

- ✓ **When plants, especially beans, are wet.** Many fungal diseases spread in moist conditions, and if you brush your tools or pant legs against diseased plants, you can transfer disease organisms to other plants down the row.

✔ **In the heat of the day, because the vegetable's texture may be limp.** For the freshest produce, harvest early in the day when vegetables' moisture levels inside the vegetables are highest and the vegetables are at peak flavor. After harvesting, refrigerate the produce and prepare it later in the day.

In the fall, wait as long as you can to dig up root crops, such as carrots, rutabagas, and beets, if you intend to store them in a root cellar or cold storage room. However, remember that while root crops can withstand frosts, you should harvest them before the ground freezes. They'll come out of the ground easiest if the soil is still slightly moist. Also, don't wash crops that are going to the root cellar; instead, just gently brush away soil crumbs. Use any blemished or cut vegetables within a few days.

Putting Away Your Vegetables

You have only two choices when you harvest your crops: Eat the veggies right away, or store them to use later. Specific vegetables need different storage conditions to maintain their freshness. These conditions can be summarized as follows:

✔ **Cool and dry:** Ideally, temperatures should be between 50 and 60 degrees Fahrenheit, with 60-percent relative humidity — conditions you usually find in a well-ventilated basement.

✔ **Cold and dry:** Temperatures should be between 32 and 40 degrees, with 65-percent humidity. You can achieve these conditions in most home refrigerators or in a cold basement or garage.

✔ **Cool and moist:** Temperatures should be between 50 and 60 degrees with 90-percent humidity. You can store vegetables in a cool kitchen or basement in perforated plastic bags.

✔ **Cold and moist:** Ideally, your storage area should be 32 to 40 degrees, with 95-percent humidity. You can create these conditions by placing your vegetables in perforated bags (vegetables in bags without ventilation are likely to degrade faster) and storing the bags in a refrigerator.

You also can create cold and moist conditions in a root cellar. An unheated basement works well as a root cellar. However, these days, most homes have heaters or furnaces in the basement, which make the conditions too warm for storing vegetables. But if you don't have a heater, or if you can section off a portion of your basement and keep temperatures just above freezing, you can store vegetables like root crops and even cabbage for long periods of time.

Make sure your vegetables are well ventilated in the root cellar; you can store onions, potatoes, and other root crops in mesh bags. Shoot for a humidity level that's as high as you can get. To increase humidity, spread moist wood shavings or sawdust on the floor but keep the vegetables elevated on wooden boxes.

In Table 19-2, I provide specifics on how to store your vegetables so that after you pick them, you quickly know what to do with them (that is, if you don't eat them right away). Table 19-2 also includes information on whether you can freeze, dry, or can vegetables, topics that I cover later in this chapter.

Table 19-2	Storing Fresh Vegetables		
Vegetable	*How to Store*	*Expected Storage Life*	*Comments*
Asparagus	Cold and moist	Two weeks	Store upright. Freeze, dry, or can.
Beans, snap	Cool and moist	One week	Pods will scar below 40 degrees. Freeze after blanching.
Beets	Cold and moist	Five months	Store without tops. Freeze, dry, or can.
Broccoli	Cold and moist	Two weeks	Freeze or dry.
Brussels sprouts	Cold and moist	One month	Freeze or dry.
Cabbage	Cold and moist	Five months	Freeze or dry.
Carrots	Cold and moist	Three weeks	Store without tops. Freeze, dry, or can.
Cauliflower	Cold and moist	Three weeks	Freeze or dry.
Corn	Cold and moist	Five days	Freeze, dry, or can.
Cucumbers	Cool and moist	One to two weeks	Will scar if stored below 40 degrees. Can be stored in a cool kitchen in a perforated bag. Don't store with apples or tomatoes. Can.
Eggplant	Cool and moist	One week	Prolonged storage below 50 degrees causes scarring. Freeze or dry.
Kohlrabi	Cold and moist	Two months	Store without tops. Freeze.

(continued)

Table 19-2 (continued)

Vegetable	How to Store	Expected Storage Life	Comments
Lettuce and other greens	Cold and moist	One week	Freeze greens such as spinach and Swiss chard.
Muskmelons	Cold and moist	One week	Freeze.
Onions	Cold and dry	Four months	*Cure* (let dry) at room temperatures for 2 to 4 weeks before storing. Keep green onions cool and moist for 1 to 4 months. Freeze, dry, or can.
Parsnips	Cold and moist	Three weeks	Will sweeten after 2 weeks at 32 degrees. Freeze.
Peanuts	Cool and dry	Four months	Pull pods after plant has dried for several weeks. Store dried in bags.
Peas	Cold and moist	One week	Freeze, dry, or can.
Peppers	Cool and moist	Two weeks	Will scar if stored below 45 degrees. Freeze, dry, or can.
Potatoes	Cold and moist	Six months	Keep out of light. Cure at 50 to 60 degrees for 14 days before storage. Freeze, dry, or can.
Pumpkins	Cool and dry	Two to five months	Very sensitive to temperatures below 45 degrees. Freeze, dry, or can.
Radishes	Cold and moist	One month	Store without tops. Freeze or dry.
Rutabagas	Cold and moist	Four months	Freeze.
Spinach	Cold and moist	Ten days	Freeze.
Squash, summer	Cool and moist	One week	Don't store in refrigerator for more than 4 days. Freeze, dry, or can.
Squash, winter	Cool and dry	Two to six months	Freeze, dry, or can.
Sweet potatoes	Cool and moist	Four months	Cure in the sun. Freeze, dry, or can.

Vegetable	How to Store	Expected Storage Life	Comments
Tomatoes	Cool and moist	Five days	Loses flavor if stored below 55 degrees. Don't refrigerate. Freeze, dry, or can.
Turnips	Cold and moist	Two to four months	Freeze.
Watermelons	Cool and moist	Two weeks	Will decay if stored below 50 degrees. Can the juice or rind.

If you want to store vegetables, make sure you harvest them at their peak ripeness. Also avoid bruising the produce, because bruises hasten rotting. The storage times in Table 19-2 are only estimates; they can vary widely depending on conditions. Store only the highest quality vegetables for long periods of time; vegetables that are damaged or scarred are likely to rot and spoil everything nearby.

If you live in an area where the ground freezes in the winter, you can actually leave some root crops — including carrots, leeks, rutabagas, and turnips — in the ground and harvest all winter long. After a good, hard frost, but before the ground freezes, cover your vegetable bed with a foot or more of dry hay. Cover the hay with heavy plastic (4 to 6 millimeters) and secure the edges with rocks, bricks, or heavy boards. The plastic keeps rain and snow from trickling down through the hay and rotting your vegetables, and it also keeps the soil from freezing solid. You can harvest periodically through winter, but be careful to re-cover the opening after each harvest.

Freezing, Drying, and Canning Veggies

You can preserve vegetables three different ways — by freezing, drying, or canning them — to make your harvest last longer than if you stored your vegetables fresh. (Refer to Table 19-2 for information on whether a particular vegetable can be frozen, dried, or canned.) I don't have room to cover all the details about these different methods, but the following list gives you a thumbnail sketch of each technique:

✔ **Freezing:** This is probably the easiest way to preserve vegetables. Heck, if you want, just puree up some tomatoes, put them in a container, and throw them in the freezer — they'll last for months. The mix is great to use in spaghetti sauce or soups.

You also can freeze some vegetables, like beans or peas, whole. But usually you have to blanch them first to preserve their color and texture. *Blanching* is simply the process of dipping the vegetables in boiling water for a minute or two and then placing them in ice water to cool them off. Then you dry the vegetables with a towel and freeze them in labeled plastic freezer bags. Simple.

✔ **Drying:** This technique can be pretty easy, but it must be done properly to prevent spoilage. Basically, you dehydrate the vegetables by laying them out in the sun to dry, by slow baking them in the oven, or by using a commercial dehydrator, which you can buy in most mail-order catalogs (see the appendix). In hot, sunny climates like California, you can dry 'Roma' tomatoes by slicing them in half and laying them out in the sun on a screen.

Spoilage is always a concern, so before drying your vegetables, you may need to get some additional information. You usually need to store dried vegetables in airtight containers; lidded jars work well. You can use dried vegetables to make soups and sauces.

✔ **Canning:** Of all preserved vegetables, I like the taste of canned tomatoes the best. Nothing tastes better in the middle of winter. But canning is a delicate and labor-intensive procedure that can require peeling, sterilizing jars, cooking, boiling, and a lot of other work. I usually set aside a whole weekend to can tomatoes and other veggies. I don't want to discourage you, but you need some good recipes, some special equipment, and probably some help if you want to can vegetables.

For help with freezing, drying, and canning vegetables and herbs, I like to refer to the bible, *The Ball Blue Book of Preserving* (Alltrista Consumer Products, 2004). Or you can check out *Canning and Preserving For Dummies* by Karen Ward. Your local Cooperative Extension Service office also is a good source of information on preserving vegetables. Finally, I have come across many great Web sites on home food preservation as well. Here are a few to try:

✔ Home Food Preservation (`foodsafety.psu.edu/lets_preserve.html`)

✔ National Center for Home Food Preservation (`www.uga.edu/nchfp`)

✔ Pick-Your-Own (`www.pickyourown.org`)

Saving Vegetable Seeds

If you have a favorite vegetable variety that's suited to your tastes or growing conditions, or if you have a particular plant that thrives in your garden, you can save those plants' seeds and possibly even improve their qualities to better fit your needs. If you collect seeds from only the best plants year after year, the qualities that you want will eventually be more present and predictable.

Hybrid seeds won't come true to type (the exact same plant) if you collect the seeds and try to grow them a year later. Open-pollinated varieties are more likely to give you what you expect.

Saving your own seeds also may be the only way to keep some heirloom varieties alive. Some heirlooms are difficult or impossible to obtain, but they have something special to offer, such as adaptation to a specific climate, certain types of disease resistance, or especially good flavor. Heirloom varieties represent a reservoir of genes that plant breeders can use to improve present and future crops.

The appendix lists organizations dedicated to heirloom varieties. Here are some Web sites that provide information on how to save some of your own vegetable seeds:

- ✔ International Seed Saving Institute (www.seedsave.org/issi/ issi_904.html)
- ✔ Cornell University (counties.cce.cornell.edu/suffolk/ HortFactSheets/factsheets/How%20to%20Save%20 Vegetable%20Seeds.pdf)

Part IV
The Part of Tens

The 5th Wave   By Rich Tennant

"That part of the garden is called 'Area 51'
because we don't know what's going on
over there."

In this part . . .

This part is all about quick lists of handy gardening tools and methods of season extending. Chapter 20 goes into details about the ten best tools to use in the garden — what's essential and what's fun to have. In Chapter 21, I talk about nearly ten good ways to extend the gardening season with row covers, cloches, cold frames, and greenhouses. It's for those gardeners who can't get enough of growing their own fresh produce.

Chapter 20

Ten Tools of the Trade

In This Chapter

▶ Identifying essential tools for your vegetable garden

▶ Using the right tool for the right situation

*Y*ou've probably heard this saying at least a hundred times: "Use the right tool for the job." It's as true in vegetable gardening as it is for any other project. The right tool allows you to finish a job faster, and even more importantly, make working in your garden easier on your body. After all, most people garden not to labor and sweat but to enjoy the vegetables and the relaxing environment.

As a new gardener, however, you may find that knowing which tools to pick is often confusing. You can spend hundreds of dollars buying tools for every imaginable use, but you may end up spending more time in your tool shed than in your garden. So when you're selecting your tools, my solution is to keep it simple — that's why I chose to highlight only ten tools in this chapter. And keep in mind that even these tools may not be appropriate for all garden situations.

Many of the items you need are probably already around your house — especially if you're working on other outdoor projects. Here's a short list of some useful gardening gear:

✔ Gloves help you grip tools better and help you avoid hand blisters. Cotton gloves are the cheapest, but the more expensive animal skin gloves — made of goat and sheep skin, for example — last longer.

✔ A good straw hat with ventilation keeps the sun off your skin and allows air to move through and cool your head.

✔ A good pocketknife or pair of pruning shears is great for cutting strings and vines.

✔ Sturdy rubber boots, garden clogs, or work boots repel water and provide support for digging.

✔ Bug repellent and sunscreen help keep you comfortable and protected while working in the garden.

Now on to the specific garden tools that you need. Depending on the size and type of garden you have, the "right tool" can vary widely. In this chapter, I describe ten essential tools and talk about the garden situations for which they're best suited. Many gardening tools are ergonomically designed to work more efficiently and put less stress on your joints. I highlight these ergonomic tools as well as provide helpful tips on how to use the tools and put less strain on your back, arms, wrists, and legs. So get ready to start digging in your garden!

To keep your metal hand tools functioning for years, clean and store them properly. After you're finished using a tool, wash all soil off it. Yearly, sharpen the blades of weeders, spades, and shovels; oil wooden handles with linseed oil; and tighten any nuts and screws on the handles.

Watering Hoses and Cans

Plants need water to grow, and if Mother Nature isn't cooperating, you need to water regularly (see Chapter 15 for watering techniques). For a large garden, you may need elaborate soaker hoses, sprinklers, and drip irrigation pipes. But for most small-scale home gardeners, a simple hose and watering can will do.

Rubber hoses are less likely to kink than vinyl or nylon hoses, but they tend to be much heavier to move around. Whatever material you choose, be sure to get a hose that's long enough to reach plants in all areas of your garden without having to shoot water across the beds to reach distant plants. Choose a hose that has brass fittings and a washer integrated into the hose; these elements make the hose less likely to fail after prolonged use.

Watering cans can be made of simple, inexpensive, brightly colored plastic or high-end, fancy galvanized metal. Plastic is lighter, but galvanized metal is rustproof and more attractive. Watering cans also come in different sizes, so try a few out for comfort before buying. Make sure you can easily remove the sprinkler head, or *rose,* for cleaning.

For watering tender seedlings, buy a can with an oval rose that points upward and applies water with less pressure. The traditional round rose is better for watering more mature plants.

Hand Trowels

Hand trowels are essential for digging in containers, window boxes, and small raised beds. The wider-bladed hand trowels, which are scoop shaped and rounded on the end, are easier to use to loosen soil than the narrower-bladed, V-pointed ones. These narrower blades are better for digging tough weeds, such as dandelions.

Hand trowel blades usually are made of steel or plastic. Steel blades are more durable, but plastic blades are lighter. Although stainless steel versions are more expensive than plastic ones, they're easier to clean and easier to find if you lose them. The handles may be steel, wooden, or plastic. Choose a trowel that's forged as one piece of metal or that has secure attachments between the blade and handle.

Try different hand trowels before buying, choosing one that feels comfortable and that fits your hand well. Ergonomic versions of hand trowels have forearm supports and cushioned grips.

Hand Cultivators

A *three-pronged hand cultivator* is a handy tool to break up soil clods, smooth seed beds, and work in granular fertilizer. Plus, after you plant your small container or raised bed, the weeds will come whether you like it or not; a cultivator serves as a great tool to remove these young weeds as they germinate. When you're digging a planting hole, a hand cultivator breaks up the soil more easily than a hand trowel.

As with a hand trowel, be sure to choose a hand cultivator that feels comfortable in your hand and that has a handle securely fastened to the blade. The steel-bladed types are the most durable.

Garden Hoes

Hoes are available for all occasions — hoes for digging furrows, hoes for weeding, hoes for wide rows, hoes for tight rows, hoes that scuffle, hoes that oscillate, and even hoes for specific vegetables such as the onion hoe. What you need largely depends on the design of your garden. The best hoes have long hardwood handles and single-forged steel blades strongly attached to their handles. Here are three favorites:

- ✔ **Common garden hoe:** This classic hoe has a broad, straight, 6-inch steel blade that's good for all types of gardening, including digging, weeding, chopping, hilling, and cultivating. Longer- and narrower-bladed versions, such as the collinear hoe, are good for weeding in tight spots.

- ✔ **Oscillating hoe (also known as a stirrup hoe):** This hoe, shown in Figure 20-1, is primarily used for weeding. Unlike other hoes — which cut weeds on the pull stroke — this hoe cuts weeds on the pull stroke *and* the push stroke, enabling you to weed faster. The 4- to 7-inch-wide steel stirrup is hinged so it moves back and forth, digging about ¼ inch deep into the soil and scalping off young weeds. This hoe works well in gardens with clearly defined rows and spaces between plants. Like all hoes, the blade works best when it's sharpened regularly.

- **Tined hoe:** This hoe is my favorite. It has 3 or 4 steel tines attached to the bottom of a 5- to 6-inch-diameter steel head. Tined hoes are good for weeding, cultivating, digging, chopping, hilling, and breaking up soil clods. They're lighter, more versatile, and easier to use than common hoes.

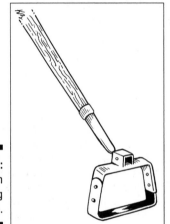

Figure 20-1: An oscillating hoe.

If hoeing gives you a sore back, try the Swan-Neck hoe. This wooden-handled, metal-bladed hoe is curved at its neck in such a way that you can stand straight up (not bending) as you work your way down those rows of beans.

Spades and Shovels

Spades and shovels are two of the most commonly used gardening tools. The difference between the two is simple: A *spade* is designed for digging, and a *shovel* is designed for scooping and throwing. Shovels traditionally have rounded and pointed blades, whereas spades have flat, straight, almost rectangular blades. A good shovel is essential in any garden for spreading compost, manure, or fertilizer. A spade is essential for edging or breaking new ground. However, many gardeners use spades for anything from cutting open fertilizer bags to hammering in stakes. Good spades are rugged.

Both spades and shovels come in short- and long-handled versions. A long handle gives you more leverage when digging holes, so keep that in mind if you're purchasing a new spade. I find that I use a short-handled shovel with a D-shaped grip more often in my garden than a spade. Choose a spade or a shovel that has a single piece of metal attached to a wooden handle with either a single socket or a single socket that runs 1 foot up the handle (referred to as a *solid-strap* connection). These models are heavier, but they're much more durable.

To get a more comfortable grip on long-handled tools like spades and shovels, try low-cost foam grippers that fit on the handles. These grippers make the diameter of a handle larger and more cushioned, reducing the amount of blistering and cramping in your hands. They're available at local garden centers or on the Internet.

Garden Forks

As handy as a spade is for turning fresh garden soil, I find that an *iron fork* is a better tool for turning beds that have been worked before. The fork digs into the soil as deep as 12 inches, and at the same time breaks up clods and loosens and aerates the soil better than a spade. Iron forks look similar to short-handled spades except that they have three to four iron tines on their heads. The best ones are those forged from one piece of steel with hardwood handles firmly attached. They're great not only for turning soil but for turning compost piles and digging root crops, such as potatoes and carrots.

Garden Rakes

After you dig soil, you need to level it, break up soil clods, and smooth the seedbeds (especially if you're growing raised beds, which are described in Chapter 3). An *iron rake* is the right tool for the job even though you may use it for this purpose only a few times a year. A 14-inch-diameter, iron-toothed rake should have a long, wooden handle that's securely attached to a metal head. You can flip the metal head over to really smooth a seedbed flat. For a lightweight but less durable version of an iron rake, try an aluminum rake.

Buckets, Wagons, and Baskets

Okay, you don't have a 1,000-square-foot garden. But you still need to carry seeds, tools, fertilizer, produce, and other items around. I love talking about storage containers because this is where the tools of the trade get really simple. Here are three essential containers:

- **Buckets:** For fertilizers, potting soil, and hand tools, a 5-gallon plastic bucket is the perfect container. You can probably get one free from a construction site; just make sure to clean it out well. For a more durable but smaller bucket, buy one made from galvanized steel.

- **Wagons:** For bulkier items, such as flats of seedlings, use a child's old red wagon. Wagons are great for moving plants and small bags of fertilizer in your garden, and the lip on the wagon bed helps hold these items in place when you cover bumpy ground. If you're interested in a wagon to move yourself (and not just equipment) around the garden, a new invention is a wagon with a seat. This type of wagon usually has a swiveling seat and is perched on four pneumatic tires, allowing you to sit and push yourself through the garden as you work (see Figure 20-2). It has storage space under the seat as well.

Figure 20-2:
A wagon with a seat and storage space is useful in the garden.

- **Baskets:** To gather all that great produce you grow and harvest, invest in a wire or wicker basket. Wire baskets are easier to use because you can wash the produce while it's still in the basket. Wicker and wooden baskets, though less durable than metal, are more aesthetically pleasing and stylish in your garden. Piling your produce in either basket is a lot more functional than trying to balance zucchinis in your arms while carrying them from your garden to your kitchen.

Wheelbarrows and Garden Carts

Invariably you need to move heavy items such as soil and fertilizer from one spot to another in your yard or garden. The two main options for moving stuff that's "larger than a bread box" are wheelbarrows and garden carts. The basic difference between the two vehicles is the wheels. *Wheelbarrows* have one wheel and an oval, metal tray; *garden carts* have two wheels and a rectangular wooden tray.

Wheelbarrows are maneuverable in tight places, can turn on a dime, and are easy to dump. A contractor-type wheelbarrow has a deeper box and is worth the extra investment because of its superior quality. For a lightweight wheelbarrow, try one with a box made out of plastic.

Garden carts are better balanced, can carry larger loads, and are easier to push than wheelbarrows. A larger-sized garden cart can easily handle loads of compost, soil, rocks, and bales of hay. Some garden carts have removable back panels that make dumping easier.

Power Tillers

The old-fashioned rear- or front-tined *power tiller* was designed to help large-scale gardeners save time turning their gardens in spring and fall. The large power tillers (more than a 5-horsepower engine) are best if you have 1,000 square feet or more to till. They also can be indispensable tools for forming raised beds and breaking sod.

If you only need to use a large tiller once a year, consider renting one from a local rental store or hiring someone to till for you.

Because home gardens have become smaller in recent years, tiller manufacturers have responded by designing a new group of tillers called *minitillers* (see Figure 20-3). These two-cycle, 1- to 2-horsepower tillers weigh only 20 to 30 pounds, are easy to handle, and can till in tight places. Not only do they have tilling tines, but they come with other attachments such as lawn aerators, edgers, and lawn dethatchers.

Minitillers work best in previously worked, loamy soil without large stones. Unlike their larger cousins, minitillers are easy to handle when you're weeding between rows of vegetables and close to plants. However, they aren't good for breaking new ground or tilling stony or heavily weeded areas in your garden. Because they're lightweight, they till raised beds and small gardens very well. Electric models are available if you don't like the noise and smell of a two-cycle engine.

Figure 20-3:
A minitiller
is perfect
for smaller
home
gardens.

Though not essential for your garden, if you like power equipment and need a little help keeping your garden looking good, check out minitillers. (See the appendix to find out where you can get minitillers.)

Chapter 21

Nearly Ten Ways to Extend Your Growing Season

....

In This Chapter

▶ Starting your veggies earlier in the season

▶ Extending your harvest into the cold-weather season

....

*A*fter you start vegetable gardening, you may get hooked on having fresh vegetables from your garden year-round. Unless you live in a mild climate, such as zones 9 and 10 (see the appendix for more on zones), the best way to get the most vegetables from your garden is to use season-extending devices. These devices protect your vegetables from deadly frosts in fall and enable you to get an earlier start in spring. Of course, selecting the right vegetables to grow also is vital to your success.

In general, greens, root crops, and cool-season cole crops are the best vegetables to grow in cold weather. (See the specific chapters on these vegetables for growing information.) However, you can extend the length of time that you harvest warm-season crops — such as melons, tomatoes, and peppers — by using the season-extending methods in this chapter. Whatever plants you grow, these techniques enable you to harvest fresh vegetables for most of the year.

Choose Clever Planting Locations

Where you plant your vegetables has as much to do with avoiding frosts and cold weather as *when* you plant. Every yard has pockets or areas that warm up earlier in spring and stay warmer later into the fall. For example, the nook near my kitchen window on the south side of my house is such a location. That area is the first place that snow melts, and plants in this location grow well past the time when frost has killed vegetables in my main garden. Find these nooks in your yard, plant cold-hardy vegetables like spinach and broccoli, and enjoy harvesting earlier and later than anyone else on the block.

Some good nook areas to check out in any yard are the south-side walls of buildings, especially if you can find a spot that's protected from wind. Courtyards are notoriously good microclimates. (See Chapter 3 for more on microclimates.) Other good spots include areas around evergreen shrubs (as long as enough sun pokes through them to grow the plants) and near paved surfaces such as driveways or walkways — especially if the pavement is dark colored.

Time Your Planting Wisely

Timing is important when you grow vegetables. Here are some guidelines to follow:

- ✔ If you want early vegetables, start your seeds indoors in late winter or early spring (as I explain in Chapter 13). Then you can transplant the young seedlings into a season extender, such as a cold frame, cloche, or hot cap (all of which I describe later in this chapter).

- ✔ If you want your vegetables to last longer into winter, start them at the end of the summer, but be sure to start them early enough that by the dark months (December and January), they'll be full-sized and edible. During these months, don't expect much growth, even in warm areas, because the light is less intense and the day is much shorter. You'll be extending the *harvest* season, not the *growing* season. (Unless, of course, you're in a warm location and trying to overwinter these vegetables for a spring harvest; see Chapter 19 for details.)

Protect Plants with Hot Caps

Hot caps are a great way to protect individual prized plants from the cold. A *hot cap* is usually a clear plastic, pyramid-shaped cone with an opening in its top to let hot air out. You can buy these cones at garden centers, or you can create your own by cutting the bottoms out of clear plastic milk jugs. If you do create your own, be sure to cut a vent at the top of the milk jugs to let hot air out on sunny days. Or use them only at night. You can cover the hole with a blanket at night if you expect chilly temperatures.

Add Elegance to Your Garden with Glass Cloches

If you really want something elegant in your garden, you can spend up to $50 on tinted glass hot caps, affectionately called *cloches,* as shown in Figure 21-1. They're sturdy and beautiful, and yes, they protect tender plants from the cold — even a little better than plastic hot caps do. However, cloches don't have vents, so during sunny days you need to remove them or prop them up to let cool air in.

Figure 21-1: A glass cloche.

Buy or Build Cold Frames

Cold frames essentially are mini-greenhouses. They're usually wooden boxes covered with windowpanes or clear plastic (see Figure 21-2). Some professional gardeners as far north as zone 5, where winter temperatures can dip down to –20 degrees Fahrenheit, can harvest vegetables every month of the year by planting cold-weather-tolerant crops in cold frames.

You can purchase a premade cold frame for $100 to $200, or you can create your own simple cold frame by following these steps:

Figure 21-2:
A sample
cold frame.

1. **Build a 3-foot-x-6-foot box from untreated lumber. Cut the box so that the back is 18 inches high, sloping to a front height of 14 inches.**

   This sloping angle enables more sun to reach the plants, and it sheds rain and snow as well.

2. **Hinge an old window sash over the top of the cold frame or make a frame by using tightly stretched clear plastic, which creates a sealed growing environment.**

   You can insulate the cold frame by adding rigid foam insulation around the insides of the cold frame and by weather stripping along the top edge.

3. **Position the cold frame so that it faces south.**

   It's best to put a cold frame next to a structure, such as a house, to protect it from cold winds.

Even though the purpose of a cold frame is to trap heat, on sunny days, even in winter, a cold frame can get so hot that it burns the plants. Check your cold frame once a day on sunny days, opening or venting the top slightly to allow hot air to escape.

Drape Row Covers over Veggies

A *row cover* can be a clear plastic cover draped over half-circle wire hoops to create a tunnel effect (see Figure 21-3), or it can be the new lightweight cheesecloth-like fabric that's so light it floats on top of your vegetables. Both plastic and floating row covers protect plants from light freezes; however, if you expect really chilly temperatures (around 20 degrees), use another protection device, such as a cloche.

Clear plastic heats up your crops faster and warmer than floating row cover material, but it needs venting to keep the plants from overheating. Floating row covers let in air, light, and water and don't overheat as easily as clear plastic row covers. You also can use both materials to protect your plants from insects.

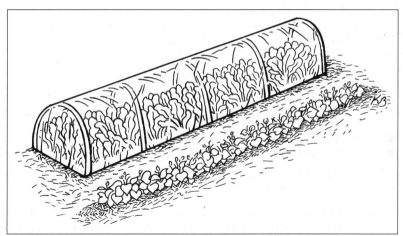

Figure 21-3:
A clear plastic grow tunnel.

Place Wall O' Waters around Plants

Wall O' Waters (see Figure 21-4) are double-walled, clear-plastic cylinders that hold narrow columns of water around your favorite vegetables. By placing Wall O' Waters around heat-loving plants, such as tomatoes, you can get a jump on spring. The water in the cylinders absorbs the warmth of the sun during the day and slowly releases the stored heat at night to protect your plants in cold temperatures. Even if the water freezes, it releases enough heat to protect your plants. Wall O' Waters have been reported to protect tomatoes in temperatures as low as 16 degrees.

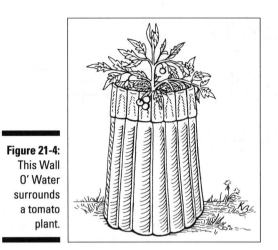

Figure 21-4:
This Wall
O' Water
surrounds
a tomato
plant.

To prevent overheating during the day, leave the tops open. For added protection at night, collapse the tops of these devices into a pyramid shape. Of course, after a plant has grown for a few weeks, it will outgrow the plastic cylinder, so you'll have to remove the Wall O' Water. But what a jump on the growing season you'll have by then!

Try Portable Greenhouses and Hoop Houses

If you really want to extend the growing season, stop fooling around with hot caps and blankets and buy a portable greenhouse or hoop house. You can find many different free-standing portable greenhouses on the market that are great for getting an early jump on the growing season and extending it into the fall. Walk-through hoop houses also have become popular because of their low cost and ease of use. They have a metal shell with clear plastic pulled over it and doors on either side. They keep the air warmer than a cold frame, but they're not as warm as a conventional greenhouse. Greenhouses and hoop houses can range in price from \$200 to \$2,000, depending on the materials and size. In the appendix, I list a number of manufacturers and suppliers that can help you choose the right greenhouse or hoop house for your location.

Appendix

Planning Guidelines and Other Resources

. . . .

*T*his appendix is vegetables by the numbers. All the distances, depths, and yields for more than 40 vegetables are listed in the section "Guidelines for Planting," which includes a chart that provides a great way for you to sketch your garden before you plant. The section "Frost Dates and the Length of the Growing Season" tells you what you need to know to avoid freezing out your veggies and stunting your crop. I also provide a guide to the hardiness zones and include a list of suppliers of vegetable seeds and other materials to get you started. And if you need even more information, I include a listing of Master Gardener organizations and Web sites by state.

Guidelines for Planting

The best way to plan your garden is to start by deciding how much produce you want. For example, if you like lettuce, 25 heads will take approximately 25 feet of row. The recommended distances between rows in Table A-1 tell you how much space to leave between crops.

Use the information in Table A-1 as a general guideline. You may choose to vary the distance between rows, for example, depending on the method of planting or cultivating. You usually can hand-hoe weeds between rows adequately in 18- or 24-inch-wide pathways; rototilling is faster, but pathways should be 30 or 36 inches wide to do so. If you garden intensively, such as in raised beds, you can space plants closer than indicated in the chart.

The days to maturity and the yield figures are averages. Depending on weather, soil fertility, pests, and weed pressure, yield and maturities in your garden can vary greatly. Just remember, you can always find friends, relatives, and bunnies who'd love some fresh, homegrown produce.

Table A-1 Planting Guide

Crop	*Seed/Plants per 100 ft. of Row*	*Frost Tolerance*	*Planting Depth (Inches)*	*Spacing between Rows (Inches)*	*Spacing between Plants (Inches)*	*Soil Temp. for Germ.**	*Avg. Days to Germ.*	*Avg. Days to Maturity*	*Avg. Yield per 10 ft. of Row*
Asparagus	1 oz./65 pl.	Very hardy (R)	6 (crowns)	36–48	18	50–95 (75)	7–21	2 years	3 lbs.
Beans, snap (bush)	½ lb.	Tender	1–1½	18–24	3–4	60–95 (85)	6–14	45–60	12 lbs.
Beans, snap (pole)	½ lb.	Tender	1–1½	36–48	4–6	60–95 (85)	6–14	60–70	15 lbs.
Beans, lima (bush)	½ lb.	Very tender	1–1½	18–24	3–4	60–85 (80)	7–12	65–80	2.5 lbs., shelled
Beans, lima (pole)	¼ lb.	Very tender	1–1½	36–48	12–18	60–85 (80)	7–12	85–90	5 lbs., shelled
Beets	1 oz. (seeds only)	Hardy	½	15–24	2	40–95 (85)	7–10	50–60	12 lbs.
Broccoli	¼ oz./45 pl.	Very hardy (P)	¼	24–36	14–24	40–95 (85)	3–10	60–80	10 lbs.
Brussels sprouts	¼ oz./55 pl.	Very hardy (P)	¼	24–36	14–24	40–95 (85)	3–10	90–100	7.5 lbs.
Cabbage	¼ oz./55 pl.	Very hardy (P)	¼	24–36	14–24	40–95 (85)	4–10	60–90	18 lbs.
Carrots	½ oz. (seeds only)	Hardy	¼	15–24	2	40–95 (80)	10–17	70–80	15 lbs.
Cauliflower	¼ oz./55 pl.	Hardy (P)	¼	24–36	14–24	40–95 (80)	4–10	70–90	10 lbs.
Celery	1/64 oz./200 pl.	Hardy	⅛	30–36	6	40–75 (70)	9–21	125	18 stalks
Chinese cabbage	¼ oz./65 pl.	Hardy (P)	¼	18–30	8–12	40–105 (80)	4–10	65–70	8 heads

Crop	Seed/Plants per 100 ft. of Row	Frost Tolerance	Planting Depth (Inches)	Spacing between Rows (Inches)	Spacing between Plants (Inches)	Soil Temp. for Germ.*	Avg. Days to Germ.	Avg. Days to Maturity	Avg. Yield per 10 ft. of Row
Corn	3–4 oz. (seeds only)	Tender	2	24–36	12–18	50–95 (95)	6–10	70–90	1 dozen
Cucumbers	½ oz./30–40 pl.	Very tender	1	48–72	24–48	60–105 (95)	6–10	50–70	12 lbs.
Eggplant	⅛ oz./50 pl.	Very tender (P)	¼–½	24–36	18–24	65–95 (85)	7–14	80–90	10 lbs.
Leeks	½ oz./300 pl.	Very hardy	½–1	12–18	2–4	45–70 (75)	7–12	130–150	12 lbs.
Lettuce, heading	¼ oz./120 pl.	Very hardy	¼–½	18–24	6–10	32–75 (75)	4–10	70–75	10 heads
Lettuce, leaf	¼ oz./400 pl.	Very hardy	¼–½	15–18	2–3	32–75 (75)	4–10	40–50	5 lbs.
Muskmelon	½ oz./50 pl.	Very tender	1	60–96	24–36	65–105 (95)	4–8	85–100	5 fruits
Okra	2 oz./50 pl.	Very tender	1	36–42	12–24	60–105 (95)	7–14	55–65	10 lbs.
Onion, seed	1 oz./300 pl.	Very hardy	½	15–24	3–4	32–95 (80)	7–12	90–120	16 lbs.
Onion, sets	400–600 pl. (no seeds)	Very hardy	1–3	15–24	3–4	NA	NA	80–120	10 lbs.
Parsley	¼ oz./150 pl.	Hardy	¼–½	15–24	6–8	50–90 (75)	14–28	70–90	4 lbs.
Parsnips	½ oz. (seeds only)	Hardy	½	18–30	3–4	32–85 (70)	15–25	120–170	10 lbs.
Peas	1 lb.	Very hardy	2	18–36	1	40–85 (75)	6–15	55–90	4 lbs.

(continued)

Table A-1 (continued)

Crop	Seed/Plants per 100 ft. of Row	Frost Tolerance	Planting Depth (Inches)	Spacing between Rows (Inches)	Spacing between Plants (Inches)	Soil Temp. for Germ.*	Avg. Days to Germ.	Avg. Days to Maturity	Avg. Yield per 10 ft. of Row
Peppers	⅛ oz./50 pl.	Very tender	¼	24–36	18–24	60–95 (85)	10–20	60–90	30 lbs.
Potatoes	6–10 lbs. seed potatoes	Very hardy (R)	4	30–36	8–10	NA	NA	75–100	10 lbs.
Pumpkins	½ oz./25 pl.	Very tender	1–2	60–96	36–48	65–105 (95)	6–10	75–100	10 lbs.
Radishes	1 oz. (seeds only)	Hardy	½	14–24	1	40–95 (80)	3–10	25–40	10 bunches
Rhubarb	20 pl. (no seeds)	Very hardy (R)	4	36–48	48	NA	NA	2 years	7 lbs.
Southern peas	½ lb.	Very tender	½–1	24–36	4–6	60–95 (85)	7–10	60–70	4 lbs.
Spinach	1 oz./300 pl.	Very hardy	¾	14–24	3–4	32–75 (70)	6–14	40–60	4–5 lbs.
Squash, summer	1 oz./40 pl.	Tender	1	36–60	18–36	65–105 (95)	3–12	50–60	25 lbs.
Squash, winter	½ oz./35 pl.	Very tender	1	60–96	24–48	65–105 (95)	6–10	85–100	15lbs.
Sweet potatoes	75–100 pl. (no seeds)	Very tender (P)	NA	36–48	12–16	NA	NA	100–130	10 lbs.
Swiss chard	1 oz./50 pl.	Hardy	½	12–15	24–36	40–95 (75)	5–16	50–60	50–75 lbs.
Tomatoes	⅛ oz./50 pl.	Tender	½	24–48	18–36	50–95 (80)	6–14	70–90	80 lbs.

Crop	Seed/Plants per 100 ft. of Row	Frost Tolerance	Planting Depth (Inches)	Spacing between Rows (Inches)	Spacing between Plants (Inches)	Soil Temp. for Germ.*	Avg. Days to Germ.	Avg. Days to Maturity	Avg. Yield per 10 ft. of Row
Turnips	½ oz. (no plants)	Very hardy	½	14–24	2–3	40–105 (80)	3–10	30–60	5–10 lbs.
Watermelon	1 oz./20 pl.	Very tender	1	72–96	36–72	65–105 (95)	3–12	80–100	4 fruits

P — plants
R — roots
NA — not applicable
Very hardy — plant outside 4 to 6 weeks before average last spring frost date
Hardy — plant outside 2 to 3 weeks before average last spring frost date
Tender — plant outside on average date of last spring frost
Very tender — plant outside 1 to 2 weeks after average last spring frost date

*Range of germination temperature in degrees Fahrenheit; optimum germination in parentheses

Frost Dates and the Length of the Growing Season

You can grow vegetables anywhere! Some of the largest, most beautiful vegetables I've ever seen are grown by avid gardeners in Alaska. If you can grow vegetables where the sun doesn't shine for 6 months of the year, you know that they must be easy to grow.

Table A-2 is a chart of the average annual first and last frost dates as well as the length of the frost-free growing season in 100 cities across the United States. Of course, this chart is only a guide, and your local climate will vary depending on many factors, including the variation in weather from year to year. Also, because of global warming, some gardeners are noticing longer growing seasons than in the past. So to get the most accurate dates, contact your local weather service or the Cooperative Extension Service office in your area. (To find your Extension Service office, check your state land grant university listings in the phone book.)

Keep in mind that just because your frost-free growing season is only so many days, many vegetables that I list can tolerate a light frost. And you can extend your growing season by using special growing techniques (described in Chapter 21). However, warm-season vegetables, such as tomatoes, don't like even a touch of frost, so Table A-2 is much more accurate for estimating how many days you have to grow your favorite heat-loving vegetables.

Table A-2	First and Last Frost Dates		
City	**Last Frost Date**	**First Frost Date**	**Length of Season**
Birmingham, Alabama	March 29	November 6	221 days
Mobile, Alabama	February 27	November 26	272 days
Juneau, Alaska	May 16	September 26	133 days
Flagstaff, Arizona	June 13	September 21	99 days
Phoenix, Arizona	February 5	December 15	308 days
Tucson, Arizona	February 28	November 29	273 days
Fayetteville, Arkansas	April 21	October 17	179 days
Little Rock, Arkansas	March 23	November 9	230 days
Fresno, California	February 22	November 25	273 days
Los Angeles, California	None likely	None likely	365 days
San Bernardino, California	February 23	December 8	294 days

City	Last Frost Date	First Frost Date	Length of Season
San Francisco, California	January 8	January 5	362 days
Sacramento, California	February 14	December 1	287 days
San Jose, California	January 22	December 25	338 days
San Diego, California	None	None	365 days
Santa Rosa, California	March 26	November 19	236 days
Denver, Colorado	May 3	October 8	157 days
Durango, Colorado	June 4	September 18	105 days
Hartford, Connecticut	April 25	October 10	167 days
New Haven, Connecticut	April 15	October 27	195 days
Dover, Delaware	April 9	October 28	202 days
Wilmington, Delaware	April 13	October 29	198 days
Washington, DC	April 10	October 31	203 days
Jacksonville, Florida	February 14	December 14	303 days
Miami, Florida	None	None	365 days
Orlando, Florida	January 31	December 17	320 days
Tallahassee, Florida	March 12	November 14	246 days
Atlanta, Georgia	March 13	November 12	243 days
Savannah, Georgia	March 10	November 15	250 days
Boise, Idaho	May 8	October 9	153 days
Pocatello, Idaho	May 20	September 20	122 days
Chicago, Illinois	April 14	November 2	201 days
Indianapolis, Indiana	April 18	October 22	186 days
Cedar Rapids, Iowa	April 29	October 7	161 days
Des Moines, Iowa	April 19	October 17	180 days
Manhattan, Kansas	April 23	October 16	176 days
Wichita, Kansas	April 13	October 23	193 days
Lexington, Kentucky	April 17	October 25	190 days
Louisville, Kentucky	April 1	November 7	220 days
New Orleans, Louisiana	February 20	December 5	288 days
Portland, Maine	May 10	September 30	143 days
Baltimore, Maryland	March 26	November 13	231 days
Amherst, Massachusetts	May 9	September 29	142 days

(continued)

Table A-2 *(continued)*

City	Last Frost Date	First Frost Date	Length of Season
Boston, Massachusetts	April 6	November 10	217 days
Detroit, Michigan	April 24	October 22	181 days
Marquette, Michigan	May 12	October 19	159 days
Minneapolis–St. Paul, Minnesota	April 30	October 13	166 days
Duluth, Minnesota	May 21	September 21	122 days
Columbus, Mississippi	March 27	October 29	215 days
Jackson, Mississippi	March 17	November 9	236 days
Jefferson City, Missouri	April 26	October 16	173 days
St. Louis, Missouri	April 3	November 6	217 days
Billings, Montana	May 12	September 23	133 days
Helena, Montana	May 18	September 18	122 days
Lincoln, Nebraska	March 13	November 13	180 days
North Platte, Nebraska	May 11	September 24	136 days
Las Vegas, Nevada	March 7	November 21	259 days
Concord, New Hampshire	May 23	September 22	121 days
Newark, New Jersey	April 4	November 10	219 days
Trenton, New Jersey	April 6	November 7	214 days
Albuquerque, New Mexico	April 16	October 29	196 days
Los Alamos, New Mexico	May 8	October 13	157 days
Albany, New York	May 7	September 29	144 days
New York, New York	April 1	November 11	223 days
Rochester, New York	May 3	October 15	164 days
Syracuse, New York	April 28	October 16	170 days
Asheville, North Carolina	April 10	October 24	195 days
Charlotte, North Carolina	March 21	November 15	239 days
Raleigh, North Carolina	April 11	October 27	198 days
Fargo, North Dakota	May 13	September 27	137 days
Akron, Ohio	May 3	October 18	168 days
Cincinnati, Ohio	April 14	October 27	195 days
Columbus, Ohio	April 26	October 17	173 days
Oklahoma City, Oklahoma	March 28	November 7	224 days
Tulsa, Oklahoma	March 30	November 4	218 days

City	Last Frost Date	First Frost Date	Length of Season
Ashland, Oregon	May 13	October 12	152 days
Pendleton, Oregon	April 15	October 21	188 days
Portland, Oregon	April 3	November 7	217 days
Allentown, Pennsylvania	April 21	October 18	179 days
Pittsburgh, Pennsylvania	April 16	November 3	201 days
State College, Pennsylvania	April 27	October 15	170 days
Kingston, Rhode Island	May 8	September 30	144 days
Charleston, South Carolina	March 11	November 20	253 days
Columbia, South Carolina	April 4	November 2	211 days
Memphis, Tennessee	March 23	November 7	228 days
Nashville, Tennessee	April 5	October 29	207 days
Amarillo, Texas	April 14	October 29	197 days
Dallas, Texas	March 18	November 12	239 days
Houston, Texas	February 4	December 10	309 days
Cedar City, Utah	May 20	October 2	134 days
Salt Lake City, Utah	April 12	November 1	203 days
Burlington, Vermont	May 11	October 1	142 days
Norfolk, Virginia	March 23	November 17	239 days
Richmond, Virginia	April 10	October 26	198 days
Seattle, Washington	March 24	November 11	232 days
Spokane, Washington	May 4	October 5	153 days
Parkersburg, West Virginia	April 25	October 18	175 days
Green Bay, Wisconsin	May 12	October 2	143 days
Milwaukee, Wisconsin	May 5	October 9	156 days
Cheyenne, Wyoming	May 20	September 27	130 days

Hardiness Zones in North America

The U.S. Department of Agriculture has helpfully divided North America into plant hardiness zones based on average annual minimum temperatures; I refer to these hardiness zones throughout this book. Planting instructions regarding depth and timing may change depending on what zone you're in. Because of global warming, as with the length of the growing season (see the previous section), some gardeners find they now can grow less hardy plants in their area. Check with local Master Gardeners and garden centers to determine which plants are best for your area, and check out www.garden. org/zipzone to find out your own zone. (I list Master Gardener resources later in this appendix.)

Your hardiness zone isn't as critical for vegetable growing as it is for growing fruits, perennial flowers, trees, and shrubs. However, knowing your hardiness zone is a good idea because in some warm areas, such as zones 7 and 8, you can grow two or three crops of the same vegetable in 1 year or even grow vegetables throughout the winter.

Where to Find Seeds and Other Resources

Vegetable seeds are available seemingly everywhere in the spring. From grocery stores to local garden centers, home centers, and hardware stores, everyone seems to sell seed packets. If you're interested in the standard vegetable varieties, these locations are great places to get them. However, if you're interested in some of the more unusual varieties that I mention in this book, try the catalog companies listed in the following sections. These companies mostly sell seeds within North America. Check other Web sites, such as www.davesgarden.com, for listings of vegetable seed suppliers in other parts of the world.

You may, however, want to avoid seed starting altogether and buy transplants. Local garden and home centers offer a broad selection of vegetable and fruit plants for sale in spring. Also, catalog companies now offer transplants through the mail. In the following sections, I indicate which companies currently offer transplants through their catalogs.

Finally, I include a list of fruit and berry nurseries for a broader selection and cheaper prices than what you may find locally as well as a list of tool and equipment suppliers for many of the products and devices I mention in this book. Part of the fun of gardening is shopping for new stuff, so check out these companies online. Or, if you like the armchair experience, write for a printed catalog. Some companies charge a small fee for their catalogs, but most are free.

Vegetables, herbs, and flowers

Abundant Life Seeds, P.O. Box 279, Cottage Grove, OR 97424; phone 541-767-9606; Web site www.abundantlifeseeds.com. This seed company is dedicated to the preservation of unusual heirloom vegetable, herb, grain, and flower seeds. The organization offers organically grown and untreated seeds.

Amishland Heirloom Seeds, Box 365, Reamstown, PA 17567; Web site www.amishlandseeds.com. This small, one-woman, organic seed company is devoted to saving heirloom varieties in the Lancaster, Pennsylvania, area.

Baker Creek Heirloom Seeds, 2278 Baker Creek Rd., Mansfield, MO 65704; phone 417-924-8917; Web site www.rareseeds.com. This company, which offers a beautiful color catalog, specializes in a wide range of unusual heirloom vegetables and flowers from around the world.

Bountiful Gardens, 18001 Shafer Ranch Rd., Willits, CA 95490; phone 707-459-6410; Web site www.bountifulgardens.org. This company specializes in untreated, unusual varieties of vegetables, cover crops, herbs, and grains.

Burrell Seed Co., P.O. Box 150, Rocky Ford, CO 81067; phone 719-254-3318; Web site www.burrellseeds.us. This seed company offers a complete line of vegetables, specializing in cantaloupes and watermelons.

The Cook's Garden, P.O. Box C5030, Warminster, PA 18974; phone 800-457-9703; Web site www.cooksgarden.com. This company provides a wide selection of culinary vegetables, herbs, and flowers, including European and hard-to-find salad greens.

Dill's Atlantic Giant Pumpkins, RR#1 400 College Rd., Windsor, N.S., Canada B0N 2T0; phone 902-798-2728; Web site www.howarddill.com. Howard Dill sells seed for the world's largest pumpkins, including 'Atlantic Giant' and other pumpkin varieties.

Dixondale Farms, P.O. Box 129, Carrizo Springs, TX 78834; phone 877-367-1015; Web site www.dixondalefarms.com. Specialists in onion plants.

Evergreen Y.H. Enterprises, P.O. Box 17538, Anaheim, CA 92817; phone 714-637-5769; Web site www.evergreenseeds.com. This company specializes in Oriental vegetables.

Fedco Seeds, P.O. Box 520, Waterville, ME 04903; phone 207-873-7333; Web site www.fedcoseeds.com. This seed company offers a full line of vegetables, including a good selection of potatoes. It also offers fruit trees, bulbs, books, tools, and products.

Filaree Farm, 182 Conconully Hwy., Okanogan, WA 98840; phone 509-422-6940; Web site www.filareefarm.com. This company offers more than 100 unique strains of garlic.

Gourmet Seed International, HC 12 Box 510, Tatum, NM, 88267; phone 575-398-6111; Web site www.gourmetseed.com. Specialists in vegetable seeds from Europe, especially Italy. The company also carries flower and herb seeds, tools, and products.

Gurney's Seed & Nursery Co., P.O. Box 4178, Greendale, IN 47025; phone 513-354-1492; Web site gurneys.com. Gurney's offers a full-line seed and nursery catalog.

Harris Seeds, 355 Paul Rd., P.O. Box 24966, Rochester, NY 14624; phone 800-544-7938; Web site www.harrisseeds.com. Through this company, you can purchase vegetable and flower seeds, gardening accessories, and vegetable transplants.

Henry Field's Seed & Nursery Co., P.O. Box 397, Aurora, IN 47001; phone 513-354-1495; Web site henryfields.com. This company offers a basic vegetable, flower, and fruit catalog with some products.

High Mowing Organic Seeds, 76 Quarry Rd., Wolcott, VT 05680; phone 802-472-6174; Web site www.highmowingseeds.com. This seed company specializes in organic vegetable, flower, and herb seeds as well as cover crop seeds.

Jersey Asparagus Farms, Inc., 105 Porchtown Rd., Pittsgrove, NJ 08318; phone 856-358-2548; Web site www.jerseyasparagus.com. This company specializes in asparagus and small fruits, such as strawberries, blueberries, raspberries, and goji berries. It also carries horseradish and rhubarb plants.

Johnny's Selected Seeds, 955 Benton Ave., Winslow, ME 04901; phone 877-564-6697; Web site www.johnnyseeds.com. Johnny's sells vegetable, herb, cover crop, and flower seeds. It also offers vegetable seeds for sprouting and organic seeds.

J.W. Jung Seed Company, 335 S. High St., Randolph, WI 53956; phone 800-297-3123; Web site www.jungseed.com. This company offers a wide selection of vegetable seeds, fruits, plants, bulbs, and products.

Native Seeds/SEARCH, 526 N. 4th Ave., Tucson, AZ 85705; phone 520-622-5561; Web site www.nativeseeds.org. This organization specializes in Native American varieties of vegetables adapted to the desert Southwest.

Nichols Garden Nursery, 1190 Old Salem Rd. NE, Albany, OR 97321; phone 800-422-3985; Web site www.nicholsgardennursery.com. This company offers Asian and unusual vegetables and a good selection of herb seeds and plants.

Nourse Farms, Inc., 41 River Rd., South Deerfield, MA 01373; phone 413-665-2658; Web site www.noursefarms.com. This farm has a good selection of small fruits and asparagus.

Park Seed Company, 1 Parkton Ave., Greenwood, SC 29647; phone 800-213-0076; Web site www.parkseed.com. This company offers a wide variety of vegetable, herb, and flower seeds. Good selection for the South.

The Pepper Gal, P.O. Box 23006, Ft. Lauderdale, FL 33307; phone 954-537-5540; Web site www.peppergal.com. The Pepper Gal offers many varieties of sweet and hot peppers as well as tomatoes and products.

Pinetree Garden Seeds, P.O. Box 300, New Gloucester, ME 04260; phone 207-926-3400; Web site www.superseeds.com. This company sells a large selection of vegetables, herbs, and flowers as well as tools and books. Small-sized packets are available at low prices.

Renee's Garden Seeds, 6116 Hwy. 9, Felton, CA 95018; phone 888-880-7228; Web site www.reneesgarden.com. Renee's Garden offers a wide variety of vegetables, herbs, and flowers. Packets often contain two or three different varieties whose seeds are color coded.

R. H. Shumway's, 334 W. Stroud St., Randolph, WI 53956; phone 800-342-9461; Web site www.rhshumway.com. This company sells a wide selection of vegetable seeds, fruits, and bulbs.

Richters Herbs, 357 Hwy. 47, Goodwood, Ontario, Canada L0C 1A0; phone 905-640-6677; Web site www.richters.com. At Richters, you can choose from an extensive selection of herb seeds, plants, and products.

Ronniger's Potato Farm LLC, 12101 2135 Rd., Austin, CO 81410; phone 877-204-8704; Web site www.ronnigers.com. This company specializes in potatoes and offers many varieties; it also has a good selection of onions and garlic.

Seed Savers Heritage Farm, 3094 N. Winn Rd., Decorah, IA 52101; phone 563-382-5990; Web site www.seedsavers.org. This farm offers a large selection of heirloom vegetable varieties from the United States and Europe. It also has herbs, flowers, and fruits and is associated with the largest nonprofit seed-saving organization in the United States: Seed Savers Exchange.

Seeds for the South, 410 Whaley Pond Rd., Graniteville, SC 29829; Web site www.seedsforthesouth.com. Through this company, you can purchase heirloom vegetable varieties that are particularly adapted to the Southeast.

Seeds of Change, P.O. Box 15700, Santa Fe, NM 87506; phone 888-762-7333; Web site www.seedsofchange.com. This company sells organic, open-pollinated vegetable, flower, and herb seeds and seeds for sprouting.

Seeds Trust, P.O. Box 596, Cornville, AZ 86325; phone 928-649-3315; Web site www.seedstrust.com. Seeds Trust offers a wide number of open-pollinated vegetables for high-altitude gardens. It also has a good selection of Russian heirloom tomatoes, herbs, flowers, and tools.

Southern Exposure Seed Exchange, P.O. Box 460, Mineral, VA 23117; phone 540-894-9480; Web site www.southernexposure.com. This company sells many varieties of heirloom and traditional vegetables, flowers, and herbs that are especially adapted in the South.

Steele Plant Company, LLC, 202 Collins St., Gleason, TN 38229; phone 731-648-5476; Web site www.sweetpotatoplant.com. The Steel Plant Company specializes in sweet potato plants.

Stokes Seeds, Inc., P.O. Box 548, Buffalo, NY 14240; phone 800-396-9238; Web site www.stokeseeds.com. This company offers a complete listing of flower and vegetable seeds, including how-to growing information.

Territorial Seed Company, P.O. Box 158, Cottage Grove, OR 97424; phone 800-626-0866; Web site www.territorialseed.com. At the Territorial Seed Company, you can purchase vegetable, herb, and flower seeds, especially varieties suited to the Pacific Northwest. It also sells transplants.

Thompson & Morgan Seedsmen, Inc., 220 Faraday Ave., Jackson, NJ 08527; phone 800-274-7333; Web site www.tmseeds.com. Through this company, you can choose from a wide selection of English flowers and vegetables. The company also sells transplants.

Tomato Growers Supply Company, P.O. Box 60015, Fort Myers, FL 33906; phone 888-478-7333; Web site www.tomatogrowers.com. Specialists in tomatoes and peppers.

Totally Tomatoes, 334 W. Stroud St., Randolph, WI, 53956; phone 800-345-5977; Web site www.totallytomato.com. Totally Tomatoes offers many varieties of tomatoes and peppers.

Vermont Bean Seed Company, 334 W. Stroud St., Randolph, WI 53956; phone 800-349-1071; Web site www.vermontbean.com. This company specializes in varieties of beans, but it also offers other vegetable seeds and fruits.

Veseys Seeds Ltd., P.O. Box 9000, Calais, ME 04619; phone 800-363-7333; Web site www.veseys.com. Veseys offers a wide selection of vegetable and flower seeds adapted to short-growing-season conditions.

W. Atlee Burpee & Co., 300 Park Ave., Warminster, PA 18974; phone 800-333-5808; Web site www.burpee.com. Through Burpee, you can choose from a wide selection of flower and vegetable seeds, plants, and supplies.

Wild Garden Seeds, P.O. Box 1509, Philomath, OR 97370; phone 541-929-4068; Web site www.wildgardenseed.com. This company offers a selection of vegetables and beneficial-insect-attracting plants. All seed is bred on the Gathering Together Farm.

Willhite Seed, Inc., P.O. Box 23, Poolville, TX 76487; phone 800-828-1840; Web site www.willhiteseed.com. Willhite Seed offers a good selection of vegetable seeds for warm growing areas. It also has a selection of Indian vegetable varieties.

William Dam Seeds Ltd., 279 Hwy. 8, RR 1, Dundas, Ontario, Canada L9H 5E1; phone 905-628-6641; Web site www.damseeds.ca. You can choose from a full line of vegetable, flower, and wildflower seeds and some products for Northern gardeners.

Wood Prairie Farm, 49 Kinney Rd., Bridgewater, ME 04735; phone 800-829-9765; Web site www.woodprairie.com. This farm specializes in potato varieties.

Seed savers

The following are some seed-saving organizations and small, nonprofit organizations specializing in historic and unusual heirloom varieties. The seed-saving organizations often have seed swaps for members so you can share and try unusual heirloom varieties from around the world. They also offer special programs promoting the reintroduction of heirloom plants. You may have to become a member to receive the seeds.

Appalachian Heirloom Seed Conservancy, P.O. Box 519, Richmond, KY 40476; phone 859-623-2765; e-mail KentuckySeeds@hotmail.com. This conservancy is dedicated to preserving Appalachia's edible heritage.

Colonial Williamsburg, P.O. Box 1776, Williamsburg, VA 23187; phone 757-229-1000; Web site www.history.org/history/CWLand/nursery1.cfm. Seeds of 18th century plants commonly grown in America are available for sale from the Colonial Nursery.

Garden State Heirloom Seed Society, P.O. Box 15, Delaware, NJ 07833; phone 908-475-2730; Web site www.historyyoucaneat.org. This society of gardeners, farmers, and historians preserves, grows, and sells heirloom varieties of seeds from the Mid-Atlantic region.

Landis Valley Museum, 2451 Kissel Hill Rd., Lancaster, PA 17601; phone 717-569-0401; Web site www.landisvalleymuseum.org/index.php. The Landis Valley Museum is home to the Heirloom Seed Project, which is dedicated to the preservation of heirloom vegetable, flower, and herb varieties grown by the Pennsylvania Dutch farmers.

Native Seeds/SEARCH. See the description for this organization in the preceding section to find out more.

Seed Savers Exchange. See the description for the Seed Savers Heritage Farm in the preceding section for more information.

Seeds of Diversity, P.O. Box 36, Station Q., Toronto, Ontario, Canada M4T 2L7; phone 866-509-7333; Web site www.seeds.ca. This organization is Canada's source for heritage seed, seed savings, and garden history.

Southern Seed Legacy, Department of Anthropology, 250A Baldwin Hall, University of Georgia, Athens, GA 30602; phone 706-542-1430; Web site www.uga.edu/ebl/ssl. The Southern Seed Legacy maintains a collection of more than 440 named varieties of southern heirloom seeds.

Thomas Jefferson Center for Historic Plants, Monticello, P.O. Box 217, Charlottesville, VA 22902; phone 434-984-9822; Web site www.monticello. org/chp/index.html. Through the Center for Historic Plants, you can find listing of flowers, trees, shrubs, vegetable, herbs, and fruits grown at Thomas Jefferson's home in Virginia.

Fruits and berries

Bay Laurel Nursery, 2500 El Camino Real, Atascadero, CA 93422; phone 805-466-3406; Web site www.baylaurelnursery.com. This nursery offers a good selection of apples, apricots, cherries, nectarines, peaches, pears, and plums for the Southwest.

Burnt Ridge Nursery & Orchards Inc., 432 Burnt Ridge Rd., Onalaska, WA 98570; phone 360-985-2873; Web site www.burntridgenursery.com. Burnt Ridge specializes in unusual and disease-resistant trees, vines, and shrubs that produce edible nuts or fruits and Northwest natives.

Edible Landscaping, 361 Spirit Ridge Ln., Afton, VA 22920; phone 800-524-4156; Web site www.ediblelandscaping.com. Through Edible Landscaping, you can choose from a good selection of unusual fruits such as kiwi, fig, and citrus.

Indiana Berry & Plant Co., 5218 W. 500 S., Huntingburg, IN 47542; phone 800-295-2226; Web site indianaberry.com. At Indiana Berry, you can find varieties of strawberries, blueberries, raspberries, blackberries, asparagus, grapes, and other unusual berries.

Ison's Nursery & Vineyards, 6855 Newnan Rd., P.O. Box 190, Brooks, GA 30205; phone 800-733-0324; Web site www.isons.com. This company offers mucho muscadines (grapes for the southern U.S.) and dozens of other fruits, large and small.

Johnson Nursery, 1352 Big Creek Rd., Ellijay, GA 30536; phone 888-276-3187; Web site www.johnsonnursery.com. Johnson Nursery sells hardy and antique fruit trees as well as grapes, berries, persimmons, pomegranates, and supplies.

Just Fruits & Exotics, 30 St. Frances St., Crawfordville, FL 32327; phone 850-926-5644; Web site www.justfruitsandexotics.com. This company offers a good selection of tropical fruits, citrus, persimmon, and many other fruit varieties adapted to warm growing regions.

Miller Nurseries, 5060 West Lake Rd., Canandaigua, NY 14424; phone 800-836-9630; Web site www.millernurseries.com. Through Miller Nurseries, you can choose from a complete selection of fruiting plants, including many varieties of antique dwarf apples.

One Green World, 28696 S. Cramer Rd., Molalla, OR 97038; phone 877-353-4028; Web site www.onegreenworld.com. This company offers a wide selection of exotic fruits from around the world as well as native Northwest fruits, nuts, and berries.

Raintree Nursery, 391 Butts Rd., Morton, WA 98356; phone 360-496-6400; Web site www.raintreenursery.com. This nursery sells fruits, nuts, vines, berries, unusual edibles, and bamboo.

Stark Bro's Nurseries & Orchards Co., P.O. Box 1800, Louisiana, MO 63353; phone 800-325-4180; Web site www.starkbros.com. At Stark Bro's, choose from fruit trees, berries, and landscape plants.

Womacks Nursery, 2551 State Hwy. 6, De Leon, TX 76444; phone 254-893-6497; Web site www.womacknursery.com. This company specializes in fruit and pecan trees.

Tools and supplies

A. M. Leonard, Inc., 241 Fox Dr., P.O. Box 816, Piqua, OH 45356; phone 800-543-8955; Web site www.amleo.com. This company offers professional nursery and gardening supplies.

Arbico Organics, P.O. Box 8910, Tucson, AZ 85738; phone 800-827-2847; Web site www.arbico-organics.com. Through Arbico Organics, you can purchase beneficial insects and other environmentally friendly products for pest control.

Charley's Greenhouse Supply, 17979 State Rt. 536, Mount Vernon, WA 98273; phone 800-322-4707; Web site www.charleysgreenhouse.com. This company has a good listing of small greenhouses and greenhouse supplies.

Fungi Perfecti, P.O. Box 7634, Olympia, WA 98507; phone 800-780-9126; Web site www.fungi.com. This company offers a full line of mushroom-growing kits and supplies.

Gardener's Supply Company, 128 Intervale Rd., Burlington, VT 05401; phone 888-833-1412; Web site www.gardeners.com. This supply company sells hundreds of innovative tools and products for gardeners.

Gardens Alive, 5100 Schenley Pl., Lawrenceburg, IN 47025; phone 513-354-1482; Web site www.gardensalive.com. A large supplier of organic pest control products.

Gempler's, P.O. Box 44993, Madison, WI 53744; phone 800-382-8473; Web site www.gemplers.com. Gempler's offers an extensive listing of tools and products for the professional and amateur gardener.

Harmony Farm Supply & Nursery, 3244 Hwy. 116 North, Sebastopol, CA 95472; phone 707-823-9125; Web site www.harmonyfarm.com. For drip and sprinkler irrigation equipment, organic fertilizers, beneficial insects, power tools, and composting supplies, check out this supply company.

Hoop House Greenhouse Kits, P.O. Box 2430, Mashpee, MA 02649; phone 800-760-5192; Web site www.hoophouse.com. This company specializes in hoop house greenhouse kits for every level of gardener, from home hobbyists to professionals.

Hydrofarm, 2249 S. McDowell Ext., Petaluma, CA 94954; phone 800-634-9990; Web site www.hydrofarm.com. One of the largest selections of indoor growing lights and hydroponic supplies available.

Kinsman Company, P.O. Box 428, Pipersville, PA 18947; phone 800-733-4146; Web site www.kinsmangarden.com. This company offers gardening supplies and quality tools.

Lee Valley Tools Ltd., P.O. Box 1780, Ogdensburg, NY 13669; phone 800-871-8158; Web site www.leevalley.com. Lee Valley Tools sells quality tools and products for home gardeners.

Natural Gardening, P.O. Box 750776, Petaluma, CA 94975; phone 707-766-9303; Web site www.naturalgardening.com. This company offers organic gardening supplies, seeds, and transplants.

Peaceful Valley Farm Supply, P.O. Box 2209, Grass Valley, CA 95945; phone 888-784-1722; Web site www.groworganic.com. Through this farm, you can choose from a large selection of organic gardening fertilizers, pest controls, cover crop seed, supplies, and quality tools.

Planet Natural, 1612 Gold Ave., Bozeman, MT 59715; phone 800-289-6656; Web site www.planetnatural.com. This company offers environmentally friendly products for your lawn, garden, or farm.

The Urban Farmer Store, 2833 Vicente St., San Francisco, CA 94116; phone 415-661-2204; Web site www.urbanfarmerstore.com. This store sells garden lighting, ponds, and drip irrigation supplies.

Walt Nicke Co., P.O. Box 433, Topsfield, MA 01983; phone 978-887-3388; Web site www.gardentalk.com. This company provides a good selection of fine and unusual gardening tools.

Worm's Way Garden Center, 7850 N. State Rd. 37, Bloomington, IN 47404; phone 800-274-9676; Web site www.wormsway.com. Worm's Way sells a wide variety of gardening supplies, including irrigation supplies, pest controls, organic fertilizers, and of course, worms for composting.

U.S. and Canadian Master Gardeners

The umbrella organization for all the regional master gardener programs is the International Master Gardener Committee (www.hort.purdue.edu/img/default.html). This committee disseminates information and helps organize international master gardener conferences. Individual state master gardener programs often have conferences, newsletters, and gatherings as well. Following is contact information for each state and participating province:

Alabama: Kerry Smith, www.aces.edu/mg

Alaska: June Riley, www.uaf.edu/ces/michele/program.html

Alberta: Devonia Botanic Garden, www.ales.ualberta.ca/devonian/master_gardener.cfm

Arizona: John Begeman, cals.arizona.edu/extension/master gardener/index.html

Arkansas: Janet Carson, www.arhomeandgarden.org/master_gardener.htm

British Columbia: MG Coordinator, Van Dusen Botanical Gardens, www.bcmastergardeners.org

California: Pam Geisel, camastergardeners.ucdavis.edu

Colorado: Dave Whiting, cmg.colostate.edu

Connecticut: Leslie Alexander, www.ladybug.uconn.edu

Delaware: Susan Barton, ag.udel.edu/extension/horticulture/index.htm

District of Columbia: Sandy Farber, www.dc-urban-gardener-news.com

Florida: Tom Wichman, hort.ifas.ufl.edu/mg

Georgia: Marco T. Fonseca, `www.caes.uga.edu/departments/hort/extension/mastergardener`

Hawaii: Rhea Hubbard, `www.ctahr.hawaii.edu/ougc/master.asp`

Idaho: Robert Tripepi, `www.ag.uidaho.edu/mg`

Illinois: Monica David, `www.extension.uiuc.edu/mg`

Indiana: Rosie Lerner, `www.hort.purdue.edu/mg`

Iowa: James Romer, `www.mastergardener.iastate.edu`

Kansas: Ward Upham, `www.oznet.k-state.edu/hfrr/MG`

Kentucky: Rick Durham, `ces.ca.uky.edu/grayson/Master%20Gardener%20Association`

Louisiana: Robert Souvestre, `www.lsuagcenter.com/en/lawn_garden/master_gardener`

Maine: Dick Brzozowski, `www.umext.maine.edu/mgmaine/welcome.htm`

Maryland: Robin Hessey, `mastergardener.umd.edu`

Massachusetts: `www.wmassmastergardeners.org`

Michigan: Mary McLellan, `www.msue.msu.edu/mastergardener`

Minnesota: Dr. Mary H. Meyer, `www.mg.umn.edu`

Mississippi: Dr. Lelia Scott Kelly, `msucares.com/lawn/master_gardener/index.html`

Missouri: Mary Kroening, `www.mg.missouri.edu`

Montana: Cheryl Moore-Gough, `gardenguide.montana.edu/mgardener/mgardenerindex.asp`

Nebraska: Anne Streich, `mastergardener.unl.edu`

Nevada: Kerrie B. Badertscher, `www.unce.unr.edu/programs/sites/mastergardener`

New Hampshire: Marcy Stanton, `extension.unh.edu/Agric/AGMastGD.htm`

New Jersey: Nicholas Polanin, `njaes.rutgers.edu/mastergardeners`

New Mexico: Curtis Smith, cahe.nmsu.edu/mastergardener

New York: Lori Bushway, www.gardening.cornell.edu/education/mgprogram

North Carolina: Erv Evans, www.ces.ncsu.edu/depts/hort/consumer/masgar

North Dakota: Ron Smith, www.ag.ndsu.edu/mg

Nova Scotia: www.atlanticmastergardeners.com

Ohio: Pam Bennett, mastergardener.osu.edu

Oklahoma: Davis Hillock, www.hortla.okstate.edu/hortla/mastergardener.htm

Ontario: Wendy Chrystian, www.mgoi.ca

Oregon: Gail Langellotto, extension.oregonstate.edu/mg

Pennsylvania: Ginger Pryor, horticulture.psu.edu/extension/mg

Rhode Island: Rosanne Sherry, www.uri.edu/cels/ceoc/ceoc_programs_mgp.html

Saskatchewan: Patricia Hanbidge, ccde.usask.ca/mastergardener

South Carolina: Tim Davis, www.clemson.edu/sandhill/page.htm?pageId=2303

South Dakota: Rhoda Burrows, hflp.sdstate.edu/mg/mgarden.htm

Tennessee: Beth Babbit, mastergardener.tennessee.edu

Texas: Douglas F. Welsh, aggie-horticulture.tamu.edu/mastergd/index.html

Utah: Debbie Amundsen, utahmastergardeners.usu.edu/home/homeMain.htm

Vermont: Nancy M. Hulett, www.uvm.edu/mastergardener

Virginia: David D. Close, www.hort.vt.edu/mastergardener

Washington: Tonie Fitzgerald, mastergardener.wsu.edu

West Virginia: John Jett, www.wvu.edu/~agexten/hortcult/master

Wisconsin: Susan E. Rice Mahr, www.hort.wisc.edu/mastergardener

Wyoming: Karen L. Panter, www.uwyo.edu/mstrgardener/info.asp?p=6258

Web Sites about Vegetables

The following sites offer a broad spectrum of general gardening information and links. (Check out additional sites for specific topics in the upcoming sections.)

Backyard Gardener (www.backyardgardener.com/veg): Extensive garden encyclopedia, blogs, articles, and links about many aspects of gardening. Special sections on tomatoes and vegetable gardening.

Dave's Garden (davesgarden.com): Articles, videos, and more than 200 discussion forums on all aspects of gardening. The site's Garden Watchdog gives customer feedback on many gardening companies.

Garden California (www.geocities.com/~jimclatfelter): A detailed monthly calendar of gardening chores for Californian gardeners. The site also has links to other sites.

Garden Guides (www.gardenguides.com): This site provides good information on vegetable and herb gardening and descriptions of and links to selected Internet gardening sites, Web pages, garden forums, and discussion groups.

Kitchen Gardeners International (kitchengardeners.org): This Web site is devoted to growing and eating good food. It has articles, blogs, video, and information on kitchen gardening from around the world.

National Gardening Association (www.garden.org): My personal favorite (but, of course, I work at the NGA)! Look to this site for everything from the largest national association of home gardeners, free regional report e-newsletters, gardening information for kids, applications for garden grants, and more.

USDA Gardening Page (www.usda.gov/wps/portal/!ut/p/_s.7_0_A/7_0_1OB?navid=GARDENING&parentnav=CONSUMER_CITIZEN&navtype=RT): This site has multiple sections, including a horticultural solutions section, lawn and garden care, a hardiness zone map, and more.

Veggie Gardening Tips (www.veggiegardeningtips.com): Gardening tips and techniques on growing vegetables, fruits, and herbs.

Weekend Gardener (www.weekendgardener.net): A site dedicated to all aspects of gardening, including seed starting. The site features videos, blogs, and lots of how-to information.

State sites

Many state Cooperative Extension Service offices have great information on home vegetable gardening. Here are some of my favorites:

Ohio State University: extension.osu.edu/lawn_and_garden/ vegetables_herbs.php

Oregon State University: extension.oregonstate.edu/catalog/pdf/ ec/ec871.pdf

Purdue University: www.hort.purdue.edu/ext/garden_pubs. html#Vegetables

Texas A & M University: aggie-horticulture.tamu.edu/extension/ TCEHomeVegFruitNut.html

University of Arizona: ag.arizona.edu/pubs/garden/mg/vegetable/ index.html

University of California: anrcatalog.ucdavis.edu/ HomeVegetableGardening

University of Florida: edis.ifas.ufl.edu/TOPIC_Vegetable_ Gardening

University of Illinois: web.extension.uiuc.edu/vegguide

University of Maryland: www.hgic.umd.edu/content/online publications.cfm#Vegetable%20and%20Herb%20Gardening

Cyber veggies

The following Web sites have information just on the specific vegetables mentioned. Some are company sponsored (such as Peas.org), some are organizations (such as the Leafy Greens Council), and others are just personal sites (such as B's Cucumber Page). Many have great links to other sites as well. The following list is only the beginning, but if you have a favorite vegetable and need to know more. . . .

Beans: Green Beans n'More, www.greenbeansnmore.com

Cabbage: The Cabbage Page, discworld.imaginary.com/lpc/links/cabbage

Carrots: The World Carrot Museum, www.carrotmuseum.co.uk

Cucumbers: B's Cucumber Page, www.lpl.arizona.edu/~bcohen/cucumbers/info.html

Garlic: Garlic Central, www.garlic-central.com

Greens: Leafy Greens Council, www.leafy-greens.org

Peas: Peas.org, www.peas.org

Peppers: How to Grow Hot Peppers, howtogrowhotpeppers.com

Potatoes: The Potato Museum, www.potatomuseum.com

Pumpkins: World Class Giant Pumpkins, www.backyardgardener.com/wcgp

Tomatoes: Growing Big Tomatoes, www.njtomato.com/indice.htm; Power Tomatoes, www.ars.usda.gov/is/tom; and On-Line Tomato Vine, www.kdcomm.net/~tomato

Index

Business/Accounting & Bookkeeping
Bookkeeping For Dummies
978-0-7645-9848-7

eBay Business
All-in-One For Dummies,
2nd Edition
978-0-470-38536-4

Job Interviews
For Dummies,
3rd Edition
978-0-470-17748-8

Resumes For Dummies,
5th Edition
978-0-470-08037-5

Stock Investing
For Dummies,
3rd Edition
978-0-470-40114-9

Successful Time
Management
For Dummies
978-0-470-29034-7

Computer Hardware
BlackBerry For Dummies,
3rd Edition
978-0-470-45762-7

Computers For Seniors
For Dummies
978-0-470-24055-7

iPhone For Dummies,
2nd Edition
978-0-470-42342-4

Laptops For Dummies,
3rd Edition
978-0-470-27759-1

Macs For Dummies,
10th Edition
978-0-470-27817-8

Cooking & Entertaining
Cooking Basics
For Dummies,
3rd Edition
978-0-7645-7206-7

Wine For Dummies,
4th Edition
978-0-470-04579-4

Diet & Nutrition
Dieting For Dummies,
2nd Edition
978-0-7645-4149-0

Nutrition For Dummies,
4th Edition
978-0-471-79868-2

Weight Training
For Dummies,
3rd Edition
978-0-471-76845-6

Digital Photography
Digital Photography
For Dummies,
6th Edition
978-0-470-25074-7

Photoshop Elements 7
For Dummies
978-0-470-39700-8

Gardening
Gardening Basics
For Dummies
978-0-470-03749-2

Organic Gardening
For Dummies,
2nd Edition
978-0-470-43067-5

Green/Sustainable
Green Building
& Remodeling
For Dummies
978-0-4710-17559-0

Green Cleaning
For Dummies
978-0-470-39106-8

Green IT For Dummies
978-0-470-38688-0

Health
Diabetes For Dummies,
3rd Edition
978-0-470-27086-8

Food Allergies
For Dummies
978-0-470-09584-3

Living Gluten-Free
For Dummies
978-0-471-77383-2

Hobbies/General
Chess For Dummies,
2nd Edition
978-0-7645-8404-6

Drawing For Dummies
978-0-7645-5476-6

Knitting For Dummies,
2nd Edition
978-0-470-28747-7

Organizing For Dummies
978-0-7645-5300-4

SuDoku For Dummies
978-0-470-01892-7

Home Improvement
Energy Efficient Homes
For Dummies
978-0-470-37602-7

Home Theater
For Dummies,
3rd Edition
978-0-470-41189-6

Living the Country Lifestyle
All-in-One For Dummies
978-0-470-43061-3

Solar Power Your Home
For Dummies
978-0-470-17569-9

Internet
Blogging For Dummies,
2nd Edition
978-0-470-23017-6

eBay For Dummies,
6th Edition
978-0-470-49741-8

Facebook For Dummies
978-0-470-26273-3

Google Blogger
For Dummies
978-0-470-40742-4

Web Marketing
For Dummies,
2nd Edition
978-0-470-37181-7

WordPress For Dummies,
2nd Edition
978-0-470-40296-2

**Language & Foreign
Language**
French For Dummies
978-0-7645-5193-2

Italian Phrases
For Dummies
978-0-7645-7203-6

Spanish For Dummies
978-0-7645-5194-9

Spanish For Dummies,
Audio Set
978-0-470-09585-0

Macintosh
Mac OS X Snow Leopard
For Dummies
978-0-470-43543-4

Math & Science
Algebra I For Dummies
978-0-7645-5325-7

Biology For Dummies
978-0-7645-5326-4

Calculus For Dummies
978-0-7645-2498-1

Chemistry For Dummies
978-0-7645-5430-8

Microsoft Office
Excel 2007 For Dummies
978-0-470-03737-9

Office 2007 All-in-One
Desk Reference
For Dummies
978-0-471-78279-7

Music
Guitar For Dummies,
2nd Edition
978-0-7645-9904-0

iPod & iTunes
For Dummies,
6th Edition
978-0-470-39062-7

Piano Exercises
For Dummies
978-0-470-38765-8

Parenting & Education
Parenting For Dummies,
2nd Edition
978-0-7645-5418-6

Type 1 Diabetes
For Dummies
978-0-470-17811-9

Pets
Cats For Dummies,
2nd Edition
978-0-7645-5275-5

Dog Training For Dummies,
2nd Edition
978-0-7645-8418-3

Puppies For Dummies,
2nd Edition
978-0-470-03717-1

Religion & Inspiration
The Bible For Dummies
978-0-7645-5296-0

Catholicism For Dummies
978-0-7645-5391-2

Women in the Bible
For Dummies
978-0-7645-8475-6

Self-Help & Relationship
Anger Management
For Dummies
978-0-470-03715-7

Overcoming Anxiety
For Dummies
978-0-7645-5447-6

Sports
Baseball For Dummies,
3rd Edition
978-0-7645-7537-2

Basketball For Dummies,
2nd Edition
978-0-7645-5248-9

Golf For Dummies,
3rd Edition
978-0-471-76871-5

Web Development
Web Design All-in-One
For Dummies
978-0-470-41796-6

Windows Vista
Windows Vista
For Dummies
978-0-471-75421-3